Gathering Places

"Inside of an Indian tent." Watercolour, pen and ink on paper, by Peter Rindisbacher, 1824. LAC, Acc. No. 1981-55-73, Bushnell Collection.

Gathering Places:
Aboriginal and Fur Trade Histories

Edited by Carolyn Podruchny
and Laura Peers

UBCPress · Vancouver · Toronto

20 19 18 17 16 15 14 13 12 11 10   5 4 3 2 1

Printed in Canada on ancient-forest-free paper (100% post-consumer recycled) that is processed chlorine- and acid-free.

Library and Archives Canada Cataloguing in Publication

Gathering places: aboriginal and fur trade histories / edited by Carolyn Podruchny and Laura Peers.

Includes bibliographical references and index.
ISBN 978-0-7748-1843-8 (bound); ISBN 978-0-7748-1844-5 (pbk.)

1. Native peoples – Canada – History. 2. Métis – History. 3. Fur trade – Northwest, Canadian – History. I. Podruchny, Carolyn. II. Peers, Laura Lynn.

E78.C2G378 2010	971.004'97	C2010-903470-8

e-book ISBNs: 978-0-7748-1845-2 (pdf); 978-0-7748-5969-1 (epub)

Canadä

UBC Press gratefully acknowledges the financial support for our publishing program of the Government of Canada (through the Canada Book Fund), the Canada Council for the Arts, and the British Columbia Arts Council.

This book has been published with the help of a grant from the Canadian Federation for the Humanities and Social Sciences, through the Aid to Scholarly Publications Programme, using funds provided by the Social Sciences and Humanities Research Council of Canada.

UBC Press
The University of British Columbia
2029 West Mall
Vancouver, BC, V6T 1Z2
www.ubcpress.ca

To Jennifer S.H. Brown,
scholar and mentor,
with gratitude and great affection

Contents

Figures

Preface and Acknowledgments

GATHERING PLACES PRESENTS AN innovative collection of essays that spans a wide range of approaches and methods of Aboriginal and fur trade history in northwestern North America. Whether discussing dietary practices on the Plateau, trees as cultural and geographical markers in the trade, the meanings of totemic signatures, issues of representation in public history, or the writings of Aboriginal anthropologists and historians, the authors link archival, archaeological, material, oral, and ethnographic evidence to offer novel explorations that extend beyond earlier scholarship centred on the archive. They draw on Aboriginal perspectives, material forms of evidence, and personal approaches to history to illuminate cross-cultural encounters and challenge paradigms of history writing.

The essays in this volume owe much to the scholarly example, leadership, mentoring, high standards, generosity, and encouragement that Jennifer S.H. Brown provided to the contributors during the course of her career. Many of us have shared either the privilege of being Jennifer's student or the experience of asking her for help only to realize her extraordinary generosity: our theses, papers, and book manuscripts have benefitted from her editorial eye and copious suggestions for further reading. These suggestions were often made while Jennifer and her husband, Wilson, fed us and put us up in their home for extended periods so that we could do research at the archives in Winnipeg. Jennifer's library has saved many of us from scholarly lapses, and her knowledge of theses, dissertations, and other unpublished work in progress has been crucial to developing conversations among budding scholars. Some of these scholars were influenced by her teaching at the University of Winnipeg, where she has for some time taught both undergraduate and graduate courses in Aboriginal history; others were graduate students whose theses she examined; some were postdoctoral fellows whom she supervised. This combination of knowledge and generosity led to the development of an important network of scholars that coalesced in the Centre for Rupert's Land Studies and its colloquia. Over time, and in various ways, Jennifer has fostered new ways of understanding and writing about the histories of the many peoples of Rupert's Land.

We also thank the contributors to the volume for their wonderful essays and assistance with plotting pesky places and tracking down citations for both obscure and obvious sources. Thanks are also due to Wilson Brown, Drew Davey, Mark Guertin, and Myra Rutherdale for a myriad of things too numerous to mention here. Jean Wilson and then Darcy Cullen at UBC Press shepherded this project along with grace and good humour. Thanks to Holly Keller for managing the production process and to Eric Leinberger for preparing the map.

A Note on Terminology: In this volume, the term "metis" refers to all descendants of European men and Aboriginal women, and the term "Metis" refers to members of the historic Metis Nation, which originated around the Red River settlement (exceptions are found in Chapters 7 and 9). Because of the inconsistencies and difficulties of naming indigenous peoples in North America, both broadly and at a local level, we opted to allow the authors of each chapter to determine their own usage rather than imposing terminology on the volume as a whole. We also decided to allow authors to use different spellings for Anishinaabemowin (Ojibwe language) words because no standardized spelling exists, and spellings vary considerably by region.

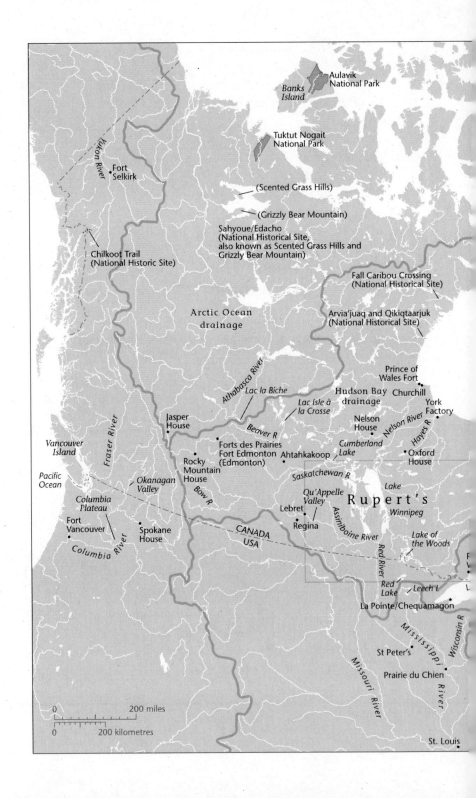

Aulavik
National Park

Banks
Island

Tuktut Nogait
National Park

(Scented Grass Hills)

(Grizzly Bear Mountain)

Sahyoue/Edacho
(National Historical Site,
also known as Scented Grass Hills and
Grizzly Bear Mountain)

Fort
Selkirk

Yukon River

Chilkoot Trail
(National Historic Site)

Arctic Ocean
drainage

Fall Caribou Crossing
(National Historical Site)

Arvia'juaq and Qikiqtaarjuk
(National Historical Site)

Prince of
Wales Fort

Athabasca River

Lac la Biche

Lac Isle à
la Crosse

Hudson Bay
drainage

Churchill

York
Factory

Nelson River

Hayes R.

Jasper
House

Beaver R

Nelson
House

Fraser River

Forts des Prairies
Fort Edmonton
(Edmonton)

Ahtahkakoop

Cumberland
Lake

Oxford
House

Vancouver
Island

Rocky
Mountain
House

Saskatchewan R.

Lake

Pacific
Ocean

Columbia
Plateau

Okanagan
Valley

Bow R.

Qu'Appelle
Valley

Lebret

R u p e r t's

Winnipeg

Fort
Vancouver

Spokane
House

Columbia River

Regina

Assiniboine River

Lake of
the Woods

CANADA
USA

Red River

Red
Lake

Leech L.

La Pointe/Chequamagon

Mississippi River

Wisconsin R.

St Peter's

Missouri River

Prairie du Chien

0   200 miles

0   200 kilometres

St. Louis

Saskatchewan River

Moose Lake

Norway House

Island Lake

Sandy Lake

Lac Bourbon (Cedar Lake)

Red Deer River Burial ▲

Red Deer River

Swan R

L Winnipegosis

Lake Winnipeg

Berens River

Poplar R

Pauingassi

Berens R

Poplar Hill

Fort Dauphin

Dauphin Lake Burial ▲

Dauphin Lake

White Horse Plains

Lake Manitoba

Assiniboine River

Brandon House

Lower Fort Garry

English River

Fort Garry, St Boniface (Winnipeg)

Lake of the Woods

Lac la Pluie/ Rainy Lake

Fort William

Red River settlement

Red River

Pembina

Pembina River

Lac la Croix

Grand Portage

Red Lake

0   50 miles

0   50 kilometres

Hudson Bay

James Bay

Hudson Bay drainage

Land

Lake Mistassini

Lower Canada

Strait of Belle Isle

St. Lawrence River

Fort William

Isle Royale

Lake Superior

Bawating/ Sault Ste Marie

Manitoulin Island

L Nipissing

French River

Montreal

Cornwall

Michilimackinac

Lake Huron

Georgian Bay

Mnjikaning (Mnjikaning/Rama)

Credit R

Alderville

Great Lakes drainage

Sarnia

L Ontario

Plymouth Colony

Atlantic Ocean

Walpole Island

Acronyms

AGS	Alberta Genealogical Society
ANF	Archives nationales de France
AO	Archives of Ontario
APS	American Philosophical Society
COIA-LR	Correspondence of the Office of Indian Affairs, Letters Received
FTC	Fur Trade Collection
HBC	Hudson's Bay Company
HBCA	Hudson's Bay Company Archives
HSMBC	Historic Sites and Monuments Board of Canada
JAF	*Journal of American Folklore*
LAC	Library and Archives Canada
MRBSC	McGill University Library, Rare Books and Special Collections
MTRL	Metropolitan Toronto Reference Library, Baldwin Room
NAM	National Archives Microfilm
NWC	North West Company
ROM	Royal Ontario Museum
UBC	University of British Columbia
UCA	United Church Archives
VUL	Victoria University Library and Special Collections
XYC	XY Company

Gathering Places

1

Introduction: Complex Subjectivities, Multiple Ways of Knowing

Laura Peers and Carolyn Podruchny

THE SON OF METHODIST missionary parents who learned too much from his Cree nurse for his parents' comfort ... The children of European fathers and tribal mothers who became, variously, Indian, halfbreed, and metis – sometimes all in the same family ... Conversations with Ojibwe people about an anthropologist their parents and grandparents taught and about a medicine man the anthropologist knew ... The different cultural perspectives that English traders and Cree hunters had about the same landscapes ... The very different expectations that North West Company and Hudson's Bay Company fathers and traders had for their fur trade "country" families. These people and their complex identities and worldviews featured nowhere in Canadian academic history until the past few decades. One of the most significant changes in Canadian historiography since the 1970s has been the development of Aboriginal history as a vibrant and challenging part of the discipline. The emergence of a scholarly focus on Aboriginal peoples, their cultural and political histories, and their relations with newcomers has changed the emphases and narratives of Canadian history. Putting Aboriginal peoples at the centre of scholarly inquiry has challenged the traditional techniques of historical research, leading to increasingly sophisticated theoretical and methodological approaches to historical sources. Two aspects of this change have been especially significant, individually and in an entwined way. First, historians have become increasingly adept at interpreting the cultural and cross-cultural meanings recorded, often implicitly and in fragmentary ways, in the archival record: in other words, the reading (and nature) of historical sources have become increasingly nuanced and cross-culturally aware. Second, the reflexive, postcolonial turn in the social sciences – with its focus on issues of power, both in the past and in the present, including the cultural and racial politics of scholarship and the production of knowledge – has had a profound effect. Recent Aboriginal history has moved far beyond older narratives in which actions by the Indian and the European were understood from scholarly perspectives that generally lacked an understanding of Aboriginal cultures.

The diverse chapters in this volume take this disciplinary history as their starting point and show the new directions in which Aboriginal history is moving. They highlight issues associated with the new methodology, especially the close reading and use of disparate kinds of sources – archival, oral, material, and fieldwork data – in tandem. They explore cross-cultural and intracultural issues of power, both in the past and in the production of scholarly knowledge in the present. They focus on the fine-grained and local as well as the broader patterns into which such case studies fit. They are reflexive about scholarly perspective, both professional (especially the cross-disciplinary use of anthropological theory and historical data) and personal, including the knowledge and stance gained from family and cultural background and experience.

The chapters explore these themes with reference to the work of one scholar, Jennifer S.H. Brown, whose publications embody these themes and have been instrumental in producing major developments in Aboriginal historiography. All of the people and topics introduced at the beginning of this chapter have featured in her work, and all of the contributors to this volume have been influenced by Brown's work, as much by the impact of her publications as through her mentorship. In the following pages, we articulate the relationship between these broad disciplinary developments, Brown's work, and the essays presented here.

Gathering Momentum: Canadian Aboriginal History

Since the late 1970s, scholarship on Aboriginal history in Canada has increased by leaps and bounds. The 1980s and 1990s saw the production of fundamental works on the histories of particular communities and regions and socio-economic and political phenomena such as the numbered treaties, agricultural programs, reserve life, and residential schools.[1] The fur trade and the rise and dispersal of metis peoples became an especially important site to study Aboriginal peoples after Arthur Ray's *Indians in the Fur Trade* (1974), Sylvia Van Kirk's *"Many Tender Ties"* (1980), and Brown's *Strangers in Blood* (1980).[2] Brown's work on the children of fur traders and Aboriginal people led her to pay careful attention to Aboriginal people, kinship, and metis ethnogenesis (see her collection co-edited with Jacqueline Peterson, *The New Peoples: Being and Becoming Metis*), and contact with Aboriginal students and scholars continues to profoundly shape her ongoing research agenda. As she explains in a recent article on metis historiography,

> Metis history keeps being made; it does not stand still. Metis scholars and family historians, in particular, are contributing to the retrieval and recognition of their historical identities. Such fine-grained and thoughtful historical work as theirs is essential in the quest for a grounded and nuanced Metis history, helping to elucidate a people's experiences, qualities, culture, and unique heritage. They also

show us that there is no single Metis core identity but rather a range along a spectrum reaching from east to west, north to south. Their research is tracing not only cores but connections, the complex links that tie together many communities and individuals who may identify as Metis, Indian, or simply as of partly Aboriginal descent.[3]

Over the past thirty-year period, the techniques of studying and producing Aboriginal history were also refined, with concepts from anthropology and sophisticated methodologies for piecing together fragmentary references and dealing with evidential bias becoming established within the field.[4] Exciting developments have come from studies that use oral and material sources as evidentiary bases to open new lines of inquiry and establish new interpretive frameworks.[5] In addition, Aboriginal histories have been incorporated into the framework of regional, national, and international texts in ways that might be startling to earlier generations of Canadian historians. Aboriginal histories do not always fit easily into these texts, and there are questions to be asked about the manner in which Aboriginal perspectives and experiences are portrayed (or not) as part of the Canadian historical narrative, but it is clear that the past several decades of scholarship have added tremendously to our understanding of the histories of Aboriginal peoples and of their relationships with various newcomers.[6]

The most advanced work on Aboriginal history in Canada, represented in recent collections, has grown out of trends in ethnohistory and cultural history. *Reading beyond Words* (1996 and 2003), edited by Jennifer S.H. Brown and Elizabeth Vibert, brings together cutting-edge ethnohistorical case studies that provide creative tools and methods for interpreting old and new evidence about Canadian Aboriginal history. As the editors explain, "intensive case studies highlight major issues surrounding the use of texts ('original' and edited writings, oral documents, images, and artefacts), as sources embedded in ever-changing contexts."[7] The collection *Earth, Water, Air and Fire: Studies in Canadian Ethnohistory* (1998), edited by David T. McNab for Nin.Da.Waab. Jig., also seeks to highlight the diversity and complexity of Aboriginal history and studies of it and to bring Aboriginal perspectives to the forefront.[8] A 2001 collection that honours the work of the late John Elgin Foster, *From Rupert's Land to Canada*, presents innovative essays on metis history, the imagined West, and Native history and the fur trade and contains studies of demographic reconstructions of Iroquois voyageurs, the genealogy of the Desjarlais family, mapping the Blackfoot world, and interrogating the authorship of Paul Kane's publications, to name a few.[9] Brown's essay "Partial Truths: A Closer Look at

Fur Trade Marriage" charts the instability of the concept of marriage in fur trade settings and underscores how fragmented evidence only lets us discover partial truths about relationships in the past.

In their introduction to *Contact Zones: Aboriginal and Settler Women in Canada's Colonial Past* (2005), Katie Pickles and Myra Rutherdale observe that "the history of colonization is a tense and difficult area to write about, but there are many vital and important stories, especially those of women, that need to be told."[10] Their collection includes essays on how women interacted with colonialism to improve their material circumstances, how colonial institutions regulated Aboriginal women's bodies, and how Aboriginal and white women staged their bodies in public settings. In *With Good Intentions: Euro-Canadian and Aboriginal Relations in Colonial Canada* (2006), editors Celia Haig-Brown and David A. Nock gather together essays that explore relationships between Aboriginal and non-Aboriginal people when colonization was at its height in Canada, from the mid-nineteenth to the early twentieth century.[11] Their focus on how social reformers and Aboriginal people tried to counter injustices makes very clear indeed the complicated knots of the colonial project.

The 2007 collection *New Histories for Old*, edited by Ted Binnema and Susan Neylan, traces the evolution of Arthur J. Ray's scholarship. The volume's essays focus on three themes related to Ray's work: indigenous people and European newcomers in the fur trade, at the treaty table, and in the Canadian judicial system. The collection explores indigenous struggles for land and resources under colonialism, Indian treaties and policies, mobility and migrations, and disease and well-being. Because the editors highlight the significance of academic research on "the present and future lives of Native peoples," they frame writing new histories for old topics as a highly charged undertaking.[12] Brown's essay "Rupert's Land, *Nituskeenan,* Our Land: Cree and English Naming and Claiming around the Dirty Sea" compares Aboriginal and English (and French) perspectives on the landscape around Hudson Bay before and after Rupert's Land was invented as a quasi colony. The fundamentally different, culturally shaped frames of reference expressed in gestures of possession and naming, which are visible in early archival sources and oral traditions, are still apparent today in language and thought.

Jennifer S.H. Brown and the Development of Aboriginal Historiography
Broad developments in the field of Aboriginal history have played out in – and have often been driven by – the work of Jennifer S.H. Brown. Examining one exemplary scholar's career – how her theoretical interests and research have developed across several decades and how her publications have challenged and inspired other scholars – helps us to understand how scholarship works as a .

collective discussion. It also shows how scholars use examples and ideas from one another and from other disciplines and how their work feeds back into collective understandings to help produce knowledge.

Trained as an anthropologist and a historian, Jennifer S.H. Brown brought fresh perspectives and theoretical interests to her analysis of differing social patterns within country families of Hudson's Bay Company (HBC) and North West Company (NWC) employees, including cultural differences among the various British heritages of traders, patterns of trader mobility and ties to Aboriginal wives and children, and the influence of factors such as education, career opportunities, and fathers on the identities of children of fur trade marriages.[13] Brown's detailed biographical work on the careers and families of HBC and NWC fur traders, which was used as the basis for reconstructing larger patterns in cross-cultural fur trade life, has been the core of her wide-ranging research. Her major early publication, *Strangers in Blood: Fur Trade Company Families in Indian Country* (1980), remains today one of the most important works ever published on fur trade social history. Her research on fur trade families and their social networks and patterns drew her immediately into studies of the children of European traders and Aboriginal women. A second focus in Brown's work thus became metis history paired with First Nations history, for she also grappled with the history of Aboriginal involvement in the fur trade. She wrote biographical entries on many individuals of various heritages for the *Dictionary of Canadian Biography,* co-edited the important volume *The New Peoples: Being and Becoming Metis* (1985), and wrote several important papers on the fluidity of identities in fur trade settings, the most recent of which questioned whether there was such a thing as fur trade society.[14]

Brown's background in anthropology brought to her work a sensitivity to nuances of cultural patterns and identity in the fur trade; it also brought a willingness to engage with theoretical debates in archive-based ethnohistorical research. Throughout the 1980s and 1990s, Brown drew into her explorations of fur trade and Aboriginal history issues of voice and representation, relations of power, and gender that were surfacing as key concerns throughout the social sciences. Brown's early training in editing and experiences growing up in an academic family also led her into editing and publishing documentary and oral sources and a series of commentaries on the problems of such work when it concerned Aboriginal peoples, whose experiences and voices are still overlooked by both the authors and the editors of documentary texts. In several important presentations that questioned the processes of editing,[15] Brown reminded us that "documentary editing is not simply copying or transcribing a text; it is a highly complex procedure which is embedded in relationships that usually go unanalyzed."[16] A central concern in her work throughout her career has been to ensure that the voices and perspectives of recorders and the recorded, of Aboriginal people and newcomers, are balanced in editing and in interpretation, that the quieter voices not be obscured by louder ones. This, she recognized, was an issue of power: "The editing of other than great men's compositions demands far more breadth and sensitivity than we have previously even imagined, as we begin to deal with texts and authors whose positioning in historical power relations is very different from that of personages whose fame, status, and education already establish their ranking and credibility among potential readers."[17] Brown has been concerned about the implications of these issues of voice, power, and representation within the production and reception of historical writing within the history profession. The dynamics of the field itself highlight, she has noted recently, issues of stereotyping, voice, mediation, representation, and appropriation that every teacher and scholar, Aboriginal or non-Aboriginal, must face:

> Who speaks for whom, in whose language, and with what evidence and authority? Asymmetries of power are endemic between and within communities (and not just along ethnic lines), often displacing local voices and local knowledge. Complex issues likewise surround language, translation, and material culture: the problems of recording, transcribing, and editing of texts from oral to written forms, the transforming and obscuring effects of translation and writing, the contesting claims that often swirl around texts and objects. Historians can neither avoid nor resolve all these issues, but we can play useful roles in the retrieval and repatriation of knowledge and texts that have often been alienated from their originating communities, in helping to counter the erosion of Aboriginal languages and oral memories, and in assisting cross-generational communications among students and elders both in universities and in communities.[18]

By the late 1980s, Brown's interest in documentary sources was leading her in several directions that have continued to play an important role in her career: Aboriginal history and documentary editing and publishing. An interest in the fur trader George Nelson, whose papers were important to her research, led her to write several papers on Nelson and his Ojibwe families and career and on the histories of Ojibwe communities around Lakes Manitoba and Winnipeg, where Nelson worked.[19] Brown has also worked with the writings of anthropologist A.I. Hallowell, whose classic work on the Berens River Ojibwe on Lake Winnipeg continues to be a source of inspiration. Brown has combined conversations along the Berens River with descendants of Ojibwe people who taught Hallowell with archival research on Hallowell's unpublished papers and notes to reconstruct a unique consideration of Aboriginal and anthropological perspectives across several generations.[20] Her engagement with members of the Berens family has contributed on a personal level to learning how knowledge is mediated and constructed in cross-cultural contexts over time, and her sensitive publications and lectures on this body of work have contributed to the development of methodology in long-term cross-cultural research within Aboriginal historiography and historical anthropology (see Figure 1.1).

Senior academics foster scholarly work through many media, and working in a field requiring interdisciplinary research has necessitated innovation. In addition to her publications and being a Canada Research Chair in Aboriginal Peoples and Histories, Jennifer Brown has since 1996 been director of the Centre for Rupert's Land Studies at the University of Winnipeg, an organization that brings together her strengths in academic scholarship and documentary editing with her skills as a networker and mentor. Publishing has been an important part of the centre's work (the centre has published eleven volumes to date with McGill-Queen's University Press and several others on its own). In another form of publishing that links traditional knowledge with emerging technology, the centre has hosted projects with Omushkego elder Louis Bird to preserve his recordings and knowledge of Cree language and culture and developed a website that makes available many of his stories in audio and textual forms.[21] Perhaps the most important contribution Brown has made to the centre, however, has been to encourage a unique format of its biennial colloquia. Not only have many of these events been held at historic fur trade communities (Fort Edmonton, Norway House, Churchill and York Factory, and Fort Selkirk), but they have also incorporated substantial participation by community-based scholars, Aboriginal and non-Aboriginal, in areas such as genealogy and community history. And they have involved epic journeys (such as the 1988 trip by bush plane from Churchill to York Factory and the day-long bus trip from Winnipeg to Norway House in 1998), during which we finally had the opportunity to talk with one another in ways that seldom happen, drawing on expertise in the scholarly and community group together and with academics and community historians challenging one another with questions we could not always answer.

The community-based parts of the colloquia have also involved searching for the historic Rat Portage at Lake of the Woods in northwestern Ontario, jigging and fiddling at Fort Selkirk in the Yukon, and rowing York boats at Norway House in northern Manitoba, activities that were, again, prompts to make scholars think about topics that often get obscured by academic conventions and documentary lapses. Together, we thought hard about the legacies of the past and the frustrating limitations of academic perspectives and archival

Figure 1.1   Jennifer S.H. Brown and Charlie Johnnie Moose, June 1992, Poplar Hill on the upper Berens River, Ontario. Brown and Johnnie Moose are standing on the site of the pavilion where anthropologist A. Irving Hallowell, in the 1930s, met the drummers who were carrying on the drum ceremony that the medicine man Fair Wind (Naamiwan) had founded at Pauingassi some years before. Photo by Maureen Matthews.

sources. We experienced first-hand what Brown observed in a 2003 article: "Aboriginal history provides constant lessons in humility. It is always reminding us of how much we do not know, given the biases, scarcities, and losses of the sources – whether they be documents oral or written, languages, memories, or material culture – and the power that intrusive outsiders have exerted over the shaping and keeping of history."[22] Oral history became part of every gathering, just as it would have been in the historical communities we studied. So did the landscape. Sensory details began to teach us, to make us think about what we might have missed in the documents about life in the past. So did the new relationships – personal and professional – that we formed. The networks within Aboriginal and fur trade communities in the past were replicated within the colloquia. This was a new way of studying the past, one that was far more holistic than archival research alone.

Colloquia and experiential, subjective ways of learning have emerged as important aspects of academia that thrive on conversations and debates, private as well as public. However objective it sets out to be, scholarship involves both personal components and subjectivities. Subjectivity and personal involvement have been central to theoretical concerns in the social sciences and humanities since the 1980s. Jennifer Brown and Elizabeth Vibert remind us that

> objectivity, then, like the historian's heaven, is an illusion. Our sources, the texts we study, present us with complex subjectivities, multiple ways of knowing the world. This is part of their fascination. The voices of our documentary texts can be listened for, articulated, balanced with one another; but only through silencing or suppression can they be melded into a single voice or unquestioned truth. Nor can we ever silence our own voices as readers and scholars. None of us is free of the social and cultural contexts in which we are embedded – of the basic human condition which one historian of ideas [James Clifford] has called our "predicament of culture."[23]

Knowing the historical and social context of one's own cultural location is crucial to appreciating the multiple perspectives of events in the past and the multiple ways they survive in evidence and can be interpreted today. Scholarship involves personal relations among scholars, a conversation among us over time. Brown observes that

> historians of immigration speak of "chain migration," whereby series of relatives lead and follow one another to a new place. People may stumble or be stopped by various obstacles, but they also find helping hands; and remarkable new

opportunities and connections may appear if they maintain a degree of faith, flexibility, patience, and an open, listening mind. Doing Aboriginal history, following the trails of others, and working with real, living people and their stories, is rather like moving along in one of those chains. It will lead somewhere interesting, but we cannot say exactly where, and the paths may wind and the destinations shift or recede. We may be favoured, however, by some good company and may do a lot of learning along the way ... Wherever the journey takes us, we can try, as academics of whatever background or homeland, to help mark out paths for the future and provide sustenance along the way for those who come after.[24]

The essays in this volume embrace this concept, weaving personal experience together with a breadth and depth of innovative methodology in ways inspired by Brown's publications, teachings, and mentoring.

The Essays Gathered Here

These essays are the fruits of interdisciplinary projects of ethnohistory and cultural history, but they also reveal new forms of scholarship and set new agendas. Ranging from dietary practices and their social implications on the plateau to fur trade customs that involved trees as cultural and geographical markers, from the unrealized dreams for a Native territory in the West to the meanings and implications of totemic signatures, from reflexive methodological concerns and issues of representation in public history to the writings of indigenous anthropologists and historians, the chapters in this volume demonstrate both individually and collectively an ability to draw on a broad sweep of local and contextual evidence to explore specific questions and issues. They bring together and integrate disparate sources and disciplinary perspectives in sometimes startling ways. They connect archival, archaeological, material, oral, and ethnographic evidence. Laura Peers and Robert Coutts, for instance, link public history practice and policy with theory on issues of representation and power, while Heidi Bohaker examines totemic drawings rather than simply the English words on treaty and other documents to understand the cultural significance and implications of signatures. Several of the chapters link personal and professional understandings of the past to show how each informs the other. Native studies, anthropology, cultural studies, and related disciplines are woven through these essays to answer theoretical and methodological concerns of historical scholarship. This interdisciplinarity goes beyond ethnohistory and cultural history, although it draws on these disciplines in particular. To have a group of authors who deploy these techniques and perspectives simply as part of their work suggests just how far the field has come since the 1970s.

Novel explorations of evidential sources are another strength of the volume, going far beyond earlier scholarship based almost exclusively on the archives. In this volume, material culture, totemic signatures, knowledge of Aboriginal languages, personal experience, and issues of identity and the personal journeys taken toward deeper understandings all take their place in sophisticated analyses alongside nuanced and culturally informed interpretations of archival evidence. These sometimes personal and reflexive sources mark a significant shift away from remnants of an older scholarly paradigm of history as an objective re-counting of the past. They go beyond the established incorporation of anthropological concepts within ethnohistorical techniques and embrace recent concerns within anthropology (and other disciplines) about authorial bias, voice, processes of understanding, and power. The incorporation of specialized evidential sources such as material culture and language and visual evidence such as totemic signatures also begins to remedy the past inability of scholars to use sources that require an entire field of study, specialized vocabulary, or knowledge of specific technologies such as the history of manufacturing processes or museum collections. Difficult though the use of such sources has been, they are critical, for they draw in perspectives and information not otherwise recorded in archival sources. Dress, for instance, was historically a critical statement about identity, alliance, and agendas within multicultural environments; to ignore material culture in such situations is folly, but that has largely been the case until recently. The incorporation of these sources in these analyses marks a shift toward the reintegration and holistic understanding of historical moments and processes such as treaty events, the records of which – wampum belts, treaty documents, commissioners' notes, diplomatic gifts – have tended to be scattered throughout different museum and archival repositories.[25] The removal of, or academic blindness to, Aboriginal signatures and artifacts as part of these historical processes and events has been part of larger disciplinary processes that have often been bound by shallow ethnocentric interpretations, for it is literal and material signatures that act as reminders of and witnesses to Aboriginal perspectives in and on the past. The failure to incorporate this evidence has functioned as part of an unconscious process of cultural translation and inscription on historical memory that emphasizes Euro-Canadian understandings of and perspectives on the past, understandings that privilege a Western textual reading of the historical record and its interpretation. Removing the wampum and presentations from a treaty gathering leaves only a limited documentary understanding of the event; the enacting of exchange relationships, aspects of performance, and the significance and intended messages of material culture are lost. Equally, the loss of the oral history from a treaty negotiation obscures the mutual understandings and meanings of the treaty; the voices of the treaty process are silenced. These chapters enable new ways of understanding integrated perspectives and forms of evidence and illustrate their implications for ongoing scholarship.

The stance that several of the contributors take in their relationships with Aboriginal peoples and in mediating broader historical dynamics through personal experience is another area of innovation in this volume. Heather Devine relates a personal journey that has led her scholarly career toward understanding her own metis identity and how that identity has placed her in relation to others over the years. Susan Elaine Gray writes about the profound ways that her understanding of northern Manitoba histories of missionization has been influenced by the process of developing relationships with people in the communities she studied: a process borrowed from anthropological fieldwork but seldom applied to historical research. The apparently simple but profoundly challenging concept that scholars should take seriously what community members tell them, that they should show respect for community members intellectually in the analysis and writing of Aboriginal histories and accredit Aboriginal intellectual property and authorship, has been discussed far more in anthropology than in Canadian history, but it has serious implications for the writing of Aboriginal histories.[26] A recent, successful experiment in collaborative research methodology in which volume editor Laura Peers was involved led to the sharing of authorship of the resulting book with members of the Kainai Nation to acknowledge the importance of the cultural knowledge they had contributed to the interpretation of historical photographs from their community. Although the text was actually written by Peers and Alison Brown, it was carefully reviewed and edited by their Kainai collaborators.[27] Other projects have made similar efforts to credit Aboriginal knowledge and facilitation of research.

Scholars are also beginning to formally acknowledge the non-institutional settings and forms of learning that affect their ability to recognize and interpret data, including ways of knowing and understanding that are personally, emotively, or bodily based.[28] Personal bases for knowledge also emerge in another underlying thread in the chapters that concerns the relationships that the authors have with Aboriginal people. Several of the authors are Aboriginal; all have had Aboriginal students, worked on reserves, or worked with Aboriginal colleagues and mentors to understand Aboriginal cultures and histories. This marks a significant change in the nature of historiography, in how historians are educated, and in the cultural politics of academia. Most historians are still non-Aboriginal, but we have had far more contact with Aboriginal people than our mentors. We no longer think that fieldwork or working with elders is confined to the discipline of anthropology. Although "we" in academia are still mostly non-Aboriginal, a significant and growing number of Aboriginal colleagues and students are shaping disciplines and research agendas in important ways. All of us, Aboriginal and non-Aboriginal alike, also have a very different understanding of the relevance of Aboriginal history than did most of our academic mentors. We know, from discussions over the years with Aboriginal students and teachers, that history matters to Aboriginal people at the immediate level of understanding reality and negotiating identity, that they play an active role in shaping and constructing history, and that they are key players in contemporary scholarly life. We have acquired an understanding of the political nature of Aboriginal history and the contestations that often occur around its construction and narrativization. We have also acquired an understanding of the implications of the past and the way it is written and interpreted for the lives of Aboriginal people today. Aboriginal history as an academic sub-discipline is a very different creature from earlier kinds of historiography, and the essays gathered in this volume exemplify the current and future nature of research in the field.

This book is divided into four parts, each of which focuses on a different aspect of new methodology. In Part 1, "Using Material Culture," two chapters on lopsticks and burials draw together a wide array of sources to interpret dramatically different objects and contexts. In "Putting Up Poles," Carolyn Podruchny, Frederic W. Gleach, and Roger Roulette draw together a disparate range of evidence from history, anthropology, linguistics, and cultural knowledge to interpret the embodied cultural practice of creating various forms of geographical and cultural markers. Their method displays the cross-cultural work necessary to understand multicultural acts and culturally hybrid objects within the fur trade. The chapter by Cory Willmott, a textile specialist and expert on Ojibwe clothing history, and Kevin Brownlee, a Cree archaeologist, "Dressing for the Homeward Journey," examines two early-nineteenth-century burials of young Aboriginal men in southern Manitoba by bringing together archaeological and material culture evidence with historical evidence from fur trade records, comparative collections, ethnographic data, and contemporary First Nations artists to help visualize reconstructions. Willmott and Brownlee link material and historical evidence to issues of identity by decoding grave goods as markers of status and identity, and they provide a detailed discussion of issues of material evidence that are often lacking in historical scholarship.

In Part 2, "Using Documents," three chapters provide dramatically different examples of how to use documentary evidence in new ways. Heidi Bohaker's "Anishinaabe Toodaims" connects Algonquian kinship systems to tribal and extra-tribal politics by using hitherto-untapped documentary evidence on totemic signatures in careful and innovative ways. In "The Contours of Everyday Life," Elizabeth Vibert, using the focal point of food and culturally based expectations pertaining to it, provides a nuanced interpretation of historical evidence to think about cross-cultural perceptions. She suggests a sophisticated theoretical structure for analyzing changing perspectives of racialization that incorporates recent work on identity, nationalism, and the processes of colonialism. Germaine Warkentin's "Make it last forever as it is" is a careful study of the little-known correspondence of the fur trader John McDonald of Garth, in which he proposes unique geopolitical plans for the western part of North America that recognize the geographic coherence of the Prairies and Subarctic and that argue for Aboriginal sovereignty. Although McDonald's proposals fell on deaf ears, his imaginative visions reveal the fluidity of fur trade social worlds, and they remind us that colonization was never inevitable or inexorable.

Part 3, "Ways of Knowing," contains two chapters that tackle head on the issues of subjectivity and personal relationships in research. Heather Devine's "Being and Becoming Métis" is an autobiographical account of the discovery of personal identity and how this process has positioned her scholarship. In "Historical Research and the Place of Oral History," Susan Elaine Gray gives an impassioned account of the embodied learning of an important methodological practice, namely, the need to pay attention to both community members and documentary evidence. Community and culturally based perceptions in the present shed light on historical issues and the construction of historical documents and accounts, and the role of fieldworker can involve mediating between sometimes very different perspectives and sources of evidence. Both chapters show that the personal commitment of fieldworkers is part of the process of researching and writing.

Part 4, "Ways of Representing," contains three chapters that explore very different contexts of representing Aboriginal people: in personal and governmental identification, in ethnographic writings, and in public commemoration. Theresa Schenck's chapter "Border Identities" explores the tricky question of identity among metis people affected by dual heritage, the international border, and local politics. By focusing on the Great Lakes and Upper Mississippi Ojibwe and their mixed-blood children, she examines how metis families south of the forty-ninth parallel struggled for recognition as Aboriginal people. In "Edward Ahenakew's Tutelage by Paul Wallace," David R. Miller describes the career and writings of Edward Ahenakew, a Cree from central Saskatchewan who went on to become an Anglican missionary and do fieldwork among the elders in his community. The chapter maps out how Paul Wallace, an English professor from Pennsylvania, shaped Ahenakew's work as an anthropologist and recorder of

Cree oral traditions by treating Ahenakew as both a student who needed guidance and as an exotic elder who demanded respect. Laura Peers and Robert Coutts' "Aboriginal History and Historic Sites" explores the interface of public history, scholarly history, and real cross-cultural politics as a backdrop against which interpretation of Aboriginal history at historic sites has developed.

Beyond their collective methodological emphasis, several cross-currents run throughout this collection. One of them involves a focus on identity and its negotiation in plural, fluid situations in which multiple cultures and languages were historically present (and on the identity of the author as it relates to the subject matter of the analysis). The meanings of lopsticks, clothing, and personal ornaments at cross-cultural boundaries; the transfer, adoption, or rejection of religious beliefs and practices; and the development of identities within Anishinaabe and metis peoples all came into being over time in response to local roots, external influences, and broader historical forces (see essays by Podruchny, Gleach, and Roulette; Willmott and Brownlee; Gray; Devine; Schenck; and Miller). Identity is especially interesting when it is considered within contexts and events that involve peoples of many cultural backgrounds making available to one another languages, beliefs, and material cultures. Writing about issues of identity throughout the British Empire during the long eighteenth century, Kathleen Wilson describes identity as a social process that often exists in the plural: it is "multiple and contingent, bound to a historical social order and both concretised and challenged through the practices of everyday life."[29] These dynamics have been true for Aboriginal histories throughout the contact period. Material culture and belief and their deployment within social contexts were crucial in the performance of identity, in creating and constantly reconstructing identity in relation to past traditions – and never more so than in cross-cultural and colonial situations faced by Aboriginal peoples.[30]

That identity processes occurred within relationships that ranged from the formal (for example, business) to the intimate and within dynamics of power between Europeans and Aboriginal peoples raises the second major set of themes in this book – cross-cultural accommodation and the shifting nature of cross-cultural relationships. Devine's thoughts on these relationships as they affected her own Metis identity, Schenck's comments on metis identity in American contexts, Bohaker's explication of diplomatic relations in Anishinaabe histories, Miller's analysis of identity issues in the relationship between Ahenakew and Wallace, and Gray's realization that the nature of relationships matters in fieldwork – all of these chapters explore the different and overlapping ways in which identities operate within cross-cultural relationships and broader colonial identity politics. These issues are linked to a third theme: the nature of representations of historical experience, recent critiques of issues of representation, and attempts to construct alternative representations. These critiques suggest a new understanding of how relations of power in colonial situations have shaped the stories we have tended to tell about the past and how European cultural constructions of Aboriginal peoples – concepts with ancient historical roots – have affected, and continue to affect, cross-cultural relationships (see chapters by Vibert; Warkentin; Miller; and Peers and Coutts). Although most of the contributors strive to discern the voices of Aboriginal people, their essays remind us that these voices can often only be reached through European sources, and we need to be ever mindful to new ways to read beyond their words.

The concerns raised in these chapters echo, and most of these authors were inspired by, Jennifer S.H. Brown's work. Her primary concern with identity and its negotiation within complex multicultural contexts; her observation – cited from one work but present in many – that there were, in such situations, "complex subjectivities [and] multiple ways of knowing"; her careful sifting of many forms of evidence to reveal the details of lives and the sweep of social patterns; and her caution to understand patterns of power in the shaping of past lives and present scholarship continue to inspire all of us.[31]

Notes

1 For overviews of the historiography of Aboriginal people in Canada, see Brown, "Doing Aboriginal History"; Carlson, Jetté, and Matsui, "An Annotated Bibliography of Major Writings in Aboriginal History"; Coates, "Writing First Nations into Canadian History"; and Trigger, "The Historians' Indian."

2 We use the term "metis" to refer to all descendants of European men and Aboriginal women and the term "Metis" for members of the historic Metis Nation, which originated around the Red River settlement. Ray, *Indians in the Fur Trade;* Van Kirk, *"Many Tender Ties";* and Brown, *Strangers in Blood.* On recent trends in fur trade and metis history, see Brown, "Noms et métaphores"; Saler and Podruchny, "Glass Curtains and Storied Landscapes"; Payne, "Fur Trade Historiography"; Pannekoek, "Metis Studies"; and Barkwell, Dorion, and Préfontaine, eds., *Metis Legacy.*

3 Brown, "Noms et métaphores," 12. Author's translation. The original French is "L'histoire métissage n'est pas figée et se réinvente constamment. Les universitaires et les généalogistes métis contribuent, en particulier, à la reconquête et la reconnaissance de leurs identités historiques. Un travail aussi minutieux et consciencieux que le leur joue un rôle essentiel dans la recherche d'une histoire métisse solide et nuancée en contribuant à mettre en relief les expériences, les caractéristiques, la culture et l'héritage unique d'un peuple. Ces Métis nous montrent également qu'il n'y a pas une identité métisse pure, mais qu'il s'agit plutôt d'une gamme d'identités, qui va de l'Est à l'Ouest et du Nord au Sud. Leurs recherches visent à révéler non seulement le coeur de ces identités mais également les liens complexes qui relient entre eux nombre de communautés et d'individus susceptibles de se déclarer Métis, Indiens ou, tout simplement, en partie d'ascendance autochtone." Brown also explores this theme in "Cores and Boundaries."

4 For an example of using innovative evidence and analysis, see Brown and Vibert, eds., *Reading beyond Words*. For innovative theoretical approaches, see Shoemaker, ed., *Clearing a Path*.

5 For examples, see Bird, *The Spirit Lives in the Mind* and *Telling Our Stories;* Cruikshank et al., *Life Lived Like a Story;* Cruikshank, *The Social Life of Stories* and *Do Glaciers Listen?;* A.K. Brown and Peers, with members of the Kainai Nation, *Sinaakssiiksi aohts-imaahpihkookiyaawa/"Pictures Bring Us Messages";* and Farrell Racette, "Sewing Ourselves Together."

6 One of the most innovative additions of Aboriginal history to a national narrative is the first volume of the new History of the American West Series (directed by Richard W. Etulain): Calloway, *One Vast Winter Count*.

7 Brown and Vibert, Introduction to *Reading beyond Words,* 1st ed., ix.

8 McNab, editor for Nin.Da.Waab.Jig., *Earth, Water, Air and Fire*.

9 See essays by Jan Grabowski and Nicole St-Onge, Heather Devine, Theodore Binnema, and I.S. MacLaren in *From Rupert's Land to Canada,* edited by Binnema, Ens, and MacLeod.

10 Pickles and Rutherdale, Introduction to *Contact Zones,* 11.

11 Haig-Brown and Nock, eds., *With Good Intentions*.

12 Binnema and Neylan, eds., *New Histories for Old,* xi.

13 See Brown, "Fur Traders, Racial Categories, and Kinship Networks," and her doctoral research, which was published as *Strangers in Blood*.

14 See, for instance, "Linguistic Solitudes and Changing Social Categories"; "Woman as Centre and Symbol in the Emergence of Metis Communities"; "Children of the Early Fur Trades"; "Diverging Identities"; and "Fur Trade as Centrifuge." Her more recent work looks at the lives and families of missionaries among indigenous peoples in northern Canada. See "Growing Up Algonquian."

15 See Brown, "Documentary Editing: Whose Voices?" and "The Blind Men and the Elephant."

16 Brown, "Documentary Editing: Whose Voices?" 3.

17 Ibid.

18 Brown, abstract for "Doing Aboriginal History," 708-9.

19 In 1988 Brown published, with Robert Brightman, a commentary by Nelson on northern Ojibwe ceremonialism: *"The Orders of the Dreamed."* She also supported the publication by Peers and Schenck in 2002 of Nelson's earliest journals: *My First Years in the Fur Trade*.

20 See her article "A Place in Your Mind for Them All"; her Introduction and Afterword in Hallowell, *The Ojibwa of Berens River;* the article, written with Maureen Matthews, "Fair Wind"; and the critical edition of *Memories Myths, and Dreams* by William Berens, as told to Hallowell (co-edited with Susan Elaine Gray). She and Gray are currently editing a collection of Hallowell's essays, *Contributions to Ojibwe Studies,* which should be published by University of Nebraska Press in 2010.

21 See OurVoices – Omushkego Oral History Project, www.ourvoices.ca.

22 Brown, "Doing Aboriginal History," 614.

23 Brown and Vibert, Introduction to *Reading beyond Words,* xi.

24 Brown, "Doing Aboriginal History," 634-35.

25 Heidi Bohaker, personal communication with the authors, December 2006, has noted this scattering of historical evidence for events. For the Great Lakes region, Ruth Phillips' Great Lakes Research Alliance for the Study of Aboriginal Arts and Cultures (GRASAC) project is creating a database that will enable these materials to be digitally re-associated.

26   See Smith, *Decolonizing Methodologies;* and Mihesuah, ed., *Natives and Academics.*
27   See Alison K. Brown, Peers, and members of the Kainai Nation, *Sinaakssiiksi aohtsimaah-pihkookiyaawa/"Pictures Bring Us Messages."*
28   For examples of embodied history, see the contributions to Pickles and Rutherdale, eds., *Contact Zones.*
29   Wilson, ed., *A New Imperial History,* 6.
30   The idea that culture, identity, and colonialism are performed – are called into being through social practices that often involve the use of material culture and dress – was developed by Judith Butler (see *Gender Trouble*) and has been examined for colonial situations by Wilson, *The Island Race,* 3; and Gosden and Knowles, *Collecting Colonialism.*
31   Brown and Vibert, Introduction to *Reading beyond Words,* xi.

Bibliography

Barkwell, Lawrence J., Leah Dorion, and Darren Préfontaine, eds. *Metis Legacy: A Metis Historiography and Annotated Bibliography.* Winnipeg: Pemmican Publications, 2001.

Berens, William, as told to A. Irving Hallowell. *Memories, Myths, and Dreams of an Ojibwe Leader.* Edited with introductions by Jennifer S.H. Brown and Susan Elaine Gray. Montreal and Kingston: McGill-Queen's University Press/Rupert's Land Record Society Series, 2009.

Binnema, Ted, and Susan Neylan, eds. *New Histories for Old: Changing Perspectives on Canada's Native Pasts.* Vancouver: UBC Press, 2007.

Binnema, Theodore. "How Does a Map Mean? Old Swan's Map of 1801 and the Blackfeet World." In *From Rupert's Land to Canada: Essays in Honour of John E. Foster,* edited by Theodore Binnema, Gerhard J. Ens, and R.C. MacLeod, 201-24. Edmonton: University of Alberta Press, 2001.

Bird, Louis. *The Spirit Lives in the Mind: Omushkego Stories, Lives, and Dreams.* Compiled and edited by Susan Elaine Gray. Montreal and Kingston: McGill-Queen's University Press, 2007.

–. *Telling Our Stories: Omushkego Lessons and Histories from Hudson Bay.* Edited by Jennifer S.H. Brown, Paul DePasquale, and Mark Ruml. Peterborough, ON: Broadview Press, 2005.

Brown, Alison K., and Laura Peers, with members of the Kainai Nation. *Sinaakssiiksi aohtsimaahpihkookiyaawa/"Pictures Bring Us Messages": Photographs and Histories from the Kainai Nation.* Toronto: University of Toronto Press, 2006.

Brown, Jennifer S.H. "The Blind Men and the Elephant: Fur Trade History Revisited." In *Proceedings of the Fort Chipewyan and Fort Vermilion Bicentennial Conference,* edited by Patricia A. McCormack and R. Geoffrey Ironside, 15-19. Edmonton: Boreal Institute for Northern Studies, University of Alberta, 1990.

–. "Children of the Early Fur Trades." In *Childhood and Family in Canadian History,* edited by Joy Parr, 44-68 and 195-98. Toronto: McClelland and Stewart, 1982. Reprinted in C.M. Wallace and R.M. Bray, eds. *Reappraisals in Canadian History: Pre-Confederation.* Scarborough, ON: Prentice Hall Allyn and Bacon Canada, 1999.

–. "Cores and Boundaries: Metis Historiography across a Generation." *Native Studies Review* 17, 2 (2008): 1-18.

–. "Diverging Identities: The Presbyterian Metis of St. Gabriel Street, Montreal." In *The New Peoples: Being and Becoming Metis in North America,* edited by Jacqueline Peterson and Jennifer S.H. Brown, 195-206. Winnipeg/Lincoln: University of Manitoba Press/ University of Nebraska Press, 1985.

–. "Documentary Editing: Whose Voices?" *Occasional Papers of the Champlain Society* 1 (1992): 1-13. Text of invited plenary talk, Toronto, 1992.

–. "Doing Aboriginal History: A View from Winnipeg." *Canadian Historical Review* 84, 4 (2003): 613-35, 708-9.

–. "Fur Trade as Centrifuge: Familial Dispersal and Offspring Identity in Two Company Contexts." In *North American Indian Anthropology: Essays on Culture and Society,* edited by Raymond J. DeMallie and Alfonso Ortiz, 197-219. Norman: University of Oklahoma Press, 1994.

–. "Fur Traders, Racial Categories, and Kinship Networks." *National Museum of Man, Mercury Series, no. 23, and Papers of the 6th Algonquian Conference* (1975): 209-22.

–. "Growing Up Algonquian: A Missionary's Son in Cree-Ojibwe Country, 1869-1876." In *Papers of the 39th Algonquian Conference,* edited by Karl S. Hele and Regna Darnell, 72-93. London: University of Western Ontario, 2008.

–. "Linguistic Solitudes and Changing Social Categories." In *Old Trails and New Directions: Papers of the Third North American Fur Trade Conference,* edited by Carol M. Judd and Arthur J. Ray, 147-59. Toronto: University of Toronto Press, 1980.

–. "Noms et métaphores dans l'historiographie métisse: Anciennes catégories et nouvelles perspectives." *Recherches Amerindiennes au Quebec* 37, 2-3 (2007): 7-14.

–. "Partial Truths: A Closer Look at Fur Trade Marriage." In *From Rupert's Land to Canada: Essays in Honour of John E. Foster,* edited by Theodore Binnema, Gerhard J. Ens, and R.C. MacLeod, 59-80. Edmonton: University of Alberta Press, 2001.

–. "A Place in Your Mind for Them All: Chief William Berens." In *Being and Becoming Indian: Biographic Studies of North American Frontiers,* edited by James A. Clifton, 204-25. Chicago: Dorsey Press, 1989. Reprinted by Waveland Press, 1993.

–. "Rupert's Land, *Nituskeenan,* Our Land: Cree and English Naming and Claiming around the Dirty Sea." In *New Histories for Old: Changing Perspectives on Canada's Native Pasts,* edited by Ted Binnema and Susan Neylan, 18-40. Vancouver: UBC Press, 2007.

–. *Strangers in Blood: Fur Trade Company Families in Indian Country.* 1980; reprint, Norman/Vancouver: University of Oklahoma Press/ UBC Press, 1998.

–. "Woman as Centre and Symbol in the Emergence of Metis Communities." *Canadian Journal of Native Studies* 3, 1 (1983): 39-46.

Brown, Jennifer S.H., and Robert Brightman, eds. *"The Orders of the Dreamed": George Nelson on Northern Ojibwa Religion and Myth.* Winnipeg: University of Manitoba Press, 1988.

Brown, Jennifer S.H., with Maureen Matthews. "Fair Wind: Medicine and Consolation on the Berens River." *Journal of the Canadian Historical Association,* new series, 4 (1994): 55-74.

Brown, Jennifer S.H., and Elizabeth Vibert, eds. *Reading beyond Words: Contexts for Native History.* Peterborough, ON: Broadview Press, 1996. Second edition published in 2003.

Butler, Judith. *Gender Trouble: Feminism and the Subversion of Identity.* New York: Routledge, 1990.

Calloway, Colin G. *One Vast Winter Count: The Native American West before Lewis and Clark.* Lincoln: University of Nebraska Press, 2003.

Carlson, Keith Thor, Melinda Marie Jetté, and Kenichi Matsui. "An Annotated Bibliography of Major Writings in Aboriginal History, 1990-99." *Canadian Historical Review* 82, 1 (2001): 122-71.

Coates, Kenneth. "Writing First Nations into Canadian History: A Review of Recent Scholarly Works." *Canadian Historical Review* 81, 1 (2000): 99-114.

Cruikshank, Julie. *Do Glaciers Listen? Local Knowledge, Colonial Encounters, and Social Imagination.* Vancouver: UBC Press, 2005.

–. *The Social Life of Stories: Narrative and Knowledge in the Yukon Territory.* Vancouver: UBC Press, 1998.

Cruikshank, Julie, in collaboration with Angela Smith, Kitty Smith, and Annie Ned. *Life Lived Like a Story: Life Stories of Three Yukon Native Elders.* Vancouver: UBC Press, 1992.

Devine, Heather. "Les Desjarlais: The Development and Dispersion of a Proto-Métis Hunting Band, 1785-1870." In *From Rupert's Land to Canada: Essays in Honour of John E. Foster,* edited by Theodore Binnema, Gerhard J. Ens, and R.C. MacLeod, 129-60. Edmonton: University of Alberta Press, 2001.

Farrell Racette, Sherry. "Sewing Ourselves Together: Clothing, Decorative Arts and the Expression of Metis and Half Breed Identity." PhD diss., University of Manitoba, 2004.

Gosden, Chris, and Chantal Knowles. *Collecting Colonialism: Material Culture and Colonial Change.* Oxford: Berg, 2001.

Grabowski, Jan, and Nicole St-Onge. "Montreal Iroquois *Engagés* in the Western Fur Trade, 1800-1821." In *From Rupert's Land to Canada: Essays in Honour of John E. Foster,* edited by Theodore Binnema, Gerhard J. Ens, and R.C. MacLeod, 23-58. Edmonton: University of Alberta Press, 2001.

Haig-Brown, Celia, and David A. Nock, eds. *With Good Intentions: Euro-Canadian and Aboriginal Relations in Colonial Canada.* Vancouver: UBC Press, 2006.

Hallowell, A. Irving. *Contributions to Ojibwe Studies: Essays, 1934-1972.* Edited with Introductions by Jennifer S.H. Brown and Susan Elaine Gray. Lincoln: University of Nebraska Press, 2010.

–. *The Ojibwa of Berens River, Manitoba: Ethnography into History.* Edited by Jennifer S.H. Brown. Fort Worth: Harcourt Brace Jovanovich, 1992.

MacLaren, I.S. "Paul Kane and the Authorship of *Wanderings of an Artist.*" In *From Rupert's Land to Canada: Essays in Honour of John E. Foster,* edited by Theodore Binnema, Gerhard J. Ens, and R.C. MacLeod, 225-48. Edmonton: University of Alberta Press, 2001.

McNab, David T., editor for Nin.Da.Waab.Jig. *Earth, Water, Air and Fire: Studies in Canadian Ethnohistory.* Waterloo: Wilfrid Laurier University Press, 1998.

Mihesuah, Devon A., ed. *Natives and Academics: Discussions on Researching and Writing about American Indians.* Nebraska: University of Nebraska Press, 1998.

Pannekoek, Frits. "Metis Studies: The Development of a Field and New Directions." In *From Rupert's Land to Canada: Essays in Honour of John E. Foster,* edited by Theodore Binnema, Gerhard J. Ens, and R.C. MacLeod, 111-28. Edmonton: University of Alberta Press, 2001.

Payne, Michael. "Fur Trade Historiography: Past Conditions, Present Circumstances and a Hint of Future Prospects." In *From Rupert's Land to Canada: Essays in Honour of John E. Foster,* edited by Theodore Binnema, Gerhard J. Ens, and R.C. MacLeod, 3-22. Edmonton: University of Alberta Press, 2001.

Peers, Laura, and Theresa Schenck, eds. *My First Years in the Fur Trade: The Journals of 1802-1804, George Nelson.* St. Paul/Kingston and Montreal: Minnesota Historical Society Press/McGill-Queen's University Press, 2002.

Peterson, Jacqueline, and Jennifer S.H. Brown, eds. *The New Peoples: Being and Becoming Metis in North America.* Winnipeg/Lincoln: University of Manitoba Press/University of Nebraska Press, 1985.

Pickles, Katie, and Myra Rutherdale, eds. *Contact Zones: Aboriginal and Settler Women in Colonial Canada.* Vancouver: UBC Press, 2005.

Ray, Arthur J. *Indians in the Fur Trade: Their Role as Hunters, Trappers and Middlemen in the Lands Southwest of Hudson's Bay 1660-1870.* Toronto: University of Toronto Press, 1974.

Saler, Bethel, and Carolyn Podruchny. "Glass Curtains and Storied Landscapes: Fur Trade Historiography in Canada and the United States." In *Bridging National Borders in North America: Transnational and Comparative Histories,* edited by Benjamin Johnson and Andrew Graybill, 275-302. Durham, NC: Duke University Press, 2010.

Shoemaker, Nancy, ed. *Clearing a Path: Theorizing the Past in Native American Studies.* New York: Routledge, 2002.

Smith, Linda Tuhiwai. *Decolonizing Methodologies: Research and Indigenous Peoples.* London: Zed Books, 1999.

Trigger, Bruce G. "The Historians' Indian: Native Americans in Canadian Historical Writing from Charlevoix to the Present." In *Out of the Background: Readings on Canadian Native History,* edited by Robin Fisher and Kenneth Coates, 19-44. Toronto: Copp Clark Pitman, 1988.

Van Kirk, Sylvia. *"Many Tender Ties": Women in Fur-Trade Society in Western Canada, 1670-1870.* Winnipeg: Watson and Dwyer, 1980.

Wilson, Kathleen. *The Island Race: Englishness, Empire and Gender in the Eighteenth Century.* New York: Routledge, 2003.

–, ed. *A New Imperial History: Culture, Identity, and Modernity in Britain and the Empire, 1660–1840.* New York: Cambridge University Press, 2004.

Part 1
Using Material Culture

The two chapters in this section use material culture – the objects around us that are made and used in contexts of cultural meaning – as a key source of evidence to understand people's lives in fur trade and Anishinaabe history. Material culture has rarely been used as a source by historians. It is found in landscapes, recovered by archaeological digging, and stored in museums rather than found in collections of papers, recovered by historical detective work, and stored in archives. It often requires specialized knowledge of materials, techniques, and regional styles of decoration and technologies and how these changed over time to understand the messages it holds about the past. Museum curators have tended to emphasize a definition of authentic indigenous material culture that excludes evidence of European contact, such as manufactured materials like metal and glass, and have downplayed (and sometimes refused to exhibit) objects that document the changing lives of Aboriginal peoples after contact with Europeans. More recently, material culture has come to be seen as an extremely useful evidential source, as a product of historical and cultural influences that can tell us much about the lives of peoples in the past and about the relationships within which objects were made, used, collected, and transferred to museums.

Some material culture has not survived in collections for study, and this aspect of the past is the most challenging of all to analyze. If we regard the landscape itself as a form of material culture, shaped and understood within cultural perspectives, then markers such as lopsticks can be considered the products of cross-cultural relationships. "Putting Up Poles," by Carolyn Podruchny, Frederic W. Gleach, and Roger Roulette offers a pioneering analysis of these marking practices, through which men were initiated into new hybrid social and labour systems in the fur trade. Podruchny is a historian of voyageur, metis, and Aboriginal societies who was raised in Manitoba and supervised by Jennifer S.H. Brown as a postdoctoral fellow and who now teaches history at York University in Toronto. Gleach is an anthropologist, archaeologist, and historian of Aboriginal societies and their interactions with Europeans in colonial Virginia, the Pacific Northwest, and the Spanish Caribbean; he is currently senior lecturer and curator of the Anthropology Collections at Cornell University. Roulette, raised in an Ojibwe family in southern Manitoba, is an Ojibwe oral historian and linguist who teaches at the University of Manitoba. Their chapter gathers Aboriginal perspectives and knowledge of relevant linguistic data with information on fur trade society, Aboriginal-European relations, and the ebb and flow of culture and identity, showing that culturally hybrid complexities can be seen only when as many diverse perspectives and sources as possible are examined.

"Dressing for the Homeward Journey" is co-authored by Cory Willmott, a textile expert and specialist in the history of Anishinaabe or Ojibwe clothing. She was trained at McMaster University in southern Ontario in anthropology and art history, studied with Jennifer S.H. Brown as a postdoctoral fellow, and currently teaches anthropology at Southern Illinois University – Edwardsville. The co-author is Kevin Brownlee, a Cree archaeologist from Norway House who was raised in a southern non-Native setting. His interest in reconnecting with his culture led him to a career in archaeology at The Manitoba Museum. By examining two early nineteenth-century burials of young Aboriginal men in southern Manitoba, Willmott and Brownlee bring together archaeological evidence from the burials with surviving comparative material from museum collections, historical records about objects in the fur trade, and ethnographic information on the meaning of dress practices to Ojibwe people. They have hired First Nations artists to create visual reconstructions of the young men to integrate all of these sources of evidence. Most importantly, by decoding grave goods as markers of status and identity, they link material and historical evidence to culture and thus tie material culture analysis to historical concerns about how the fur trade shaped the lives of Aboriginal peoples. Read in this way, the burials provide strong evidence that Anishinaabe people both adapted to new opportunities in terms of status and interpreted the new trade goods within much older cultural perspectives.

2

Putting Up Poles: Power, Navigation, and Cultural Mixing in the Fur Trade

Carolyn Podruchny, Frederic W. Gleach, and Roger Roulette

MATERIAL OBJECTS HAVE ALWAYS been central to the fur trade. Felt hats, fur pelts, blankets, and copper kettles were the raisons d'être of centuries of trade between Europeans and indigenous peoples in northern North America. As a sideline to amassing the valuable fur pelts, Europeans also collected vast arrays of objects from the many Aboriginal cultures they encountered, and Canadian antiquarians had a special fetish for fur trade artifacts that enabled many museums to house substantial fur trade collections. All these objects constitute a chorus of voices that recalls the long history and great expanse of this mercantile enterprise. In a 1982 catalogue for the Minnesota Historical Society exhibit "Where Two Worlds Meet," scholar Bruce White observes that "the fur trade ... thrived on communication – not simply through a language of words, but also through a language of objects."[1] More recently, in her study of an 1840s embroidered and beaded bag from central Rupert's Land, Laura Peers has shown that items of clothing had different layers of meaning that derived from the diverse heritages of the people making and wearing them.[2] The fur trade is filled with innumerable multivocal objects, and most attention has been focused on those found in archaeological digs or preserved in European cabinets of curiosities. This chapter takes a slightly different track by examining an object that was rooted in place, that was not collectable, and that had a relatively short shelf life in archaeological terms: partially denuded trees fashioned into poles called lopsticks. These poles had a variety of meanings and uses among indigenous and European societies, and these meanings and uses collided in the fur trade. All who made and encountered these poles performed rituals with them; consequently, the poles became sites where identities were articulated and negotiated. We argue that those working in the fur trade drew on both indigenous and European traditions to create lopsticks as navigational tools; in doing so, they articulated a creole identity.

In his 1848 narrative, Hudson's Bay Company (HBC) clerk Robert Ballantyne recalls that he encountered a cluster of lopsticks as he travelled from York Factory on the western shore of Hudson Bay to Norway House at the northern end of Lake Winnipeg:

At sunset we put ashore for the night, on a point covered with a great number of lopsticks. These are tall pine-trees, denuded of their lower branches, a small tuft being left at the top. They are generally made to serve as landmarks, and sometimes the voyageurs make them in honour of gentlemen who happen to be travelling for the first time along the route, and those trees are chosen, which, from their being on elevated ground, are conspicuous objects. The traveller for whom they are made is always expected to acknowledge his sense of the honour conferred upon him, by present[ing] the boat's crew with a pint of grog, either on the spot or at the first establishment they meet with. He is then considered as having paid for his footing, and may ever afterwards pass scot-free.[3]

The conspicuous objects that Ballantyne described were variously called lopsticks, lobsticks, mais, and maypoles in the documentary record from at least the eighteenth century to the early twentieth century.[4] Figures 2.1 and 2.2, photographs from the first quarter of the twentieth century, show lopsticks that have had their central branches lopped off. In other cases, branches were cut down to the base of the tree, resulting in a long, living pole with only a leafy tuft at the top remaining. In all cases, the trees were left alive.

Lopsticks are still in use today by some indigenous groups, but we restrict our analysis to lopsticks that were constructed during the fur trade, found along the major trade routes of the rivers and lakes in the boreal forests and in the northern prairies, and lasted into the early twentieth century. As Ballantyne's quotation makes clear, in the fur trade the poles were used primarily as directional markers and as ritual objects to express the hegemonic order, which required servants to honour their masters and masters to provide for their servants. But a host of secondary meanings came to be associated with lopsticks. We argue in this chapter that the mixed function of the lopsticks can be understood because multiple traditions came to bear on their making.

Indigenous Traditions of Pole Making

Poles had a variety of meanings and uses among Aboriginal peoples. Poles were most commonly used in the construction of dwellings, such as teepees (made of straight poles and covered with birch bark), smaller temporary shelters covered with brush, the Anishinaabe *waaginogaan(an)* (a dome-shaped structure made of bent poles and covered with birch bark), and the *zhaabandawaan(an)* (an elongated waaginogaan).[5] Since these poles were both readily obtainable and subject to deterioration over time, they were often left behind when a village or camp was moved. The architectural debris of abandoned Aboriginal campsites was therefore probably often seen along fur trade routes.[6]

Figure 2.1 Lopstick, Hayes River, ca. 1910. A.V. Thomas Collection, A.V. 134 (N8208), Archives of Manitoba, Winnipeg.

Figure 2.2   Lopstick, Separation Creek, close to Flin Flon, Manitoba, ca. 1923.
J.A. Campbell Collection, 117, Archives of Manitoba, Winnipeg.

Many Algonquian speakers also created poles as points of reference or *gik-inawaajichigan(an)* in Anishinaabemowin. These poles would be used as markers for travelling. Many of the gikinawaajichigan constituted named travel routes and landscape features, and physical markers were erected for outsiders and newcomers. The preferred material for gikinawaajichigan was stones, but Anishinaabeg frequently relied on denuded trees.[7] Likewise, the same practice may be found among other indigenous groups in the boreal forest. The fur trader and explorer Alexander Mackenzie reported seeing trees stripped of all their branches "to the top like an English may-pole" at a well-used fishing site and in front of indigenous winter abodes along the Mackenzie River. These were probably made by Dene.[8]

Some poles had a deeper significance. Among the western Anishinaabeg, poles were a central feature of the *Madaa'idiwin(an)* or give-away ceremony, which was a means of wealth distribution. Gifts would be pooled together and given away according to need. All community members decided on how wealth and tools were to be distributed, and a designated facilitator, usually a male elder and medicine man, would provide the means of distribution. These ceremonies were held in the transition period between seasons, usually at the beginning or end of summer when it was easier for large groups of people to congregate. Both on the plains and in the woodlands, preparations for the Madaa'idiwin involved felling a tree, removing its branches, and decorating it with feathers, ribbon, and cloth. The beginning of the ceremony was announced by mounting the pole. The facilitator would face the pole and sing to echo the past season and announce the coming season, while the participants would dance around the pole.[9]

Generally, among Algonquian-speakers, poles were considered cosmological axes that provided a means of communication among different worlds. Anishinaabeg, for example, lived in a tripartite universe that comprised a world above, a world on earth, and a world below.[10] Living human beings resided only on the level of earth, and other-than-human beings, known as *manidoog*[11] (spirits), could move among these worlds, though some manidoog stayed only in the level where their power was greatest; for instance, thunderers (formless spirits representing thunder and lightning called *Animikiig*)[12] and thunderbirds *(Binesiwag)*[13] stayed in the world above, and the Great Panther *(Mishibizhiw)*[14] stayed in the world below.

Although most adult males engaged in communication with their personal spirits, much communication between human beings and other-than-human beings was conducted by religious specialists known as medicine people, conjurors, or shamans. These practitioners had access to a great number and variety of spirits, including powerful ones who could effect great actions. They used a variety of means – such as dreaming, vision quests, and shaking tent ceremonies – to access the spirit world. The shaking tent itself roughly resembled a pole. A small cylindrical or barrel-shaped structure, it was typically about eight feet tall and a couple of feet in diameter. The practitioner entered the tent to establish connections with his or her spirits. The shaking tent served as a conduit between the human and spirit worlds.[15] In Anishinaabemowin, the word for shaking tent in the south, "*Gosaabanijigan*," translates literally as "that which induces visual subconsciousness," but the term used in the north, "*Jiisakaan*," translates literally as "that which pierces the earth," denoting passage among worlds. The relationship between mental states and the physical domains is clear.[16]

In the Great Lakes and northern Plains area, many Anishinaabe religious specialists belonged to the Midewiwin, a sacred society that trained medicine people to hone their skills in communication with manidoog. Although the Midewiwin is generally not well described in print, there are mentions in some texts of the use of poles in Mide ceremonies.[17] In 1888, W.J. Hoffman wrote:

> The average size of [a Midewiwin lodge] is about seventy-five feet long, twenty
> feet wide, and fifteen feet high. The framework of the structure is of poles and
> saplings, the sides being closed by the close arrangement of branches and pieces
> of birch bark or blankets, while the roof is generally of birch bark. Near the top
> of the interior and running lengthwise is a pole, intended for the exhibition of
> such presents as can be suspended therefrom. A cedar pole is erected in the lodge
> about sixty feet from the entrance, upon which is placed a rudely-mounted bird
> about the size of a pigeon.[18]

Both William Warren and George Copway describe poles mounted in the interior of Midewiwin lodges. In an explanation of a Mide ceremony, Warren wrote: "The novice in the process of initiation, sat in the centre on a clean mat facing the Me-da-wautig, a cedar post planted in the centre of the lodge, daubed with vermillion and ornamented with tufts of birds' down."[19] Copway recorded that "in the centre of the lodge is a pole, which we call a meeting pole, or *Me-day Wahtick*. It has painted on it a representation of the Great Spirit."[20] In his record of Ojibwe logograms of pictographs, Copway records the following symbol for

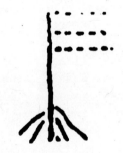

Worship, medicine, pure.

Figure 2.3 Logogram of "worship, medicine, pure." From George Copway's
The Traditional History and Characteristic Sketches of the Ojibway Nation (1850).

"worship, medicine, pure," which was probably inspired by medicine poles (see Figure 2.3).

Although many details and specifics varied, similar features can be found in other Algonquian settings. Perhaps best documented is the Big House ceremony of the Lenape (or Delaware) Indians, an eastern Algonquian group.[21] Like the Mide lodge, the Big House in which this ceremony took place was centred by a carved post. In this case, the post is clearly symbolic, with the dance floor representing the everyday world, the arched roof of the Big House the levels of the spirit world, and the earth beneath the floor the levels of the underworld. The central post bridges these domains, and the path of the dancers, the White Path, represents the course of human life within this universe. In a structural analysis of Delaware culture, Jay Miller describes the contextual meanings of the central post:

> The source for mediators along the vertical axis of the Delaware cosmos was the Cosmic Tree, which grew from the back of the Cosmic Turtle. Important mediators in Delaware culture such as sticks and poles seem to be metonyms of this tree. As the building used for the Big House Rite was a metaphor for the Cosmos, so the carved center post was a metaphor for the Cosmic Tree as *axis mundi*. The Cosmic Tree grew at the exact center of the world and the center post recreates its formal position as the center for the Delaware cultural world. In the same way, the center of the world is paralleled by the belief that the heart is the center of the person. The center post is the nexus of the macrocosm as the heart is the nexus of the personal microcosm.[22]

Frank Speck's study of the Big House ceremony as practised in Oklahoma in the late 1920s includes an account dictated in Delaware by Wi·tapano'xwe (James C. Webber), who describes the central post in somewhat different terms but with similar place of precedence in the culture: "And now the Big House when first built, they say of it, was the one great prayer-creed, that this carved post in the middle of the House, standing there reaches to the above through as many as ten and two strata. And the strata of the sky light are as high as that post, it is said, this being the fastener. That is the Creator's staff. From that very staff, branch off all prayer-creeds of the red people given to them, whence come all other prayer-creeds of the world."[23] The Big House Ceremony also featured a trimmed tree outside the Big House on which meat was hung, to maintain the purity of the Big House.[24]

The ritual use of poles was also found in medicine practices, especially those connected to warfare and hunting. According to John Tanner, while Anishinaabe war chiefs prayed to discover the whereabouts of their enemies, warriors would mount offerings to manidoog on poles.[25] After battle, Anishinaabe warriors placed the hair or skulls of their enemies on poles to signify victory in war.[26] In one case, in northwestern Ontario near Lac Seul, when a French Canadian fur trader tried to cheat Anishinaabeg, they killed him and mounted his head on a pole to send a message to other unethical traders. To this day, the site is referred to as Frenchman's Head.[27] In the 1680s, Nicholas Perrot noted that before Anishinaabeg embark on voyages, "they are careful to kill some dogs with their clubs and to hang the bodies from a tree or a pole; sometimes also they suspend thus dressed skins of elk, or moose, or deer, which they consecrate to the sun or the lake, in order to obtain fair weather."[28] Egerton R. Young in 1869 visited a site in northern Manitoba also related to a dog ritual:

> We had been journeying on for ten or twelve days when one night we camped on the shore of a lake-like river. While my men were busily employed in gathering wood and cooking the supper, I wandered off and ascended to the top of a well wooded hill which I saw in the distance. Very great indeed was my surprise, when I reached the top, to find myself in the presence of the most startling evidences of a degraded paganism.
>
> The hill had once been densely covered with trees, but about every third one had been cut down, and the stumps, which had been left from four to ten feet high, had been carved into rude representations of the human form. Scattered around were the dog-ovens ... Here and there were the tents of the old conjurers and medicine men ... I wandered around and examined the idols, most of which had in front of them, and in some instances on their flat heads, offerings of tobacco, food, red cotton, and other things.[29]

Although Young's religious biases dominate the text, the association of these poles with offerings is also clear.[30] The practice had a long history: Father Allouez reported in 1666 that Crees "pay idolatrous worship to the Sun, to which they are wont to offer sacrifice by fastening a dog to the top of a pole and leaving it thus suspended until it rots."[31] The Menominee bear ceremony concluded with the ritually treated skull hung in a tree, and at least to the late twentieth century Mistassini Crees would hang the skulls of hunted animals in trees as a respectful treatment of their prey.[32] In the 1930s, Regina Flannery observed the James Bay Cree spring feast and noted that first kills were displayed on a pole strikingly like the lopstick: "Near the door of the tent which faced the rising sun a 'mast' or 'flagpole' was set up for the permanent exhibition of the decorated animal remains ... The mast consisted of a freshly cut tree about 15 ft tall which was debarked except for the new growth at the crown (the tree's acahkw) and to which a crosspiece was attached about 6 ft from the ground."[33] The use of poles for ritual purposes is widespread beyond the Algonquian-speaking world. The totem poles of the Pacific Northwest are better understood as honouring and mnemonic devices that record through the stories represented not only a clan totem but also entire sets of relationships and histories. Scaffolds and other kinds of elevated burials that used poles to raise the deceased were also widespread. The sun dance – which reached into Plains Cree and Anishinaabe country, although it did not originate with them – features a centre pole that is prepared in a similar fashion to a lopstick. Branches are stripped, but a fork or branches left on top represent Thunderbird's nest.[34]

An interesting parallel to sacred poles that are set in the ground is Umon'hon'ti, the sacred pole of the Omaha tribe, which was not only a physical object made from cottonwood but also a living person. Robin Ridington and Dennis Hastings (In'aska) explain that the sacred pole "served to symbolize the tribe's unity at a time when they were moving from one place to another. He continued to stand for their tribal identity during the good times when they controlled the trade up and down the Missouri River."[35] Umon'hon'ti resided for over a century at the Peabody Museum at Harvard but was returned to the Omaha people in 1989.

Although none of these examples is precisely the same as a lopstick, taken together they document a range of traditions involving poles among Algonquian and other Aboriginal groups in North America. In particular, the Anishinaabe give-away ceremony seems closest to lopsticks, for they both involve a pole created specifically for a ceremony that involves exchange and represents power. In addition, lopsticks most likely descended directly from indigenous traditions that used denuded trees as geographical markers. By the late nineteenth century, some travellers – such as Caspar Whitney, an American sports journalist who published an account of his trek through the northern Canadian barren lands in 1896 – were attributing lopsticks solely to Aboriginal people. In northern Alberta near McMurray, Whitney recorded that the Indians made a lopstick to honour him.[36] But poles have significance in many parts of the world, and Europeans brought their own traditions of making marker poles to North America.

European Maypole Traditions

Poles honouring important people were common in Lower Canada and had deep roots in Europe. On the first of May, bushes, trees, or poles were arranged in front of the houses of priests, seigneurs, and young women with eager suitors. And poles could also honour the election of aldermen. Those honoured with a pole were required to provide treats in the form of food or alcohol.[37] Anthropologist Arnold Van Gennep suggested that the maypole ritual was a reciprocal exchange that could mark the successful completion of a relationship of obligation. For example, at the end of a harvest, agricultural labourers sometimes erected a maypole for their employer, who then provided them with a banquet, which signified that both parties were satisfied.[38]

Maypole traditions were widespread in Europe and elsewhere in the world. In a general sense, they were tied to fertility and pagan tree spirits, but in western Europe, by at least the seventeenth century, the maypole had become primarily a sign of the exuberant joy attendant on the rebirth of spring. Its erection was accompanied by dancing and merrymaking that attracted the ire of Puritans.[39] The traditional maypole, like the lopstick, had its trunk smoothed, but a tuft of branches was left at the top, where ornaments were placed. In some cases, when the pole was left in place from year to year, a fresh bush was attached to the top each May.

One of the most interesting uses of the maypole occurred in Plymouth Colony (Massachusetts) in 1627 and 1628. Colonist Thomas Morton drew the ire of Puritan leaders by erecting and celebrating a maypole at his trading post, which he called Ma-re Mount and is generally known as Merry Mount.[40] This pole was eighty feet tall, decorated with ribbons and flowers, and had a pair of stag's horns at the top. Morton's chief antagonist, Governor William Bradford, wrote: "They also set up a maypole, drinking and dancing about it many days together, inviting the Indian women as their consorts, dancing and frisking together like so many faeries, or furies, rather; and worse practices. As if they had anew revived and celebrated the feasts of the Roman goddess Flora, or the beastly practices of the mad Bacchanalians."[41] Morton considered Aboriginal people to be admirable (although he wrote that they lacked religion) and kept close consort with them, both in his trade and in his life. He seems to have found Aboriginal people more friendly and humane than his fellow colonists. He traded guns to Aboriginal people, against Puritan mandate, and profited well by the trade. Morton included Aboriginal people in the construction and ceremonies of his maypole. Michael Zuckerman reports that "he and his men ate and drank with the Indians, spoke their language, and kept sexual company with them."[42] Morton exalted nature and considered the local environment a New Canaan, while the Puritan colonists held it in fear. Morton thus constituted a threat to the Puritans' very way of life. He was arrested and sent back to England, and the pole was torn down. But in using the English pagan tradition of the maypole to celebrate his association with the Aboriginal people among whom he lived, he presaged some of the uses of lopsticks by fur traders in Canada.

French settlers brought the practice of putting up maypoles to the St. Lawrence Valley. As in France, habitants honoured seigneurs by placing maypoles in front of their residences in return for feasts. Not all seigneurs were so honoured, and by the eighteenth century seigneurs began inserting clauses in deeds that required habitants to erect maypoles for them. In the tumultuous years before the 1837 rebellion in Lower Canada, habitants used maypoles to honour locally elected militia captains. Historian Allan Greer, citing Van Gennep, explains that in these cases the meaning of maypole ceremonies was reciprocity: "The men presented their captain with a symbol of his authority, while he for his part had to make a gesture of repayment. In accepting the symbol of power, the captain also accepted the responsibility it implied, responsibility, that is, towards the men under his command, rather than towards his superiors."[43]

French or English, the maypole traditions emphasized among other things a state of community, a network of interactions among people who may be of different classes or kinds. Aboriginal peoples and Europeans alike probably recognized the similarities between the maypole tradition and pole traditions in Aboriginal societies, and the transformation of these practices into lopsticks represents precisely the kind of creolization to be expected in a context of cultural interaction.

Lopsticks in the Fur Trade Context

Fur traders created lopsticks for a variety of purposes. The most obvious use for a lopstick was as a directional marker along fur trade routes. For example, on 2 October 1819, the famous Arctic explorer John Franklin, who was being transported by voyageurs, sighted a lopstick at White Fall, along the Hayes River between Hudson Bay and Lake Winnipeg: "We observed a conspicuous *lop-stick,* a kind of land-mark, which I have not hitherto noticed, notwithstanding its great use in pointing out the frequented routes."[44] In 1892, Warburton Pike, an Englishman who spent most of his life travelling in the barrens with indigenous people, recalled that "these lop-sticks are easily distinguished landmarks, well known to the voyageurs, and many an appointment has been kept at Campbell's, Macdougal's, or Macfarlane's tree. In giving directions to a stranger it is hopeless to describe the points and bends of a monotonous river highway, but a lop-stick does the duty as a signpost and at once settles the question of locality."[45] As recently as 1941, historian Grace Lee Nute reported that "lob pines are said to be standing on the Kaministikwia route between Fort William and Lac La Croix, on Knife Lake, Cecil Lake, and at other points."[46] The lopsticks reminded travellers of those who had gone that way before. As Alexander Ross's brigade passed a lopstick at the mouth of Berens River in the 1820s, one of the men in his crew recalled building it eighteen years earlier. Almost sixty years later, the site at the mouth of Berens River was still known as Lobstick Island.[47]

Other places in the landscape came to be associated with or named for lop-sticks. In 1872, George M. Grant, travelling with the engineer-in-chief of the Canadian Pacific and Intercolonial Railways, wrote about Lobstick River, named after the great number of lopsticks along the waterway, flowing into the Pembina River on the Prairies.[48] An island in Rainy Lake is still known today as Maypole Island. Other places include Lobstick Lake in Saskatchewan, northeast from Saskatoon; a village named Lobstick in Alberta, west of Edmonton; Lobstick Creek at the southern edge of the Northwest Territories, between the Little Buffalo and Slave Rivers; and Lobstick Lake in Labrador, which is now under the Smallwood Reservoir. There is also a Lopstick Lodge in New Hampshire; a Lobstick Lodge in Jasper, Alberta; and a Lobstick Golf Course in Waskesiu, Saskatchewan.[49]

A second common use of lopsticks in the fur trade was for servants, and in some cases indigenous trappers, to honour those considered to have power or a high social status. Poles were navigational markers not only for fur trade routes but also for power relationships among participants in the fur trade.[50] Lopstick ceremonies were practised mainly by French Canadian voyageurs, who created maypoles for their masters. The lopstick ritual allowed masters to claim author-ity and permitted servants to demand material rewards. In the quotation at the beginning of this chapter, HBC clerk Robert Ballantyne wrote that voyageurs sometimes created the lopsticks to honour masters who were travelling along a fur trade route for the first time. In return for the lopstick, the honouree was expected to provide a pint of grog for all the men on the crew.[51] This dramatic performance of authority had different meanings for different participants. The bourgeois demonstrated their superiority over their servants in part by reward-ing voyageurs who performed a difficult and dangerous task for no apparent benefit other than to assert the masters' own eminence. The voyageurs, on the other hand, probably welcomed the occasion to rest from paddling and enjoyed the treats and revelry that accompanied the ceremony. In 1821, Nicholas Garry, who became deputy governor of the HBC from 1822 to 1835, noted that the voyageurs who created a lopstick for him at Oxford House (on the way from Norway House to York Factory) also named the immediate area around the lopstick Garry's Point to honour him further.[52]

The lopstick ceremony was not restricted to fur trade masters. Some travellers in voyageur canoes, who owed voyageurs nothing except payment for a safe passage, were honoured with a maypole. One intriguing example was the wife of Sir George Simpson, the governor of the HBC after its merger with the North West Company (NWC) in 1821. A lopstick was raised in honour of Frances Simpson in 1830 at Norway House while she journeyed from York Factory to Red River. She wrote in her diary that the Voyageurs agreed among themselves to cut a "May Pole," or "Lopped Stock" for me; which is a tall Pine Tree, lopped of all its branches excepting those at the top, which are cut in a round bunch: it is then barked: and mine (being a memorable one) was honored with a red feather, and streamers of purple ribband tied to a poll, and fastened to the top of the Tree, so as to be seen above every other object: the surrounding trees were then cut down, in order to leave it open to the Lake. Bernard (the Guide) then presented me with a Gun, the contents of which I discharged against the Tree, and Mr. Miles engraved my name, and the date, on the trunk, so that my "Lopped Stick" will be conspicuous as long as it stands, among the number of those to be seen along the banks of different Lakes and Rivers.[53]

Frances Simpson was among the first white women to live in the Northwest. Historian Sylvia Van Kirk explains that, "with the arrival of Frances Simpson, the [HBC] Governor [George Simpson] seemed determined to create an all-white elite in the [Red River] settlement. Mrs. Simpson's female society was restricted to those few white women whose husbands possessed social standing."[54] The voyageurs might have been trying to make a good impression on the governor. The voyageurs may also have been awed by the exotic Mrs. Simpson, who represented the alien world of upper-class British society. Another traveller deemed worthy of a lopstick was Paul Kane, an artist from Toronto who travelled through the Northwest in the late 1840s, sketching indigenous people and the environment.[55] In 1872, George M. Grant explained that a "lobstick is the Indian or half-breed monument to a friend or a man he delights to honour ... You are expected to feel highly flattered and make a handsome present in return to the noble fellow or fellows who have erected such a pillar in your honour."[56] In another example, while travelling with the HBC close to York Factory in June 1842, voyageurs honoured John Birkbeck Nevins with a lopstick. Nevins reported that "this is a complimentary ceremony, which is performed for most strangers, the first time of their traveling up the country ... which the stranger returns, by making them a present of a gallon of rum, or something of equal value, on arriving at the first fort."[57] Nevins then described a case in which two men, who "professed tee-total principles," refused to provide alcohol to the men who cut them lopsticks. The next time the two men travelled by the site of their lopsticks, they had been cut down. When they expressed indignation, the canoemen retorted, "they were not yours; you never paid for them."[58] The ceremony generally resembled other common rituals in the trade that featured the firing of guns and cheering. In Simpson's case, the addition of feathers and streamers to the maypole suggests possible Aboriginal influences.

Some traders made their own lopstick or ordered labourers to construct one for them. In 1790, trader Peter Pangman created a lopstick for himself at Rocky

Mountain House in sight of the Rocky Mountains to mark the farthest extent of traders' discoveries along the Saskatchewan River. The lopstick came to be known as Pangman's Tree.[59] In another example, fur trader Alexander Ross wrote:

> It is a habit among the grandees [bourgeois] of the Indian trade to have May-poles with their names inscribed thereon on conspicuous places, not to dance round, but merely to denote that such a person passed there on such a day, or to com-memorate some event. For this purpose, the tallest tree on the highest ground is generally selected, and all the branches are stripped off excepting a small tuft at the top. On Mr. McKay's return from his reconnoitring expedition up the river, he ordered one of his men to climb a lofty tree and dress it for a May-pole. The man very willingly undertook the job, expecting, as usual on these occasions, to get a dram.[60]

On an expedition to explore the Prairies in 1857, Henry Youle Hind described a site near Cat Head on Lake Winnipeg: "A spruce tree growing on this peninsula has been trimmed into a 'lopstick,' by Angus Macbeth, from which the locality has derived the name of Macbeth's point."[61]

The context in which lopsticks were made and used in the fur trade was a culture of encounter and creolization that involved a mixing of indigenous traditions from Aboriginal populations and European traditions brought by settlers, trappers, and traders.[62] Lopsticks have strong antecedents among French and English colonists and among Algonquian-speaking people, particularly Anishinaabe, that likely converged to form this specific tradition. The general term for all poles in Anishinaabemowin is *"badakijiganaak(oog)*," an animate term that means that the poles were living beings with access to power. Both English and French had specific terms for ritual poles – "maypoles" and *"les mais."* Lopsticks in the fur trade drew from a number of traditions to act as navigational markers for both geography and hegemony.

Conclusion

The use of poles in ceremonies was a common practice all over the world, in particular among western Europeans and Algonquian speakers in northern North America. The hybrid practice of lopsticks in the fur trade bore remark-able resemblances both to badakijiganaakoog (poles) in the Madaa'idiwin (give-away ceremony) among Anishinaabeg and to maypole ceremonies in the St. Lawrence Valley. In some cases, the names of the ceremonies became blurred. For example, while travelling around western Ontario (then Manitoba) in 1877, Mary Fitzgibbon observed lopsticks and recorded in her journal that "Indians formerly made them to commemorate some great event but now will make one for a bag of flour or a feast."[63] She likely witnessed a Madaa'idiwin. Over time, the practice of creating lopsticks might have drifted back into indigenous communities that the fur trade routes travelled through, such as the northern Cree communities south of Lake Athabasca observed by George Grant in the 1870s and by the American sportswriter Caspar Whitney in the 1890s. Yet the lopsticks may also have been old traditions, mimicked in the fur trade, that continue to the present day. The poet and playwright Charles Mair, who was secretary to the Metis Scrip Commission that travelled with the Treaty 8 commissioners, noted while he travelled in the Mackenzie River basin at the turn of the twentieth century that "the Indian's lop-stick, called by the Cree piskootenusk, is a sort of living talisman which he connects in some mysterious way with his own fate, and which he will often go many miles out of his direct course to visit. Even white men fall in with the fetish, and one of the three we saw was called 'Lambert's lop-stick.' I myself had one made for me by Gros Oreilles, the Saulteau Chief, nearly forty years ago, in the forest east of Pointe du Chene, in what is now Manitoba."[64]

In all of these contexts – in the land of the Anishinaabeg and the Cree, in the St. Lawrence Valley, and along the travel routes of fur traders – poles served a variety of purposes. They acted as navigational markers for travellers. They symbolized power and represented a transfer of wealth from the prosperous to those in need. In the fur trade, they became poignant symbols of the complex negotiation of power inherent in the master and servant relationship. As time went on, servants began to honour not only their masters but also European wives of fur trade officials, such as Sir George Simpson's wife, Frances, and European artists such as Paul Kane.

At first glance, the poles seem to be anomalous creations to honour a few bourgeois. But on closer inspection, the making of lopsticks reflects the multivocality of the fur trade. Lopsticks could be used as maypoles and gikinawaajichigan, but they also developed as a creolization of traditions in the context of interactions between Algonquian-speakers and Euro-Canadians. Lopsticks articulated practices of honouring and sharing that resonated with both French Canadian and Anishinaabe traditions and acted as sites of cultural conjunction that fostered the building of common understandings and shared meanings, yet Europeans and Aboriginals could continue to use the poles in ways that made sense to them. One is reminded of Jennifer S.H. Brown's description of the fur trade as centrifuge: mixed European and Aboriginal families were pulled in many directions and developed an array of identities that were situational and fluid. As she recently explained:

Trading brought people together for exchanges both tangible and intangible, but the dynamics of the fur trade also eventually propelled them in many different directions. There was no unitary or bounded "fur trade society"; that construct can use some scrutiny. Aboriginal communities remained self-governing in the context of the fur trade, and the traders themselves came from diverse backgrounds and were subject to varied forms of control and authority, depending on their employers and living conditions. They had to adapt locally, and their values varied widely ... In sum, the trade was built upon and spawned a broad spectrum of Aboriginal, mixed, and newcomer communities that related with one another in diverse, complex ways that changed over time. Working forward from the past, we are often tracing families and groups that were flung in different directions as the fur trade expanded and contracted and as fur trade fathers were moved, or lost or changed employment, or died, leaving families on their own. The centrifugal forces were many and strong.[65]

All of these examples show us that the fur trade was not a monolithic constant; rather, it was diverse, fluid, and unstable. Although the poles were used in a process of creolization and developed meanings specific to the fur trade context, Europeans and Anishinaabe peoples could continue to use them in distinct ways. Putting up poles was one of many activities in the fur trade that involved disparate meanings and heritages.

Notes

This chapter originated as a presentation by Carolyn Podruchny at the Thirty-Fifth Algonquian Conference in 2003. Frederic Gleach and Roger Roulette were pleased to contribute to this version. The authors would like to thank all those who have commented on the various versions, particularly Kevin Alstrup, Charles Bishop, Alicia Colson, Karl Hele, John S. Long, Peter Jan L. Loovers, Victor Lytwyn, Cath Oberholzer, Richard Preston, Nicholas Smith, Rhonda Telford, Terry Wilde, and members of the Toronto Area Early Canada and Colonial North America Seminar. We also heartily thank Jennifer S.H. Brown for years of support, collegiality, and collaboration, on this and other projects.

1 White, "Parisian Women's Dogs," 121.
2 Peers, "Many Tender Ties," 293.
3 Ballantyne, *Hudson's Bay*, 191-92.
4 "Lobstick" is a simple consonant shift from the original "lopstick"; "lop" refers to the removal of branches from a trunk, typically with an axe. "Maypole" derives from the European tradition, discussed below. "Mai" is probably from the French and also related to the idea of the maypole.
5 See, for example, Hallowell, "Dwellings and Households," 102-7.
6 Kohl, *Kitchi-Gami*, 10.
7 Roger Roulette, fieldwork with Plains and Woodland Anishinaabe (western Ojibwe) in 1990 for the Manitoba Museum of Man and Nature; in 1992-94 for the CBC documentary "Fairwind's Drum," with Maureen Matthews; and in 1995-97 for Treaty One Oral History, Manitoba Indian Cultural Education Centre. See also Matthews and Roulette, "Fairwind's

Dream." For reference to broader Aboriginal cultural practices in the eastern United States, see Shoemaker, *A Strange Likeness,* 26-27.

8 Mackenzie, *Voyages from Montreal,* 56, 69.
9 Roger Roulette, fieldwork with Plains and Woodland Anishinaabe (western Ojibwe).
10 Although not always attested to in print, this general pattern is widespread among Algonquian groups. For more extensive descriptions of Anishinaabe religious beliefs, see Smith, *The Island of the Anishnaabeg Thunderers;* Hallowell, "Ojibwa Ontology, Behaviour, and World View"; and Bohaker, "Nindoodemag." On Menominee cosmology, see Skinner, "Cosmology and Medicine Bundles."
11 The singular is *"manidoo."* The term was found in Algonquian languages and cultures from the northern prairies of Canada to the Atlantic coast of New England and even to the southeastern Algonquian groups of Virginia and North Carolina. For a brief survey, see Gleach, *Powhatan's World,* 40-42.
12 The singular form is *"animikii."*
13 The singular form is *"binesi."*
14 The plural form is *"mishibizhiwag"* and also refers generally to underwater panthers.
15 On the shaking tent, see, for example, Hallowell, *The Role of Conjuring* and "Dwelling and Households," 69-71, and Brown and Brightman, eds., *"The Orders of the Dreamed,"* 146-58.
16 Roger Roulette, fieldwork with Plains and Woodlands Anishinaabe (western Ojibwe).
17 General overviews can be found in Landes, *Ojibwa Religion and the Midéwiwin;* Densmore, *Chippewa Customs,* 86-97; and Hoffman, "Notes on Ojibwa Folk-Lore."
18 Hoffman, "Pictography and Shamanistic Rites," 219.
19 Warren, *History of the Ojibway People,* 77.
20 Copway, *The Traditional History,* 166.
21 On the Big House ceremony, see Speck, *A Study of the Delaware Indian Big House Ceremony* and "Additional Notes to the Big House Ceremony," and Harrington, *Religion and Ceremonies of the Lenape.*
22 Miller, "A Strucon Model," 799-800.
23 Speck's translation, in *A Study of the Delaware Indian Big House Ceremony,* 87.
24 Speck, *A Study of the Delaware Indian Big House Ceremony,* Fig. 4, 34; see also his description of the ceremony and discussion of the concept of purity.
25 Tanner, *A Narrative of the Captivity,* 123-24.
26 Roger Roulette, fieldwork with Plains and Woodland Anishinaabe (western Ojibwe), and Kohl, *Kitchi-Gami,* 247.
27 Ningewance, *Talking Gookom's Language,* 187.
28 Perrot, "Memoir on the Manners," 60.
29 Young, *By Canoe and Dog Train,* 84-85.
30 These poles represented the spirits and provided a locus for offerings from humans who had ties to them. See Brightman, *Grateful Prey,* 116.
31 Allouez, "Father Allouez's Journey to Lake Superior," 134.
32 Skinner, *Associations and Ceremonies of the Menomini Indians,* 213. Brightman describes similar practices among the Rock Cree in *Grateful Prey,* 207. The Mistassini Cree practice is documented on Richardson's film *Cree Hunters of Mistassini.*
33 Flannery and Chambers, "Each Man Has His Own Friends," 10.
34 Mandelbaum, *The Plains Cree,* 188-90.
35 Ridington and Hastings, *Blessing for a Long Time,* xvii.
36 Whitney, *On Snow-Shoes,* 321. Also see Grant, *Ocean to Ocean,* 196. In another example, James Southesk, the earl of Carnegie, attributed the making of lopsticks to half-breeds. Southesk, *Saskatchewan and the Rocky Mountains,* 44, 251. The journal *Lobstick: An*

Interdisciplinary Journal of Creative Thought, Social Commentary, Scholarly Research, and Debate, published at Grande Prairie Regional College in Alberta, states that lopsticks are "strongly associated with northern Cree nations." See the journal's website.

37 See Greer, *The Patriots and the People,* 107-13.

38 Van Gennep, *Le folklore du Daphiné (Isère),* 1:300-1. Also cited in Greer, *The Patriots and the People,* 111. For the European roots to maypole ceremonies in Canada, Greer cites Van Gennep, *Manuel de folklore français contemporain,* 1:516-75, and Ozouf, *La fête révolutionnaire,* 293.

39 See, for example, Cooper and Sullivan, *Maypoles, Martyrs and Mayhem,* 133; Hardwick, *Traditions, Superstitions, and Folk-Lore,* 83-95; and Frazier, *The Golden Bough,* 73-85.

40 For the original accounts, see Bradford, *Of Plymouth Plantation,* 204-10, and Morton, *A New English Canaan,* 132-36. Morton's spelling was intended to *imply* the sense of "merry" when spoken while conveying literally "mount by the sea." See also Cohen, "Morton's Maypole and the Indians"; Zuckerman, "Pilgrims in the Wilderness"; and Demos, "The Maypole of Merry Mount."

41 Bradford, *Of Plymouth Plantation,* 205-6.

42 Zuckerman, *Pilgrims in the Wilderness,* 263.

43 Greer, *The Patriots and the People,* 112.

44 Franklin, *Narrative of a Journey,* 2 October 1819, 40. For other examples of lopsticks as geographical markers, see Macdonell, "The Diary of John Macdonell," 16 August 1793, 102, and Ballantyne, *Hudson's Bay,* 91-92.

45 Pike, *The Barren Ground,* 209. For an example of a lopstick marking a place in a forest, see J.B. MacDougall's comment from Ontario: "And over all rises some giant lobstick pine with branching top standing sentinel over his perennial domain, for we are in the heart of the Timagami Forest Reserve." MacDougall, *Two Thousand Miles of Gold,* 89.

46 Nute, *The Voyageur's Highway,* 49.

47 Ross, *Fur Hunters,* 2:242; Morris, *The Treaties of Canada,* 157.

48 Grant, *Ocean to Ocean,* 196. This river, originating in west central Alberta, retains its name today.

49 Walpole Island in Ontario is also known as Warpole Island, although it is not clear that the multiple posts that once stood there were the same as lopsticks. See *Memorial of the Chippeway Indians.*

50 For a discussion of lopsticks as part of the master and servant relationship in the Montreal-based fur trade, see Podruchny, *Making the Voyageur World,* 134-42.

51 Ballantyne, *Hudson's Bay,* 191-92. Also see Begg, *"Dot It Down,"* 220-21.

52 Garry, *Diary of Nicholas Garry,* 149. For another example of naming a landscape feature after the honouree of a lopstick, see the explanation for Macbeth's Point in Hind, *Narrative of the Canadian Red River Exploring Expedition,* 489.

53 Nute, "Journey for Frances," 17.

54 Van Kirk, *"Many Tender Ties,"* 204.

55 Kane, "Journal," 48, and *Wanderings,* 236.

56 Grant, *Ocean to Ocean,* 196.

57 Nevins, *A Narrative,* 90.

58 Ibid., 90-91.

59 Henry (the Younger), *New Light,* 1:269 and 2:507, 640, 662.

60 Ross, *Adventures of the First Settlers,* 2 May 1811, 78-79.

61 Hind, *Narrative of the Canadian Red River Exploring Expedition,* 489.

62 "Creolization" refers to a process of blending elements from distinct cultures in a context of cultural contact. Although never purely egalitarian, it is a less oppressive process than

many forms of colonial interaction. The term originated in linguistics but is now commonly applied to other domains of mixing as well. It is analogous to *"metíssage"* in French contexts and *"mestizaje"* in Spanish contexts but avoids the genetic or racial implications of those terms by focusing explicitly on cultural rather than biological interactions. The literature on linguistic creolization is vast. See, for example, Le Page and Tabouret-Keller, *Acts of Identity;* Thomason and Kaufman, *Language Contact, Creolization, and Genetic Linguistics;* and Spears and Winford, eds., *The Structure and Status of Pidgins and Creoles.* For examples of analyses based on creolization in extra-linguistic domains, see Kulikoff, *Tobacco and Slaves,* and the contributors to *Historical Archaeology* 34, 3 (2000), a special issue on the subject that includes a piece on Métis log buildings by David V. Burley.

63 Fitzgibbon, *A Trip to Manitoba,* 199-200.
64 Mair, *Through the Mackenzie Basin,* 126.
65 Brown, "Noms et métaphores," 8-9. Translation by Jennifer S.H. Brown. The original French is as follows: "Le fait de commercer a permis de réunir les gens à l'occasion d'échanges, à la fois matériels et immatériels, mais la dynamique du commerce des fourrures a aussi fini par les entraîner dans de nombreuses autres directions. Il n'y eut pas de 'société de la traite de fourrures' unifiée ou bien délimitée, une hypothèse qui se mériterait d'être approfondie. Les communautés autochtones demeurèrent autonomes dans le cadre du commerce des fourrures et les marchands eux-mêmes, aux origines diverses, furent soumis à plusieurs formes de contrôle de pouvoir qui dépendaient de leur employer et de leurs conditions de vie. Il leur fallut s'adapter aux usages locaux alors que leurs valeurs respectives différaient grandement relativement ... En somme, le commerce avait prospéré en donnant naissance à une vaste série de communautés amérindiennes, mixtes ou constituées de nouveaux arrivants qui interagissaient entre elles de manière complexe, diversifiée et évolutive dans le temps. L'étude du passé permet souvent de découvrir la trace de familles et de groupes qui furent projetés dans des voies au gré du sort reserve aux pères, lesquels pouvaient être mutes, perdre ou changer d'emploi, ou mourir, abandonnant ainsi leur famille à leur proper sort. Les forces centrifuges étaient nombreuses et importantes."

Bibliography

Allouez, Jean Claude. "Father Allouez's Journey to Lake Superior, 1665-1667." In *Early Narratives of the Northwest, 1634-1699,* edited by Louise Phelps Kellogg, 93-138. New York: Charles Scribner's Sons, 1917.

Ballantyne, Robert Michael. *Hudson's Bay or Every-Day Life in the Wilds of North America during Six Years' Residence in the Territories of the Honourable Hudson's Bay Company.* Edinburgh: William Blackwood and Sons, 1848.

Begg, Alexander. *"Dot It Down": A Story of Life in the North-West.* Toronto: Hunter, Rose, 1871.

Bradford, William. *Of Plymouth Plantation, 1620-1647.* New York: Modern Library, 1967.

Brightman, Robert. *Grateful Prey: Rock Cree Human-Animal Relationships.* Berkeley: University of California Press, 1993.

Brown, Jennifer S.H. "Noms et métaphores dans l'historiographie métisse: Anciennes catégories et nouvelles perspectives." *Recherches Amerindiennes au Quebec* 37, 2-3 (2007): 7-14.

Brown, Jennifer S.H., and Robert Brightman, eds. *"The Orders of the Dreamed": George Nelson on Cree and Northern Ojibwa Religion and Myth, 1823.* St. Paul: Minnesota Historical Society Press, 1988.

Bohaker, Heidi. "Nindoodemag: The Significance of Algonquian Kinship Networks in the Eastern Great Lakes Region, 1600–1701." *William and Mary Quarterly,* 3rd series, 63, 1 (2006): 23-52.

Burley, David V. "Creolization and Late 19th-Century Métis Vernacular Log Architecture on the South Saskatchewan River." *Historical Archaeology* 34, 3 (2000): 49-56.

Cohen, Matt. "Morton's Maypole and the Indians: Publishing in Early New England." *Book History* 5 (2002): 1-18.

Cooper, Quentin, and Paul Sullivan. *Maypoles, Martyrs and Mayhem: 366 Days of British Customs, Myths and Eccentricities.* London: Bloomsbury, 1994.

Copway, George. *The Traditional History and Characteristic Sketches of the Ojibway Nation.* Toronto: Prospero, 2001 [1850].

Demos, John. "The Maypole of Merry Mount." *American Heritage* (October-November 1986): 83-87.

Densmore, Frances. *Chippewa Customs.* Introduction by Nina Marchetti Archabal. St. Paul: Minnesota Historical Society Press, 1979 [1929].

Fitzgibbon, Mary. *A Trip to Manitoba, or, Roughing It on the Line.* Toronto: Rose-Belford Publishing Company, 1880.

Flannery, Regina, and Mary Elizabeth Chambers. "Each Man Has His Own Friends: The Role of Dream Visitors in East Cree Belief and Practice." *Arctic Anthropology* 22, 1 (1985): 1-22.

Franklin, Sir John. *Narrative of a Journey to the Shores of the Polar Sea in the Years 1819, 20, 21 and 22.* London: J.M. Dent and Sons, 1819.

Frazier, James G. *The Golden Bough.* New York: Gramercy Books, 1993 [1890].

Garry, Nicholas. *Diary of Nicholas Garry, Deputy-Governor of the Hudson's Bay Company from 1822-1835: A Detailed Narrative of His Travels in the Northwest Territories of British North America in 1821.* S.l: s.n.

Gleach, Frederic W. *Powhatan's World and Colonial Virginia: A Conflict of Cultures.* Lincoln: University of Nebraska Press, 1997.

Grant, George M. *Ocean to Ocean: Sanford Fleming's Expedition through Canada in 1872: Being a Diary Kept during a Journey from the Atlantic to the Pacific with the Expedition of the Engineer-in-Chief of the Canadian Pacific and Intercolonial Railways.* Toronto: J. Campbell, 1873.

Greer, Allan. *The Patriots and the People: The Rebellion of 1837 in Rural Lower Canada.* Toronto: University of Toronto Press, 1993.

Hallowell, A. Irving. "Dwellings and Households along the Berens River [1935-36]." In *The Ojibwa of Berens River, Manitoba: Ethnography into History,* edited by Jennifer S.H. Brown, 100-10. Fort Worth: Harcourt Brace College Publishers, 1992.

–. "Ojibwa Ontology, Behaviour, and World View." In *Culture in History: Essays in Honor of Paul Radin,* edited by Stanley Diamond, 22-52. New York: Columbia University Press, 1960.

–. *The Role of Conjuring in Saulteaux Society.* New York: Octagon Books, 1971 [1942].

Hardwick, Charles. *Traditions, Superstitions, and Folk-Lore, (Chiefly Lancashire and the North of England): Their Affinity to Others in Widely-Distributed Localities; Their Eastern Origin and Mythical Significance.* Manchester/London: A. Ireland/Simpkin, Marshall and Co., 1872.

Harrington, Mark R. *Religion and Ceremonies of the Lenape.* Indian Notes and Monographs. New York: Museum of the American Indian, Heye Foundation, 1921.

Henry (the Younger), Alexander. *New Light on the Early History of the Greater Northwest: The Manuscript Journals of Alexander Henry.* Edited by Elliott Coues. 2 vols. Minneapolis: Ross and Haines, 1897.

Hind, Henry Youle. *Narrative of the Canadian Red River Exploring Expedition of 1857 and of the Assiniboine and Saskatchewan Exploring Expedition of 1858*. London: Longman, Green, Longman, and Roberts, 1860.

Hoffman, W.J. "Notes on Ojibwa Folk-Lore." *American Anthropologist* 2, 3 (1889): 215-24.

–. "Pictography and Shamanistic Rites of the Ojibwa." *American Anthropologist* 1, 3 (1888): 209-30.

Kane, Paul. "Journal of Paul Kane's Western Travels, 1846-1848." Transcribed by I.S. MacLaren. *American Art Journal* 21, 2 (1989): 23-62.

–. *Wanderings of an Artist among the Indians of North America from Canada to Vancouver's Island and Oregon through the Hudson's Bay Company Territory and Back Again*. London: Longman, Brown, Green, Longmans, and Roberts, 1859.

Kohl, George Johann. *Kitchi-Gami: Life among the Lake Superior Ojibway*. Translated from the German by Lascelles Wraxall. Introduction by Robert E. Beider. St. Paul: Minnesota Historical Society Press, 1985 [1859].

Kulikoff, Allan. *Tobacco and Slaves: The Development of Southern Cultures in the Chesapeake, 1680-1800*. Chapel Hill: University of North Carolina Press, 1986.

Landes, Ruth. *Ojibwa Religion and the Midéwiwin*. Madison: University of Wisconsin Press, 1968.

Le Page, R.B., and Andrée Tabouret-Keller. *Acts of Identity: Creole-Based Approaches to Language and Identity*. Cambridge: Cambridge University Press, 1985.

Macdonell, John. "The Diary of John Macdonell." In *Five Fur Traders of the Northwest*, edited by Charles M. Gates, 61-119. St Paul: Minnesota Historical Society, 1965.

MacDougall, J.B. *Two Thousand Miles of Gold, from Val d'Or to Yellowknife*. Toronto: McClelland and Stewart, 1946.

Mackenzie, Alexander. *Voyages from Montreal on the River St. Laurence, through the Continent of North America, to the Frozen and Pacific Oceans, in the Years 1789 and 1793: With a Preliminary Account of the Rise, Progress and Present State of the Fur Trade of That Country*. London: R. Noble, 1801.

Mair, Charles. *Through the Mackenzie Basin: An Account of the Signing of Treaty No. 8 and the Scrip Commission, 1899*. Edmonton: University of Alberta Press/Edmonton Historical Society, 1999 [Toronto: W. Briggs, 1908].

Mandelbaum, David G. *The Plains Cree: An Ethnographic, Historical and Comparative Study*. Canadian Plains Studies 9. Regina: Canadian Plains Research Center, 1979.

Matthews, Maureen, with Jennifer S.H. Brown. "Fairwind's Drum." Produced by Margaret Ingram for Canadian Broadcasting Corporation's *Ideas*. First aired 11-12 May 1993.

Matthews, Maureen, and Roger Roulette. "Fairwind's Dream: *Naamiwan Obawaajigewin*." In *Reading beyond Words: Contexts for Native History*, edited by Jennifer S.H. Brown and Elizabeth Vibert, 330-60. Peterborough, ON: Broadview Press, 1996.

Memorial of the Chippeway Indians of Port Sarnia, Warpole Island, Kettle Point, and Sauble, Touching Their Claim of the Grant of 1,100 Currency Perpetual Annuity to His Excellency the Governor General in Council that the Foreign Indians May Participate in the Annuity. London: n.p., ca. 1871.

Miller, Jay. "A Strucon Model of Delaware Culture and the Positioning of Mediators." *American Ethnologist* 6, 4 (1979): 791-802.

Morris, Alexander. *The Treaties of Canada with the Indians of Manitoba and the North-West Territories, Including the Negotiations on Which They Were Based*. Toronto: Belfords, Clarke, 1880.

Morton, Thomas. *A New English Canaan*. Amsterdam: Jacob Frederick Stam, 1637.

Nevins, John Birkbeck. *A Narrative of Two Voyages to Hudson's Bay; With Traditions of the North American Indians*. London: Society for Promoting Christian Knowledge,

1847.

Ningewance, Patricia M. *Talking Gookom's Language: Learning Ojibwe.* Lac Seul, ON: Mazinaate Press, 2004.

Nute, Grace Lee. "Journey for Frances." *The Beaver* (Summer 1954): 12-18. For the rest of the published excerpts of Frances Simpson's diary, see *The Beaver* (December 1953): 50-59, and (March 1954): 12-17.

–. *The Voyageur's Highway: Minnesota's Border Lake Land.* St. Paul: Minnesota Historical Society Press, 1941.

Ozouf, Mona. *La fête révolutionnaire, 1789-1799.* Paris: Gallimard, 1976.

Peers, Laura. "'Many Tender Ties': The Shifting Contexts and Meanings of the S BLACK Bag." *World Archaeology* 31, 2 (1999): 288-302.

Perrot, Nicholas. "Memoir on the Manners, Customs, and Religion of the Savages of North America." In *The Indian Tribes of the Mississippi Valley and the Region of the Great Lakes,* edited by Emma Helen Blair, 23-272. Lincoln: University of Nebraska Press, 1996.

Pike, Warburton. *The Barren Ground of Northern Canada.* London: Macmillan, 1892.

Podruchny, Carolyn. *Making the Voyageur World: Travelers and Traders in the North American Fur Trade.* Lincoln/Toronto: University of Nebraska Press/University of Toronto Press, 2006.

Richardson, Boyce. *Cree Hunters of Mistassini.* Ottawa: National Film Board of Canada, 1974.

Ridington, Robin, and Dennis Hastings. *Blessing for a Long Time: The Sacred Pole of the Omaha Tribe.* Lincoln: University of Nebraska Press, 1997.

Ross, Alexander. *Adventures of the First Settlers on the Oregon or Columbia River: Being a Narrative of the Expedition Fitted Out by John Jacob Astor, to Establish the "Pacific Fur Company," with an Account of Some Indian Tribes on the Coast of the Pacific.* Ann Arbor: University Microfilms, 1966 [London: Smith, Elder and Co., 1849].

–. *Fur Hunters of the Far West: A Narrative of Adventures in Oregon and the Rocky Mountains.* 2 vols. London: Smith, Elder and Co., 1855.

Shoemaker, Nancy. *A Strange Likeness: Becoming Red and White in Eighteenth-Century North America.* Oxford: Oxford University Press, 2004.

Skinner, Alanson. "Cosmology and Medicine Bundles." In *Social Life and Ceremonial Bundles of the Menomini Indians,* 73-161. Anthropological Papers of the American Museum of Natural History, Vol. 13, Pt. 1. New York: The Trustees, 1913.

Smith, Theresa S. *The Island of the Anishnaabeg Thunderers and Water Monsters in the Traditional Ojibwe Life-World.* Moscow: University of Idaho Press, 1995.

Southesk, James Carnegie, Earl of. *Saskatchewan and the Rocky Mountains: A Diary and Narrative of Travel, Sport, and Adventure during a Journey through Hudson's Bay Company's Territories in 1850 and 1860.* Toronto: J. Campbell, 1875.

Spears, Arthur K., and Donald Winford, eds. *The Structure and Status of Pidgins and Creoles.* Amsterdam: John Benjamins, 1997.

Speck, Frank G. "Additional Notes to the Big House Ceremony." *Oklahoma Delaware Ceremonies, Feasts and Dances.* Memoirs of the American Philosophical Society, Vol. 7. Philadelphia: American Philosophical Society, 1937.

–. *A Study of the Delaware Indian Big House Ceremony.* Publications of the Pennsylvania Historical Commission, Vol 2. Harrisburg: Publications of the Pennsylvania Historical Commission, 1931.

Tanner, John. *A Narrative of the Captivity and Adventures of John Tanner (U.S. Interpreter at the Saut de Ste. Marie) during Thirty Years Residence among the Indians in the Interior of North America*. Edited by Edwin James. New York: G. and C. and H. Carvili, 1830.

Thomason, Sarah G., and Terrence Kaufman. *Language Contact, Creolization, and Genetic Linguistics*. Berkeley: University of California Press, 1988.

Van Gennep, Arnold. *Le folklore du Daphiné (Isère): Étude descriptive et comparée de psychologie populaire*. 2 vols. Paris: Librarie Orientale et Américaine, 1932.

–. *Manuel de folklore français contemporain*. 4 vols. Paris: J. Picard, 1937-49.

Van Kirk, Sylvia. *"Many Tender Ties": Women in Fur-Trade Society, 1670-1870*. Winnipeg: Watson and Dwyer Publishing Ltd., 1980.

Warren, William W. *History of the Ojibway People*. Edited by W. Roger Buffalohead. St. Paul: Minnesota Historical Society Press, 1984 [1885].

White, Bruce M. "Parisian Women's Dogs: A Bibliographical Essay on Cross-Cultural Communication and Trade." In *Where Two Worlds Meet: The Great Lakes Fur Trade*, edited by Carolyn Gilman, 120-26. St. Paul: Minnesota Historical Society, 1982.

Whitney, Caspar. *On Snow-Shoes to the Barren Grounds: Twenty-Eight Hundred Miles after Musk-Oxen and Wood-Bison*. New York: Harper and Brothers, 1896.

Young, Egerton Ryerson. *By Canoe and Dog Train among the Cree and Salteaux Indians*. Toronto: W. Briggs, c. 1890.

Zuckerman, Michael. "Pilgrims in the Wilderness: Community, Modernity, and the Maypole at Merry Mount." *New England Quarterly* 50, 2 (1977): 255-77.

3

Dressing for the Homeward Journey: Western Anishinaabe Leadership Roles Viewed through Two Nineteenth-Century Burials

Cory Willmott and Kevin Brownlee

ABOUT TWO HUNDRED YEARS ago, two Western Anishinaabe youths were dressed in their finest apparel for their final homeward journey to the Land of the Dead. One was carefully arranged in fetal position, and the other was in an extended position, but they were both decked with their most sumptuous ornaments. Well prepared for their reception among their deceased relatives, they set off on their journeys from their gravesites near two fur trade posts in present-day Manitoba. In 1938, one of these youths was disturbed and recovered by construction workers. In 1966, the other youth was discovered and excavated by a team of archaeologists from the University of Saskatchewan. Today, an interdisciplinary team is studying the physical remains and grave goods. Once the team has completed the analysis, everything will be turned over to the community of Pine Creek for reburial.[1]

The silverwork adornment and trade cloth dress worn by these two individuals are characteristic of the Great Lakes Ojibwe and Odawa (Anishinaabeg in their own language) at the height of their involvement with the fur trade (c. 1780-1820). Other inhabitants of the region, notably the Cree and Assiniboine, did not care as much for the cloth and silverwork sold by the traders.[2] Many Anishinaabeg moved to present-day Manitoba during this period, in part to follow the fur trade as the beaver began to be trapped out in their own hunting territories.[3] In the Red River region, they came to be known as Saulteaux because of their supposed origins around Sault Ste. Marie.[4] Because this appellation oversimplifies the complex histories of these migrants, however, we maintain the indigenous term "Anishinaabe," which includes the Ojibwe, Odawa, and Potawatomi.

With the understanding that Western Anishinaabeg dress their dead in order to "make a decent appearance before their relations" on arrival in the Land of the Dead,[5] we have reconstructed their social identities through an interpretation of their accoutrements. Analysis of the dress and burial goods of these two Western Anishinaabe youths provides an unusual opportunity to widen and deepen our understanding of Anishinaabe worldview and social structure in the Manitoba fur trade during a period of rapid change. The textual record and material evidence surrounding these burials complement and enlarge upon each other in unique ways. Fortuitously, for example, these youths belonged to the groups discussed in the extraordinarily rich narratives of Alexander Henry the Younger, a North West Company (hereafter NWC) partner, and John Tanner, a captive raised by an Odawa family. These sources provide greater insight into the social and cultural context of these youths' lives than is typical of the unpublished fur trade journals from the region. Inventories of trade goods flowing into the region complement these narratives by providing a material and economic context for the trade goods used in the burials.

Most importantly, these two burials had an unusual amount and variety of extant textiles that enable us to gain a clearer picture of their dress than is normally possible. Analysis of dress reveals social structural relations because dress functions to articulate individual and social identities along lines of age, gender, ethnicity, occupation, rank, lineage, personal accomplishments, and other aspects of status.[6] Moreover, in the fur trade context, dress "provided an important means of cultural mediation" because its capacity for self-fashioning facilitated cultural mobility within the "middle ground" of European-Native relations.[7] Richard White defines the middle ground as a "new set of common conventions" in relationships between Amerindians and Europeans that governed "suitable ways of acting" that did not necessarily reflect shared understandings.[8] Because of the tenuous nature of Europeans' initial foothold in North America, the outer forms of these conventions were largely determined by First Nations or by a blend of First Nations and European cultural protocols. We can therefore interpret middle ground ceremonial forms through Aboriginal cultural norms.

Items of material culture provide tangible and objective evidence of Anishinaabe practice at a level of minute detail and specificity that one rarely, if ever, finds in textual sources. The reasons are twofold. First, textual and visual sources are iconic and/or symbolic representations that are filtered through the perspectives and interests of their creators. In contrast, although they are iconic and/or symbolic as vehicles for expression, artifacts also bear an indexical relation to their referents, by which means they provide unequivocal and highly detailed empirical facts.[9] As John Ewers reminds us, the "history of Indian-white relations was not really *written,* it was *enacted;* and ... artifacts played important roles in that acting."[10] As trade goods, presents, annuity payments, weapons, and so on, artifacts did important things for historical actors. Second, whereas textual and visual sources are typically produced by and for men of European descent, material culture reflects indigenous practices and perspectives even if it was produced from European goods and/or for European consumers. Fur trade journals and inventories represent modes of exchange at the intersection between European and indigenous worlds. In contrast, material culture provides windows into modes of exchange and use value within indigenous communities, thereby opening vistas into Aboriginal agency and worldview unobtainable through textual sources alone.

In contrast to ethnology collections assembled by European collectors and institutions, archaeological assemblages are especially valuable because they represent Aboriginal individuals' self-fashioned biographical statements. Each item in these burial assemblages represents a series of choices in accordance with indigenous criteria, both practical and symbolic. Together, these choices provide alternative histories of people whose lives form the substance of in-cremental change in daily life rather than the exceptional moments of rapid and decisive historical transformation normally the subject of history. Material culture preserves a record of non-events that contemporaneous participants and observers take for granted and therefore neglect to include in their narratives.[11]

In this chapter, we explore these two Western Anishinaabe youths' grave goods for the light they shed on intercultural power relations at the height of the fur trade (c. 1780-1820). We draw on ethnographies, archaeology reports, fur trade journals, fur trade inventories, and ethnological artifact collections to place the youths' lives in historical and cultural context. We agree that First Nations consumers and diplomats held the upper hand in intercultural relations during periods of economic and/or political competition.[12] Nevertheless, both the material traits of the youths' grave goods and the cultural context to which they point suggest that the fur trade offered unprecedented opportunities for personal growth and expression while at the same time introducing harmful influences into Anishinaabe society that ultimately undermined collective political power and autonomy when the fur trade gave way to agricultural settlements composed of European colonists.

The Circumstances of Death

The two burials were both relatively close to NWC posts, one on the Red Deer River and the other near Dauphin Lake (see map). Their proximity to the posts is one of many indications of these individuals' close association with the fur trade. As we learn from the narratives of John Tanner, Alexander Henry the Younger, and others, it was customary for these recently immigrated Anishin-aabeg to visit the trading posts during fall and spring to dispose of their furs.[13] Drunken "frolics" were an inevitable part of these biannual visits.[14] Additionally, some families temporarily camped near the posts for a variety of other reasons, including the promise of help during periods of starvation, safety for the women and children when men went on the warpath, protection from Sioux war parties when men were not on the warpath, and the ability to trade provisions for liquor on a regular basis.[15]

The Red Deer River burial was not at the post but five or six miles upstream from it.[16] In this case, the family might have chosen a hunting camp near the post in order to maintain continuous commerce. In George Nelson's Dauphin River journal, for example, all the Anishinaabeg who took debts from him encamped within a day's journey from his post so that NWC men could travel to their camps to exchange liquor and trade items for meat and/or furs.[17] The Dauphin Lake burial, by contrast, was adjacent to the post. It was quite common for burials to take place at fur trade posts. For example, in his autobiography, Tanner relates that his adoptive father and brother were buried at Grand Portage.[18] Henry (the Younger) makes frequent reference to burials taking place at the "burying grounds" just outside his fort.[19] In one instance, the body of a prominent man's son was brought from an outpost for burial at the fort at Pembina.[20] The Hudson's Bay Company (HBC) trader Peter Fidler noted this burial ground when he passed through the region in 1809.[21] In 1795 at Fort Dauphin, the HBC trader John Best was called on to transport two Western Anishinaabeg killed during a "drinking match" from their camp to his fort for burial.[22] On these occasions, fur traders were expected to supply a blanket or cloth and vermilion for the dead and rum for the relatives.[23]

Physical anthropologists examined the human remains of the two Western Anishinaabe youths twice: once when they were excavated (Dauphin Lake, 1938; Red Deer River, 1966) and again under Kevin Brownlee's direction. The analyses suggest that the Dauphin Lake burial contained the remains of a male youth about seventeen to twenty years old, while the Red Deer River burial's occupant was a male only twelve to fourteen years old. The physical remains do not yield conclusive evidence about the causes of death. The Dauphin Lake youth's skull, however, has signs of a severe ear infection (mastoiditis), which might have been caused by a fatal illness.[24] Several epidemics occurred in this region during the period in question. For example, Tanner recounts in detail the widespread effects of a disease that rendered him unconscious for days and deaf for a few weeks in 1804:

> I was awakened by a dreadful pain in my ears. It appeared to me that something was eating into my ears, and I called Wa-me-gon-a-biew to look, but he could see nothing. The pain became more and more excruciating for two days; at the end of which I became insensible ... Though my health soon became good, I did not recover my hearing, and it was several months before I could hunt as well as

I had been able to do previous to my sickness; but I was not among those who suffered most severely by this terrible complaint. Of the Indians who survived, some were permanently deaf, others injured their intellects, and some, in the fury occasioned by the illness, dashed themselves against trees and rocks, breaking their arms, or otherwise maiming themselves. Most of those who survived, had copious discharges from the ears, or in the earlier stages had bled profusely from the nose. This disease was entirely new to the Indians, and they attempted to use few or no remedies for it.[25]

The Red Deer River youth's skull was missing the right mastoid, suggesting that he might have suffered from a similar disease. He also had a puncture in his skull above the right ear, which is an unlikely place for an accidental wound. If it occurred while he was alive, it would have caused death, for there is no evidence of healing.[26] But it cannot be determined if it happened before or after death, during the burial process. Death by warfare is unlikely. The Red Deer River youth was too young to have been on the warpath himself. Therefore, if the wound was inflicted by enemies, it would have occurred at the site of an enemy attack. Peter Fidler reports that there were attacks by the "Fall Indians" in this region when he was posted there in 1802.[27] Even if the youth was wounded in battle, however, he probably would not have been buried intact because enemies customarily mutilated or burned their casualties on the battlefield to deprive them of a happy afterlife.[28] Alternatively, the death might have been alcohol related. Many Anishinaabeg met untimely deaths at one another's hands during drinking bouts at fur trade posts.[29] We consider this the most likely scenario for the Red Deer River youth. Unfortunately, there is no definitive answer to the cause of death for either youth. Nevertheless, their physical traits enable us to explore the range of possibilities inherent in their fur trade lifestyle and the intercultural circumstances of its enactment.

Dauphin Lake and Red Deer River Material Culture Assemblages

The cosmology of the Great Lakes and Western Anishinaabeg included a Land of the Dead, where souls travelled after departure from their earthly lives. Souls had to overcome a variety of challenges on their way, including traversing a narrow and/or undulating log stretched across a deep ravine. Travellers could see in the turbulent river below the souls of those who had been greedy or cruel during their lives. After successfully reaching the other side and crossing a wide plain, souls entered a land of abundance, where they met all of their ancestral relations and joined them in a perpetual celebration of song and dance.[30] Anishinaabeg therefore referred to this route as the homeward road.[31]

Table 3.1

Composition of grave goods described in twelve historical sources from 1720 to 1860

Item	Number[1]	Item	Number[1]
Weapons and hunting tools[2]	12	Fire steel, flint	2
Domestic utensils[3]	8	Tobacco	2
Ornaments	7	Pipe	2
Best clothes	6	Tobacco pouch	2
Blanket	3	Axe	2
Face painting	2	Money	1
Face paint	2	Drum	1
Medicine bag	2	Same clothing as when living	1

Sources: Perrot, "Memoire," 78, 81; Cameron, "The Nipigon Country," 259; Carver, *Carver's Travels,* 399; Grant, "The Saulteaux Indians," 364; Jones, *History of the Ojebway Indians,* 98-99; Keating, *Narrative,* 113; Kohl, *Kitchi-Gami,* 217; Long, *Voyages,* 49; McDonnell, "The Red River," 276; Nelson, *My First Years,* 113; Schoolcraft, *Historical and Statistical Information,* 1:355; and Warren, *History of the Ojibway People,* 72-73.

1 Represents the number of sources that mentioned the item in question.
2 Rifles, knives, war clubs, and bows and arrows.
3 Spoons and kettles.

These beliefs about the afterlife influenced how the Western Anishinaabeg buried their dead. During the eighteenth century, Great Lakes Ojibwe and Odawa funerary practices changed from ossuary style communal graves with few grave goods to individual graves with an increasing number of grave goods, the majority of which were trade goods.[32] By the turn of the nineteenth century, it was customary, although not universal, to dress the deceased in their finest clothing and ornaments and provide them with weapons and hunting implements, domestic utensils, and a variety of other articles deemed desirable or necessary for a man or a woman on a four-day journey.[33] Table 3.1 shows the types of grave goods that twelve historical sources mention in their descriptions of Anishinaabe funerary practices. These sources most frequently mention weapons, hunting tools, and domestic utensils, closely followed by ceremonial dress and ornaments.

The term "assemblage" refers to all the items of material culture found in close proximity; the relation among them reveals more than the individual items. This term is particularly apropos for the personal items interred with Anishinaabeg, since they included those things that collectively expressed an individual's identity, that is, his or her social roles and statuses. With the exception of the absence of axes and guns,[34] both the Dauphin Lake and Red Deer

River youths' assemblages fall well within the parameters for burial goods established in Table 3.1. Although neither had a rifle, spear, war club, bow, or arrow, both had knives and gunflints. The Dauphin Lake youth had two strike-a-lights, and the Red Deer River youth had four musket balls and seventy-two shot pellets. Arguably, the knives were multipurpose hunting implements rather than strictly weapons, although "domestic utensils" in Table 3.1 includes only kettles and spoons.

The Dauphin Lake youth was better equipped with domestic utensils than was the Red Deer River youth, for he had scissors, a file, a copper kettle, a sugaring spoon, and two clamshells. He might have used the latter as trays to prepare vermilion face paint. Vermilion was present in the Dauphin Lake burial but not in the burial at Red Deer River. Both youths had mirrors, and the Red Deer River youth also had a comb. They both had pipes, but while the Red Deer River youth had a metal tobacco container, the Dauphin Lake youth might have had a cloth tobacco pouch. This is suggested by the presence of some fine broadcloth fragments that are rarely found on whole garments such as leggings and breechcloths.[35] The Red Deer River grave lacked evidence of two types of frequently described items: domestic utensils and blankets. As we will discuss, this grave appears to be exceptional in its focus on status as opposed to practical items.

Table 3.2 shows the grave goods associated with the Dauphin Lake and Red Deer River burials in the categories of silverworks, modified silver, beads, other accoutrements, and textiles. This comparative overview illustrates that the Red Deer River youth had far more variety and amounts of adornment and status markers than did the Dauphin Lake youth, but the latter had more variety in textiles. Rather than attempt a detailed analysis of every item in these assemblages, we will focus on the most significant artifacts, which are those items on which dating depends and those that can be read as ethnic markers or in terms of a culturally specific dress code.

For the Dauphin Lake youth, the significant artifacts are shell hair pipe beads, silverworks, the textiles that made up a red chief's coat with metallic braid trimming and blue cuffs and collar, peacock and ostrich feathers, a gauze head or neck scarf, and a wooden spoon. In particular, he had a pair of shell hair pipe beads, which were three and a quarter inches long and which he probably wore on tiny braids on either side of his face.[36] He had a moderate amount of silver – only twenty-eight pieces – including two bracelets, seventeen broaches, and three pieces of modified silver that were cut into rectangular shapes (see Figure 3.1).

The Dauphin Lake burial had a greater variety of extant textile types than the Red Deer River burial – seven types in all, including silk gauze, blanketing, red

Table 3.2

Comparison of Dauphin Lake and Red Deer River assemblages

Category	Artifact	Dauphin Lake	Red Deer River
Silverworks	Wristbands (RC Montreal)	2	2
	Wristbands (NR)		2
	Three-quarter-inch broaches	13	30
	One-half-inch broaches	10	50
	One-and-one-half-inch broach		1
	Ear bobs		56
	Gorget		1
	Small double-bar cross (RC)		14
	Hearts (RC)		2
	Hatband (RC Montreal)		1
	Heart ear wheel (RC)		2
	Six-pointed star ear wheel (NR)		2
Modified silver	New bands	2	
	Silver with holes	1	2
	Scrap	1	2
Beads	White seed beads	321	> 3,000
	Shell hair pipe beads	2	3
	Shell wampum	18	2,193
	Bone hair pipe beads		11
	Perforated lynx claw		1
Other accoutrements	Rings		3
	Hawk bells		32
	Brass neck ring		1
	Ostrich feathers	1 cluster	
	Peacock feather	1	
Textiles	Common red stroud	Yes	Yes
	Fine red stroud	Yes	
	Common blue stroud		Yes
	Fine blue stroud	Yes	
	Silk gauze	Yes	
	Blanketing	Yes	
	Metallic braid (lace)	Yes	Yes
	Ribbon	Yes	Yes
	Gartering	Yes	Yes

Note: This table does not include the full range of artifacts associated with each grave, but it does show all of those in the categories represented. Although we will not discuss all of the artifacts shown here, we think it is important to provide a complete record at least for the categories on which we focus.

Figure 3.1   Two pieces of modified silver from the Dauphin Lake assemblage. © The Manitoba Museum, Winnipeg, MB.

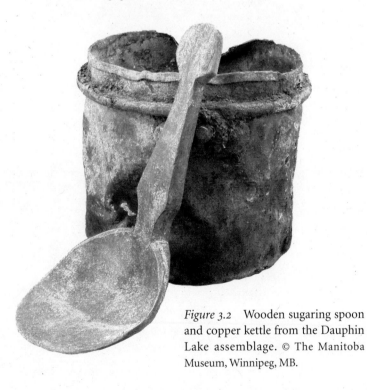

Figure 3.2   Wooden sugaring spoon and copper kettle from the Dauphin Lake assemblage. © The Manitoba Museum, Winnipeg, MB.

and blue common strouds, fine red broadcloth, metallic braid or "lace," silk ribbon, and gros grain binding. Another interesting feature of this assemblage is a fully intact copper kettle and a carved wooden spoon (see Figure 3.2). The remarkable preservation of perishable materials buried with this individual is attributed to this kettle.[37]

The significant artifacts for the Red Deer River youth are his shell hair pipe beads, silverworks, a wampum belt, and the textiles that make up a blue chief's coat with metallic braid trimming and red cuffs and collar. In contrast to its Dauphin Lake counterpart, the Red Deer River assemblage includes a profuse amount of silverworks – 179 pieces in all – including a crescent gorget with a bear motif and an "NR" mark (for Montreal silversmith Narcisse Roy) (see Figure 3.3). The individual had a wampum belt wrapped around his neck that consisted of approximately 2,057 to 2,193 mass-produced shell wampum beads (seventeen strands, each of which was from 121 to 127 beads long). Attached to it were fourteen tiny silver crosses with "RC" marks (for Montreal silversmith Robert Cruikshank), eight silver ear bobs, and two silver hearts with "RC" marks. There was also a lynx claw attached to the belt (see Figure 3.4).[38] This thirteen-year-old youth also had multiple indications of wealth or status markers, including a lead pipe bowl, a brass neck ring, piles of scrap silver, and two hanks of white seed beads. Finally, he was wearing an elaborate and apparently unique crown-like headdress that might have indicated wealth or status.[39]

Both of these assemblages are remarkable for their opulence. The sheer quantity of trade goods and variety of adornment and status items suggest that

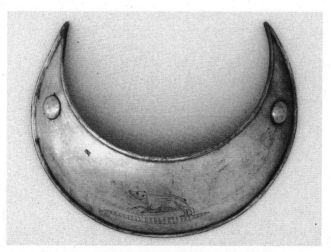

Figure 3.3   Trade silver gorget with a bear motif from the Red Deer River assemblage.
© The Manitoba Museum, Winnipeg, MB.

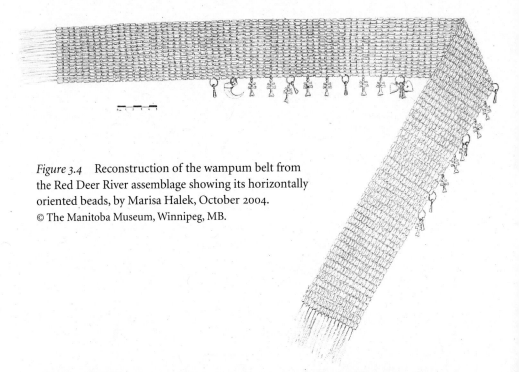

Figure 3.4   Reconstruction of the wampum belt from
the Red Deer River assemblage showing its horizontally
oriented beads, by Marisa Halek, October 2004.
© The Manitoba Museum, Winnipeg, MB.

these youths were interred during the very height of the Manitoba fur trade, which represents a relatively small window in time. When David Thompson travelled through the Swan River region in 1797, he met an elderly Anishinaabe man who foretold the demise of the beaver. Thompson concurred.[40] Decline in the NWC trade began to be evident in the region west of Lake Winnipeg by 1808, when fur traders' journals and the minutes from the annual meeting at Fort William reported radical reductions in returns.[41] In 1812, the NWC partners bemoaned the "gloomy" state of the trade, and in 1813 they resolved to cut back expenses by reducing orders for goods by one quarter and by laying off 150 men.[42] Besides shrinking beaver populations and political strife, factors such as climate change and epidemic diseases adversely affected the Manitoba fur trade in the second decade of the nineteenth century.[43] We suggest that these two opulent burials probably occurred before the decline in the trade, specifically in the first decade of the nineteenth century.

Given that the egalitarian Anishinaabe social structure nevertheless had a pronounced age hierarchy,[44] it is noteworthy that both of these youths were dressed in chief's coats. This raises questions about the types and roles of leaders in indigenous Anishinaabe political systems and the ways in which political and economic relations with Europeans caused changes in these leadership roles. Historically, Great Lakes Anishinaabeg had a variety of leadership roles, none of which conferred the authority and power to enforce laws or wishes or even the right to remain in power unless the leaders could continually prove their worthiness.[45] The Anishinaabe word for chief – "*ogimaa*," which means leader or boss – describes positions of both ascribed and achieved status.[46] Civic chiefs – also called natural, political, or peace chiefs – were the hereditary leaders of totemic groups. Although this leadership position typically passed to a son of the chief, it went to the most worthy among them rather than the oldest. If none of the sons was deemed worthy, then the chief, either alone or with the support of his or her followers, would select another person.[47] The several known instances of female chiefs were the exceptions rather than the rule, as is to be expected in a patrilineal descent system.[48] Civic chiefs were assisted in their duties by sub-chiefs (*aanike-ogimaag*, literally "those who are second in succession" or, in modern usage, "vice-presidents"), functionaries such as the spokesperson (*giigidoowinini*, literally "speaker man" or, in modern usage, "councillor"), and the messenger (*oshkaabewis*, in modern usage often a spiritual practitioner's helper), all of which were hereditary positions from which new chiefs were sometimes selected.[49] Despite the hereditary basis of these positions, an ineffective chief could be replaced by a chief with stronger support from the community.

In addition to these ascribed roles in civic governance, Anishinaabe society had a number of achieved leadership positions, such as the war chief (*meyosiwinini*, literally "foremost man" or "upright man," or *nigaanossewinini*, literally, "first, foremost, walks at the head of a company"), the hunting chief, the rice-gathering chief, and the economic aid to the chief (*mishinowa*, a "steward, administrator of property, or manager").[50] Attainment and retention of these roles depended wholly on trustworthiness as well as demonstrated and continuing efficacy in the particular domain of the leadership role.[51] Most prominent among the achieved leaders were the war chiefs, who not only exemplified the male cultural value of bravery but were also called temporarily to civic duty in times of strife. Whereas civic chiefs, sub-chiefs, and their assistants tended to represent village elders, the war chiefs tended to represent the young men of the village. Insofar as the functions of civic and war chiefs were opposed, and each community had both, there was a continual, dynamic tension within Anishinaabe society between peaceful elders (ascribed chiefs) and militant youths (achieved chiefs and officers) and their respective interests in peace and war.[52]

During the historical period, there was a gradual shift from villages composed of a single patrilineal totemic group and its affines to multi-clan villages. This shift occurred in part because sons of chiefs who did not succeed to leadership positions split from the main group and founded their own villages in new regions to the west, as did ambitious young men who gained followings through their achievements in the domains of war, hunting, and healing. The former type of village had a single totemic head chief and totemic group composed of his assistant and headmen (aanike-ogimaag) and their families. The later villages had head chiefs of multiple totems with their assistants and sub-chiefs, as well as the families of diverse totems that were associated with these leaders.[53] European diplomats at first found the plethora of chiefs inconvenient for developing political relationships, particularly in forming alliances in times of war. The French government officials, however, followed by those of the English and Americans, soon found the flexibility of the system conducive to creating chiefs of their own choosing on whom they could depend to act in their best interests.[54] Their tendency to bestow chieftainships on Anishinaabeg of all social roles and ranks led to an overabundance of generic chiefs, a development that confused and undermined the indigenous political system.[55]

Fur traders, often acting as official or unofficial emissaries of their nations, also made chiefs of those on whom they could rely to repay the credits they received in fall, supply provisions, act as guides and interceders, and bring in the best returns because of their hunting skills and loyalty to the company. Fur trade companies such as the HBC, the NWC, and the XY Company (XYC) continued this practice on a wide scale, distributing their own distinctive emblems of chiefdom such as clothing, flags, and medals.[56] For example, Alexander Henry the Younger preferred to appoint his own chiefs because chiefs who claimed authority through indigenous criteria could not be counted on to act in the interest of the fur company.[57]

The context in which European diplomats and traders recognized or created chiefs was the gift-giving ceremony, which formed the core of the shared middle ground ceremonial culture. When representatives of the two groups met, Anishinaabe chiefs gave gifts of furs and other indigenous products, and Europeans responded with gifts of clothing, tobacco, and alcohol. The chiefs redistributed the latter to their followers. These ceremonial exchanges initiated and renewed alliances based on a kinship model. Gift giving thereby established the intimacy and trust that were necessary for barter trade to take place. Europeans also gave chiefs insignia that consisted of flags, medals, and chiefly dress, which included, at minimum, a coat but could also include a hat, feather, gorget, shirt, and/or leggings. Chiefs sometimes redistributed these personal gifts but typically retained at least some of the insignia as visible symbols of their status as chiefs. The ceremonial context for the mutual recognition of social roles and statuses provided fertile ground for European diplomats and fur traders to manipulate leaders and leadership positions in Anishinaabe society.[58]

Anishinaabeg sometimes called "made chiefs" *ogimaakaan*. The suffix *"kaan"* means "not the actual entity but a substitute that has that appearance," and in this case it was a specific reference to the red coat given to signify leadership.[59] In the fur trade, chiefs whose position had been bestowed by traders were sometimes referred to more specifically as *adaawagani-ogimaa-kaan,* literally, "bartering person with the appearance of a chief."[60] These chiefs often had little to no authority among their own people,[61] although they might have been respected as hunting chiefs whose decision-making powers were temporary and limited to those activities related directly to hunting and trapping.[62] There are several recorded instances in which individuals refused to accept chieftainship from Europeans.[63] Nevertheless, some made chiefs were recognized by their people, and by mid-century they played prominent leadership roles within their communities. For example, Father Nicholas Frémiot reported that in 1849 a Fort William chief, the Illinois, was "simply one of the fur-trading chiefs appointed by the Hudson's Bay Company," which is why he was nicknamed Miskouakkonayé (literally, "clothed in red"). Nevertheless, the "people like to look upon [him] as their Chief."[64] At a meeting with government representatives, the Illinois performed the traditional role of orator *(giigidoowinini)* by leading the pipe ceremony and reciting the history of relations between the two nations. Although the Illinois was respected in this ceremonial role, the government officials were unsuccessful in their attempt to oust the hereditary head chief and make the Illinois the civic chief in his stead. Similarly, Paul Kane reported in 1848 that the head chief of the Michipicoton Ojibwe posed for him "in his red coat trimmed with gold lace." The coats, he continued, were "given by the [Hudson's Bay] Company to such Indian chiefs as have been friendly and serviceable to them, and are very highly prized by their possessors."[65] In both instances, these made chiefs were distinguished by their red, not blue, coats.

In 1804, at the height of competition among the NWC, the HBC, and the XYC,[66] traders' journals suggest that chief's coats were neither rare nor exclusively reserved for hereditary chiefs. Henry the Younger complained: "Thus, by our obstinate proceedings, we had spoiled the Indians. Every man who had killed a few skins was considered a chief and was treated accordingly; there was scarcely a common buck to be seen among them; all wore scarlet coats, had large kegs and flasks, and nothing was purchased by them but silver works, strouds and blankets."[67] That same year, the NWC partner in charge of the Nipigon District, Duncan Cameron, remarked that "if an Indian is a good hunter ... you must make a chief of him to secure his hunt, otherwise your opponents will debauch him from you, and you are sure to lose him."[68]

An examination of NWC and XYC inventories of goods sent to posts, however, suggests that Henry and Cameron might have exaggerated the number of chief's coats in circulation during this period. Although we cannot tell the exact ratio of men with chief's coats to men without them, the inventories reveal how many chief's coats were shipped to various posts in proportion to other forms of men's outerwear such as blankets and capots. By considering the total number of men's outerwear garments on extant NWC and XYC fur trade inventories from 1804 to 1821, we can arrive at a fairly accurate picture of the proportion of status to functional garments, which will help situate the status garments of these two youths in their socio-cultural context. In Figure 3.5, a set of 1804 XYC inventories represents trade goods sent to posts and outposts during a period of heightened fur trade competition and high-volume trade, while NWC inventories from between 1814 and 1821 represent goods sent to depots, posts, and outposts during a period of relative decline. Although the XYC and NWC were in competition during the earlier period and were merged during the latter period, their business practices were comparable, and throughout both periods

Figure 3.5

Comparison of percentages of men's outerwear, 1804 vs. 1814-21

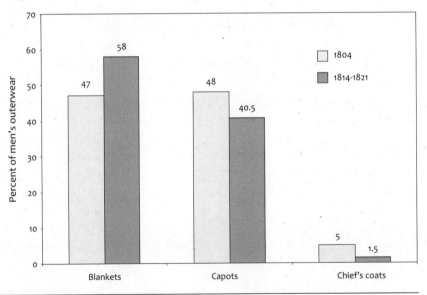

Note: This figure is based on a table that records all the outerwear on thirty-eight NYC and XYC inventories in the sizes and styles worn by men – specifically chief's coats, capots, and blankets – the latter two in sizes two and half ells or higher. Smaller sizes were for women and children, whose dress is not directly relevant to this discussion.

Sources: Malhiot, "A Wisconsin Fur-Trader's Journal," 221; AO, FTC, Fonds F431, Microfilm MS 312, Reels 1-3, "Archives du Seminaire de Quebec," No. 5, "Invoices of Goods Shipped from Montreal," and No. 6, "Invoices of Goods Shipped from Montreal"; HBCA, F.4/3, Reel 5M2, NWC Account Book, 1812; HBCA, F.4/6, Reel FM3, NWC Account Book, 1814; HBCA, F.4/9, Reel 5M3, NWC Account Book, 1817; HBCA, F.4/12, Reel 5M4, NWC Account Book, 1818; and AO, FTC, North West Company Collection, Furs Inventory, 1815, MU2201, Box 6-3.

they had the same suppliers. In the latter period, competition between the NWC and the HBC escalated as fur returns diminished.

Figure 3.5 shows that there were substantially fewer chief's coats than there were blankets or capots in both 1804 and the period between 1814 and 1821, although there were relatively more chief's coats in the earlier period than the later period (5 percent versus 1.5 percent). Although 5 percent of the total number of men's outwear garments distributed to posts annually does not support Henry's claim that every man was given a chief's coat, other factors might have raised the number of coats in actual circulation at any given time. If trading chiefs received one coat per year, they might have gradually accumulated a surplus. Because of the need to demonstrate generosity to authenticate and maintain their powers, chiefs gave coats away to the young men in their bands.[69] The traders may not have given the Dauphin Lake and Red Deer River youths their chief's coats. It is more likely that youths their age would have received them from an elder chief or "leading man" in their band. In George Nelson's journal, for example, the traders honoured only older men by clothing them. The older men's grown and married sons, as well as their sons-in-law, were often not even mentioned by name but rather by their relation to the principal older man.[70] Tanner relates an incident in which the traders delivered his step-mother's chief's coat to him because she was too drunk to receive it herself.[71] The traders honoured her with a coat because she was a chief and an elder, even though Tanner was the primary hunter of the group.[72] Young men could also acquire chief's coats in barter exchanges. For example, Tanner's brother attempted to trade a chief's coat and some other valuables for a horse.[73] Chief's coats may also have been available for purchase, although we do not believe this was a common practice.[74] In the case of burial, fine dress and ornaments were often provided by family members.[75] The youths' chief's coats therefore may not have been their own while they were alive.

In a variety of ways, young men who had no particular claim to status came to possess chief's coats. These practices introduced ambiguity into the dress code that made it appear as though every hunter wore a chief's coat, although only a few of them were given coats as emblems of authority. Nevertheless, we must conclude that chief's coats were relatively rare in comparison to other forms of men's outerwear, even during the height of competition among the fur trade companies, the period when we believe these two burials took place. These two youths therefore probably belonged to a relatively small subset of high-status members of Western Anishinaabe society. As Henry the Younger suggests, however, some men had both a chief's coat and a blanket; the former was a status marker, and the latter was a functional outerwear garment. This was indeed the case for the Dauphin Lake youth. In contrast, since most capots were made from blanketing materials, they could serve instead of a coat and blanket combination, functioning simultaneously as status markers and functional outerwear garments. The reduction in chief's coats therefore cannot explain the rise in blankets in the period of decline, although the reduction of both chief's coats and capots suggests fewer status garments in circulation.

For an accurate sense of the proportion of status versus functional garments in a complex system of clothing symbolism, one must clarify the ambiguous and multivalent roles of capots. Capots differed from coats in a number of ways: they had a less tailored cut, no vent in the skirt back, came to the knee (making them a little longer), were typically unlined (although some have been described or pictured with lining), and had a hood instead of a collar (the most significant diagnostic feature, even though some have been described or pictured without them).[76] Common capots were made from blanketing materials such as molton, duffel, and point blankets. They were functional garments that were comparable to blankets. The NWC also manufactured and distributed various kinds of decorated capots that functioned as status garments.[77] Unlike common capots, decorated capots were sometimes distributed as gifts much like chief's coats, except they served as status markers for intermediate leadership roles such as hunting chiefs, speakers, messengers, and other principal men. For example, NWC trader François Malhiot spent the season of 1804 to 1805 among the Anishinaabeg of Wisconsin. His "Statement of the Goods Given to the Savages for Nothing" records his gifts of chief's coats and "laced capots" to chiefs and their bands. Whereas he gave each of three chiefs one chief's coat, two chief's shirts, one chief's plume, one chief's hat, and one laced capot, he gave each of two other chiefs only one chief's shirt and one laced capot.[78] Malhiot's journal states that he gave a laced capot to Grand Canard and to La Loutre through his aide-de-camp (*Michinaois,* see translation of "michinowa" above) before regaling them with a speech about glory and company loyalty.[79] In the same region the previous year, XYC trader Michel Curot noted that his rival trader gave Le Grand Mâle a laced capot in the fall with the promise that he would receive a chief's coat in the spring if he brought in a good return.[80] Curot faithfully records the day in May when the rival bestowed the promised chief's coat. These examples suggest that traders reserved chief's coats for higher honours than the laced capots, although we think they were typically given to different individuals in a band, not the same person at different seasons.

Figure 3.5 shows that, whereas in 1804 there were almost the same number of blankets and capots (47 percent and 48 percent, respectively), the relative number of blankets rose (from 47 percent to 58 percent) for the period between 1814 and 1821, while the relative number of capots declined (from 48 percent to 40.5 percent). These trends may be interpreted in terms of gifted (chief's coats

Figure 3.6

Percentage of chief's coats and capots by colour and type, 1813-21

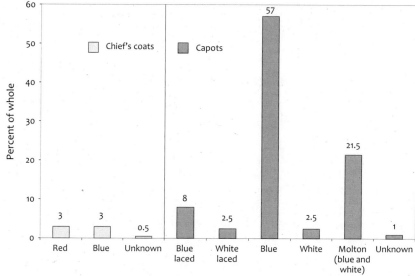

Types and colours of men's outerwear

Note: This figure is based on the same sources as Figure 3.5, except that it excludes inventories from Fort William because these outfits are clearly geared toward employee markets. Since none of the 1804 inventories mentions the colour of the garments, Figure 3.6 shows the relative percentages of red, blue, white, and unknown men's chief's coats and capots in extant NWC inventories from 1813 to 1821. We have counted all Illinois capots as blue because blue is the only colour mentioned in connection with them. Although molton cloth was shipped from England in red and green, as well as in blue and white, only the latter colours are mentioned in connection with molton capots, which were typically more blue than white. AO, FTC, Fonds F431, Microfilm MS 312, Reels 1-3, "Archives du Seminaire de Quebec," No. 4, "Invoices of Goods Shipped from England to Montreal."

and some capots) versus bartered (blankets) items, the former being more abundant in times of tough competition and high-volume trade, the latter rising in importance with the reduced volume in furs. Insofar as relative power may be measured by the need to secure allegiance through the bestowal of gifts, these figures suggest that, whereas Aboriginal consumers had the upper hand in the earlier period, in the latter period the fur traders gained political ascendancy even as they suffered economic losses.

Despite the similarity of time, place, and fur trade company affiliation, the different colour of the two youths' coats raises questions about the colour symbolism of chief's coats and how it relates to that of capots. As Figure 3.6 shows, chief's coats came in red and blue, while the capots that were shipped to posts were primarily blue and white.[81] Red coats were unambiguously in the minority compared with blue and white outer garments. Insofar as chief's coats were the only outer garments available in red, these must have been more visually outstanding than the blue chief's coats. The latter were visually similar to the majority of capots, which were also blue. Any status attached to the blue coats that might have arisen because of their scarcity would have been offset significantly by the ambiguity introduced by their similarity to the high-status fine blue broadcloth capots worn by company clerks, the laced blue capots given to intermediate-level Anishinaabe leaders, and the medium- to low-status blue molton and Illinois cloth capots worn by voyageurs and Anishinaabeg alike. This may be one reason why in nineteenth-century colloquial English "red coat" became almost synonymous with "chief's coat."

Insofar as chief's coats and laced capots simulated military uniforms, one must ask whether the blue and red colours of the coats were linked in a significant way to specific time periods and/or the nationality of the fur traders. That the NWC distributed both blue coats with red trim and red coats with blue trim simultaneously between 1813 and 1821 suggests that their supply of coats did not change from one colour to the other during this time period.[82] We do not know, however, when these companies started or ended this practice. During the American Revolutionary War from 1775 to 1783 and the War of 1812, red coats signified the British army, and blue coats signified that of the United States.[83] The British military, however, was divided into dozens of discrete units, some of which wore red uniforms and some of which wore blue. Moreover, these colour assignments changed over time.[84] In the late eighteenth century, blue with red trim was popular with George III as the quasi-military Windsor uniform.[85] Hence, it was a common colour for the chief's coats that the British distributed with George III medals. Three paintings of Huron chiefs suggest that the British might have continued to distribute blue chief's coats well into the nineteenth century.[86] By the time of the numbered treaties with Manitoba Anishinaabeg in 1875, however, the colonial Canadian government was only distributing red coats.[87] Conversely, in 1804 the American officials Lewis and Clark gave out red coats with blue trim, and an American fur company's inventory for 1831 listed twice as many red coats as blue ones.[88] We therefore conclude that neither time period nor national affiliation explains the meaning of the colour of chief's coats. We may also rule out differentiation by rank based on British military precedence because the officers wore uniforms of the same colour as their men.[89]

We suggest instead that the Anishinaabe worldview and social structure might have been the basis for the colour symbolism of the chief's coats and laced capots, at least for the period between the Revolutionary War and the War of 1812. For historic Anishinaabeg, the colour red signified an active spiritual power that could be directed toward specific ends but was best applied in small quantities or for very special occasions and people.[90] As anthropologist Mary Black points out, one would not want to advertise more personal spiritual power than one was sure of exercising or than one had acquired legitimately.[91] The reason for this assumed modesty was to avoid spiritual or physical attacks from jealous rivals that could cause illness or death to oneself or one's family.[92] Indeed, Tanner recounts an instance in which he did not hold the usual and expected feast when he killed a buffalo because he feared retribution from his wife's jealous male relatives.[93] Insofar as red was associated with willful direct action, the colour's symbolism would tend to link red chief's coats to status acquired through individual achievement. Therefore, we argue that the red chief's coats indicated made chiefs, chosen by traders on account of their individual exertions and loyalty to the company.

In contrast, blue in the Anishinaabe worldview indicated a passive and potential spiritual power that relied on the principle of reciprocity to receive power from spirits who took pity on one's poor and humble state.[94] The symbolism of the colour blue tends to link blue chief's coats to the ascribed status of hereditary chiefs in that there was a parallel relation between humans and spirits on the one hand and chiefs and their followers on the other. Both cases involved reciprocal relations in which the persons with inferior status expected to receive gifts from the chief or other-than-human person in return for their support or other demands. We therefore speculate that, in line with a middle-ground culture in which behaviours but not necessarily meanings are shared, the NWC and XYC conformed to Aboriginal protocol by reserving blue chief's coats for hereditary chiefs when they were able to, or chose to, acknowledge these positions. Over time, however, this sartorial system might have been difficult to maintain because of poor communication between wintering partners and clerks who worked closely with their Anishinaabe customers and the company suppliers in Montreal who ordered and shipped the merchandise. Moreover, as mentioned, fur traders and diplomats alike had ulterior motives for using their own criteria to confer chiefly status on those whom they believed were most deserving. Finally, since Anishinaabeg who participated in the War of 1812 received red chief's coats from the British, the nationalist basis for colour symbolism was reinforced for both Amerindians and Euro-Americans, and the semiotic system of the military and diplomatic alliance rather than that of the commercial context of the fur trade is what remains in our collective memories today.[95]

Dauphin Lake Interpretation

The artifacts in the Dauphin Lake assemblage reveal information about the youth's ethnic and commercial affiliations as well as his status within his group. The wooden spoon is of a type associated with the Great Lakes Anishinaabeg, who used it to make maple sugar. It is therefore referred to as a "sugaring spoon," although Carrie Lyford suggests that men also brought the spoons to feasts along with wooden bowls.[96] In either case, the implement's inclusion in the grave supports the ethnic attribution of the individual as a recently arrived Great Lakes Anishinaabe immigrant to Manitoba. Writing from first-hand experience, Tanner, Henry, and the HBC trader Alexander Kennedy refer to sugar making among the Western Anishinaabeg in early spring each year.[97] Perhaps this youth's death occurred during the spring sugar-making season. Regardless of whether the spoon pertained to sugar making, its inclusion with the copper kettle in the grave suggests the youth was indeed prepared for a feast upon his arrival in the Land of the Dead.

The Dauphin Lake youth was wearing a red chief's coat with blue trim and metallic lace, which suggests his own, or his father's, status as a fur trade made chief. Additional symbols of his status as a trade chief include eighteen loose wampum beads that might have composed a single wampum string, and ostrich and peacock feathers, which were typically among the items associated with clothing a chief.[98] As is shown in Table 3.2, the Dauphin Lake youth's dress included a variety of textiles aside from the three employed on the chief's coat (course red stroud, course blue stroud, and fine blue broadcloth).[99] Of these other textiles, the scrap of fringed gauze is of most interest because of its rarity. The term "gauze" generally refers to fabrics that are so loosely woven that one can see through them. This term accurately describes one of the protein-based fabrics found at the Dauphin Lake site. At thirty-five times magnification, the fabric has the smooth surface and high lustre of silk fibres (see Figure 3.7).[100]

"Plain, striped and flowered silk gauze" was manufactured in England and imported to America in the late eighteenth century.[101] In addition to its variation on a twill weave, the Dauphin Lake textile appears to have a striped pattern. Interestingly, the NWC carried a product that they called gauze. Among the inventories studied, however, the term appears only on those for central depots, specifically Grand Portage in 1804 and Fort William in 1821.[102] Although 1821 is too late for these two burials, these inventories demonstrate the continuing rarity of the fabric. If this gauze is the product in question, then the youth might have obtained it at Grand Portage and then travelled to the Red River region, where he met his untimely death. This interpretation is strengthened by the fact that in 1804 foxtail feathers (that is, ostrich feathers) were also only available at Grand Portage.

Figure 3.7 Gauze textile at thirty-five times magnification from the Dauphin Lake assemblage. Photograph by Kevin Brownlee. © The Manitoba Museum, Winnipeg, MB.

As noted above, the Dauphin Lake youth's silverworks were not significant in terms of quantity, variety, or type compared with those of the Red Deer River youth. But they were opulent compared with two other Manitoba burials thought to be from the subsequent decade.[103] Interestingly, both the Dauphin Lake and the Red Deer River burials contained pieces of scrap silver that Anishinaabeg modified into their present forms. Several of the modified pieces in the Dauphin Lake site were rectangular with holes poked with an awl on two or four of the corners, evidently intended to secure the pieces on thongs or ribbons (see Figure 3.1). Initially, we interpreted these pieces as parts of a neck and chest ornament, in which case the gauze would be worn as a headscarf (see Figure 3.8). An alternative interpretation is that the scrap pieces were cut to form ornamentation for a hairstyle similar to that described by Peter Grant in 1804: "The young men allow several long locks to fall down over the face, ornamented with ribbands, silver broaches, etc.; they gather up another lock from behind the head into a small club wrapped up with very thin plates of silver, in which they fix the tail feathers of the eagle, or any other favorite bird."[104] Although the first interpretation is plausible, the second is preferable because it enables us to

Figure 3.8   Dauphin Lake Youth, by Terrakian WinterMoon, April 2006.
© The Manitoba Museum, Winnipeg, MB.

account for a series of three-quarter-inch broaches secured to grosgrain binding, a series of half-inch broaches attached to silk ribbon, and a number of loose
half-inch broaches that are part of this assemblage. We suggest that these
broaches were also attached to the hair ornament, along with the ostrich and
peacock feathers, while the gauze served as a neck handkerchief.

The silverworks are important for establishing the youths' affiliation with the
NWC or the XYC and for helping to date the burials. Several of the silverworks
associated with the Dauphin Lake youth are marked "RC" for Robert Cruikshank
(1767-1809), a Montreal silversmith who sold his wares to the NWC and the
XYC.[105] Given that Cruikshank died in 1809, the last year his work was sold on
the market was 1810.[106] Although silverworks certainly circulated within Native
communities long after their initial purchase, the remarkable absence of scrapes,
dents, or other indicators of use on the bracelets and other pieces suggests that
the youth's death occurred in or before 1810. This date accords with the period
of opulence that characterizes these assemblages more generally.

Two shell hair pipes helped us to determine the earliest date for the burials.
Manufactured in New Jersey, these items were first introduced to the Montreal-
based trade by McGill and Co. in 1799. This was followed in 1802 by purchases

by Forsyth Richardson and Co. and Donald Sutherland of the XYC. McGill, Forsyth, and Richardson were Montreal-based merchants who dealt with both the XYC and the NWC.[107] This means that both burials took place no earlier than 1800 and likely occurred in 1803 or later. After the merger of the XYC and the NWC in 1804, the latter continued to stock shell hair pipes in large quantities. That year, the NWC purchased 3,971 hair pipes.[108] In 1806, they purchased an unidentified number at a slightly higher cost than in 1804. These purchases were from a New York merchant, John Murray and Sons, who also supplied the company with white and black wampum and sold the NWC's furs on consignment on the New York market.[109] Made from the same type of shell, these hair pipes carried the political and spiritual connotations of wampum. The Montreal-based companies' commerce with the New York market is a notable example of their efforts to secure products and markets that would give them an advantage over the HBC. Neither the fur trade merchandise nor indigenous styles were stagnant but rather represented dynamic change in a manner similar to fashion today. The gauze and shell hair pipes suggest that the Dauphin Lake youth was fashion conscious and dressed in the latest styles of his day.

Red Deer River Interpretation

Like the Dauphin Lake burial, the Red Deer River burial included "RC" silverworks and shell hair pipes that linked the individual to the XYC or the NWC. Additionally, several silver pieces were marked "NR" for Narcisse Roy (1765-1814), another Montreal silversmith who dealt with the XYC and the NWC. Following the same reasoning that we applied to the Dauphin Lake burial, we can assume that the youth's death occurred during or before 1810 and probably later than 1803. In contrast to the Dauphin Lake assemblage, however, this youth possessed a substantial amount of silverworks (Table 3.2). A group of scrap silver pieces and two hanks of white seed beads might have been included purely as markers of wealth, for they served no apparent practical or decorative function. Some items associated with this youth suggest that he held a political rank, specifically that he was the son of a hereditary chief. It is important to distinguish between symbols of political authority or leadership and those of wealth because civil chiefs frequently dressed to avoid ostentation, while ambitious youths often displayed the most signs of wealth. Given that Anishinaabe social structure emphasizes an age hierarchy in which youths are at the bottom, this feature of the dress code appears to be contradictory. But chiefs acquired and maintained high status through generous gift giving, whereas youths did so by proving their hunting prowess, which was manifested in the amount and value of trade goods in their possession.[110]

Figure 3.9   Detail of Red Deer River youth's collar and metallic lace, by Terrakian WinterMoon, 2005. © The Manitoba Museum, Winnipeg, MB.

The Red Deer River youth wore a blue chief's coat with red collar and cuffs. As explained above, the blue colour of the coat might have indicated his status as the son of a hereditary chief. Curiously, the metallic braid that trimmed the top edge of the collar and the bottom edge of the cuffs was rolled back and hand sewn under so that it was not visible (see Figure 3.9). This puzzled us for a long time until we realized that the coat had a standing collar. Perhaps the collar was too tall and the sleeves were too long for the boy, so they were shortened. Evidently, comfort outweighed glamour in this instance.

Foremost among the symbols of hereditary civil chieftainship in the youth's assemblage is the wampum belt of over two thousand beads and attached silver ornaments, which the youth wore around his neck (see Figures 3.4 and 3.10).

Figure 3.10   Red Deer River Youth, by Elaine McIntosh, 2004. © The Manitoba Museum, Winnipeg, MB.

According to Anishinaabe historian William Warren, these belts were worn around the necks of Ojibwe totemic chiefs as "badges of their honor."[111] Johann Kohl adds that influential or respected chiefs and *jessakid* (medicine men) wore "heavy masses of them round the neck" and that white wampum beads signified peace.[112] According to Peter Grant, the symbolism of this item of adornment was so well known that a wampum belt worn on special occasions was often the only article of dress that distinguished a chief from others in his group.[113]

Multiple strands of wampum beads worn around the neck could serve a similar function. When Anna Jameson met the Anishinaabe chief White Deer at Mackinac Island in 1837, for example, he wore a capot, a cloth hood with eagle feather decorations, and "about fifty strings of blue wampum around his neck. The other two [his companions] were similarly dressed, with the exception of the wampum and feathers."[114] Considering this evidence of Anishinaabe chiefs wearing wampum belts or strings as badges of their chieftainship, it is remarkable how little has been written about wampum as an element of dress, its role in signalling political rank, and its use among Anishinaabeg more generally.[115]

Other elements of the Red Deer River youth's adornment also suggest his chiefly status. For example, silver crescent gorgets were mostly worn by chiefs.[116] The NWC carried two styles, which were called gorgets and moons. Both types came in sets of five or fewer.[117] The moons were circular, while the gorgets were crescent-shaped.[118] The bear motif on the gorget worn by the Red Deer River youth (see Figure 3.3) might have referred either to the youth's totem or to his guardian spirit. For the Odawa and Ojibwe alike, totems were ascribed at birth, whereas guardian spirits were acquired later in life. They bore no relation to each other.[119] Unfortunately, there is no certain way to differentiate between totemic emblems and guardian spirits on images that were worn as adornment.[120] It was customary, however, to represent one's guardian spirit by some token of esteem such as "a feather, a claw, a piece of cloth or a bird's head," which could be placed within a small medicine pouch or suspended from a belt.[121] We therefore speculate that the lynx claw on the youth's wampum belt might have referred to a guardian spirit.

It is more likely, however, that the bear motif on the gorget referred to the youth's totem, for gorgets were customarily given to chiefs. Those given to chiefs by political authorities were often inscribed with French, British, or American national insignia such as monarchs' crests and floral or faunal emblems.[122] In contrast, trade gorgets were often engraved with animals.[123] Because civil chiefs were leaders of their totemic lineages, the animal motifs might have represented the recipients' totems.[124] Members of the bear totem were among the Great Lakes Anishinaabeg who migrated to Manitoba in this period. For example, Tanner notes that not long after his family arrived on the Prairies, they found some birch-bark messages, one of which featured "the figure of a bear, and on the others, those of other animals. Net-no-kwa [his adoptive mother] immediately recognized the totems of Pe-shau-ba, Waus-so, and their companions."[125] Years later, when the War of 1812 prevented him from travelling east to find his birth family, Tanner encountered another birch-bark message. This time, it revealed to him that his brother Wa-me-gon-a-biew had killed a man whose totem was the bear: "As there were few of the bear totem in our band, I was confident the man he killed was a young man called Ke-zhe-zhoons."[126]

Although there might have been few of the bear totem in Tanner's band, there were certainly leaders of the bear totem in the region. One of them, Ouchidoat or the Premier, signed the Treaty of Selkirk in 1817.[127] HBC trader Peter Fidler exulted that even La Sonnet, a NWC company chief, had signed the treaty, even though the NWC "used every persuasion to prevent" him.[128] The Premier, however, was also a NWC chief. George Nelson reports that in the fall of 1808, NWC trader Mr. Cameron gave the Premier presents and credit at Fort Dauphin, which functioned as a depot during this period, after which he and his band left and "promise[d] not to be back 'till near next spring.'" A few days later, Nelson himself gave several chiefs at his wintering post gifts of laced coats, shirts, leggings, rum, and gorgets.[129] Hence, given that there were bear totem chiefs in the region and that NWC traders gave them gorgets, and given that animal motifs on trade gorgets most often indicated totems, we believe that the bear motif on the Red Deer River gorget indicated the totem of the youth's lineage. It seems appropriate that his future leadership claims would be advertised in the Land of the Dead even though his death prematurely cut off his succession to leadership in the world of the living.

The Red Deer River youth's headdress certainly indicated great wealth and may also have signified chiefly status. It consisted of two silver bands that were attached to a base of red common strouds. These silver bands were modified from their original form. They were both cut in half length-wise to form narrower bands. In the process, the lower parts of the stag and butterfly motifs were cut off so that only their heads remain. In contrast to David Meyer's interpretation of a headdress of silver bands with separate ear ornamentation,[130] we suggest that the two sets of ear wheels were attached to the silver bands with ribbons to form an integral part of the headdress. The extant textile scraps suggest that ribbons hung from the headdress at either side, on which were attached a pair of large silver ear wheels with a heart motif and a smaller pair of silver ear wheels with a star motif. The former had many ear bobs pierced through ribbons attached to the lower rims. Together, these appendages would have hung down to the youth's shoulders. Arranged across the individual's forehead and attached to the lower band was a ribbon with a row of thirty-one silver broaches, each three-quarter-inches wide. A similar headdress is depicted in a painting of Sir John Caldwell in 1780.[131] Likewise, a photograph in Hamilton shows a headscarf with broaches and ear wheels attached at the sides with ribbons.[132] Three hair pipes were found with hair running through them, suggesting that these were attached directly to the youth's hair and not associated with the headdress.

Although we cannot be sure about many of the details, we can be fairly certain that the combination of artifacts in the Red Deer River assemblage could belong only to a member of a chief's family. Because of the young age of the Red Deer River individual, we assume that he had not yet had time to acquire a position as chief or a spiritual office through his own actions. Since spiritual offices and the position of war chief were always achieved statuses, this means that he must have been the son of a civil (that is, hereditary) chief.

Conclusion

We find that it is possible to reconstruct the clothing and adornment of these two youths to a remarkable degree by studying and analyzing contemporaneous documents and analogous material culture. Moreover, we find that we can read these assemblages as individuals' social identities. In particular, we interpret both the Dauphin Lake and the Red Deer River youths as recent immigrants to the region. The Dauphin Lake youth's father or father-in-law was likely appointed as a trading chief by a NWC or XYC trader. Although this honour was probably bestowed on an older male relative, the youth was old enough to contribute substantially to the subsistence of his family and friends. He might have been assisting with sugar-making operations at the time of his death. Although he had little authority, the youth's assemblage shows that he was relatively wealthy at a time when most Anishinaabeg in the region still enjoyed successful hunting and trapping. He was a fashion-conscious individual who adorned himself in the most current and attractive fashions for young Western Anishinaabe men. He and his relations used his emblems of achieved status to show his social identity to best advantage in the Land of the Dead. The Red Deer River youth displayed numerous emblems of chiefly status, even though he was but a boy. This suggests that he was the son of a hereditary chief of a totemic line, most likely the bear. His family was profusely wealthy at the time of his death and spared no measures to ensure that he received a fitting reception in the Land of the Dead.

Although the families of these youths dressed them to encounter their ancestors in the Land of the Dead, the opportunity to study their assemblages today helps us to understand the meaning and value of their lives and deaths. At the height of the fur trade, the Western Anishinaabeg lived within a complex cultural middle ground that was neither entirely indigenous Anishinaabe nor foreign European; it was, nevertheless, uniquely Anishinaabe. These two archaeological assemblages enable us to reflect on historical events through the lived experience of individual Anishinaabeg. While the Red Deer River youth's assemblage portrays the relatively conservative leadership role of a civic hereditary chief of a totemic line, that of the Dauphin Lake youth suggests the colonial influence on indigenous leadership structures that was embodied in "made chiefs." The process of fission that brought the youths and their families to the region was probably an organic one irrespective of colonial influence. Additionally, the fur traders' raising up of complicit individuals to leadership roles within the context of a robust fur trade had little immediate impact on Anishinaabe culture and society because Anishinaabeg, as consumers, had the upper hand.

As the colonial economy shifted to agriculture, however, the balance of power shifted, and the colonizers' political power to assign leadership combined with their new economic supremacy to undermine Anishinaabe autonomy. Questions of colonial power relations must be refined to distinguish clearly between fur trade and political-diplomatic contexts, even though these boundaries were often blurred at the time because of their common use of middle-ground protocols and ceremonies. An adaptive culture trait imperceptibly became maladaptive as individuals such as these two youths gained personal honour and status as fur trade consumers while their nation was on the brink of losing collective power as a political unit. The blue coat, which represented the indigenous mode of reciprocal exchange, gave way to the red coat, which represented the colonial market mode of exchange in which achieved status, rather than kinship relations, was the primary index of identity.

Focusing on material culture sheds new light on colonial relations; it also enables us to catch sight of indigenous leadership practices within and among totemic and national groups. As the quotidian foundations of everyday life, the wearing of wampum, ostrich feathers, or fringed gauze is not remarked upon in historical documents. Yet this practice draws our attention to new questions surrounding socio-political processes and structures within Anishinaabe society, as well as those pertaining to the historical movement of indigenous groups within the contact period. Hopefully, the lives and deaths of these two youths will serve as beacons for these new lines of inquiry.

Notes

The authors would like to extend their sincere thanks to Kirsten Brooks, Jennifer Brown, Alan Corbiere, Anne Lindsay, Kate Peach, Mark Peck, Myra Sitchon, and Lorrie Storr for invaluable help with research and sources. We would also like to thank Marisa Halek, Elaine MacIntosh (Ojibwe/Metis), and Terrakian WinterMoon (Cree) for their artistic contributions. Finally, we would like to thank the Manitoba Heritage Grants Program, the Manitoba Museum, the Department of Anthropology at the University of Manitoba, and the Office of Research and Programs at Southern Illinois University Edwardsville for financial support for this project.

1 This chapter focuses on a portion of a larger project coordinated by Kevin Brownlee, curator of archaeology, Manitoba Museum of Man and Nature, Winnipeg. The wider project concerns the physical remains and material culture associated with four Western Anishinaabe burials recovered in Manitoba between 1938 and 1991. All four burials appear to be of First Nations individuals who were interred between 1803 and 1819. Two of them, however, contained an unusual amount and variety of extant textiles, which enabled us to gain a deeper understanding of the individuals and their culture than is normally possible.

2 Harmon, *A Journal*, 73; McDonnell, "The Red River," 277; D. McGillivray, *The Journal*, 47; and Blackstock, "Nineteenth-Century Fur Trade Costume," 199. Also see the Hudson's Bay Company Archives (hereafter HBCA), B.199/A/1, Reel 1M139, John Sutherland Journal, Shell River Post, 1794-95.

3 Peers, *The Ojibwa*, 14-18; and Thompson, *David Thompson's Narrative*, 149, 156.

4 Schoolcraft, *Historical and Statistical Information*, 5:144.

5 Cameron, "The Nipigon Country," 258; D. McGillivray, *The Journal*, 34.

6 Silverstein, "Clothed Encounters," 31.

7 Shannon, "Dressing for Success," 18.

8 White, *The Middle Ground*, 50, 52.

9 For an explanation of the terms "index," "icon," and "symbol" in Peircian semiotics, see Danesi, *The Quest for Meaning*, 41-47.

10 Ewers, "Artifacts and Pictures," 101.

11 Fogelson, "The Ethnohistory of Events and Nonevents," passim.

12 Axtell, *Beyond 1492*, 125-51; Carlos and Lewis, "Marketing in the Land of Hudson's Bay"; Jaenen, "The Role of Presents," 234; Ray, "Indians as Consumers"; Rich, *The Fur Trade*, 135; and Thistle, *Indian-European Trade Relations*.

13 Tanner, *A Narrative*, 57, 93, 98, 101-2, 164; and Henry (the Younger), *The Manuscript Journals*, 48, 59, 196, 203.

14 HBCA, B.51/a/1, Folios 2a–20a, Reel 1M41, John Best Journal, Fort Dauphin, 1795-96; Cameron, "The Nipigon Country," 299; Long, *Voyages and Travels*, 49-50, 56, 85; Harmon, *A Journal*, 37, 38, 87; Henry (the Younger), *The Manuscript Journals*, 56, 95, 103-5, 162, 180, 196, 203; and D. McGillivray, *The Journal*, 30-31.

15 HBCA, B.199/A/1, Reel 1M139, John Sutherland Journal, Shell River Post, 1794-95; Harmon, *A Journal*, 48; Henry (the Younger), *The Manuscript Journals*, 95, 103-5, 168, 180, 196; McDonnell, "The Red River," 268; and Tanner, *A Narrative*, 48, 54, 68-69, 76, 82, 86, 118.

16 Meyer, "The Red Deer River Grave," 6.

17 Metropolitan Toronto Reference Library, Baldwin Room (hereafter MTRL), George Nelson Papers, Dauphin River Journal, 1808-10.

18 Tanner, *A Narrative*, 42-43.

19 Henry (the Younger), *The Manuscript Journals*, 203, 204, 209, 258, 275, 429.

20 Ibid., 229.

21 HBCA, E.3/3, Folio 58, Reel 4M103, Peter Fidler, "Journal of a Journey from Swan to the Red River and Down It."

22 HBCA, B.51/a/1, Folios 2a-20a, Reel 1M41, John Best Journal.

23 Sayer, *John Sayer's Snake River Journal*, 46, 48; Henry (the Younger), *The Manuscript Journals*, 187, 190; Long, *Voyages and Travels*, 56; and Nelson, *My First Years*, 113.

24 Brownlee et al., "Four Historic Burials."

25 Tanner, *A Narrative*, 111, 113.

26 Brownlee et al., "Four Historic Burials."

27 HBCA, E.3/2, Folio 71, Reel 4M103, Peter Fidler, "Journal from the Mouth of the South Branch." NWC partner Archibald McLeod reported threats by the Fall or Rapid Indians at Fort Alexandria in April 1801 (see Gates, ed., *Five Fur Traders*, 172, 178, 183), while NWC clerk Daniel Harmon reported that by August 1801 the Cree around Fort Alexandria had left to make war upon them (see Harmon, *A Journal*, 51). He adds that they call themselves Paw-is-tick I-e-ne-wuck in their own language. Fort Alexandria was situated to the southwest of Red Deer River, within a few days journey.

28 Kinietz, *The Indians*, 325; Henry (the Younger), *The Manuscript Journals*, 262; and Warren, *History of the Ojibway People*, 162. Indeed, Fidler noted that the ten Iroquois and two Canadians killed by the Fall Indians were all "scalped, and several were cut to pieces limb from limb – their nose, private parts – etc. mangled in the most shocking manner." HBCA, E.3/2, Folio 71, Reel 4M103, "Journal from the Mouth of the South Branch."

29 Sayer, *John Sayer's Snake River Journal*, 42-43, 47; Cameron, "The Nipigon Country," 11, 287; Henry (the Younger), *The Manuscript Journals*, 105, 156, 160, 162, 168, 186, 194, 209, 243, 257, 429; Nelson, *My First Years*, 54, 114-15; and Tanner, *A Narrative*, 42, 46.

30 Perrot, "Memoire," 89-91; Jones, *History of the Ojebway Indians*, 104; Kohl, *Kitchi-Gami*, 217-22; and Warren, *History of the Ojibway People*, 73.

31 Warren, *History of the Ojibway People*, 73.

32 Mainfort, "Indian Social Dynamics," 294-313; and White, *The Middle Ground*, 102.

33 Cameron, "The Nipigon Country," 111; Grant, "The Saulteaux Indians," 364; and McDonnell, "The Red River," 276.

34 No gun was present in the Red Deer River burial, and it is unlikely that one occurred in the Dauphin Lake burial. Red Deer River was properly excavated, and no gun was present. Dauphin Lake burial was recovered in 1938, and there were various newspaper articles written about the discovery. None mentioned a gun – only silver bands, a kettle, a spoon, and a bison hide.

35 Willmott has drawn this conclusion from an examination of bags and clothing articles in museum collections and a quantitative analysis of fabric types in fur trade inventories. The evidence from museum collections for the use of superfine cloth on small items such as bags, but not on items of clothing, is not in itself enough to demonstrate this trend because the ethnological record is incomplete. More convincing is the fact that superfine cloth appears on inventories in extremely small amounts in comparison to coarser woolens. See Willmott, "From Stroud to Strouds," 223.

36 See, for example, Catlin, *Letters and Notes*, 1: Plate 35, *Shakopee, The Six, Chief of the Ojibbeways*, and 2: Plate 260, *Chee-me-na-na-quet, Great Cloud, Son of Grizzly Bear (Menominee)*.

37 Brownlee et al., "Four Historic Burials."

38 Ibid. Identification of the claw courtesy of Kate Peach.

39 Hamilton, *Silver in the Fur Trade*, 99-102.

40 Thompson, *David Thompson's Narrative*, 155, 157.

41 HBCA, E.3/3, Folio 54-55d, Reel 4M103, "Journal of a Journey from Swan to Red River"; MTRL, George Nelson Papers, Dauphin River Journal, 1808-10; and Wallace, ed., *Documents*, 157-258.

42 HBCA, B.22/a/19, Folio 1-2d, Reel 1M17, "Journal at Brandon House, Ossiniboyne River"; S. McGillivray, *The Northwest Company*, 25-29; and Wallace, ed., *Documents*, 273.

43 Brownlee et al., "Four Historic Burials."

44 Kugel, *To Be the Main Leaders*, 5.

45 Schenck, "*The Voice of the Crane Echoes Afar*," 72-73.

46 Treuer, *Living Our Language*, 266.

47 Schenck, "*The Voice of the Crane Echoes Afar*," 74-75; and Vennum, *Wild Rice*, 177.

48 Patrilineal descent systems are not necessarily patriarchal. The term *"ogimaakwe"* means either "female chief" or "the wife of a chief," see Nichols and Nyholm, eds., *A Concise Dictionary*, 105, and many women rose to positions of influence if not chieftainship. Given that descent and residence patterns depend on tracing the male line, however, it is more convenient for leadership to also pass through the male line. We know of only a few examples of female chiefs. Besides John Tanner's adoptive mother, Netnokwa, Peter Jones published an engraving of a female Mississauga chief in the mid-nineteenth century, *The Rippling Stream*, see Jones, *History of the Ojebway Indians*, 57. Around the same time, Chief Flat Mouth offered his chieftainship to his daughter because his son was too young at the time of his passing; however, the daughter gave it to her brother when he came of age, see Dietrich, *Ojibway Chiefs*, 9.

49 Baraga, *A Dictionary*, 36, 48, 239, 335; Kohl, *Kitchi-Gami*, 85, 161-62; Nichols and Nyholm, eds., *A Concise Dictionary*, 161; and Vennum, *Wild Rice*, 177-78.

50 Baraga, *A Dictionary*, 206, 236, 287; Chute, *The Legacy*, 14; and Jenness, *The Ojibwa Indians*, 2, 4.

51 Vennum, *Wild Rice*, 177.

52 Johnston, *Ojibway Heritage*, 64, 68; and Kugel, *To Be the Main Leaders of Our People*, 4-5.

53 Chute, *The Legacy*, 13-14; Hickerson, *The Chippewa*, 44-50; and Schenck, "*The Voice of the Crane Echoes Afar*," 78-80.

54 Kohl, *Kitchi-Gami*, 270-71; and Schenck, "*The Voice of the Crane Echoes Afar*," 73.

55 Schenck, "*The Voice of the Crane Echoes Afar*," 74.

56 Silverstein, "Clothed Encounters," 159.

57 Henry (the Younger), *The Manuscript Journals*, 241.

58 Ibid., 56-57; Jaenen, "The Role of Presents," 235, 239; and White, *The Middle Ground*, 113-14.

59 Matthews and Roulette, "Fair Wind's Dream," 283.

60 Hallowell, *The Ojibwa of Berens River*, 27.

61 Kohl, *Kitchi-Gami*, 270-71; and Warren, *History of the Ojibway People*, 371-72.

62 Tanner, *A Narrative*, 172.

63 Nelson, *My First Years*, 89-91; and Schenck, "*The Voice of the Crane Echoes Afar*," 81.

64 Cadieux, ed., *Letters*, 130-33.

65 Kane, *Wanderings*, 323.

66 During the mid-1790s, HBC traders John Best, John Sutherland, and Peter Fidler complained of intense competition with traders from the "South Company." See Cadieux, ed., *Letters*, 130-33; HBCA, B.199/A/1, Reel 1M139, John Sutherland Journal, Shell River Post, 1794-95; and HBCA, E.3/2, Folios 40-46, Reel 4M103, Peter Fidler, "A Journal from the Long Point Cedar Lake, 1795." The XYC was based in Montreal under the direction of Sir Alexander MacKenzie and others. It operated in opposition to the NWC between 1798 and 1804, when the two companies merged.

67 Henry (the Younger), *The Manuscript Journals*, 256.

68 Cameron, "The Nipigon Country," 278.

69 Jaenen, "The Role of Presents," 239; and Smith, *Something More than Mere Ornament*, 48.

70 MTRL, George Nelson Papers, Dauphin River Journal, 1808-10.

71 Tanner, *A Narrative*, 102.

72 Although the NWC trader Daniel Harmon describes Tanner as a "young man of about twenty years of age" who is "said to be an excellent hunter" and "regarded as a chief among that tribe" (see Harmon, *A Journal*, 53), Tanner's only claim to chieftainship was that a civic chief appointed him hunting chief for one winter, see Tanner, *A Narrative*, 172.

73 Tanner, *A Narrative*, 149.

74 Hanson, "Laced Coats and Leather Jackets," 106.

75 Perrot, "Memoire," 78.

76 Beaudoin-Ross, "A la Canadienne," 71, 73; and Blackstock, "Nineteenth-Century Fur Trade Costume," 195.

77 The types of cloth used for capots, as well as the laced and gartered varieties, are documented in the same sources cited for Figure 3.5.

78 Malhiot, "A Wisconsin Fur-Trader's Journal," insert (no page numbers).

79 Malhiot, "Journal du Fort Kamanaitiquoya," 244.

80 Curot, "A Wisconsin Fur-Trader's Journal," 420, 464.

81 The only reference to red capots we have seen is in the 1821 outfit of the combined NWC and HBC to the Western Districts, which includes 16 red laced capots out of a total of 1,385 capots in men's sizes (see Simpson, *Journal of Occurrences*, 145-46). It seems likely that at an earlier decade voyageurs primarily wore grey capots (see Thompson, *David Thompson's Narrative*, 40), the national dress of the French Canadian habitants from whose ranks they were recruited (see Beaudoin-Ross, "A la Canadienne," 73). By the 1800s, however, we have reason to believe that blue had become the voyageurs' preferred colour. In 1808, the NWC partners reported at their annual meeting that employees were dissatisfied with their ratteen capot allotments, so they resolved to replace these with blue cloth when the ratteen in stock ran out (see Wallace, ed., *Documents*, 253). In NWC and XYC shipments from England to Montreal, ratteen came in blue but mainly in the "sad" colours of "mixed" (mottled grey), grey, brown, and green (see Archives of Ontario [hereafter AO], Fur Trade Collection [hereafter FTC], Fonds F431, Microfilm MS 312, Reels 1-3, "Archives du Seminaire de Quebec," No. 4, "Invoices of Goods Shipped from England to Montreal, 1798-1804.") Also, much later (1867), HBC clerk Isaac Cowie explained that the "approved uniform for clerks" was a "grayish blue cloth 'Illinois' capote with silver-plated buttons" (see Cowie, *The Company of Adventurers*, 116). The question of company employee dress is outside the parameters of the present discussion except in the case of Illinois capots, which might have been worn by both voyageurs and Amerindians.

82 HBCA, F.4/3, Reel 5M2, NWC Account Book, 1812; HBCA, F.4/12, Reel 5M4, NWC Account Book, 1818; and AO FTC, Fonds F431, Microfilm MS 312 Reels 1-3, "Archives du Seminaire de Quebec," No. 6., "Invoices of Goods Shipped from Montreal for Various Outfits, 1821."

83 Catlin, *Letters and Notes*, 1:240; Kohl, *Kitchi-Gami*, 115; and Montgomery, *Textiles in America*, 192.

84 Carman, *British Military Uniforms*, 87, 106; and Lawson, *A History of the Uniforms*, 17, 32, 35.

85 Blackman, "Walking Amazons," 53.

86 The three paintings are as follows: Edward Chatfield, *Three Chiefs of the Huron Indians, Residing at La Jeune Lorette, near Quebec, in Their National Costume*, 1825, Library and Archives Canada (hereafter LAC), C-6042; Edward Chatfield, *Nicholas Vincent Isawanhonhi*, 1824, LAC, C-038948 (see Hamilton, *Silver in the Fur Trade*, 114; and Karklins, *Trade Ornament Usage*, Plate 4); and Henry D. Thielcke, *The Presentation of a Newly Elected Chief of the Huron Tribe, Canada*, 1841, LAC, C-041373 (see Hamilton, *Silver in the Fur Trade*, 115). Hanson states that the British continued to distribute blue coats "under their treaty obligations" but does not reveal his sources or reasoning, see Hanson, "Laced Coats and Leather Jackets," 108.

87 LAC, Indian Affairs, RG 10, Reel C-11123, "Treaty 3."

88 Hanson, "Laced Coats and Leather Jackets," 106.

89 Carman, *British Military Uniforms*, 111, 113; and Lawson, *A History of the Uniforms*, 39.

90 Silverstein, "Clothed Encounters," 210-15.

91 Black, "The Ojibwa Power Belief System," 147-48.

92 Rogers, *The Round Lake Ojibwa*, Section D, 29-31.

93 Tanner, *A Narrative*, 230.

94 Silverstein, "Clothed Encounters," 200-10.

95 A "Red Chief's Coat" in the Dr. Oronhyatekha Collection at the Royal Ontario Museum (hereafter ROM) is attributed to Anishinaabe Chief Oshawana for his service under Tecumseh in the War of 1812, see ROM 911.3.119. The 1904 catalogue to this collection states that the Canadian government gave red chief's coats to Indian chiefs with their annuity payments, see Cumberland, *Catalogue*, 135. In 1822, Chief Peshikee told British officials at Drummond Island that he was "not one of those children who change their Allegiance as often as they meet with different coloured coats." In the same passage, he refers to the Americans as "black coats," see Peshikee in Corbiere, "Ojibwe Chief Peshikee," 8.

96 Lyford, *Ojibwa Crafts*, 31. A search for "Ojibway" and "spoon" at the Minnesota Historical Society's website revealed that the Ayer Collection has five similar wooden spoons, several of which have residue of maple sap on them. Informants suggested in oral interviews with Ayers that the spoons were used for skimming the maple sap in the process of making maple sugar.

97 Tanner, *A Narrative*, 92, 96, 109; Henry (the Younger), *The Manuscript Journals*, 170, 428-49; and HBCA, B.176/a/1, Reel 1M119, Alexander Kennedy Journal, Red Deer River Post, 1812-13.

98 Identification of the feathers by Mark Peck, Centre for Biodiversity and Conservation Biology, Royal Ontario Museum, personal communication, 26 October 1999. NWC inventories of goods sent to posts in 1804 include five terms for feathers: "cock," "circle," "chiefs," "foxtail," and "ladies." The last two appear only on the Grand Portage inventory, suggesting that the NWC did not ship them to the interior. Circle and chiefs feathers are clearly the same item, for they cost the same (fifteen shillings each, as compared with four shillings each for cock feathers and six shillings each for foxtail feathers) and appear in direct proportion to the number of chief's coats on the inventories for each of the inland posts, see AO, FTC, Fonds F431, Microfilm MS 312, Reels 1-3, "Archives du Seminaire de Quebec," No. 5, "Invoices of Goods Shipped from Montreal, 1804." In the spring of 1803, George Nelson included a "splendid circular feather" among the items in a chief's outfit offered to a man the XYC wished to make a chief, see Nelson, *My First Years*, 89. We believe that the term "circle" describes the circular motif on peacock feathers. Likewise, the term "foxtail" describes the appearance of ostrich feathers. The latter interpretation is supported by the fact that a NWC inventory of goods on hand at Grand Portage in 1797 includes "26 dozen black ostrich feathers," "22¼ dozen cock plumes," and "44 chiefs feathers." See MTRL, Northwest Company Collection, "Inventory of Goods." These items correspond directly to the foxtail, cock, and circle feathers mentioned in the inventories of 1804. Our interpretation of "circle" and "foxtail" as peacock and ostrich feathers, respectively, is also supported by the pictorial record. Both George Catlin and Charles Bird King illustrate chiefs wearing ostrich and peacock feathers in their headdresses, the former much more often than the latter. See Catlin, *Letters and Notes*, Plates 199, 206, 241, 258, 260, 268, 298; and Viola, *The Indian Legacy*, 57, 58, 60, 94.

99 For a detailed analysis of the differences between stroud and broadcloth (a.k.a. cloth), see Willmott, "From Stroud to Strouds."

100 In an analysis performed by the Parks Canada Textile Conservation Centre, Lynn Storr confirmed our opinion that the fabric is silk. These results are not entirely conclusive, however, because there remains a minute possibility that it is worsted wool. What can be said with certainty is that it is a protein-based fibre.

101 Montgomery, *Textiles in America*, 246.

102 AO FTC, Fonds F431, Microfilm MS 312, Reels 1-3, "Archives du Seminaire de Quebec," No. 5, "Invoices of Goods Shipped from Montreal, 1804," and No. 6, "Invoices of Goods Shipped from Montreal, 1821." Gauze also appears on the 1804 inventory of St. Valier Mailloux, a Montreal merchant who hired men to work for the XYC. During the winter, he travelled to Grant Portage to sell merchandise to the employees of both the XYC and the NWC, see Nelson, *My First Years*, 213.

103 Brownlee et al., "Four Historic Burials."

104 Grant, "The Saulteaux Indians," 317. Similar modified silver scraps are also interpreted as men's hair ornaments in Hamilton, *Silver in the Fur Trade*, 95-98, 118.

105 AO, FTC, Fonds F431, Microfilm MS 312, Reels 1-3, "Archives du Seminaire de Quebec," No. 3, "Accounts Current of Expenditures, 1805-1813."

106 Hamilton, *Silver in the Fur Trade*, 206, 211-13.

107 Although John Ewers's research is remarkably thorough and meticulous, he was mistaken that the Forsyth Richardson Co. was composed of traders, see Ewers, *Hair Pipes*, 47. Rather, they were Montreal merchants who supplied the NWC until the formation of the XYC, when the latter became their primary client. It is also worth mentioning that in 1797 the NWC had fifteen masses (i.e., hanks) of pipe beads and eight silver hair pipes in its store at Grand Portage, see MTRL, Northwest Company Collection, "Inventory of Goods, 1797." Also see Hamilton, *Silver in the Fur Trade*, 98-99 for examples of silver hair pipes. These products might have been the forerunners of shell or wampum hair pipes, in which case they show how the shell variety was developed specifically for the fur trade market.

108 Ewers, *Hair Pipes*, 46-47.

109 AO, FTC, Fonds F431, Microfilm MS 312, Reels 1-3, "Archives du Seminaire de Quebec," No. 3, "Accounts Current of Expenditures, 1805-1813."

110 Jameson, *Winter Studies and Summer Rambles*, 385; and Silverstein, "Clothed Encounters," 68-74.

111 Warren, *History of the Ojibway People*, 48.

112 Kohl, *Kitchi-Gami*, 136.

113 Grant, "The Saulteaux Indians," 350.

114 Jameson, *Winter Studies and Summer Rambles*, 27.

115 Another unusual aspect of this wampum belt is its construction technique. An in situ photograph reveals that the Red Deer River youth's belt was constructed with the beads oriented horizontally (Meyer, "The Red Deer River Grave," Figure 15). This means that it could not be loom woven, as are the vast majority of wampum belts. This technique might be peculiar to the belt's function as an element of dress, a regional variation, or the creative ingenuity of the individual who made it. Unfortunately, further details regarding both the form and the function of this wampum belt are beyond the scope of the present discussion.

116 Hamilton, *Silver in the Fur Trade*, 69; and Karklins, *Trade Ornament Usage*, 26.

117 AO, FTC, Fonds F431, Microfilm MS 312, Reels 1-3, "Archives du Seminaire de Quebec," No. 5, "Invoices of Goods Shipped from Montreal, 1804."

118 Hamilton, *Silver in the Fur Trade*, 66.

119 Schenck, "*The Voice of the Crane Echoes Afar*," 57-60; Silverstein, "Marks of Identity." This differs from contemporary usage in which the term "totem" is often used to refer to a guardian spirit.

120 Silverstein-Willmott, "A Picture's Worth."

121 Hilger, *Chippewa Child Life*, 45.

122 Hamilton, *Silver in the Fur Trade*, 69; Karklins, *Trade Ornament Usage*, 26.

123 Hamilton, *Silver in the Fur Trade,* 70-74.
124 Gilman, *Where Two Worlds Meet,* 77; and Hamilton, *Silver in the Fur Trade,* 69-74.
125 Tanner, *A Narrative,* 60.
126 Ibid., 175.
127 Morris, *The Treaties of Canada,* 298, 300. See Bohaker, "*Nindoodemag,*" for a discussion of Algonquian totemic emblems in the context of treaty signatures.
128 HBCA, B.22/a/20, Peter Fidler Journal, Brandon House Post, 1817-18.
129 MTRL, George Nelson Papers, Dauphin River Journal, 1808-10.
130 Meyer, "The Red Deer River Grave," 10-15.
131 Karklins, *Trade Ornament Usage,* 25.
132 Hamilton, *Silver in the Fur Trade,* 53.

Bibliography

Archival Sources

Archives of Ontario (AO)

Fur Trade Collection (FTC). Fonds F431, Microfilm MS 312, Reels 1-3, Archives du Seminaire de Quebec, Documents relatifs à la Compagnie du Nord-Ouest et Sir Alexander MacKenzie:

No. 3, "Accounts Current of Expenditures on the Yearly 'Outfits' and the 'Adventures' in the Various Districts of the West; Sir Alexander MacKenzie & Co., Account Current Book, 1805-1813."

No. 4, "Invoices of Goods Shipped from England to Montreal for the New North West Co., Forsyth Richardson & Co., and Sir Alexander MacKenzie & Co., and of the Goods Shipped to Them to the Western Country; also Invoices of Furs Sent by Them to England, 1798-1804."

No. 5, "Invoices of Goods Shipped from Montreal to the Various Western Posts by Sir Alex. MacKenzie and Co., 1804."

No. 6. "Invoices of Goods Shipped from Montreal for Various Outfits by McTavish MacGillivray and Co., 1821."

North West Company Collection

Furs Inventory, 1815. MU2201, Box 6-3.

Hudson's Bay Company Archives (HBCA)

B.22/a/19, Folio 1-2d, Reel 1M17, Peter Fidler Journal. "Journal at Brandon House, Ossiniboyne River Lat 49°52' with Some Account of the Notorious Conduct of the NWCo in Employing Half Indians to Destroy the Red River Settlement, also Astronomical Observations Made at the Same Place by Peter Thomas and Charles Fidler, also the Abstract of a Thermomitrical Journal Kept at the Same Place with Occasional Remarks on the Seasons Productions &c & Copies of a Few Letters from Mr Robt Semple by Peter Fidler."

B.22/a/20, Peter Fidler Journal, Brandon House Post, 1817-18.

B.51/a/1, Folios 2a-20a, Reel 1M41, John Best Journal, Fort Dauphin, 1795-96.

B.176/a/1, Reel 1M119, Alexander Kennedy Journal, Red Deer River Post, 1812-13.

B.199/A/1, Reel 1M139, John Sutherland Journal, Shell River Post, 1794-95.

E.3/2, Folios 40-46, Reel 4M103, Peter Fidler, "A Journal from the Long Point Cedar Lake to Swan River House, Somerset and Carleton Houses, also the Upper Parts of the Red River in 1795."

E.3/2, Folio 71, Reel 4M103, Peter Fidler, "Journal from the Mouth of the South Branch of the Saskatchewan River to the Confluence of the Bad and Red Deer's Rivers, Where Chesterfield House Is Situated, by Peter Fidler."

E.3/3, Folio 54-55d, Reel 4M103, Peter Fidler, "Journal of a Journey from Swan to Red River."

E.3/3, Folio 58, Reel 4M103, Peter Fidler, "Journal of a Journey from Swan to the Red River and Down It in a Canoe from the Elbow to Its Entrance into Lake Winnipeg, & along the South and Eastern Shores to Its Discharge into the Elongation of the Saskatchewan River or Nelson's Bay. By Peter Fidler."

F.4/3, Reel 5M2, NWC Account Book, 1812.

F.4/6, Reel 5M3, NWC Account Book, 1814.

F.4/9, Reel 5M3, NWC Account Book, 1817.

F.4/12, Reel 5M4, NWC Account Book, 1818.

Library and Archives Canada (LAC)
Documentary Art Collection:
C-6042, Edward Chatfield, *Three Chiefs of the Huron Indians, Residing at La Jeune Lorette, Near Quebec, in Their National Costume*, 1825.

C-038948, Edward Chatfield, *Nicholas Vincent Tsawanhonhi*, lithograph from a painting published in 1824.

C-041373, Henry D. Thielcke, *The Presentation of a Newly Elected Chief of the Huron Tribe, Canada*, 1841.

Indian Affairs. RG 10, Reel C-11123, "Treaty 3 – Commissioner J.A.N. Provencher Reports that Due to a Misunderstanding the Indians Will Be Issued a Full Suit of Clothes Rather than Just a Coat."

Metropolitan Toronto Reference Library, Baldwin Room (MTRL)
George Nelson Papers. Dauphin River Journal, 1808-10.

North West Company Collection. "Inventory of Goods Taken in the Grand Portage 1797."

Royal Ontario Museum (ROM)
Dr. Oronhyatekha Collection. 911.3.119, "A Red Chief's Coat Attributed to Anishinaabe Chief Oshawana for His Service under Tecumseh in the War of 1812."

Published Sources
Axtell, James. *Beyond 1492: Encounters in Colonial North America.* New York: Oxford University Press, 1992.

Baraga, Frederic. *A Dictionary of the Ojibway Language.* St. Paul: Minnesota Historical Society, 1992 [1878 and 1880].

Beaudoin-Ross, Jacqueline. "A la Canadienne: Some Aspects of 19th-Century Habitant Dress." *Dress* 6 (1980): 71-82.

Black, Mary. "The Ojibwa Power Belief System." In *The Anthropology of Power*, edited by R.D. Fogelson and R.N. Adams, 141-51. New York: Academic Press, 1977.

Blackman, Cally. "Walking Amazons: The Development of the Riding Habit in England during the Eighteenth Century." *Costume* 35 (2001): 47-58.

Blackstock, Pamela. "Nineteenth-Century Fur Trade Costume." *Canadian Folklore* 10, 1-2 (1988): 183-208.

Bohaker, Heidi. "*Nindoodemag:* The Significance of Algonquian Kinship Networks in the Eastern Great Lakes Region, 1600-1701." *William and Mary Quarterly,* 3rd series, 63, 1 (2006): 23-52.

Brownlee, Kevin, Pat Badertscher, Barb Hewitt, Robert Hoppa, Linda Larcombe, Christopher Meiklejohn, Deidre White, and Cory Willmott. "Four Historic Burials from Early Nineteenth-Century Manitoba." Paper presented at the Canadian Archaeological Association, Hamilton, Ontario, May 2003.

Cadieux, Lorenzo, ed. *Letters from the New Canada Mission, 1843-1852.* Part 2, *Letters No. 45-93.* Ottawa: William Lonc, 2001.

Cameron, Duncan. "The Nipigon Country, 1804." In *Les bourgeois de la Compagnie du Nord-Ouest: Recits de voyages, lettres et rapports inedits relatifs au Nord-Ouest Canadien,* vol. 2, edited by L.R. Masson, 231-300. New York: Antiquarian Press, 1960.

Carlos, Ann M., and Frank D. Lewis. "Marketing in the Land of Hudson's Bay: Indian Consumers and the Hudson's Bay Company, 1670-1770." *Enterprise and Society* 3, 2 (2002): 285-317.

Carman, William Y. *British Military Uniforms from Contemporary Pictures, Henry VII to the Present Day.* New York: Arco Pub. Co., 1958.

Carver, Jonathan. *Carver's Travels through North America in the Years 1766, 1767 and 1768.* New York: Dover Reprints, 1974 [1778].

Catlin, George. *Letters and Notes on the Manners, Customs, and Conditions of North American Indians.* 2 vols. New York: Dover Reprints, 1973 [1844].

Chute, Janet. *The Legacy of Shingwaukonse: A Century of Native Leadership.* Toronto: University of Toronto Press, 1998.

Corbiere, Alan. "Ojibwe Chief Peshikee (Buffalo) aka Keche-Waishkee." *Ojibwe Cultural Foundation News* 3, 1 (2009): 8.

Cowie, Isaac. *The Company of Adventurers: A Narrative of Seven Years in the Service of the Hudson's Bay Company during 1867-1874.* Lincoln: University of Nebraska Press, 1993 [1913].

Cumberland, F. Barlow. *Catalogue and Notes of the Oronhyateckha Historical Collection.* Toronto: Independent Order of Foresters, 1904.

Curot, Michel. "A Wisconsin Fur Trader's Journal, 1803-1804." In *Collections of the State Historical Society of Wisconsin,* vol. 20, edited by Reuben Thwaites, 396-471. Madison: Wisconsin Historical Society, 1911.

Danesi, Marcel. *The Quest for Meaning: A Guide to Semiotic Theory and Practice.* Toronto: University of Toronto Press, 2007.

Dietrich, Mark. *Ojibway Chiefs: Portraits of Anishinaabe Leadership.* Rochester, MN: Coyote Books, 1999.

Ewers, John C. "Artifacts and Pictures as Documents in the History of Indian-White Relations." In *Indian-White Relations: A Persistent Paradox,* edited by Jane F. Smith and Robert M. Kvasnicka, 101-11. Washington, DC: Howard University Press, 1976.

–. *Hair Pipes in Plains Indian Adornment: A Study of Indian and White Ingenuity.* Anthropological Papers No. 50. Bureau of American Ethnology Bulletin 164. Washington, DC: US Government Printing House, 1996 [1957].

Fogelson, Raymond D. "The Ethnohistory of Events and Nonevents." *Ethnohistory* 36, 2 (1989): 133-47.

Gates, Charles M., ed. *Five Fur Traders of the Northwest: Being the Narrative of Peter Pond, and the Diaries of John MacDonell, Archibald N. McLeod, Hugh Faries and Thomas Connor.* St. Paul: Minnesota Historical Society, 1965.

Gilman, Carolyn. *Where Two Worlds Meet: The Great Lakes Fur Trade.* St. Paul: Minnesota Historical Society Press, 1982.

Grant, Peter. "The Saulteaux Indians, about 1804." In *Les bourgeois de la Compagnie du Nord-Ouest: Recits de voyages, lettres, et rapports inedits relatifs au Nord-Ouest Canadien,* vol. 2, edited by L.R. Masson, 307-66. New York: Antiquarian Press, 1960.

Hallowell, A. Irving. *The Ojibwa of Berens River, Manitoba: Ethnography into History.* Edited by Jennifer S.H. Brown. New York: Harcourt Brace Jovanovich, 1992.

Hamilton, Martha Wilson. *Silver in the Fur Trade, 1680-1820.* Chelmsford, MS: Martha Hamilton Publishing, 1995.

Hanson, James A. "Laced Coats and Leather Jackets: The Great Plains Intercultural Clothing Exchange." In *Plains Indian Studies: A Collection of Essays in Honor of John C. Ewers and Waldo R. Wedel,* edited by Douglas H. Ubelaker and Herman J. Viola, 105-17. Smithsonian Contributions to Anthropology No. 30. Washington, DC: Smithsonian Institution, 1982.

Harmon, Daniel. *A Journal of the Voyages and Travels in the Interior of North America between the 47th and 58th Degrees of N. Latitude Extending from Montreal Nearly to the Pacific, a Distance of about 5,000 Miles.* New York: A.S. Barnes and Co., 1903.

Henry (the Younger), Alexander. *The Manuscript Journals of Alexander Henry, Fur Trader of the Northwest Company, and of David Thompson, Official Geographer and Explorer of the Same Company, 1799-1814.* Vol. 1. Edited by Elliot Coues. Minneapolis: Ross and Haines, 1965 [1897].

Hickerson, Harold. *The Chippewa and Their Neighbors: A Study in Ethnohistory.* 2nd ed. Prospect Heights, IL: Waveland Press, 1988.

Hilger, M. Inez. *Chippewa Child Life and Its Cultural Background.* St. Paul: Minnesota Historical Society Press, 1992 [1951].

Jaenen, Cornelius J. "The Role of Presents in French-Amerindian Trade." In *Explorations in Canadian Economic History: Essays in Honour of Irene M. Spry,* edited by Duncan Cameron, 231-50. Ottawa: University of Ottawa Press, 1985.

Jameson, Anna B. *Winter Studies and Summer Rambles in Canada.* Toronto: McClelland and Stewart, 1990 [1838].

Jenness, Diamond. *The Ojibwa Indians of Parry Island: Their Social and Religious Life.* Bulletin No. 78, Anthropological Series No. 17. Ottawa: National Museum of Canada, 1935.

Johnston, Basil. *Ojibway Heritage.* Toronto: McClelland and Stewart, 1976.

Jones, Peter, Rev. *History of the Ojebway Indians with Especial Reference to Their Conversion to Christianity.* Freeport, NY: Books for Libraries Press, 1970 [1861].

Kane, Paul. *Wanderings of an Artist among the Indians of North America.* New York: Dover Publications, 1996 [1859].

Karklins, Karlis. *Trade Ornament Usage among the Native Peoples of Canada: A Source Book.* Ottawa: Environment Canada Parks Service, 1992.

Keating, William H. *Narrative of an Expedition to the Source of the St. Peter's River, Lake Winnepeek, Lake of the Woods, &c Performed in the Year 1823.* Minneapolis: Ross and Haines, 1959 [1824].

Kinietz, Vernon W. *The Indians of the Western Great Lakes, 1615-1760.* Ann Arbor: University of Michigan Press, 1965.

Kohl, Johann Georg. *Kitchi-Gami: Life among the Lake Superior Ojibway.* St. Paul: Minnesota Historical Society Press, 1985 [1860].

Kugel, Rebecca. *To Be the Main Leaders of Our People: A History of Minnesota Ojibwe Politics, 1825-1898.* East Lansing: Michigan State University Press, 1998.

Lawson, Cecil C.P. *A History of the Uniforms of the British Army; with Many Drawings by the Author.* New York: A.S. Barnes, 1962 [1940].

Long, John. *Voyages and Travels of an Indian Interpreter and Trader.* Toronto: Coles, 1971 [1791].

Lyford, Carrie A. *Ojibwa Crafts.* Stephen's Point, WI: Schneider Publishers, 1982 [1943].

Mainfort, Robert C. "Indian Social Dynamics in the Period of European Contact: Fletcher Site Cemetery Bay County." *Michigan State University Archaeology Series* 1, 4 (1979): 269-418.

Malhiot, François. "Journal du Fort Kamanaitiquoya à la rivière Montréal." In *Les bourgeois de la Compagnie du Nord-Ouest,* vol. 1, edited by L.R. Masson, 226-63. New York: Antiquarian Press, 1960.

–. "A Wisconsin Fur-Trader's Journal, 1804-1805." In *Collections of the State Historical Society of Wisconsin,* vol. 19, edited by Reuben Thwaites, 163-233. Madison: Wisconsin Historical Society, 1910.

Matthews, Maureen, and Roger Roulette. "Fair Wind's Dream: *Naamiwan Obawaajigewin.*" In *Reading beyond Words: Contexts for Native History,* edited by Jennifer S.H. Brown and Elizabeth Vibert, 263-92. 2nd ed. Peterborough, ON: Broadview Press, 2003.

McDonnell, John. 1960. "The Red River (about 1797)." In *Les bourgeois de la Compagnie du Nord-Ouest,* vol. 1, edited by L.R. Masson, 267-81. New York: Antiquarian Press, 1960.

McGillivray, Duncan. *The Journal of Duncan M'Gillivray of the North West Company at Fort George on the Saskatchewan, 1794-5.* Edited by Arthur S. Morton. Fairfield, WA: Ye Galleon Press, 1989 [1929].

McGillivray, Simon. *The Northwest Company in Rebellion: Simon McGillivray's Fort William Notebook, 1815.* Edited and introduced by Jean Morrison. Thunder Bay, ON: Thunder Bay Historical Museum Society, 1988.

Meyer, David. "The Red Deer River Grave: An Historic Burial." *Na'pao: A Saskatchewan Anthropological Journal* 4, 1 (1973): 3-28.

Montgomery, Florence M. *Textiles in America, 1650-1870.* New York: W.W. Norton and Co., 1984.

Morris, Alexander. *The Treaties of Canada with the Indians of Manitoba and the North-West Territories.* Toronto: Belfords, Clarke and Co., 1971 [1880].

Nelson, George. *My First Years in the Fur Trade: The Journals of 1802-1804.* Edited by Laura Peers and Theresa Schenck. St. Paul: Minnesota Historical Society Press, 2002.

Nichols, John, and Earl Nyholm, eds. *A Concise Dictionary of the Minnesota Ojibwe.* Minneapolis: University of Minnesota Press, 1995.

Peers, Laura. *The Ojibwa of Western Canada, 1780 to 1870.* Winnipeg: University of Manitoba Press, 1994.

Perrot, Nicolas. "Memoire sur les moeurs, coustumes et religion des sauvages de l'Amérique Septentrionale; Publié pour la première fois le R.P.F. Tailhan, de la Compagnie de Jesus (Paris, 1864)." In *The Indian Tribes of the Upper Mississippi Valley and Region of the Great Lakes,* edited by Emma Helen Blair, 25-272. Lincoln: University of Nebraska Press, 1996.

Ray, Arthur. "Indians as Consumers in the Eighteenth Century." In *Old Trails and New Directions: Papers of the Third North American Fur Trade Conference,* edited by Carol M. Judd and Arthur J. Ray, 255-71. Toronto: University of Toronto Press, 1980.

Rich, E.E. *The Fur Trade and the Northwest to 1857.* Toronto: McClelland and Stewart, 1967.

Rogers, Edward S. *The Round Lake Ojibwa.* Toronto: Royal Ontario Museum, 1962.

Sayer, John. *John Sayer's Snake River Journal, 1804-05.* Edited by Douglas A. Birk. Minneapolis: Institute for Minnesota Archaeology, 1989.

Schenck, Theresa M. *"The Voice of the Crane Echoes Afar": The Sociopolitical Organization of the Lake Superior Ojibwa, 1640-1855.* New York: Garland, 1997.

Schoolcraft, Henry Rowe. *Historical and Statistical Information Respecting the History, Condition and Prospects of the Indian Tribes of the United States.* Vols. 1 and 5. New York: Palladin Press, 1969 [1851, 1855].

Shannon, Timothy J. "Dressing for Success on the Mohawk Frontier: Hendrick, William Johnson, and the Indian Fashion." *William and Mary Quarterly,* 3rd series, 53, 1 (1996): 13-42.

Silverstein, Cory. "Clothed Encounters: The Power of Dress in Relations between Anishnaabe and British Peoples in the Great Lakes Region, 1760-2000." PhD diss., McMaster University, 2000.

–. "Marks of Identity: Anishnaabe Totemic Emblems in Historical Perspective." Paper presented at the 32nd Algonquian Conference, Montreal, 27 October 2000.

Silverstein-Willmott, Cory. "A Picture's Worth: Algonquian Totemic Emblems in Multiple Contexts of 'Picture-Writing.'" Paper presented at the American Society for Ethnohistory, Quebec City, 17 October 2002.

Simpson, George. *Journal of Occurrences in the Athabasca Department by George Simpson, 1820 and 1821, and Report.* Edited by E.E. Rich. Toronto: Champlain Society, 1938.

Smith, Erica. "Something More than Mere Ornament: Cloth and Indian-European Relations in the Eighteenth Century." Master's thesis, University of Winnipeg, 1991.

Tanner, John. *A Narrative of the Captivity and Adventures of John Tanner.* Edited by Edwin James. New York: Garland Publishing, 1975 [1830].

Thistle, Paul C. *Indian-European Trade Relations in the Lower Saskatchewan River Region to 1840.* Winnipeg: University of Manitoba Press, 1986.

Thompson, David. *David Thompson's Narrative, 1784-1812.* Edited by Richard Glover. Toronto: Champlain Society, 1962.

Treuer, Anton. *Living Our Language: Ojibwe Tales and Oral Histories.* St. Paul: Minnesota Historical Society Press, 2001.

Vennum, Thomas, Jr. *Wild Rice and the Ojibway People.* St. Paul: Minnesota Historical Society Press, 1988.

Viola, Herman J. *The Indian Legacy of Charles Bird King.* New York/Washington, DC: Doubleday/Smithsonian Institution Press, 1976.

Wallace, Stewart W., ed. *Documents Relating to the North West Company.* Toronto: Champlain Society, 1934.

Warren, William. *History of the Ojibway People.* St. Paul: Minnesota Historical Society Press, 1984 [1885].

White, Richard. *The Middle Ground: Indians, Empires, and the Republics in the Great Lakes Region, 1650-1815.* Cambridge: Cambridge University Press, 1991.

Willmott, Cory. "From Stroud to Strouds: The Hidden History of a Fur Trade Textile." *Textile History* 36, 2 (2005): 196-234.

Part 2

Using Documents

Although archival documents have always been the major source for historians, scholars are developing new ways to work with them to incorporate culturally specific perspectives and information. In an important breakthrough, historian Heidi Bohaker has compared totemic signatures – sketches of totemic animals used by Anishinaabe treaty signatories – to develop a system for reading these aspects of documentary evidence, which have rarely been examined carefully by historians. Bohaker uses ethnographic evidence to illuminate relationships between Algonquian kinship systems and tribal and extra-tribal politics, making it possible to see how the individuals who signed treaties with their totemic signatures were pursuing kin-based and regional agendas in their interactions with Europeans. Bohaker currently teaches history at the University of Toronto and is a founding member of the Great Lakes Research Alliance for the Study of Aboriginal Arts and Cultures (GRASAC), a collaborative research partnership that is building databases of digitized museum collections, research sources, and scholarship to elicit and serve as a repository for knowledge that has been carried in living memory, indigenous languages, and oral traditions.

Cross-cultural perspectives also inform "The Contours of Everyday Life" by Elizabeth Vibert, a historian of the cultural construction of race and gender who teaches at the University of Victoria and has co-edited two editions of *Reading beyond Words* with Jennifer S.H. Brown. Vibert examines European perceptions of Aboriginal diet and how these perceptions shaped European assumptions about the moral and physical abilities and relative states of evolution of Aboriginal peoples. In particular, the contrast between the British ideal of a game-based diet and the Plateau reality of a fish-oriented diet led Europeans to view Aboriginal peoples as inferior. Vibert reminds us that food is not simply a biological mandate – it can be culturally constructed – and that many of our expectations about sociality are linked to culturally based beliefs about food and how it should be consumed. She suggests a sophisticated theoretical structure for analyzing changing perspectives on racialization that incorporates much recent work on identity, nationalism, and the processes of colonialism.

Germaine Warkentin is professor emerita at the University of Toronto, where she taught English literature for many years. She has published widely on Renaissance writing and libraries, early Canadian exploration literature, and the history of the book. In the chapter "Make it last forever as it is," she examines the little-known correspondence of the fur trader John McDonald of Garth (1771-1866), in which he proposed, in 1857, a plan to ensure that the western part of North America remained sovereign Aboriginal homelands. His ideas were regarded as folly because at that time the British government was sending survey expeditions to explore the potential of the West for British settlers. They are important, however, for they show us the extent to which settler society and the processes of colonialism were not monolithic. And they remind us that many British citizens hoped for a just provision of lands and resources for Aboriginal peoples.

4

Anishinaabe Toodaims: Contexts for Politics, Kinship, and Identity in the Eastern Great Lakes

Heidi Bohaker

> *I have remarked that when the English speak of the different nations of Indians they generally call them tribes; which term is quite erroneous, as each nation is subdivided into a number of tribes or clans, called "toodaims."*
>
> – PETER JONES, *HISTORY OF THE OJEBWAY INDIANS*

THE NINETEENTH-CENTURY Mississauga-Anishinaabe leader and Methodist missionary Peter Jones (Kahkewaquonaby) explained in his posthumously published 1861 *History of the Ojebway Indians* that the Anishinaabeg were organized politically into divisions by clan identities (as a type of extended family kinship) that they had inherited from their fathers and their fathers' fathers.[1] Jones, who had been born and lived much of his life on the northwestern shores of Lake Ontario, was personally familiar with the following clan identities: "Eagle, Reindeer, Otter, Bear, Buffalo, Beaver, Catfish, Pike, Birch-bark, White Oak Tree, Bear's Liver, &c, &c."[2] All referred to flora and fauna common in the region, including the buffalo or wood bison, an animal that had ranged into the woodlands of the northeast until the middle of the eighteenth century. Likewise, reindeer (woodland caribou) had historically ranged south along the full extent of the Canadian Shield into what is now southeastern Ontario.[3] Jones characterized these *toodaims* as gifts bestowed by the Great Spirit to ensure that the mobile Anishinaabeg would find kin wherever they went. "When an Indian, in travelling, meets with a strange band of Indians," Jones notes, "all he has to do is to seek for those bearing the same emblem of his tribe; and having made it known that he belongs to their 'toodaim,' he is sure to be treated as a relative." By reflecting on the usefulness of the toodaim identity as a sort of traveller's aid society, Jones was making no particular comment on any larger political significance. Only in the quotation cited in the epigraph does he define "toodaim" as a tribe or clan, as a subset of a larger national polity.[4] But throughout the rest of his book, and particularly in chapters devoted to discussions of Anishinaabe governance, Jones writes frequently about the importance and centrality of the tribe to Anishinaabe politics and decision making. A rereading of Jones's *History*, substituting "toodaim" for "tribe," reveals that toodaim shaped all aspects of Anishinaabe political life, from the band to the local council and to larger regional councils, and defined the leadership roles that individuals could play in those contexts. Leading ethnohistorians – including Jennifer S.H. Brown, Elizabeth Vibert, and Nancy Shoemaker – have all called for the use of culturally specific categories of analysis. In this chapter, I argue that the toodaim identity as described by Peter Jones is one such category and that it is of fundamental importance to understanding and writing Anishinaabe histories.[5]

In addition to Jones, other nineteenth-century Anishinaabe writers, including William Warren, understood both the centrality and the political importance of toodaim.[6] Jones's contemporary and fellow Anishinaabe missionary, George Copway, also equated tribe with clan. He noted that "a tribe is a band of Indians whose sign or mark is the same; for example, such as wear the sign of the *crane* [sic], recognize each other as relatives."[7] In present-day Anishinaabemowin, "toodaim" is usually written "*nindoodem*," which translates as "my clan."[8] Copway's reference to signs and marks reflects that the Anishinaabeg historically communicated their nindoodem identity on a wide range of media. Such pictographs appear on rock art and were made on treaty documents with the French as early as the late seventeenth century. Nindoodem images appear on the signature page of the Great Peace of Montreal in 1701, on nearly every Anishinaabe treaty signed with the British from 1764 to 1867, on those treaties signed with the United States from 1784 to 1818, and on many petitions from Anishinaabe communities to British, American, and Canadian governments to the late nineteenth century.[9] The example in Figure 4.1 is the signature page and a detail of an 1806 sale of land by the Mississauga-Anishinaabeg to the British Crown of eighty-five thousand acres on the north shore of Lake Ontario.[10] The pictographs on that document represent seven headmen of the Eagle clan, one headman of the Otter clan, one headman of the Pike clan, and one headman of the Ox (Bison) clan.[11]

In the Great Lakes region, kinship, political affiliation, and personal identity – categories viewed as being separate in Western patterns of thought – are incorporated by the Anishinaabe into one: the nindoodem identity, which is also the mechanism through which people negotiated their claims to specific places. Families, marriages, alliances, migration, and access to land and resources were shaped by nindoodem. The *migiziwaaz* (white-headed eagle), *nigig* (otter), *kinoozhe* (pike), and *bizhiki* (bison) pictographs in Figure 4.1 represent just four of the twenty-seven distinct nindoodem pictographs recorded on treaties and land cessions signed by eastern Great Lakes Anishinaabe on documents from the late seventeenth to the twentieth centuries.[12] The ox referred to in Figure 4.1 is the same as the buffalo or bison listed by Peter Jones. In nineteenth-century Anishinaabemowin usage, *pjiki* (bizhiki) could mean "ox," "bull," "cow," or "buffalo."[13]

(a)

(b)

Figure 4.1

a Signature page, 6 September 1806 sale of eighty-five thousand acres west of what is now the City of Toronto.

b Detail, showing pictographs.

Library and Archives Canada.

In studying these nindoodemag as important assertions of political identity, I follow the groundbreaking work of Anishinaabe historian Darlene Johnston, who was raised with her grandmother's narratives about the importance of clan identities. As a lawyer who assists her community in Aboriginal rights litigation, Johnston was required to demonstrate to Canadian courts that the Chippewa of Nawash First Nation had cultural and political continuity with pre-contact people on the Bruce Peninsula. Johnston faced an archival challenge, for the name "Chippewas of Nawash" did not appear in the documentary record until the 1830s. Johnston did know that her grandmother's clan identity was Otter (nigig); she had been told that as a small child. While researching nineteenth-century treaties, Johnston found evidence on the manuscript copies that her great-great-grandfather had signed with a pictograph of an otter. This chain of continuity was strengthened when Johnston uncovered references in seventeenth-century records to the presence of a people named "Nikikouek" in Georgian Bay. *"Nikik"* (nigig) is Anishinaabemowin for "otter." Subsequent research revealed continuity with and connections to other pictographs on treaties signed by the ancestors of her First Nation and a larger connection to Anishinaabe spirituality, their conception of nationhood, and ties to particular landscapes. Johnston argued persuasively on the basis of these findings and other evidence that a chain of continuity could indeed be made visible, that ancestors of the Chippewa of Nawash had called the Bruce Peninsula home since time immemorial.[14]

Building on Johnston's important insights, this chapter connects two important yet discrete threads in Great Lakes history: studies of leadership and political history and scholarship on kinship, families, and clan systems. Academic debates about the Anishinaabe clan system have focused on the question of whether the clan system itself existed before contact with Europeans (Hickerson; Bishop) or rose in response to it (Schenck).[15] My research has engaged with these questions, and I conclude that the nindoodem identity that Jones described was both an old political tradition that predated the arrival of Europeans and a tradition that was flexible enough to accommodate change. Other scholars have discussed clan identity as but one part of an important web of Anishinaabe families. In their essay "There is no end to relationship among the Indians," published in 1994, Laura Peers and Jennifer Brown briefly discussed clan identity in a larger work that focused on the ways in which kinship shaped all aspects of daily life, was a resource when travelling, and offered support during difficult times. Brown and Peers showed that clans created "broader kinship networks" that "overlaid immediate and regional kinship networks, situating the individual within the broadest possible web of relatives."[16] But the repeated efforts of Anishinaabe individuals to communicate their clan identities in what were in effect national and international diplomatic contexts raise intriguing questions about the other roles and functions that these identities also served.

Although many scholars are familiar with Jones's *History,* the writings of William Warren and other nineteenth-century Anishinaabe authors, and the presence of pictographs on manuscript documents, historians are just beginning to consider the political significance of kinship to the Anishinaabeg. In the most significant and widely read work on the region to date, *The Middle Ground* (1991), Richard White argues that the upheaval that followed the collapse of the Wendat (Huron) and other confederacies in the Great Lakes in the mid-seventeenth century created new refugee villages in which local realities took precedence over older kinship ties. White writes that "tribal identity and the technicalities of kinship reckoning thus did not dictate political behaviour in this world of refugees."[17] Kinship as a category of analysis played no significant role in White's interpretation of these events.

Anishinaabe political histories and governance strategies have also been approached through biographies of important leaders. In Donald Smith's biography of Peter Jones, Janet Chute's biography of Shingwaukonse, and Catherine Sim's essay on Assance, the clan identity of each leader is identified, but the political implications are not discussed.[18] A more substantial interrogation of the political function of clan identity can be found in Mark Walters' "'According to the Old Customs of Our Nation': Aboriginal Self-Government on the Credit River Mississauga Reserve, 1826-1847." Walters concludes that the Mississauga-Anishinaabe government during this nineteen-year period was a flexible amalgam of indigenous and Western governance practices. Walters acknowledges the existence of clan identities but remains unsure of whether "a formal clan government existed or not"; consequently, the identity itself does not form part of his analysis. Walters was also, as I will show, studying the Mississauga-Anishinaabeg during a period of tremendous change that affected how Anishinaabe people made use of clan identities.[19]

The life story of Peter Jones provides a window into the centrality of his nindoodem identity and the flexibility embedded within the system to accommodate change. Jones was born in 1802, the son of Tubenequay and a Welsh surveyor, Augustus Jones, on the Burlington Heights near the northwestern corner of Lake Ontario. By strict definition, Jones was born without a toodaim because his father was not Anishinaabe. But his maternal grandfather, Wabenose, bestowed a name – Kahkewaquonaby or Sacred Feathers – on the infant that was the property of the migiziwaaz (eagle) nindoodem. In giving his grandson this name, Wabenose claimed Jones as a member of the Eagle nindoodem. Tubenequay later permitted her son's adoption by Adjutant, the Eagle *ogimaa* (head or principal chief) at the Credit River. Through this adoption,

Jones could legitimately claim his own eventual role as a community leader and *anikeogimaa* (step below chief). Although Jones received formal education in English as a teenager, at the behest of his father, and then converted to Christianity and became a Methodist missionary in 1820, throughout his life he held fast to his clan identity, his nindoodem as Eagle. He signed documents with an eagle pictograph alongside his written name and wore a similarly styled image of an eagle embroidered on his suit when he was presented to Queen Victoria in 1844.[20]

As a case study, Peter Jones and the Mississauga-Anishinaabeg of southern Ontario provide a fascinating window into the important relationship between nindoodem and leadership from the late 1790s to 1847 (when the Mississauga left the Credit River for a new reserve near the Six Nations on the Grand River). In 1830, the reserve community at Credit River adopted a written constitution and moved toward an elected system of governance. People lived in houses quite similar to their white settler neighbours and practised farming. Yet the presence and relative position of pictographic signatures on land surrenders, petitions, and other documents provide evidence of the continuity of Anishinaabe political tradition in one community (Credit River) that by the 1830s was being celebrated as a model of seemingly near-complete acculturation to Western ways.[21] Anishinaabe leadership, even during this period of significant change and external stress, remained grounded in clan identity, which had deep roots in a centuries-old tradition.

Origins: Language and Stories

Evidence for the origin, antiquity, and centrality of the nindoodem comes from both Anishinaabe narratives of origin and the language in which these stories were told (Anishinaabemowin). Together, language and narratives of origin shape social practices and construct relationships between peoples and landscapes.[22] The linguistic evidence for nindoodem reaches back to Proto-Algonquian, a common ancestor to the variety of Algonquian languages spoken in northeastern North America.[23] Nindoodem functions grammatically as kinship terminology in Anishinaabemowin and belongs to a class of nouns that is both very old and related to close personal possessions.[24] Narratives of origin told to seventeenth-century Jesuits and French traders date the creation of nindoodem identities to the beginning of known time as an event that followed the creation of the world.

Nicolas Perrot, a French fur trader and interpreter for the Crown, and Sebastian Râles, a Jesuit missionary, both recorded detailed creation stories in the earth diver genre that explained the origins of nindoodem identity and made evident the expanded Anishinaabe concept of personhood, which included persons who inhabited floral or faunal forms. In these earth diver narratives, people existed first in animal form; there were no people in human bodies. The world consisted of water, and the land animals floated together on a large raft. Perrot was likely told this story while he was actively working in and travelling through the Great Lakes region from the late 1660s to 1696. He spent significant time in the central part of the region, near Michilimackinac.[25] In the version he recounted, after Michabous (the Great Hare) created the world (and the land) from soil returned by the earth-diving muskrat, the first beings relocated to the place best suited "for having their pasture or prey." When these first beings died, Michabous created descendants from their corpses. He created beaver people, for example, in beaver form and then in human form. The two were linked together as kin through their apical ancestor, the first beaver.[26] In a slight variation, the Jesuit priest Sebastian Râles, who worked in the New France mission field from the 1680s until his murder in New England in 1724, was told explicitly that the Carp people sprang into being from eggs laid by a female carp on the bank of a river, while the Bear *(makwa)* people were descended from the paw of the first bear.[27] These narratives of origin connected people to the land where ancestral members of their nindoodem first came into being and with living members who shared their nindoodem, regardless of their physical form.[28] Jones recounted a substantively similar story in his history some two hundred years later when he noted that Nanabozho (Michabous) placed the various tribes (toodaims) in their own distinct territories.[29] These narratives of origin, which explain the beginnings of this kinship system, also firmly tie identities to specific locations and were used to express a relationship to place.

Anishinaabe elders might have told these stories to French visitors in an effort to remind them exactly who had the authority to regulate access to the land and its resources. In doing so, they reinforced the connection between clan and place. In 1671, Perrot attended a ceremony organized by French officials at Sault Ste. Marie, at which the French publicly attempted to claim the Great Lakes region in the name of the king. Delegates of the Otter, Sturgeon, Caribou, and other nindoodemag attended and signed a document with the marks of their families. According to the French, through this action the signatories recognized French sovereignty.[30] But in his manuscript memoirs, Perrot recorded another narrative that indicates that the Anishinaabeg did not accept French claims to the land and its waterways. Perrot reveals that people from Lake Nipissing and around the shores of Georgian Bay had told him that the "Amikoüs" (Amikwa), "which means descendants of the beaver," were the proprietors of the waterway that Perrot and other Europeans had named the French River. "*Amik*" is Anishinaabemowin for "beaver." Perrot was told that these people "took their creation from the corpse of the Great Beaver, from where emerged the first man of that nation." The Great Beaver created the landscape of the pond-rich country around Lake Nipissing by constructing dams; he made a suitable habitat for his descendants, who took both animal and human form.[31] The Anishinaabeg used narratives of origin to remind Perrot that the French could not claim the land and its resources, for it was already the country of the Beaver people.

The Anishinaabeg also used nindoodem identities to articulate new relationships to places. Peter Jones's ancestors, for example, likely moved to the Credit River sometime around the beginning of the eighteenth century. The political stability of the eastern Great Lakes was severely damaged, beginning in 1639, as a wave of smallpox epidemics swept through the region, producing a high mortality rate; losses were compounded by wars in the region. The Wendat Confederacy, the Tionontaté, the Neutral, the Wenro, and the Erie were among the hardest hit. Although the Haudenosaunee Confederacy also lost many of their own, they successfully incorporated captive adoptees from other nations to rebuild their population. Christianity played an important role too, for those Wendat who had not been captured split in 1649 into Christians (who relocated with their priests to Quebec) and traditionalists (who moved west to Lake Superior with their Tionontaté and Anishinaabe allies).[32] Other Anishinaabeg in the eastern Great Lakes, although less severely affected in terms of gross mortality than the Wendat, also found it prudent to move north and west. Anishinaabe clan ties provided a social safety net. In addition to accessing resources of their own clans in the central and western Great Lakes, eastern Anishinaabe men could also claim the assistance of their wives' kin, since women, when they married, kept the identities they had inherited from their fathers.[33]

Within a decade, eastern Anishinaabeg began to move back to their historical territories. However, the presence of Haudenosaunee villages on the north shore of Lake Ontario limited occupation of the Ontario peninsula. An initial peace treaty between the Haudenosaunee and the Anishinaabeg, recounted in several nineteenth-century sources, set Parry Island on the eastern side of Georgian Bay as the dividing line. But in the decades that followed, the Anishinaabeg grew increasingly frustrated with Haudenosaunee raids on their people. Anishinaabe leaders chose to attack and pushed the Six Nations back to south of the Great Lakes. In the peace agreement that followed, some Anishinaabe people moved into southern Ontario.[34] In many cases, these were lands to which they had been historically connected. In the first half of the seventeenth century, for example, both Samuel de Champlain and the Jesuits reported on the close alliances between certain Anishinaabe headmen and specific Wendat and Tionontaté villages. These Anishinaabe bands had provided fish and furs to their Iroquoian-speaking allies in return for corn and other produce, and they typically wintered near their allies' villages. Eastern Ontario, on the other hand, had historically been Anishinaabeg territory.[35]

As part of the peace agreement with the Haudenosaunee in the latter part of the seventeenth century, the confederacy agreed to recognize specific Anishinaabe claims to the lands. In the agreement itself, the locations were defined through nindoodem identities. Particularly, the agreement articulated new relationships between specific clans and specific places. The peace agreement itself was renewed multiple times over the eighteenth century and again in January 1840, at a large regional council convened at the Credit River. The extant record of the agreement comes from that meeting, when the peace agreement was again renewed. Peter Jones was at the meeting and recorded minutes of the session. He provides a description of the wampum belt that affirmed the peace. The belt, about three feet long and four inches wide, was woven with unspecified symbols, one for each new council fire (or national seat) established by the agreement, and connected by a white line (the path or road) through the middle of the length of the belt, which symbolized the connection between the council fires. Chief Yellowhead from Rama, whose family was the official keeper of the wampum and therefore charged with keeping the memory of the alliance itself, explained the terms of the agreement. In his oration, Yellowhead identified the symbols on the belt as symbols of the clans he named, each of which was placed, in Yellowhead's words, at a specific location and charged with the responsibility for watching their respective fires. The first emblem represented the location where the original council for the alliance met on Lake Superior. The second symbol represented the fire of the beautiful white fish on Manitoulin Island. The third, a beaver, "placed on an Island opposite Penetanguishene Bay," represented the formal kindling of a council fire at that location. The fourth symbol stood for a "white rein deer [caribou], placed at Lake Simcoe." To the Reindeer (Caribou) clan, Yellowhead noted, was "committed the keeping of this Wampum talk." The last mark "represents the Council fire which was placed at this River Credit where a beautiful White headed Eagle was placed upon a very tall pine tree, in order to watch the Council fires and see if any ill winds blew upon the smoke of the Council fires." The terms of the agreement were then confirmed by John Johnson, who represented the Six Nations. When Johnson spoke, he reiterated Yellowhead's speech nearly verbatim and, by doing so, confirmed the Six Nations' own memory of the alliance agreement. Johnson also used each named clan identity as a metaphor for a role or value related to the treaty, stressing, for example, that the eagle at the Credit River also "denotes *watching, and swiftness* in conveying messages.[36]

Thus, this wampum belt explains, in terms of specific Anishinaabe nindoodem identities, which clans were responsible for and were, in English terms, the proprietors of specific places and therefore the keepers of these important council sites (fires). In the regional language of diplomacy the Anishinaabeg shared with the Haudenosaunee, references to fires and council fires were metaphors that could mean, depending on the context, the place where a family lived (where smoke arose) or, more broadly, a nation or people. The terms also referred to those locations designated for treaty councils. The council fire had related metaphors. To kindle a fire was to establish a location for councils; to cover the fire was to adjourn discussions; to extinguish the fire was to stop using the place for negotiations. Since people sat in council grouped by nation, to eat across the fire was a symbol of unity. To cross the fire meant to change sides; informal negotiations were those that happened in the bush – away from the fire itself.[37]

As the renewal ceremony concluded, the Six Nations orator John Johnson also employed the metaphors of fire and clans. When the Six Nations next wished to have a meeting with the Anishinaabeg, Johnson explained that they would follow the protocol of the alliance and "let the eagle know that he may take the message to the white deer, who would decide when the council should be held."[38] Johnson meant that the Eagle nindoodem at the Credit River was specifically responsible for contacting the leaders of the Caribou nindoodem at Mnjikaning (Rama) when the Six Nations requested a meeting. By this treaty, those of the Eagle nindoodem were recognized not only as the proprietors of the lands and fishery resources at the Credit River but also as the keepers of the peace and a council site and as messengers for the larger alliance.

Significantly, other treaties and petitions signed with Anishinaabe peoples in the eastern Great Lakes support this connection between clan identity and a regional system of land tenure. The evidence for this argument comes from a review of all treaties signed by Anishinaabe peoples in the eastern Great Lakes region from 1783 to 1867 that currently form part of the Indian Treaties and Surrenders collection at Library and Archives Canada.[39] On the two cessions with pictographs dealing with lands around Garden River (near Sault Ste. Marie), one in 1798 and the other in 1859, Crane chiefs head the list of signatories.[40] Theresa Schenck has demonstrated the longstanding occupation and pre-eminence of the Crane nindoodem at that location.[41] On six cessions and one provisional agreement concerning lands around Lake Simcoe and the Narrows between Lake Simcoe and Lake Couchiching, images of caribou are the first pictographs.[42] And finally, for all cessions concerning lands around the Credit River and the north shore of Lake Ontario, pictographs representing Eagle nindoodem identities match the pattern of those at Lake Simcoe and Garden

River: pictographs of eagles are positioned first in the list of signatories.[43] Nindoodem identities for these cessions match the placement of fires acknowledged in the 1840 renewal of the longstanding peace between the Anishinaabeg and the Haudenosaunee Confederacy. And for eastern Ontario, George Copway noted that, after the peace agreement had been made, some members of the Crane nindoodem claimed the Rice Lake region. Copway writes, "The *Crane tribe* became the sole proprietors of this part of the Ojebwa [sic] land; the descendants of this tribe will continue to wear the distinguishing sign; except in a few instances, the chiefs are of this tribe."[44] Indeed, crane pictographs appear frequently on treaties, petitions, and other documents pertaining to this region, and a leading ogimaa from this area, Chief Paudash, was himself a Crane.[45]

Pictographs and Politics

The placement of pictographs on treaties, petitions, and other documents also suggests important intersections between clan identities, specific locations, and Anishinaabe systems of governance and leadership roles. On treaties concerning land sales, the pictograph typically represented the headman of an extended family group or band. As other scholars have long documented, the core unit of Anishinaabe political life was an extended family group of anywhere from ten to twenty or more related people who were led by a headman or principal man. This group typically comprised people who wintered together. Historically, Anishinaabe peoples relocated seasonally, dispersing into smaller bands in their hunting territories in the winter and gathering in the spring and fall in much larger groups to participate in the fishery, to conduct ceremonies, and to have large social gatherings. This pattern of changing residences appears to be quite old, predating the seventeenth century.[46] Men within each family group would typically have the same nindoodem identity. Each extended family group managed its particular hunting territories, sugar bushes, and other resources. Among the Mississauga-Anishinaabeg around Lake Ontario, the headmen and their respective families would claim as their jurisdictions the lands around a particular river system that was important to the spring and fall fisheries. In addition to the Credit River, the Sixteen Mile Creek and Fourteen Mile Creek (both located west of the Credit and emptying into Lake Ontario) had bands who fished the waters and who considered these locations their specific domains.[47]

The Mississauga-Anishinaabeg's way of life was disrupted by colonists earlier than more northerly Great Lakes peoples. With the end of the American Revolution in 1783 and the creation of Upper Canada as a separate British province in 1791, newcomers flooded into the region. Initially, these Loyalist colonists remained toward the eastern end of Lake Ontario, but the British colonial government sought cessions from Anishinaabeg who lived in the remainder of the peninsula. In 1805, the Mississauga-Anishinaabeg of the Credit River were approached to surrender a large portion of their territory along the north shore. After much discussion and negotiation, they consented, but not before they reserved the fishery of the three rivers for their own use and selected the lands along the Credit River itself as the site of the reserve.[48] Even when they "settled" on reserve communities, residence patterns and practices did not change overnight. Until the growing white settler population destroyed enough forest cover to make hunting difficult, Credit River families continued to participate in winter hunts. Even after hunting ceased to be sustainable, data from the Credit River community suggests that family members who conformed to the idea of the Anishinaabe extended family group lived in close proximity to one another. The marriage registers of the Methodist church, to which many Credit River people belonged by the late 1820s, indicate that brothers continued to live in the same community, while the old marriage practice of women coming from other communities, or at the very least belonging to a different nindoodem, continued.[49] The reserve system did result in changes over time, and year-round settlement worked against the practice of clan exogamy, but change did not occur immediately.[50]

Census returns taken by British Indian Department officials for the purposes of monitoring present and treaty annuity payment distributions provide a snapshot of Anishinaabe band organization in the early nineteenth century. In a census of the Mississauga gathered at the Humber River for a present-giving ceremony in 1818, 209 individuals were counted. The census is in the form of a table, with the name of each headman and his tribe (nindoodem) on the left side. Each row represents one extended family under the leadership of its headman, and individuals are tabulated in columns under the headings "men," "women," "boys," and "girls." The first entry lists Adjutant (who was the ogimaa, or principal chief). The document identifies him as both Eagle and chief of the other bands on the list. In the same row, the census also records two other men, four women, four boys, and four girls, for a total of sixteen members in Adjutant's band. In addition, the census lists six other bands of the Eagle nindoodem: three Otter, two Bear, one Ox (Bison), one Goose, one Bittern, one Bark (Birch Bark), and one Clay.[51] Band sizes ranged from five to nineteen individuals, with anywhere from one to five men and two to nine women. A similar census taken in 1824 only counts bands by nindoodem and does not name individual headmen but is otherwise similar in structure to the 1818 census. This 1824 document lists one Goose, one Otter, one Pike, one Reindeer (Caribou), and five Eagle bands. On average, these bands were slightly larger than those listed in the 1818 census. For example, those of the Pike nindoodem enumerated on the second census reported three fewer women, three more men, and two more children. Assuming that this is indeed the same band as on the 1818 census, the difference in numbers can be explained by the deaths or out marriages of three adult women, the maturity of the three boys counted in the previous census, and the birth of five new children, all of which is quite possible in a six-year period.[52]

Evidence suggests that headmen historically managed their own distinct lands or districts. In what is now southern Ontario, band territories covered lands reserved especially for winter hunting and important rivers for fishing. George Copway explained that "the Ojebwas [sic] each claimed, and claim to this day, hunting grounds, rivers, lakes and whole districts of country. No one hunted on each other's ground. My father had the northern fork of the river Trent, above Bellmont Lake."[53] Specific bands were associated with particular locations. Adjutant, born in 1769, was forty-nine years old when the census was taken in 1818. He had been ogimaa at the Credit River since 1810, when he had been raised to the position at a common council. At the council, he was also described as "the chief of this river."[54] At least one band of Otters had been for decades, or longer, the proprietors of Twelve Mile Creek, which was closer to the west end of Lake Ontario.[55] In Methodist baptismal records that date from 1802 to 1857, newly converted Anishinaabe Christians who had been born prior to the establishment of year-round settlements on reserves identified their place of birth (and they did give the place with a high frequency) as near or at a particular body of water: a river, a creek, a lake, or a bay.[56]

After the band, the next level of governance was a common or local council that represented headmen from a particular area. According to Jones, local councils historically met at least in the spring and the fall as part of larger festivals. Jones noted that the spring gathering typically took place after 1 May, when maple sugaring was complete.[57] Local councils could and did include headmen with clan identities other than the one situated historically at that location. But the relative importance of the original proprietors continued in the nineteenth century. According to Jones's explanation of how the Mississauga-Anishinaabeg organized their local governments by nindoodem, it is likely that the five Eagle bands that had their census taken in 1818 at the Humber River acknowledged Adjutant as their ogimaa. In fact, the distribution of bands on that census likely represented the composition of a local council. As keepers of their respective council fires, each regional ogimaa would have had particular authority in councils held at the locations for which they were responsible: the Eagle ogimaa at the Credit River, the Caribou ogimaa at Mnjikaning, and the Crane head chiefs at Sault Ste. Marie and Rice Lake. In spite of this, the authority of any ogimaa was, according to Francis Assiginack, another nineteenth-century

Anishinaabe author, entirely nominal. Authority was always fluid and shifting and depended to no small degree on the abilities of the chiefs in question to command respect through their generosity, accomplishments in war, and ability to channel spiritual power. A family could produce noted leaders for several generations and, as a result of their influence, could shape the agenda of councils. Other families, as Francis Assiginack observes (somewhat wryly it seems), achieved notice not for their bravery or eloquence but for "their filibustering propensities."[58]

At this level of the local council, leadership roles appear to have been both flexible and structured by tradition. In her 1999 study of Anishinaabe leadership, Janet Chute identifies five key leadership roles in local councils: the ogimaa or head chief, already discussed; the step-below chief or anikeogima; the *mishinaway* (data collector); the *kekedowenine* (mediator and conflict resolver); and the *oskabewis* (speaker and messenger). Group decision making might have been shaped by the ideas of the ogimaa and anikeogima, but Chute found that the other three roles were almost as important.[59] Jones, writing from the Credit River, describes only two historical roles in his text – the ogimaa and the mishinaway. According to Jones, the duties of ogimaag were to "settle all the disputes which arise among the people, watch over their territories, regulate the order of their marches, and appoint the time for their general rendezvous." The mishinaway was to "deliver the messages of the chief, call a council, attend to all the necessary preparations."[60] Further research is required to determine if the differing leadership roles associated with Credit River and Garden River communities in the nineteenth century reflected any significant difference between political organization in the northern and southern regions of the Great Lakes or if Jones instead simplified a complex reality for his non-Native readers. What can be said is that throughout his adult life Jones appeared to have filled at least three of the roles defined by Chute, that of anikeogima (when he was signing documents below the name and pictograph of Ogimaa Joseph Sawyer), that of mishinaway (when he was assisting in councils and interacting with British Indian Department officials), and that of oskabewis (when he was given the task, by the Mississauga-Anishinaabe leaders meeting in council, of carrying petitions to British government authorities). Although Jones was certainly an important leader among the Mississauga-Anishinaabeg, he never served as ogimaa. Jones consistently signed his signature and pictograph on documents in the place below that of the Credit River ogimaa Joseph Sawyer, who held the position of ogimaa from 1826 until after Jones's death in 1856. This signature placement pattern is evident on the council minutes, petitions, and correspondence that Jones authored on behalf of the Credit River community.[61]

In his history, Jones identifies the regional council as another important level of governance, one in which ogimaag and other leaders from a much larger geographical area met on an as-needed basis to discuss regional concerns. Again, in Jones's explanation of the general council, the independence of local headmen and the connection between nindoodem identity and land are clear. On general councils, Jones writes that "each band or community has its own chiefs, and manages its own affairs, within the limits of its territory, quite independently of other tribes of the same nation; but in matters which affect the whole nation, a general council is called, composed of all or a majority of the chiefs of the different tribes."[62] Responsibility for hosting the council itself fell to the "head chief of the tribe in whose territory the council is convened."[63] The councils opened with a set of rituals that opened the meeting: the council fire was kindled, the peace pipe was smoked, and a ceremony of condolence was conducted to remember those who had died since the last council. The purpose of the general councils, according to Jones, was to form larger unions or alliances, declare war or peace, make or renew treaties, and revise or make new territorial boundaries.[64] Jones himself participated in these general or regional councils. Documents produced as a result of these meetings, including petitions to be sent to the governor general or the queen to address specific grievances, include the signatures and pictographs of leaders from each of the local councils who had attended the general council.[65]

The pattern, number, and diversity of nindoodem pictographs on treaty documents, petitions, annuity payment receipts, and other documents further reflect the distinction between local and regional councils that Jones describes. Throughout the first half of the nineteenth century, when the vast majority of land surrenders in the eastern Great Lakes were made, it appears that the local council did have responsibility for land cessions. In contrast to the plethora and variety of pictographs on documents produced in regional councils, land sale agreements made between British officials and local councils have pictographic signatures that correspond in number and clan composition to the membership of each local council – the layer of governance that, according to Jones, was responsible for the territories and for "the sale and division of their lands."[66] In 1795, a sale of 3,450 acres to Joseph Brant by the Mississauga for lands near the west end of Lake Ontario was signed by pictographs that represented six headmen: Wabakanyne (Eagle ogimaa), Wabanip (Eagle), Wanipanant (Eagle), Tabandan (Eagle), Okemapenasse (Eagle), and Potaphquan (an ungulate, either Caribou or Bison). In 1806, the cession of lands in what are now the cities of Oakville and Mississauga, just west of Toronto, was signed by Cheechalk (the next Eagle ogimaa), Quenepenon (Otter), Wabukanyne (presumably different from Wabakanyne in 1795, since that Wabakanyne had died after an assault by a British soldier in 1796), Okimapenasse (Eagle), Wabenose (Eagle), Kebonecence (Eagle), Osenego (Eagle), Acheton (Eagle), Patequan (an ungulate, either Caribou or Bison), and Wabakegego (Pike).[67] In 1818, the cession of most of the remainder of Mississauga-Anishinaabe lands, which left only a reserve of land on the Credit River itself, was signed by Adjutant (formerly Acheton, Eagle ogimaa after Cheechalk), Weygishigomin (formerly Okimapenasse, Eagle anikeogima), Cabibonike (Otter), Pagitaniquatoibo (Otter), and Noiwahkitakquibi (Pike). Not only do Eagle headmen predominate on these land sale treaties, but there is also consistency among these documents in the pattern of other nindoodemag who appear on the treaties. Only Otters, Pike, and either Bison or Caribou are signatories on treaties relating to land sales with the local council at the Credit River, a trend that demonstrates the relative consistency, over a twenty-three-year period from 1795 to 1818, of the composition of that local council. It should also be noted that the headmen of the other nindoodem identities who were listed on the 1818 and 1824 enumerations – such as Bark, Goose, and Bittern – do not appear as signatories to these treaties. People with these identities might have lived in or near the Credit River area, but it appears that they did not have the authority to participate in matters concerning land.

Individual and nindoodem identities can sometimes be difficult to determine. In the case of Potaphquan (or Potoquan), the name appears next to the distinctive track mark of the caribou on one cession (1795) and next to an image of a bison on the other (1806). In the 1818 enumeration, however, a Pattaquan is listed as Ox. The latter two are not a real problem, for the Anishinaabemowin word "bizhiki" could refer either to a bison or a cow and could also be translated as either animal. But the confusion between the Caribou and Bison nindoodem is a problem. It is not yet clear to which nindoodem Potoquan belongs or if the differences in nindoodem actually reflect the presence of two different individuals with the same name or very similar names. Both interpretations are possible, for the Bison (Ox) identity is mentioned on both the 1818 census discussed previously and the 1826 register of the Methodist Society at Grand River. The Reindeer (Caribou) nindoodem is listed on the 1824 census taken at the Humber River.[68]

Other challenges with the identification of individuals stem from the fact that Anishinaabe people could receive and use different names in their lifetimes.[69] Weygishigomin (Possessor of Day), the second Eagle signatory on the 1818 Mississauga cession, is actually the person named Okemapenasse on the 1795 and 1806 cessions. Okemapenasse had received a new name (a not uncommon occurrence) sometime between 1806 and 1818. Peter Jones's baptismal records for the Credit River mission indicate that Okemapenasse was born at the Credit

River in 1764. He took at least one other new name, John Cameron, when he was baptized in 1810 at the age of forty-six, but he always signed documents with his eagle pictograph.[70] Nindoodem pictographs can sometimes aid in the confirmation of individual identity, at least at the level of the clan, even in cases in which a person has changed his or her name.

Reconstructing Leadership for the Credit River

It is now possible to reconstruct a history of the leadership for one local council area, the Mississauga of the Credit River, based on the pattern of pictographs on treaty and other documents from the 1690s to 1847, from the founding of the council fire to the year when the Credit River community was relocated to its current location adjacent to the Six Nations on the Grand River (the New Credit Reserve). For the Eagle nindoodem people living around the northwestern shore of Lake Ontario, leadership was vested in their ogimaa, who was also a headman of his own band, at the Credit River. As Jones himself noted, although the office of ogimaa was a hereditary position in the family that was the keeper of the council fire, the title did not necessarily pass to the eldest son. The local or common council decided on the suitability of an individual, and leadership could and did pass to a younger son, a brother, or a nephew.[71] Tracing the history of ogimaag of the Eagle nindoodem at the Credit River demonstrates both continuity of the cultural preference for a hereditary system and the flexibility inherent in the practice that ensured the transfer of responsibility to a suitable individual.

The earliest known Mississauga leader from the Credit River who can clearly be identified as belonging to the Eagle nindoodem was Wabicommicot, who attended councils with Sir William Johnson on the Mohawk River in the 1760s. Wabicommicot seems to have been widely respected and was most likely ogimaa at the Credit River, although I have not yet been able to confirm this fact. Wabicommicot signed a treaty at Detroit in 1764, working on behalf of Sir William Johnson to secure the alliance of the western nations (including other Anishinaabeg) after Pontiac's War.[72] On a clerk's copy of the peace treaty made in the aftermath of the conflict, Wabicommicot's presence is represented by a pictograph of an eagle wearing two medals around its neck. The medals likely refer to the King George III medals that were given to Wabicommicot by Johnson in recognition of Wabicommicot's role as a British-allied chief.[73] Wabicommicot died in 1764 and may have been succeeded directly by Wabakayne, whose eagle pictograph appears on the cession for a strip of land on the north side of the Niagara River in 1781.[74] As ogimaa, Wabakayne signed several treaties, including the original sale for the lands around what is now Toronto in 1787. Wabakayne was murdered in 1796 and was succeeded by Wabanip, who had signed cessions in 1792 and 1795 in the second position below Wabakayne. Wabanip had likely filled the role of anikeogima before he became ogimaa. Cheechalk then became ogimaa sometime after 21 August 1797, the date of the last document on which I have found Wabanip's name and pictograph.

After Cheechalk's death around 1810, his brother Adjutant (Captain Jim) became ogimaa. Adjutant served during the War of 1812, when battles fought on Mississauga lands made times difficult. By the early 1820s, some Mississauga had already begun to convert to Christianity. In 1829, Adjutant (also known as Adjutance or Acheton) died; he was succeeded by Joseph Sawyer (Nawuhjegee-zhegwabe or Sloping Sky). Sawyer was forty-three years old and, as the son of Wabanosey, Jones's maternal grandfather, Peter Jones's uncle. By this time, Jones was twenty-seven, and because of his fluency in written English, he was already taking on some leadership roles. On subsequent petitions and letters written in council on behalf of the Mississauga-Anishinaabeg at the Credit River community, Jones consistently signed his eagle pictograph below that of Sawyer's (except on those occasions when Jones was travelling in the Great Lakes on mission trips or was out of the country). Jones never filled the role of ogimaa despite his public profile, and Sawyer remained ogimaa until after Jones's own death in 1856. Sawyer himself was widely regarded as a leader and on two occasions served as a regional leader, as "elected president of the Ojibwa Grand Council of Upper Canada."[75] Even during the mid-nineteenth century, a period of tremendous cultural change and adjustment for southern Ontario Anishinaabeg, leadership continued to reflect Anishinaabe cultural priorities and historical practices.

When settlement pressure began to increase in southern Ontario, Anishinaabe leaders worked to protect those places that had particular significance for their people.[76] They aimed to preserve lands and access to resources such as key fishing sites, for these locations were important both culturally and politically.[77] The annual fishery gatherings were times for councils, celebrations, games, and young people to meet potential marriage partners. Access to the fisheries was crucial for maintaining both cultural integrity and a subsistence base; indeed, petitions to the Crown in this period by Credit River and other families indicate a consistent desire to protect the fishery against the encroachment of white settlers.

People were also clear in their desire to secure their right to hunt on traditional hunting territories.[78] The first lands the Credit River Anishinaabeg were willing to part with, for example, were those from Niagara west to the Thames River, lands well away from the heart of their own country.[79] In 1805, when the colonial government expressed interest in purchasing the lands directly north of the Credit River, Cheechalk and his headmen had concerns. In the provisional agreement they negotiated at the Credit River on 2 August 1805, they agreed to sell the land in question but reserved "to ourselves and the Mississague [sic] Nation the sole right of the fisheries in the Twelve Mile Creek, the Sixteen Mile Creek, the Etobicoke River, together with the flats or low grounds on said creeks and river, which we have heretofore cultivated and where we have our camps. And also the sole right of the fishery in the River Credit with one mile on each side of the River."[80] In a speech in council with Indian Department officials, Quenepennon, the Otter headman from Twelve Mile Creek, acted as oskabewis (speaker) and reminded William Claus, the deputy superintendent of the Indian Department, that at previous councils "our old Chiefs at the same time particularly reserved the fishery of the River."[81]

As Loyalist and American settlers moved into the region, they effectively surrounded the Anishinaabeg in their reserve communities and depleted the fisheries and other resources on which the Anishinaabeg depended. The Credit River community was hit particularly hard and by the 1830s was facing a shortage of timber on its reserve lands. The community, however, hung on at that location, resisting pressure to move. Simply put, the Credit River location had a deep symbolic importance to all the Anishinaabeg in the region as the site of an important council fire. In addition, the close proximity of the Credit River to the seat of the Upper Canadian government at Toronto had reinforced the importance of the Credit location. In 1840, the union of Lower and Upper Canada made Kingston a more logical choice for the seat of colonial government. The Anishinaabeg of southern Ontario were greatly upset by the proposed plan, and they wrote a petition to the governor general in which they explained their concerns.[82] Unfortunately, their petition was unsuccessful. With the loss of the immediate connection to representatives of the British colonial government, and facing serious resource depletion, the people of the Eagle nindoodem at the Credit River could not, from their perspective, sustain the council fire any longer. In 1847, they accepted the invitation of the Six Nations to move to Grand River territory, a reciprocal gesture for the kindness shown them by the Mississauga in 1783.[83] The community of the New Credit was born.

In the second half of the nineteenth century, Anishinaabe peoples became increasingly Christianized, and the new Dominion of Canada grew more coercive in its approach to Aboriginal peoples generally. Over time, many Anishinaabeg adopted surnames; sometimes people chose the name of their immediate family's headman or ogimaa, and sometimes people chose their nindoodem identity. The 1871 census of Canada reveals Anishinaabe families with the following surnames, which were likely derived from nindoodemag: Goose, Beaver, Partridge, and Snake.[84] But these names do not always correspond to an individual's nindoodem identity. On one document from 1840, James Mahshkenozha (whose last name translates as "pike"), did indeed sign with an image of a pike fish, but on the same document George Snake signed with a turtle.[85] There are many other such examples. Family names recorded by nineteenth-century census takers must be checked against pictographs for nindoodemag on treaties and other documents to confirm these identities.

Even in the twentieth century, nindoodem identities did not disappear entirely. Some ogimaag continued to sign documents with these images. The most recent example found to date was written to Prime Minister Borden during the First World War.[86] Early-twentieth-century anthropologists found mixed information about the continuity of nindoodem identities among their informants. Some reported that the clan system was still in use; others described it as being in decline. Elders from Parry Island to Walpole Island to the Michigan Peninsula to Thunder Bay explained to these anthropologists that the violation of the incest taboo against intra-nindoodem marriage had been, they felt, a significant factor that contributed to their current state of poverty and isolation.[87] Nindoodem remained a potent category of causation and explanation, even if people no longer retained or used the identity themselves. In the nineteenth century, as Christianity spread, the stories that linked nindoodem identity to descent from other-than-human beings were passed down only through the practitioners of traditional teachings. But even the most ardent converts to Christianity, such as Peter Jones, kept and asserted their nindoodem identity. It was the core of a centuries-old political tradition that expanded to accommodate even massive sea changes in worldview.

Notes

1 Anishinaabe women kept their clan identities when they married. People who call themselves Anishinaabeg today include people who may also identify or be described separately as Ojibwe (principally in Canada), Chippewa (principally in the United States), Odawa or Ottawa, Potawatomi, Mississauga (principally in southern Ontario), or Algonquin. As a term of reference, I use "Anishinaabe" (or "Anishinaabeg" in the plural) because it is an indigenous term of identity, a collective noun that connects people who speak closely related dialects of the same language: Anishinaabemowin. I use a compound form, such as Mississauga-Anishinaabeg, in cases where identification is useful to the reader.
2 Jones, *History of the Ojebway Indians*, 138.
3 Rezendes, *Tracking and the Art of Seeing*, 279-301.
4 Jones, *History of the Ojebway Indians*, 138.
5 Brown and Vibert, eds., Introduction to *Reading beyond Words*, xxiii; Shoemaker, "Categories."
6 Warren's history contains many references to Anishinaabe clans. See, for example, his description of clan identities being related to human characteristics. Warren describes those of the bear clan as being short-tempered and keeping black hair into old age and "those of the catfish and other fish clans having little body hair," *History*, 49, 46.
7 Copway, *Life, History and Travels*, 58.

8 Pronunciation is straightforward: "nindoodem" as nin-doh-dem and the plural "nindoo-demag" as nin-doh-dem-ag. In Anishinaabemowin, a speaker would actually say "*odoode-man*" to express the meaning "his or her clan." I apologize to speakers of Anishinaabemowin, who will read the construction "their nindoodem" with a double possessive pronoun ("their my clan"). This spelling follows linguistic conventions.

9 The continuous pictographic expression of nindoodem identity, methods for reading the images (as Crane, Eagle, and so on), and the sources I consulted are documented in Bohaker, "*Nindoodemag*: Anishinaabe Identities."

10 Sale of 85,000 acres in the Home District of Upper Canada, 6 September 1806, Indian Treaty No. 42, Library and Archives Canada (hereafter LAC), Indian Affairs fonds (RG 10), Indian Treaties and Surrenders series, vol. 1842.

11 Although the pictograph appears to represent a cow, Buffalo is listed as one of the clans belonging to Christian converts in 1826. List of names of the members of the Methodist Society at the Upper Mohawk Grand River, 10 January 1826, New Credit Indian Mission fonds, folios 4-6, United Church of Canada Archives, Victoria University (hereafter UCA). The initial Anishinaabe converts lived near the Grand River before they returned to the Credit River in April 1826, see Smith, *Sacred Feathers*, 73.

12 See Bohaker, "*Nindoodemag*: Anishinaabe Identities," 151. More precisely, nindoodem identity is a system of categories such as race, because race contains categories (white, black) that can be used to structure historical analysis. Likewise, nindoodem identity contains its own categories: eagle, otter, pike, and so on. Nancy Shoemaker explains this difference in "Categories."

13 Baraga, *Dictionary*, 351.

14 Johnston, "Litigating Identity."

15 Hickerson, *The Chippewa and Their Neighbors*; Bishop, "The Question of Ojibwa Clans," 56; and Schenck, *Voice of the Crane*.

16 Peers and Brown, "There is no end," 534-35.

17 White, *The Middle Ground*, 18.

18 See, specifically, Smith, *Sacred Feathers*, in which Peter Jones is identified as a member of the Eagle clan; Chute, *The Legacy of Shingwaukonse*, in which Shingwaukonse is identified as a member of the Plover clan; and Sims, "Exploring Ojibwa History," in which Assance is identified as a member of the Otter clan.

19 Walters, "According to the Old Customs," 11.

20 Smith, *Sacred Feathers*, 3-5, 35-65, 212; and Willmott, "Clothed Encounters," 477.

21 See Walters, "According to the Old Customs."

22 Howe, "The Story of America," and Cruikshank, "Oral History."

23 In Proto-Algonquian, "o:te" is a root form that likely means "to dwell together as a group or village"; "ninto:te-m," by extension, would have meant "my fellow group or clan member." Callender, "Great Lakes-Riverine Sociopolitical Organization," 15:611.

24 "Nindoodem" belongs to a class of nouns that can only appear with a possessive prefix; therefore, the linguistic convention is to use the first-person pronoun in combination with the root form when referring to the term in another language, such as English. "Nindoodem" also takes the possessive suffix "-m"; Anishinaabemowin linguist Rand Valentine explains that these words are exceptional nouns that "appear to represent items of great cultural antiquity and close personal possession." Valentine, *Nishnaabemwin Reference Grammar*, 106-7, 202. See also Cuoq, *Lexique*.

25 *Dictionary of Canadian Biography Online*, s.v. "Nicolas Perrot" (by Claude Perrault).

26 Perrot, *Mémoire sur les moeurs*, 5-6, in Blair, ed., *The Indian Tribes*, 1:35-37.

27 Thwaites, ed., *Jesuit Relations and Allied Documents* (hereafter *JR*), 1:11; Sebastian Râles, "Lettre à Monsieur son Frère," 12 October 1723, *JR*, 67:153-57.

28 For a thorough discussion of the importance of souls to the Anishinaabeg and a persuasive argument for the connections among souls, nation, and land, see Johnston, "Litigating Identity."

29 Jones, *History of the Ojebway Indians,* 35.

30 Potherie, *Histoire de l'Amérique septentrionale,* 347.

31 Perrot, *Mémoire sur les moeurs,* in Blair, ed., *Indian Tribes,* 1:63.

32 See Trigger, *Children of Aataentsic;* Brandão, "Your Fyre Shall Burn No More"; Richter, *Ordeal of the Longhouse.*

33 Bohaker, "*Nindoodemag:* The Significance of Algonquian Kinship Networks," 23-52.

34 MacLeod, "Anishinaabeg Point of View," 194-210.

35 On trading fish for corn, see *JR,* 21:239-41. For eastern Ontario, see Bohaker, "*Nindoodemag:* Anishinaabe Identities," Chapter 2, and Champlain, *Works,* vol. 3.

36 Minutes of a general council held at the River Credit, 16 January 1840, Chief George Paudash Papers, Part B, Band Minutes, 1834-42, LAC, RG 10, vol. 1011, pp. 69-92. Although Donald Smith mentions this council in *Sacred Feathers,* I would like to thank Darlene Johnston for sharing her insight with me that this peace agreement described the establishment of council fires by nindoodem identity.

37 See Jennings et al., *The History and Culture of Iroquois Diplomacy,* 118.

38 Jones described this council in his *History of the Ojebway* and summarized the comments of Johnson's remarks, 133.

39 I undertook a complete survey of this entire collection. See Bohaker, "*Nindoodemag:* Anishinaabe Identities."

40 The two treaties form part of the Indian Treaties and Surrenders collection, LAC, RG 10. For the first, see Deed of Conveyance of the Island of St. Joseph, 30 June 1798, Indian Treaty 35, RG 10, vol. 1841. Regarding the second, thirty-six individuals signed the agreement for the sale of lands around what is now Garden River First Nation; thirty-four signed with an *x*. Only the first two, Thomas Ogista and Henry Pahgwahgenine, signed with crane pictographs. See 10 June 1859, Indian Treaty 230, LAC, RG 10, vol. 1845. The major treaty for this region is known as the Robinson-Huron Treaty. It was signed in 1850 and is, like its associated agreement the Robinson-Superior Treaty, an anomaly in the region, for neither treaty has pictographs. This may be because the chief negotiator, William Benjamin Robinson, was not the usual representative from the Indian Department and was not familiar with previous protocols. See Robinson-Huron Treaty, 7 September 1850, RG 10, vol. 1844; Robinson-Superior Treaty, 9 September 1850, Indian Treaty 148, RG 10, vol. 1844.

41 See Schenck, *Voice of the Crane.*

42 The following documents are all from LAC, RG 10, and are listed by date and the internal series number assigned by the archive: 19 May 1795, Indian Treaty 19, vol. 1841; 22 May 1798, Indian Treaty 17, vol. 1841; 17 October 1818, Indian Treaty 55, vol. 1842; 26 November 1836, Indian Treaty 126, vol. 1844; 17 June 1852, Indian Treaty 152 (for a twenty-acre lot), vol. 1844; 5 June 1856, Indian Treaty 188, vol. 1845; and 28 March 1857, Indian Treaty 192, vol. 1845.

43 Leaders from the Credit River and north shore of Lake Ontario appear as signatories on treaties made with the British as early as 1764 and on numerous documents and petitions from that time. See, for example, pictographic signatures on five treaties in LAC, RG 10, that range in date from 1795 to 1830: 10 October 1795, Indian Treaty 8, vol. 1840; 21 August 1797, Indian Treaty 29, vol. 1841; 1 August 1805, Indian Treaty 38, vol. 1841; 28 October 1818, Indian Treaty 59, vol. 1842; and 22 January 1830, Indian Treaty 72, vol. 1842.

44 Copway, *Life, History and Travels*, 14 (emphasis in original).

45 See, for example, Paudaush's crane pictograph on the sale of the Rice Lake islands, 24 June 1856, Indian Treaty 195, LAC, RG 10, vol. 1845.

46 Bishop, "Question of Ojibwe Clans."

47 Bohaker, "*Nindoodemag*: Anishinaabe Identities," 211, 217-18.

48 Smith, *Sacred Feathers*, 29-34.

49 Marriages, Indian Village, Township of Toronto, Home District, 1836-46, UCA, New Credit Indian Mission fonds, folios 9-16.

50 A more detailed investigation of these nineteenth-century changes in marriage practices and family composition forms part of my current research project into the intersection of Mississauga-Anishinaabe family and political histories.

51 The clay or white clay nindoodem is also listed on a 1736 French census of the Great Lakes as being one of the clans from the Lake Nipissing area. See dénombrement des nations sauvages, 1736, Archives nationales de France (hereafter ANF), fondes des colonies, Série C11A, vol. 66, folios 236-56v.

52 The two census documents are "Return of the Mississauga Nation of Indians Taken 26th of August 1818 at the River Humber" and "Return of the Mississauga Indians Taken August 15, 1824 at the Humber," LAC, RG 10, vol. 42, p. 2671, and vol. 42, p. 2668, respectively.

53 Copway, *Life, History and Travels*, 12.

54 Proceedings of a meeting with the Missisawque Indians at the River Credit, 3 October 1810, LAC, RG 10, vol. 27, n.p.

55 Bohaker, "*Nindoodemag*: Anishinaabe Identities," 211.

56 Common birth places listed include the Credit and Humber Rivers; Twelve Mile, Six Mile, and "Tobecox" (Etobicoke) Creeks; the head of Lake Ontario; and Rice and Mud Lakes: Baptisms, 1802-57, UCA, New Credit Indian Mission fonds, folios 18-90.

57 Jones, *History of the Ojebway*, 109.

58 Assiginack, "Legends and Traditions," 116.

59 Chute, "Shingwaukonse," 68.

60 Jones, *History of the Ojebway*, 107-9.

61 Peter Jones, Entry Book, 1831-48, LAC, RG 10, Chief George Paudash Papers, vol. 1011.

62 Jones, *History of the Ojebway*, 39.

63 Ibid., 105.

64 Ibid.

65 "An Address of the River Credit Indians to the King and Public of England, 3 February 1831." Copy of "An Address of the Chiefs at Lake Huron – To the Christians of England, Lake Huron, 17 February 1831," Victoria University Library and Special Collections (hereafter VUL), Peter Jones fonds, Petition to the Queen, 19 October 1844, Series 1, Indian Petitions and Addresses, (1826-44), box 1, folder 9.

66 Jones, *History of the Ojebway*, 106.

67 *Dictionary of Canadian Biography Online*, s.v. "Wabakayne" (by Donald B. Smith); see treaties cited in Note 42. The spelling of names is taken directly from the manuscript treaty documents.

68 "Return of the Mississauga Nation of Indians Taken 26th of August 1818 at the River Humber" and "Return of the Mississauga Indians Taken August 15, 1824 at the Humber"; Members of the Methodist Society at the Upper Mohawk Grand River, 10 January 1826, UCA, New Credit Indian Mission fonds, folios 4-6.

69 See Bohaker, "*Nindoodemag*: Anishinaabe Identities," 192-96.

70 Smith, *Sacred Feathers*, 272n9.

71   Jones, *History of the Ojebway,* 107.
72   "Transaction of a Congress Held with the Ottawas and Chippewa Nations with Several Others, 7 September 1764," Centre for Kentish Studies, Maidstone, Amherst Papers, vol. U1350. My thanks to Darlene Johnston for bringing this document to my attention. This document is a clerk's copy.
73   For information on this practice, see Prucha, *Indian Peace Medals.*
74   *Dictionary of Canadian Biography Online,* s.v. "Wabicommicot" (by Jane E. Graham).
75   Ibid., s.v. "Nawahjegezhegwabe" (by Donald B. Smith).
76   Walters, "According to the Old Customs."
77   Surtees, *Indian Land Surrenders,* 111.
78   Ibid.
79   Sale of land, Niagara to the Thames River, 7 December 1792, Indian Treaty 5, LAC, RG 10, vol. 1840.
80   Sale of lands in Peel and Halton counties reserving the Credit River, 2 August 1805, Indian Treaty No. 41, LAC, RG 10, vol. 1840.
81   Proceedings of a meeting with the Mississaugas at the River Credit, 31 July 1805, LAC, RG 10, vol. 1, pp. 288-309.
82   Petition to Governor Thompson, 24 January 1840, LAC, RG 10, vol. 72, pp. 66801-4.
83   Smith, *Sacred Feathers,* 212-14.
84   Canadian Federal Census of 1871 (Ontario Index), LAC, see online collection.
85   Petition to Governor Thompson, 24 January 1840, LAC, RG 10, vol. 72, pp. 66801-4.
86   The signatories were the chiefs and councillors of the Ojibwa Nation whose communities had been included in the 1850 Robinson-Huron and Robinson-Superior treaties. See "Petition to the Honourable Robert Laird Borden, Premier of the Dominion of Canada," n.d., LAC, RG 10, vol. 6743, file 420-8, p. 3.
87   J.B. Peuessie, Fort William, John Perrot, Fort Francis, to William Jones, ethnographic and linguistic field notes on the Ojibwa Indians, c. 1903-5, American Philosophical Society, in Jenness, *Ojibwa Indians of Parry Island,* vi, 115.

Bibliography

Archival Sources

Archives nationales de France (ANF)
Fondes des colonies.

Centre for Kentish Studies, Maidstone
Amherst Papers.

Library and Archives Canada (LAC)
Indian Affairs fonds, RG 10.
   George Paudash Papers.
   Indian Treaties and Surrenders.

United Church of Canada Archives, Victoria University (UCA)
New Credit Indian fonds.

Victoria University Library and Special Collections (VUL)
Peter Jones fonds.

Published Sources

Assiginack, Francis. "Legends and Traditions of the Odahwah Indians." *Canadian Journal of Industry, Science and Arts, n.s.* 3 (1858): 115-25.

Baraga, Frederic. *A Dictionary of the Otchipwe Language.* Cincinnati, OH: J.A. Hemann, 1853.

Bishop, Charles. "The Question of Ojibwa Clans." In *Actes du Vingtième Congrès des Algonquinistes,* edited by William Cowan, 43-61. Ottawa: Carleton University Press, 1989.

Bohaker, Heidi. "*Nindoodemag:* Anishinaabe Identities in the Eastern Great Lakes Region, 1600 to 1900." PhD thesis, University of Toronto, 2006.

–. "*Nindoodemag:* The Significance of Algonquian Kinship Networks in the Eastern Great Lakes Region, 1600-1701," *William and Mary Quarterly,* 3rd series, 63, 1 (2006): 23-52.

Brandão, José António. *"Your Fyre Shall Burn No More": Iroquois Policy towards New France and Its Native Allies to 1701.* Lincoln: University of Nebraska Press, 1997.

Brown, Jennifer S.H., and Elizabeth Vibert, eds. *Reading beyond Words: Contexts for Native History.* Peterborough, ON: Broadview Press, 1996.

Champlain, Samuel de. *The Works of Samuel de Champlain.* Edited by Henry P. Biggar. 6 vols. Toronto: Champlain Society, 1922-36.

Callender, Charles. "Great Lakes-Riverine Sociopolitical Organization." In *Handbook of North American Indians,* vol. 15, *The Northeast,* edited by Bruce G. Trigger, 610-21. Washington, DC: Smithsonian Institution, 1978.

Chute, Janet. *The Legacy of Shingwaukonse: A Century of Native Leadership.* Toronto: University of Toronto Press, 1998.

–. "Shingwaukonse: A Nineteenth-Century Innovative Ojibway Leader." *Ethnohistory* 45, 1 (1998): 65-101.

Copway, George. *The Life, History and Travels of Kah-ge-ga-gah-bowh (George Copway).* Albany, NY: n.p., 1847.

Cruikshank, Julie. "Oral History, Narrative Strategies, and Native American Historiography: Perspectives from the Yukon Territory, Canada." In *Clearing a Path: Theorizing the Past in Native American Studies,* edited by Nancy Shoemaker, 43-61. New York: Routledge, 2002.

Cuoq, J.A. (Jean André). *Lexique de la langue Algonquine.* Montreal: J. Chapleau, 1886.

Hickerson, Harold. *The Chippewa and Their Neighbours: A Study in Ethnohistory.* Edited and with an Introduction by Jennifer S.H. Brown. Prospect Heights, IL: Waveland Press, 1988.

Howe, LeAnne. "The Story of America: A Tribalography." In *Clearing a Path: Theorizing the Past in Native American Studies,* edited by Nancy Shoemaker, 29-49. New York: Routledge, 2002.

Jenness, Diamond. *The Ojibwa Indians of Parry Island: Their Social and Religious Life.* Ottawa: Canada Department of Mines/National Museum of Canada, 1935.

Jennings, Francis, William N. Fenton, Mary A. Druke, and David R. Miller. *The History and Culture of Iroquois Diplomacy: An Interdisciplinary Guide to the Treaties of the Six Nations and Their League.* Syracuse, NY: Syracuse University Press, 1985.

Johnston, Darlene M. "Litigating Identity: The Challenge of Aboriginality." Master's thesis, University of Toronto, 2003.

Jones, Peter. *History of the Ojebway Indians with Especial Reference to Their Conversion to Christianity.* London: A.W. Bennett, 1861.

MacLeod, D. Peter. "The Anishinabeg Point of View: The History of the Great Lakes Region to 1800 in Nineteenth-Century Mississauga, Odawa and Ojibwa Historiography." *Canadian Historical Review* 73, 2 (1992): 194-210.

Peers, Laura, and Jennifer S.H. Brown. "'There is no end to relationship among the Indians': Ojibwa Families and Kinship in Historical Perspective." *History of the Family* 4, 4 (2000): 529-55.

Perrot, Nicolas. *Mémoire sur les moeurs, coustumes et religion des sauvages de l'Amérique septentrionale*, edited by Jules Tailhan. Leipzig: A. Franck, 1864. Translated in *The Indian Tribes of the Upper Mississippi Valley and Region of the Great Lakes*, edited by Emma Blair. 2 vols. Cleveland: Arthur H. Clark Company, 1911.

Potherie, Claude Charles Le Roy de la, Sieur de Bacqueville. *Histoire de l'Amérique septentrionale*. Vol. 2 of *The Indian Tribes of the Upper Mississippi Valley and Region of the Great Lakes*, edited by Emma Blair. Cleveland: Arthur H. Clark Company, 1911.

Prucha, Francis Paul. *Indian Peace Medals in American History*. Lincoln: University of Nebraska Press, 1971.

Rezendes, Paul. *Tracking and the Art of Seeing: How to Read Animal Tracks and Signs*. New York: Harper Perennial, 1999.

Richter, Daniel. *The Ordeal of the Longhouse: The Peoples of the Iroquois League in the Era of European Colonization*. Chapel Hill: University of North Carolina Press, 1992.

Schenck, Theresa. *The Voice of the Crane Echoes Afar: The Sociopolitical Organization of the Lake Superior Ojibwa, 1640-1855*. New York: Garland Publishing, 1997.

Shoemaker, Nancy. "Categories." In *Clearing a Path: Theorizing the Past in Native American Studies*, edited by Nancy Shoemaker, 51-76. New York: Routledge, 2002.

Sims, Catherine. "Exploring Ojibwa History through Documentary Sources: An Outline of the Life of Chief John Assance." In *Gin Das Winan: Documenting Aboriginal History in Ontario*, edited by David McNab and Dale Standen, 5-47. Toronto: Champlain Society, 1996.

Smith, Donald B. *Sacred Feathers: The Reverend Peter Jones (Kahkewa-Quonaby) and the Mississauga Indians*. Toronto: University of Toronto Press, 1987.

Surtees, Robert. *Indian Land Surrenders in Ontario, 1763-1867*. Ottawa: Treaties and Historical Research Centre, 1984.

Thwaites, Reuben Gold, ed. *The Jesuit Relations and Allied Documents*. 73 vols. Cleveland: Burrows Brothers, 1896-1901 [1610-1791]. Reprint, New York: Pageant Books, 1959.

Trigger, Bruce. *The Children of Aataentsic: A History of the Huron People to 1660*. Kingston and Montreal: McGill-Queen's University Press, 1976.

Valentine, J. Randolph. *Nishnaabemwin Reference Grammar*. Toronto: University of Toronto Press, 2001.

Walters, Mark D. "'According to the Old Customs of Our Nation': Aboriginal Self-Government on the Credit River Mississauga Reserve, 1826-1847." *Ottawa Law Review* 30, 1 (1999): 1-45.

Warren, William. *History of the Ojibways Based upon Traditions and Oral Statements*. Minneapolis: Ross and Haines, 1957.

White, Richard. *The Middle Ground: Indians, Empires, and Republics in the Great Lakes Region, 1650-1815*. New York: Cambridge University Press, 1991.

Willmott, Cory Silverstein. "Clothed Encounters: The Power of Dress in Relations between Anishinaabe and British Peoples in the Great Lakes Region, 1760-2000." PhD diss., McMaster University, 2000.

5

The Contours of Everyday Life:
Food and Identity in the Plateau Fur Trade
Elizabeth Vibert

IN *DOMESTIC MEDICINE*, ONE of the most influential British home health care manuals of the late eighteenth and early nineteenth centuries, Dr. William Buchan declared that "the whole constitution of [the] body may be changed by diet alone." The balance and configuration of the fluids and solids believed to determine physical and emotional health and the very outward appearance of the body itself rested on "a proper regimen of diet."[1] The wide social acceptance of the notion that food made the body – the status of this discourse as basic common sense – is revealed in much contemporary writing about the physical condition of the poor in Britain and the so-called backward races in Britain's colonial domains. This chapter takes Buchan's observations on the connection between food and health as the starting point for an examination of the role of food and food practices in the making of colonial discourses of race, class, and gender difference.[2] The ways in which the membership of the nation was defined historically through internal hierarchies of race, ethnicity, gender, and class – as well as through the presence of a constitutive outside, in particular colonized peoples – has recently been the focus of many historians of empire. In this chapter, drawing on a selection of British fur traders' writings about the food practices of indigenous communities in northwestern North America in the early decades of the nineteenth century, I contend that food was a principal grammar of difference within colonial discourses, a crucial way of identifying who belonged to one's community and who did not.[3]

The observation that food is a marker of difference in colonial discourse should come as little surprise to readers familiar with some of the foundational texts of European travel writing. From the philosophizing-from-afar of a work such as Montaigne's "Of Cannibals" to gripping first-person accounts of the African interior, early modern writers contemplated at length the unfamiliar food practices – real and imagined – of indigenous peoples in newly colonized realms.[4] Yet scholars of the colonial past have tended to overlook the power of these narratives in the construction of European and colonial identities. Scholars concerned, as I am, with the representational strategies that supported European imperialism and the exercise of colonial power – those who study the ways in which Europeans constructed their own identities in part by imagining non-Europeans as profoundly, often irremediably, inferior – have not paid sufficient attention to the pernicious power of European discourses about food. Anthropologists have a longer history of attending to the roles of food in cultural systems; historians are relative newcomers to the fray. A book in honour of Jennifer Brown, a scholar whose work brilliantly transcends the boundary between anthropology and history, seems an ideal place for a historian to think about food and difference. And it is high time: as anthropologist Mary Douglas insisted a quarter century ago, food is a key medium not only of community but also of social exclusion.[5] In this chapter, I investigate the mechanisms by which food functioned as a boundary marker between the fur traders' "us" and the indigenous "them."

A growing body of research in recent years has turned to the centrality of food practices to national and other forms of cultural identification. Whereas influential theorists could once dismiss food as less cultural than other expressions because of its basic physiological dimensions,[6] they must now recognize food as a constellation of practices and products so intimately enmeshed in the social order "that society cannot be imagined without them." In her recent book on the history of French food culture, for instance, Priscilla Parkhurst Ferguson demonstrates how cuisine provides direct support to nationalism. Precisely because it is part of everyday life, she argues, food allows people to practise their nationalism without even thinking about it. The fundamental importance of particular foods to daily routine "gives the culinary an immense advantage over cultural products that require more self-conscious ideological direction."[7] Food shares something here with clothing, another embodied element of material culture that has fruitfully engaged the interest of historians.[8] Because food is so embedded in everyday life, it is a regularly visited site of national memory. The very ordinariness of boiled beef, garlic, or raisin scones as signs of national belonging goes a long way toward explaining the resonance of such identifications.[9]

Food is a symbol of national (and regional and local) identity, but it is not symbol alone. It is not irrelevant that beef, potatoes, and wheat sustain life. As anthropologist Sidney Mintz observes, it is only because so many of us in the West are so well fed and have never known intense hunger that we "too easily forget the astonishing, at times even terrifying, importance of food and eating."[10] Food writes its effects on the body in a more profound and lasting way than most other cultural traits: the emaciated frames of refugees of war in Darfur, Sudan, and the increasingly obese bodies of North Americans raised on processed foods are stark contemporary examples. In her powerful study of Canadian Aboriginal health in the early twentieth century, historian Mary-Ellen Kelm examines the visible and often dreadful bodily effects of loss of access to traditional food resources and poor food in residential schools. Although they speak to biological functions, these examples are rooted in global and national political and economic realities.[11] Human relationships to food go far beyond the physiological. The intriguing questions about historical food habits are, in the main, moral and social. The cultural historian, for instance, seeks to understand the working out of complex social codes and imperatives by which refined wheat becomes a sought-after human staple and potatoes, the food of so many, come to be viewed as hog feed.[12] Except in situations of dire constraint, humans choose what to eat, when to eat, and with whom. In making these choices, individuals and communities make strong statements about who they are and, just as importantly, who they are not. Food is as important as shelter for sustaining life; it is as powerful a tool of inclusion or exclusion "as gates and doors."[13] Food choices, food rituals, and discourses about good and bad food are shot through with material *and* cultural implications, with physiological imperatives and power.

The assertion of any identity requires a marking of distinction between insider and outsider, between us and them. Discourses of difference, by which I mean beliefs and practices that define who does *not* belong to a given community, are a fundamental aspect of ideologies of national identity.[14] A recognizable British identity coalesced throughout the eighteenth century, not so much as a result of internal political or cultural consensus but in reaction to the "other" beyond British shores (and by the nineteenth century, in response to growing numbers of immigrant "others" within Britain itself). As historian Linda Colley puts it, "a strong sense of dissimilarity from those without" was the essential cement that allowed for the formation of the British nation.[15] British identity came into being in repeated confrontations with a French nation whose identity materialized, in part, through food, and it came into being in interaction with the peoples of the British colonies whose food practices became symbols of their non-Britishness.

Identity is defined here, above all, as a relational concept. It is a product of "where one is placed and where one places oneself within social networks" that is worked out on the shifting ground between what is possible in a given time and place and what is forbidden or not yet conceivable. The image of shifting ground is important: identity is not stable or continuous – it is a dynamic historical process.[16] Approaching national identity in this way, as a historical process of becoming as much as of being,[17] and as an individual as well as a collective mode of consciousness, allows us to analyze differing ideas about national belonging and exclusion in distinct times and places and among groups and individuals who might on the surface appear to be rather marginal to the ideological projects of national identity formation. Identity is not given from on high: it involves a broad circulation of social energies through a culture.[18]

The particular categories on which identity hinges change over time. In the early twenty-first century, race, read mainly through physical markers, remains a primary referent. So does gender. Religion has re-emerged as a defining concept of national identity in an era of economic and political struggle cloaked as holy war. In late-eighteenth- and early-nineteenth-century Europe, the question of where one was placed and where one placed oneself within social networks tended to be defined through rather different categories. Nation was starting to be attached to political and territorial entities, but this understanding jostled with older ideas about nation as breed or stock and the broader notion of a people being defined by class, geography, political institutions, religious affiliation, and stage of civilization. In the endless debates of the eighteenth century about the roots of human difference, the island of Britain emerged as a central focus of identity.[19] Within the island, and in the more and more closely entwined reaches of the British Empire, manners and customs were fundamental markers of identity and difference. The prolific essayist Oliver Goldsmith wrote in the 1760s that the British were distinguished from the rest of the world by their superior "manners, dispositions, and turn of thinking" (he felt that these were traits that indigenous people and Africans could match, though, if offered the healthful British climate and better nourishment). "Manners" tended to mean the shared practices and traits, including moral character, that came to define a people who lived in a common territory with a common language, laws, and political institutions. Others wrote of "the common arts of life" that defined national character.[20] Britons abroad, including the British explorers and traders who traversed western North America in this era, adopted the language of manners and customs when they organized their narratives.[21]

Then as now, identities were negotiated through the practices of everyday life.[22] And although identity is now widely theorized as performative – as based on everyday gestures and practices that actually constitute "the very subject [they are] purported to express"[23] – identity could (and can) seem to its practitioners both universal and immutable. Identity has frequently been understood as an essence, as an irreducible core of individual, group, or national character. This kind of thinking about difference, thinking that consigns whole groups of people to fixed and unalterable otherness, is what is meant by "racializing discourse." It is racializing in the sense that it defines communities or collectivities by some imagined set of signifiers that sets them distinctly apart from others (including those who purvey the discourse). Racializing discourse seeks to ground difference, to "fix and secure and guarantee the truth of differences"; in this way, it assists in the management of racialized power relations.[24] Racializing discourse has political implications for those being described – for those who are not members of the chosen political community, be it the British nation or Western civilization, and do not merit full membership. They are represented as lesser, perhaps savage, and certainly inferior. We will see in the discussion that follows how British fur traders – most of them Scots and some of them only tenuously connected to a newly British nation – deployed prevailing understandings of appropriate food and cultural manners to secure their own identities and distance themselves from the indigenous peoples among whom they moved. And we will see how concerted was the effort: these traders, after all, were in many instances entirely dependent on Aboriginal people for their food and security.

To the Sources

In this study, the indigenous peoples of North America figure as the "outside" that helped to constitute European identities in the Age of Empire. I examine most closely the writings of British explorers and fur traders in the Columbia Plateau region of the Pacific Northwest in the early nineteenth century. My focus is on two interrelated aspects of colonial discourses on food: the role of Aboriginal food practices in defining and affirming (and at times undermining) British understandings of their own purportedly elevated stage of civilization and the ways in which British travellers sought to demonstrate and activate their own class, gender, race, and national identities through their food habits. "Stage of civilization" refers to the influential set of theories of this period that held that societies developed through four distinct stages, defined broadly as hunting and gathering, pastoral, agricultural, and commercial. The commercial stage was viewed as the apex of human social development, and the commercially minded and hard-working British middle class was its highest expression.[25]

Although my focus is on British travellers to the interior regions of the Pacific Northwest, other colonial sites colour the background. The writings of earlier European travellers provided an archive of expectations on which nineteenth-century travellers drew. More generally, the experience of imperial exploration, commerce, and settlement – the experience of being an imperial power – profoundly influenced the responses of Britons abroad in the imperial era. The idea that the colonies were useful sources of commodities – from human labour to sugar, from timber to furs – was complicated by the notion that the colonies were profoundly different. The imagined right to extract resources and amass wealth from these territories and peoples was based on "the gap between metropole and colony: civilisation here, barbarism/savagery there."[26] The supposed savagery or backwardness of indigenous peoples helped to justify their colonization; the texts that delineated that backwardness, in the smallest details of daily life, were vital tools in the arsenal of empire.

Food was one of the first cultural practices remarked upon by Europeans abroad. Missionaries, explorers, soldiers, settlers, and administrators had a good deal to say about the remarkable food practices of those they encountered in the far reaches of empire. The practice, real or imagined, that drew harshest condemnation was cannibalism. As historian Olive Dickason has noted, cannibalism ranked with nudity as a characteristic of indigenous peoples that most unsettled Europeans.[27] More frequent and less vexed were ruminations on the everyday foods of the indigenous peoples of distant parts. Jacques Cartier, the first French explorer to describe the peoples of the east coast of present-day Canada (1534), focused on the cultural practices of the peoples, including, centrally, their dress and mode of sustenance. In a lovely example of early modern preoccupation with a narrow range of practices, Cartier's opening account of the Mi'kmaq people he met at Baie de Chaleur, in present-day New Brunswick, fixed on the food offerings of the area and the people's ripeness for conversion:

> There is not the smallest plot of ground bare of wood, and even on sandy soil, but is full of wild wheat, that has an ear like barley and the grain like oats, as well as of pease, as thick as if they had been sown and hoed; of white and red currant-bushes, of strawberries, of raspberries, of white and red roses ... Likewise there are many fine meadows with useful herbs, and a pond where there are many salmon. I am more than ever of the opinion that these people would be easy to convert to our holy faith.[28]

The passage makes clear the link between food and religion, between food and identity, in this era. The people Cartier describes had access to an abundance of what the visitor regarded as fine and familiar foods, *and* they would be easy to convert to that highest expression of French identity, Roman Catholicism. Their food bounty and the familiarity of foodstuffs that appeared "as if sown and hoed" marked these Mi'kmaq for special attention. They might not be civilized farmers now, but they were not far from it in the visitor's view. These people were rendered all the more promising in contrast to the other indigenous people encountered at Baie de Chaleur in the summer of 1534. Shortly after his glowing depiction of the Mi'kmaq, Cartier wrote of the sorry Stadaconan fishers he met farther north in the bay.[29] Described as being not at all of the same race or language as the Mi'kmaq, these people were depicted shaving their hair into top-knots, sleeping in their canoes, and eating their meat a tad rare for the Frenchman's taste. They ate it, he noted, "almost raw, only warming it a little on the coals; and the same with their fish."[30] "Almost raw" meant almost lacking the most basic veil of civility. If the Mi'kmaq were close to agriculture, these

Stadaconans were too close to nature. There is no mention of their amenability to civilization, which was expressed in this period most powerfully through Christianity. Food practices were a primary consideration in the explorer's definition of axes of difference.

Food is saturated with beliefs about cultural identity and vigour. As Parama Roy has written about emigrants from India to North America and Britain, those who leave their homeland may be especially attached to traditional practices of consumption: "Expatriates are adamant, entirely passionate about such matters as the eating habits of the motherland."[31] Adamant and deeply rooted cultural assumptions about what constitutes good and proper food underpinned the writings of British travellers to the Pacific Northwest in the early nineteenth century. At isolated interior fur trade posts, though, day-to-day practical concerns came very much into play. Although fur traders' careers might depend on the trade in fur-bearing animals, their survival depended on regular supplies of country food, most of it produced by Aboriginal people. As historian George Colpitts shows so well for the Prairies and subarctic West, European traders were in a condition of perpetual dependency on Aboriginal provisioners of meat, fish, and other country produce. Traditional seasonal production cycles determined what foods traders might expect to eat and when; the Native communities' own sustenance needs determined the quantity and quality of produce that would be left for trade at the posts. At many posts, winter shortages were common, and "the energies of all" were frequently directed at mere survival.[32] Fur traders' writings from the Interior Plateau betray this sense of vulnerability about food. Anxiety about where the next meal would come from informed traders' views of the Native people of the region. Indigenous food ways could have major implications for trade as well: traders in the Plateau quickly found that communities that gained a substantial portion of their diet from fishing were in no hurry to become trappers of furs.[33]

Yet these writers' minds were not guided by practical concerns alone. A broader concern with the palpable cultural difference displayed in food practices colours many of these writings. Difference, however, is never stable; the lines between colonizer and colonized were never as neat as these binary terms suggest. As students of colonialism have shown repeatedly in recent years, colonies were spaces defined by intimate frontiers as much as by segregation. Research by Jennifer Brown and Sylvia Van Kirk more than twenty-five years ago anticipated the recent fascination with the social and cultural middle ground, where intimate relationships between colonizer and colonized – sexual, familial, or domestic in form – defined and, at times, challenged binary classifications and the categories of colonial rule.[34] In the fur trade domains of northwestern North America, explorers and traders depended for their survival on assistance and support, in myriad forms, from indigenous communities. Fur traders married Aboriginal women, fathered mixed-race children, and lived for long periods alongside Aboriginal communities. Aboriginal and metis wives and partners were essential to the trade posts for economic and diplomatic purposes and for the many tender ties that softened life at the post. The children of these marriages formed a vital part of the fur trade work force.[35] In addition, Native hunters, Native trappers, Native guides, and Native suppliers of foodstuffs, leather, cord, and many other materials literally kept the trade running. Surely the constitutive nature of the outside – the ways in which the other becomes a defining element of the self – must be close to the surface in such a setting. Such contradictions surface often in the pages of traders' writings.

By the 1820s, fur trade social practices such as intermarriage were coming under increasing censure from permanent settlers, missionaries, and a new generation of fur trade officials. This was an era of hardening racial distinctions in the British Empire; within the fur trade, it was an era of sharpening racial and class distinctions. Food practices provided a ready means to shore up social boundaries. Not only Indianness, but also civilized, respectable, middle-class whiteness was rendered in an accessible, easy-to-read form through food. In this decade, the London-based authorities of the Hudson's Bay Company (HBC), as part of a wide-ranging reorganization and rationalization of company operations after amalgamation with the North West Company, introduced new regulations to protect the officers in the service from threats to their racial and class status. Rules to limit social and racial mixing at table were key among them.[36] In the same period, the company issued a standard questionnaire to guide the reportage of traders in the field. Food practices were an important category for reflection in the questionnaire.[37]

Hierarchies of Meat and Fish

Fur traders' depictions of the food practices of those Interior Plateau communities that relied heavily on fish provide transparent examples of the fixing and securing function of discourses of difference. As I have demonstrated elsewhere, traders elaborated a distinct hierarchy of indigenous peoples in the Plateau. Those they described as fishing tribes of the Interior were generally depicted as lazy, feckless, physically weak, and prone to starvation. Those defined as hunters, particularly the buffalo hunters of the southeastern Plateau, meanwhile, were said to be brave, manly, and industrious. Nevertheless, even the virtue of the hunters was marked by savagery: they remained, after all, in the first stage of social development.[38] The Indian hunter might be brave, manly, and productive, but he was, at base, a representative of a savage race – a race defined in part by physical features, but more profoundly by stage of civilization and the cultural practices that attended it.[39]

A powerful assumption shared by early visitors to the Plateau was the notion that with minimal effort the fishing tribes could have ample deer and other meat at their disposal. Fishing peoples such as the Lower Nlaka'pamux, who provided rations for Simon Fraser's party during its journey down the Fraser River in 1808, were denigrated for offering food that was "commonly wretched if not disgusting." Many other traders in the region decried a diet heavy in fish and criticized the peoples who partook of it. Surely they were "indolent and lazy to an extreme" if they were willing to content themselves with such a diet.[40] First Nations assessments of a diet high in fish protein are very different: as Mary-Ellen Kelm found in her research on twentieth-century Aboriginal nutrition in British Columbia, First Nations depictions of the strength of their communities always come back to food – with fish being high on the list of essential ingredients for physical and community health.[41]

Fur traders' aversion to fish had deep roots both in the fur trade and in British culture. Within the Columbia Interior district, complaints about food were constant and tended to focus on the privations of a steady diet of dried salmon. Similar complaints had long been heard throughout fur trade country. Service at so-called fish posts east of the Rockies was generally considered a penance.[42] In the 1840s, servants at the Plateau post at Kamloops went on strike to protest their reliance on dried salmon. They did indeed consume large amounts: the daily ration provided to each company servant was three pounds of dried fish, roughly the equivalent of ten pounds of fresh. Servants' rations were supplemented with wheat flour, pulses, and whatever game, vegetables, or other country produce was available. Fresh meat and vegetables, however, tended to go first to the gentlemen of the company – the officer class – and there was often little left for the labouring men.[43] Fish was the staple, and as one trader put it, "God help him that passes many years on such poor stuff."[44]

Complaints about this poor stuff must be read in light of contemporary class- and gender-based food ideologies. Those beliefs are laid bare in *Domestic Medicine,* a text that went through myriad editions in Britain between 1769 and 1846. In Scotland, the childhood home of many fur traders who wound up in the Interior Plateau, it was said that there was "scarcely a cottage but what contains on its shelf the Domestic Medicine."[45] Dr. Buchan emphasized that the best rule of diet was to "avoid all extremes": meat, bread, and vegetables in moderate combination were most wholesome, but "to gorge, beef, mutton, pork, fish, and fowl, twice or thrice a day, is certainly too much."[46] His point of reference is those with sufficient wealth to support such extravagance: echoing contemporary middle-class critiques of aristocratic dissipation and French-style over-indulgence, Buchan cautioned against "poignant sauces [and] rich soups," noting that they "are only incentives to luxury ... [and] prove almost a poison" to the British body.[47] Although certainly not luxurious, a diet built around a three-pound daily ration of dried salmon (with occasional variation when supplies lasted beyond the officer rank) qualified as extreme in the good doctor's calculus.

Fish in whatever quantity suffered from a deeply rooted perception that it was an inferior form of sustenance to red meat. Although angling for salmon was by this time a popular pursuit for wealthy gentlemen in places such as the Scottish Highlands (where fishing by poor and middling folk was considered poaching), received wisdom and medical orthodoxy held that fish was a relatively weak or even feminine food. In most of Britain, fish consumption had plunged dramatically following the break with the Catholic Church.[48] Medieval and Renaissance understandings of a natural hierarchy that placed land animals well above fish on a great chain of being appear to have persisted well into the modern period.[49] Historian Stephen Mennell has shown that by the early nineteenth century class differences in meat consumption in Britain were as pronounced as they had been in the medieval period, when the famously prodigious quantities of meat consumed at the banquets of the wealthy stood in marked contrast to the meagre, cereal-based diet of the peasantry.[50] Yet, by the turn of the nineteenth century, growing numbers of middling folk in Britain were willing to spend disposable income on meat.[51] Meat was a marker of social standing that bore substantial cultural weight.

Red meat was not only valued for its class connotations, but also viewed as a quintessentially healthful food – for men. Red meat has long been construed in Western and other traditions as strong food, in part because the eating of it implies incorporation of some measure of the powers of the animal consumed – the strength, aggression, and sexual potency that define the animal nature of humans.[52] Yet the thinking in this period, drawing in part on the theory of the four humours, called for moderation. Dr. Buchan advised that animal flesh, being "solid, with a sufficient degree of tenacity, is most proper for the state of manhood." "Laborious" men, in particular, needed sufficient red meat to fuel their bodies. Those who "labour hard without doors" (peasants are his case in point) required high-energy foods that were "almost indigestible to a citizen"; citizens, on the other hand, could subsist on foods on which a peasant would starve. The contemporary gloss on "citizen" included a man of the town as opposed to a farmer; in Samuel Johnson's lexicon, a citizen was a man involved in commercial activities.[53] The very bodies of peasants, then, were adapted to the consumption of red meat. Training diets for soldiers and athletes also called for enormous quantities of the stuff: men who carried arms for the nation were to protect the national vigour by consuming plenty of meat. The bodies of citizens, whose demands were more cerebral and less physical, could manage with substantially less.[54] There is more than a hint of stadial theory here: those who lived and worked closest to the land had the highest need for animal foods; those at greater remove – those who had achieved that summit of civilization, the commercial stage – had also achieved some distance from the physiological need for meat. The need, however, was not removed. Convictions about the indispensability of meat to hardy manhood had broad reach in British imperial culture. The British in India in the nineteenth century came to view Hindu men as weakened and effeminate, the result of an array of cultural practices, including, importantly, insufficient consumption of meat.[55]

The mighty Englishman might wear the benefits of his carnivorous ways, but Dr. Buchan cautioned that even for labouring men there were limits: too much red meat was too great a stimulus to the system, causing "too great fulness [sic]" of the blood vessels.[56] It was a common view in nineteenth-century Britain that meat was heat producing and stimulated the passions. Vigorous vegetarian movements called for strict limitations on meat eating as a way, among other things, to contain the potentially dangerous male libido.[57] Doctors not of the vegetarian persuasion, including Dr. Buchan, urged patients of delicate constitution – women, children, and the old and infirm – to choose lighter foods such as chicken, fish, and eggs.[58] Intriguingly, people of supposedly delicate constitution had for centuries been directed to foods that can be considered the symbolic opposite of red: white foods such as chicken breast, eggs, almonds, and milk were widely prescribed for the ill, women, and the elderly.[59] These prescriptions indicate a highly gendered code of foods, one in which red meat grounded the masculine pole.

These cultural assumptions undergird the writings of fur traders from the Interior Plateau in the early nineteenth century. The gentlemen of this regional trade, meaning the men of the officer class who oversaw the posts and kept the records on which historians rely, were almost all of British extraction. Most were Scots.[60] The majority came from tenant-farming or trades families, a social standing below or precariously within the margins of the middling ranks. In fur trade society, they could achieve a social rank well beyond their roots. But in the difficult cultural and class setting of the fur trade, where it was a daily struggle to maintain the vestiges of British middle-class civility, that status was highly vulnerable. Their jealous guarding of the privileges of middle-class identity was undoubtedly amplified by this sense of vulnerability. The continual rehearsal of the customs and rituals of middle-class consumption and the conspicuous display of the trappings of respectability were the central means by which traders produced and confirmed their privilege. As historical geographer Cole Harris emphasizes, these rituals were also the central means of producing and confirming power: trade posts, Harris argues, bristled with power, a key modality of which was the pervasive discipline of daily routine.[61]

Relatively few markers of respectability were available to men who had First Nations wives and families, who often had to share housing with company servants, and who had at best sporadic access to imported goods from Britain. The daily rituals of the table provided a key venue for the performance and reproduction of class and racial status. Although they faced many challenges in their attempts to perform and secure their identity, it must be said that the British gentlemen of the trade fared better materially than those of other ethnic backgrounds. The men of the servant class in the Columbia Interior were mainly French Canadians, Scots from the Highlands and outer islands, metis, Aboriginals, and Hawaiians.[62] These men faced much less attractive prospects than their superiors. They entered the company as labourers, and only a few made it to the officer ranks.

Although no fur trader that I have read quoted Buchan, it is apparent that prevailing medical ideology informed their views on the nutritional qualities of fish. Traders were not only sick of fish; many were convinced it threatened their masculine vigour. Jules Quesnel believed that the dire effects of this mauvaise nourriture accounted for the declining health of his colleagues in the field. Thomas Dears complained that a diet of fish had left him so emaciated he was in danger of "slipping through my Breeks." John McLean warned of the unfortunate medicinal effects a steady diet of dried salmon might produce in the uninitiated: it worked its way through the system like "a dose of Glauber salts."[63] McLean's warning reminds us that there were real physical effects from the change of diet traders faced in the Plateau. A steady diet of fish and little else would have indeed been a challenge for many. In the thinking of the day, the fact that it was dried fish added to the challenge. Salted and smoke-dried foods came in for special censure in *Domestic Medicine*. Buchan cautioned that preserved foods were "hard of digestion" and exacerbated melancholic tendencies, liver disease, hysteria, and a host of other maladies.[64] Dried salmon, then, was problematic for many reasons. Yet this diet was hardly more monotonous than the daily fare of young men raised in the Highlands and outer islands of Scotland.[65] Those from the eastern shores of Quebec might have been accustomed to a more varied diet, although evidence from that region points to a regime laden with wheat flour.[66] Many in the servant class in the Plateau had previously served at posts east of the Rockies. These men were well accustomed to repetitious fur trade rations. In the Prairies, for instance, they would have consumed large amounts of dried meat (pemmican) and substantial quantities of fish.

Complaints about the monotonous fish diet of the Plateau need to be read in this broader context and in the context of what was absent. Traders were missing meat.

Traders' representations of the indigenous peoples of the Interior Plateau are strongly shaped by prevailing ideologies about the special powers of meat. Indian bodies – particularly the bodies of those (incorrectly) believed to subsist on fish – were widely reported to be weakened by diet. Terms such as "wretches," "miserable," "poor," "starving," "slovenly," and "indolent" were frequently used to describe fishing Indians. That these people lived in territory many traders found barely habitable only confirmed this view. Fishing peoples of the Columbia Interior, traders asserted, were weak, wretched, and depleted, as was their land. Explorer David Thompson expressed succinctly the view that fish was inferior sustenance. In his words, "fish however plenty can never compensate the want of Deer, Sheep, and Goats." In a phrase that could have come straight from *Domestic Medicine,* Thompson insisted that those who ate meat were simply "more full in form."[67] The weakness of those believed to lack access to meat was written on their bodies and their character.

The image of the impoverished, famished fishing Indian was persistent in fur trade writings from the Plateau throughout the first half of the century. A dozen years after Thompson, Alexander Kennedy wrote from Spokane House in the 1820s that the Lower Kootenay (Ktunaxa) were still fishermen, and, as a result, they were "half starved and half naked." George Simpson described these same people as "small decrepit and dirty."[68] If fish in any form was second-rate food, salmon on its gruelling upriver journey to spawn was viewed as particularly useless. People who ate this "putrid" stuff were described as desperate salmon eaters indeed. The eating of this type of fish was generally equated with starvation, even though lean post-spawning fish are most suitable for air and smoke drying and store well for long periods. Kennedy came to understand the complementary role of fine and bad salmon in the annual round of Interior peoples. In the fall, he noted, lean and dying fish were "never rejected by the Natives ... they are eagerly sought after and hung up in their natural state, to be used when necessity requires."[69] In addition, there is much evidence in oral histories, anthropological accounts, and trader writings to demonstrate that so-called fishing tribes followed a complex seasonal round of food production activities and consumed a varied diet. The food-production cycle took fishing communities well beyond the banks of the river as they tracked game into the hills, harvested vast stores of roots and vegetables, and traded with neighbouring communities.[70] Many of these activities took place beyond the view of fur traders. Numerous foods routinely stored and consumed by Plateau First Nations were not even recognized by most traders as fit to eat. Roots, mosses and lichens, and other vegetable foods – most of which were produced by women – loom large in this category. Fishing tribes of the Plateau ate far more than fish, just as hunters ate more than meat. Although some traders made note of varied production activities, few showed Kennedy's sensitivity to seasonal and local variation in indigenous diets.

As I have discussed elsewhere, most instances of what traders called starvation in the Plateau appear to have been what anthropologist Mary Black-Rogers has labelled technical starvation. I found no evidence in the local fur trade record, spotty as it is, of people dying of hunger. Instead, there is a good deal of evidence that the people whom the fur traders described as starving were either eating food the traders considered inadequate or were too busy procuring their own food to take an interest in working for the traders. As Samuel Black put it bluntly on one occasion, "the tribes of the Columbia do nothing in winter, but procure a livelihood, and the latter with a great deal of trouble."[71] The season when they were "doing nothing" was the very time when traders wanted them to trap furs. This focus on the semantics of starvation is not meant to downplay the terrible bodily effects of food shortage. Although I found no evidence of deaths from starvation, there is evidence of people suffering from shortage, especially in late winter. As one commentator on Plateau food ways has put it, "the margin of safety for winter survival was not overly generous."[72] This was particularly the case in inland regions distant from major fishing, hunting, or gathering grounds. Communities made use of an array of foods that outsiders viewed as barely edible, including "half-rotten" fish and lichen gathered from trees, partly as a hedge against suffering when few fresh foods were available.

As Black's "do nothing" remark suggests, indolence was a trait closely associated with fish eating in trader writings. Native people who chose to eat fish rather than hunt game were routinely derided as too lazy to hunt. The common view was that the abundance of the fishery on the Columbia River and its tributaries permitted Interior peoples to "indulge their sloth."[73] Preference for fishing over hunting and trapping was an annoyance to fur traders for practical reasons, as noted above. But the derision went deeper than this. Fishing seemed to require minimal effort in much of the Columbia. Traders were aware that salmon runs were seasonal and that supplies could run low in late winter and spring. Yet so prolific was the resource in summer that those who suffered hardship were viewed as the authors of their own misfortune. John McLeod, commenting on the Northern Okanagan people, claimed they were "such an indolent and improvident Set, that altho' their country in summer abound with Trout and Salmon ... [they] are starving for most part of winter and Spring ... living on roots and a kind of Moss."[74] Fishing was viewed as an easy living, if only the Indians would plan ahead.

Many traders shared McLeod's mystification at the failure of fishing communities to lay in enough dried salmon to get through the winter. The explanation most frequently invoked was humankind's natural aversion to labour. This notion had a long history and wide currency in Britain. The writings of Thomas Malthus, among others, helped in the early nineteenth century to solidify the idea that torpor and corruption were the original state of humans. A common argument held that the poor, much like Native peoples, were wretched and indolent because they had never learned the civilized – and particularly middle-class – habits of industry and foresight: their wretchedness was a moral failing.[75] Remaining sunk in their torpor, the poor, like Native people, were responsible for their own weakness. David Thompson made explicit reference to this "axiom of the civilised world, that Poverty begets Poverty."[76] Narratives from other colonial settings demonstrate the power of this concept of original lassitude. Images from the South Pacific of languid Natives occasionally dipping a hand into a brimming sea or reaching for a piece of ripe fruit are well known. The age-old trope of the lazy Native was frequently invoked by British observers of enslaved and formerly enslaved people in the West Indies.[77] Here, in the less hospitable climate of the Plateau, were Native people of similar propensities. The fishing peoples of the Plateau were not well suited to labour, traders believed, and they did not have the moral character to bear it.

I have written elsewhere about the much more positive image of the hunting Indian in fur trader accounts. Buffalo hunters of the eastern Plateau, in particular, were viewed as manly, at times threateningly so; that manliness comprised industriousness, moral fortitude, and physical vigour.[78] But Native people were measured most immediately against the character of the British middle-class man. The moral character of such a man was spelled out by George Simpson during his sojourn in the Plateau. The overseas governor of the Hudson's Bay Company defined a gentleman as a man of zeal, hard work, industry, and restraint.[79] Simpson drew on the ideal of the middle-class man that powerfully defined the British nation in this era. For this new man of enterprise, proper manhood derived from individual effort (as opposed to family wealth or property), piety, sobriety, self-discipline, and dedication to family. Manhood rested above all on the ability to "work for oneself ... to trust in the dignity of labour."[80] Aboriginal people who were seen – in spite of the great complexity and exertions inherent in their seasonal cycle of food production activities – as "doing nothing" much of the year and relying on the beneficence of nature did not fare well by such a yardstick.

The gentlemen of the fur trade performed and confirmed their race, gender, and class status in a dense array of daily rituals. Perhaps the most powerful of these centred on food. Where conditions allowed, traders established vegetable gardens to supply their tables with the familiar foods of home. Gardens also helped to mark off crucial symbolic boundaries. Agriculture, after all, was an art of civilized men: a carefully tended garden offered traders a fine opportunity to display their civility, both to themselves and to the hunter-gatherers of the region.[81] The cultivation of this boundary was rendered more potent by the view that the so-called New World was a vacant plot waiting to be tilled, an ideology in broad circulation in contemporary Britain.

Dining arrangements at company posts offered another vital opportunity for the display of class and racial privilege. At all but the smallest posts, it was customary for the gentlemen of the service to dine separately from the men of the labouring ranks (and for traders' wives to dine entirely apart). Alexander Ross wryly observed that, at the officers' hall at North West Company posts, "strict rules of subordination" were in place – for instance, "you take your seat, as a Chinese Mandarine [sic] would take his dress, according to your rank." Even the most prosaic of beverages was class specific: there were three grades of tea and as many of sugar.[82] Ross's remarks bring vividly to mind the observation by scholar Sidney Mintz that sugar, tea, and tobacco, vital products of empire, "conveyed with their use the complex idea that one could *become* different by *consuming* differently."[83] One became a gentleman by consuming the goods that attended that status. The Hudson's Bay Company took rituals of social sorting as seriously as its rival, the North West Company. In the early 1820s, shortly after the amalgamation of the two companies, the HBC's governing council issued a stern call for the more stringent policing of social boundaries at company posts. Practices viewed as "derogatory to the dignity of the Chief Factors and Chief Traders" were to be terminated immediately, and scrupulous efforts were to be made to "draw a line of distinction" between officers and servants. An important site for the drawing of boundaries was the table. Guides and interpreters, men in the upper echelon of the servant rank, were prohibited from dining with the gentlemen. Skilled and high ranking as they might have been, they were not to be confused with their superiors. What was more, these guides and interpreters were usually French Canadian or Aboriginal. Their presence at officer tables threatened not only the dignity of the officers but also their status as white gentlemen of British roots.[84]

The gentlemen not only messed separately from those deemed to be of inferior class and race but also dined far more lavishly when circumstances allowed. Fresh produce from post gardens went first to the officers' tables, as did any fresh meat. That local produce occupied a similar station to coveted imported goods in the hierarchy of fur trade foods is worth noting: fresh country produce, particularly fresh meat, was "as much an index of class as consumption of imported Teneriffe wines, Madeira, and double Gloucester cheese."[85]

So ingrained, so commonplace, was this class-specific distribution of food, that it drew little attention. John Tod, officer at Kamloops, was oblivious to the irony of his remark that fresh venison brought in by First Nations hunters was served to the officer's family, while "an old lame horse [was served] as beef for the men."[86] The officers' choice is not surprising: fresh venison was likely more palatable than the flesh of an old horse. Venison had special advantages, according to Buchan. The flesh of animals that "take sufficient exercise" occupied the top rung of his hierarchy of wholesome meats; it was far preferable to the flesh of animals that were penned up or "feed grossly" (hogs, ducks). The superior manliness of Plateau hunters was no doubt linked to their regular consumption of superior meat. Gentlemen traders likewise sought to benefit from its special properties.

Visitors were alert to the class concerns on display at western trade posts. An American visitor to the gentlemen's hall at Fort Vancouver in 1839 saw the signifiers of class privilege in sharp relief: "At the end of a table twenty feet in length stands Governor McLaughlin [Chief Factor John McLoughlin], directing guests and gentlemen from neighbouring posts to their places, at distances from the Governor according to their rank in the service ... Roast beef and port, boiled mutton, baked salmon, boiled ham; beets, carrots, turnips, cabbage and potatoes, and wheaten bread, are tastefully distributed over the table among a dinner-set of elegant queen's ware, burnished with glittering glasses and decanters of various colored Italian wines."[87]

This performance needs little decoding. It was all part of the constant theatre of the fur trade, a set of self-conscious performances that extended beyond food to dress, personal conduct, and cross-cultural ceremony.[88] Although the symbolism is quite apparent, what is less obvious is the practical function of the display. Performances such as McLoughlin's banquet asserted and reinforced social and racial hierarchies and were aimed at Native people as much as company servants. This type of ritual created the post as a symbol of power for surrounding populations (who, for the most part, were barred from entry) and served as a vital tool in the regulation of the labour force. The allocation of food, the tradition of high table, the arrangement of chairs around tables, the absence of women – this matrix of carefully articulated inclusions and exclusions served as bodily and spatial cues that asserted the authority of the officers and provided daily reminders to the labouring men of their place in the structure.[89] The rituals of everyday life both symbolized and enabled the hierarchical class, race, and gender relationships that structured fur trade society.

As noted earlier, the need for ritual was felt more keenly in this quasi-colonial setting than at home in Britain or in the settled eastern colonies. In fur trade country, officers and servants worried not only about asserting and defending their hard-won social status but also about the dangers of "going native" – of compromising their racial status. Fear of going native weighed heavily on the mind of Alexander Ross in the southern Plateau in the 1810s. Ross observed with disdain the social and cultural lapses of Donald McKenzie, the first British trader to travel into the Nez Percé and Shoshone regions of the present-day American northwest. So affected was McKenzie by this wild country that he had become a man "only fit to eat horse and shoot at a mark."[90] Ross himself stooped to eating horse when there was no alternative, but he could not understand those who actively chose it over buffalo, venison, fowl, or fish. Still more incomprehensible were the French Canadians, who would "leave their rations of good venison and eat dogs' flesh!" The only explanation Ross could offer for this jarring transgression was that the Canadians were habituated to the country; they had come to live "almost as Indians."[91] By willingly eating horse or dog, the men had crossed the precious boundary between traders and Indians. McKenzie and the Canadians had gone native.

By the 1820s and 1830s, fears of going native had spread to the intimate confines of fur trade family life. Like so many other practices that blurred the lines of race and class identity, marriages to Aboriginal women came to be seen as a threat. New pressures were brought to bear in fur trade country as outsiders swept into the region and as economic and political shifts in Britain and the United States increasingly pointed to the demise of the western fur trade. The arrival of missionaries to the Plateau in the 1810s brought virulent attacks on the moral and social acceptability of cross-cultural marriages. High-ranking officers in the HBC were the first to follow missionary admonitions to choose chaste and proper white wives.[92] By the 1830s, just as metis women had earlier displaced Native women as wives of choice, white women came to displace association with metisse as key accoutrements of proper fur trade manhood. White women, whose bodies were potent symbols of respectability, introduced to this fledgling colonial society a new constellation of the trappings of civility. Their clothing, their artistic skills, and, not least, their knowledge of the civilized arts of the table helped usher in a new era in fur trade society. As the fur trade gave way to settler colonialism, food practices would remain an important way of marking the boundaries between the British and their colonial others.[93]

Conclusion

One of the most insistent ideological projects of empire was the effort to define the boundaries between colonizer and colonized. Food was a fundamental element in the colonial grammar of difference. Food practices, embedded as they are in both the most humble activities of the everyday and the most elaborate public displays, were vital tools in the construction of European self and indigenous other in the long era of imperial expansion and national integration. Food's importance as an axis of identity has been long overlooked by historians, likely because its uses and meanings are so mundane as to be taken for granted. Yet its mundaneness is precisely what gives food such social power: the seeds of imperialism "were most fruitfully sown in the contours of everyday life."[94]

The fur trade of the Columbia Plateau provides a fascinating case study of the uses of food in the building of national, class, racial, and gender identities (in all their interactions). Officers at Plateau posts engaged in the project of marking difference on a daily basis as they struggled to perform and protect their status as civilized, respectable white men. The marking of difference was central to the process of defining Britishness in its fur trade variant; more broadly, knowledge of non-British others was the essential cement that constituted Britishness at home and abroad. As secure as that identity may seem in the confident pronouncements of colonial officials, its ambiguities were never far from the surface. Fur trade officers might have wished to be fine gentlemen in the British style, but they lived in a setting where their dependence on indigenous people was constantly apparent. Those who adapted well to the environment could be accused of going native; even when they guarded their distance, they relied on indigenous expertise for the necessities of life – from food to love. In spite of these tensions – or, perhaps more to the point, because of them – traders elaborated a deeply racialized image of indigenous peoples in the Plateau. Fishing Indians came in for special censure. With bodies as weak as their moral character, the fishing Indians of the Interior represented everything British traders were not. They were seen as lazy, feckless, and wasted in physical form in contrast to the traders' industry, self-discipline, and vigour. Their fish diet and the activity of fishing itself seemed to condemn them to poverty and indolence. Although in theory Indians might have been able to rise up from this backward state (the fishing Indian having barely entered the first stage in the progressivist model of social development), and although traders acknowledged their admiration for particular individuals or communities, in practice trader discourse left little room for improvement. Indians were defined by their difference, a difference rooted in part in the powerful symbolism of food. Indian difference was profound, and it played a central role in the definition of civilized British manhood.

Notes

1 Buchan, *Domestic Medicine*, 62, and see *The New Domestic Medicine*.
2 Race should be understood as if the term were embedded in scare quotes, as should other socially constructed categories such as gender and civilization. I work with a discursive definition of race, viewing it as a historically situated or sliding signifier of difference.

Race has no biological or other transparent meaning: it exists as a representation of difference organized – in distinctive ways in different times and places – through language, through systems of meaning, and through power relationships that result in material inequalities. For a useful presentation of this position, see Hall, *Race: The Floating Signifier.*

3   By food practices, I mean food preferences, cultural and personal, and everyday and often subconscious rituals of preparation and consumption. The phrase "grammar of difference" is from Frederick Cooper and Ann Laura Stoler's now classic "Between Colony and Metropole," 7. On the broader questions, see Hall, "The Rule of Difference," and her "Introduction" to *Cultures of Empire.* I am aware that it is problematic to speak of Britishness when Englishness, Scottishness, and other elements of that larger identity were so distinct from one another. For the purposes of this chapter, when both Scots and English loom large, British is the most useful denomination.

4   Montaigne, "Of Cannibals." For African exploration texts, see Pratt, *Imperial Eyes.* European observations were diverse and not all pejorative. Cortes and other early Spanish explorers of present-day Mexico, for instance, were awed by the variety and quality of foods consumed in the Aztec city of Tenochtitlan, and the salivations of French and British visitors to the South Pacific are well known.

5   See Douglas, "Standard Social Uses of Food," 36. Until recently, there has been limited attention to the specific ways in which the symbolic power of food has been invoked in the construction of regional and national identities. For wonderful insights, see Gabaccia, *We Are What We Eat.* In her effort to demonstrate that American food has long been defined by its multi-ethnicity and culinary tolerance, Gabaccia pays less attention to food as a tool of social exclusion (but see Chapter 5). See also the useful review of recent literature in Scholliers, "Meals, Food Narratives, and Sentiments of Belonging." Some of the new historical work is canvassed below.

6   The observation was made by Williams in *Keywords,* among others.

7   Ferguson, *Accounting for Taste,* 81, 1.

8   For a recent suggestive work on clothing and identity in a British colonial setting, see Kupperman, "Reading Indian Bodies," Chapter 2 in her *Indians and English.* See also Wrigley, *The Politics of Appearances;* and Tarlo, *Clothing Matters.* For stimulating reflections on material culture as a historical source, see Auslander, "Beyond Words."

9   Absence of sufficient food and deprivation can also be stamped on national identity in poignant ways. As Hasia Diner argues, Irish social history in the era of British colonialism is so intimately connected with long-term food want that Ireland failed to develop an elaborate national food culture. The Irish, wrote James Joyce, were "outcast from life's feast." See Diner, *Hungering for America,* Chapter 4. Others note how American national identity has been shaped by abundance; see, for example, Bentley, "Reading Food Riots."

10 Mintz, *Tasting Food, Tasting Freedom,* 4.

11 Kelm, *Colonizing Bodies.* For a powerful demonstration of how present-day famine and hunger are the result of inequities of resource distribution rather than food scarcity, see Sen, *Poverty and Famines.* The number of people worldwide facing chronic hunger is growing steadily and surpassed 850 million in 2004. See Milanovic, *Worlds Apart.*

12 This was the case in turn-of-the-nineteenth-century southern England. For insights, see Thompson, *The Making of the English Working Class,* and "The Moral Economy of the English Crowd"; and Gallagher and Greenblatt, "The Potato in the Materialist Imagination." The importance of this homely crop from the Americas to European material and cultural history – and to many European poor – cannot be overstated. Potatoes were moving up the social scale in England by the late 1700s; they had long been consumed by

all social ranks in Spain, where they were introduced in the sixteenth century from the Americas. See Lehmann, *The British Housewife,* 158-59; and Sarasúa, "Upholding Status," 48-49.

13 Douglas, "Standard Social Uses of Food," 12. See also Grignon, "Commensality and Social Morphology."

14 See Hall, "Conclusion: The Multi-Cultural Question," 234.

15 Colley, *Britons,* 6, 17. Colley calls roast beef the "archetypal food of [British] patriots" in the eighteenth century. She argues that by the 1750s the terms "British" and "Great Britain" had come to dominate official and everyday vocabulary (13), eclipsing particular referents such as "English" or "Scottish." Colonial historians insist on the centrality of the colonial outside to the forging of national identity, a factor Colley underplays. See Colley, *Captives;* Hall, *Civilising Subjects;* Cooper and Stoler, "Between Metropole and Colony"; and Wilson, *The Island Race.*

16 Wilson, *The Island Race,* 3. This point has been made widely. See, for instance, Foucault, *Discipline and Punish;* Said, *Orientalism;* and Hall, "William Knibb and the Constitution of the New Black Subject."

17 Hall, "Cultural Identity and Diaspora," 22.

18 The phrase "social energies" is from Gallagher and Greenblatt, "Introduction," *Practicing New Historicism,* 13.

19 See Wilson, *The Island Race,* 4-5n20, on the centrality of the island to identity in this era.

20 Oliver Goldsmith, "A Comparative View of Races and Nations" (1760), and John Millar, *The Origin of the Distinction of Ranks* (1806). Both are quoted in Wilson, *The Island Race,* 5-7; and Goldsmith is quoted in Kidd, *The Forging of Races,* 91. See the *Oxford English Dictionary* for the moral aspects of the term "manners" in the eighteenth and nineteenth centuries.

21 Traders' writings from the Columbia Plateau region come to us in a variety of forms, from daily field notes, log-book entries, letters, and annual reports written in their own hands to posthumously published volumes that bear the marks of literary editors. I distinguish among these forms of writing in Vibert, *Traders' Tales.*

22 For brilliant insights, see Bourdieu, *Outline of a Theory of Practice,* 72-73, 95, 159-97; de Certeau, *The Practice of Everyday Life;* Lefebvre, *Critique of Everyday Life;* and Holt, "Marking: Race, Race-Making and the Writing of History," 9, 10.

23 Butler, *Gender Trouble;* see also Bourdieu, *Outline of a Theory;* and Hall, "Conclusion: The Multi-Cultural Question." The now classic analysis of the process of imagining a nation is Anderson's *Imagined Communities.*

24 Wilson, *The Island Race,* 11-12; and Hall, *Race: The Floating Signifier.* This definition also draws on Peter Hulme's characterization of colonial discourse as an ensemble of practices "unified by their common deployment in the management of colonial relationships." Hulme, *Colonial Encounters,* 2.

25 Four-stages theory was widely professed by Scottish thinkers of the late eighteenth century. Smith, *Lectures on Jurisprudence;* Meek, *Social Science and the Ignoble Savage;* Kidd, *Forging of Races;* and Wilson, *The Island Race,* Introduction and Chapter 1.

26 Hall, *Civilising Subjects,* 10.

27 Dickason, "Europeans and a New World," 14-15. The vast majority of indigenous peoples of the Americas did not consume human flesh; some societies performed ritual consumption for various religious and political reasons. For useful insights into the heritage of European ideas about cannibalism, its polysemy, and anthropological interpretations, see Jahoda, *Images of Savages,* especially Chapters 8 and 9; Pagden, *The Fall of Natural Man;* and for Britain, Guerrini, "A Diet for a Sensitive Soul." Many travel accounts report Natives

warning of cannibals nearby. For a colourful example, see Purchas, "North Virginia Voyages, 1606-1608," especially 350.

28 Cartier, "First Account of the New Land," 22-23.

29 The Stadaconans are known widely as the St. Lawrence Iroquois and appear to have disappeared from the region between Cartier's visit and the founding of New France.

30 Cartier, "First Account of the New Land," 24-25.

31 Roy, "Reading Communities and Culinary Communities," 471. The quotation is from Sara Suleri's *Meatless Days*. On the power of the familiar in immigrant foods, see Eidinger, "Gefilte Fish and Roast Duck with Orange Slices."

32 Colpitts, *Game in the Garden*, 22, Introduction, and passim.

33 For a detailed account of the ways material concerns shaped traders' perceptions, see Vibert, *Traders' Tales*.

34 Brown, *Strangers in Blood*; Van Kirk, "*Many Tender Ties*." See Stoler's provocative review article, "Tense and Tender Ties." For a sampling of other recent work, see Ballantyne and Burton, eds., *Moving Subjects*.

35 "Metis" means, literally, "mixed" and refers to the offspring of traders and their Aboriginal wives.

36 The new rules were codified in 1828 in "Standing Rules and Regulations," Hudson's Bay Company Archives (hereafter HBCA), D.4/92, folios 88-90d. See also Fleming, ed., *Minutes of Council*, 218-31.

37 Queries Connected with Natural History, HBCA, PP 2035. Prior to the introduction of the standard questionnaire, traders would have been guided by convention and the archive of trader writings that preceded them.

38 See Marshall and Williams, *The Great Map of Mankind*, 146-48; and Meek, *Social Science and the Ignoble Savage*.

39 For an extended discussion of this hierarchical representational strategy and its tensions, see Vibert, *Traders' Tales*, and "Real Men Hunt Buffalo." "Indian" is used here as a figment of trader language to indicate that it is the *representation* of indigenous people that is at issue.

40 Fraser, *The Letters and Journals; Sir George Simpson's Journals, 1824-41*, HBCA, D.3/1, folios 61-62; and Simpson, "Journal, 1824-25," 94-95.

41 Kelm, *Colonizing Bodies*, Chapter 2.

42 George Simpson's Correspondence Inward, HBCA, D.5/19, folio 299; Payne, "Daily Life on Western Hudson Bay," 439-40; and Colpitts, *Game in the Garden*, Introduction.

43 See extended discussion of these issues in Vibert, *Traders' Tales*, 176-79.

44 James McMillan, quoted in Kamloops Post Journal, 1822-45, HBCA, B.97/a/1, folio 5.

45 Lawrence, "William Buchan: Medicine Laid Open," 32; and Lehmann, *The British Housewife*, 146.

46 Buchan, *Domestic Medicine*, 63-65.

47 Ibid., 67.

48 Flandrin, "Dietary Choices and Culinary Technique." Fish consumption remained much higher in France and other Catholic countries, partly because of religious obligations.

49 For details, see Grieco, "Food and Social Classes." Fish consumption increased again when the transportation revolution of the mid-1800s made fresh fish more widely available.

50 Mennell, *All Manners of Food*, 62, 303, Chapter 8. Sarasúa shows similar class differences for nineteenth-century Spain in "Upholding Status," 42-44. Meat consumption by the masses in Europe decreased throughout the early modern period (especially post-1700) as a result of land enclosure for grain production and a reduction of range land for animals: Flandrin, "Introduction: The Early Modern Period."

51 Thompson, *Making of the English Working Class*, 348-49; and Burnett, *A History of the Cost of Living*, 167-68.

52 Fiddes, *Meat: A Natural Symbol*, 2 and passim; and Douglas, *Implicit Meanings*.

53 According to the *Oxford English Dictionary*: "A townsman as opposed to a countryman ... a civilian as distinguished from a soldier"; according to Samuel Johnson: "A man of trade, not a gentleman." According to humoural theory, the four humours – blood, phlegm, and black and yellow bile – were believed to rise and recede in response to environmental factors and the food one consumed; the balance of these fluids had a large role in regulating health. For the persistence of this theory into the nineteenth century, see Wheeler, *The Complexion of Race*.

54 Buchan, *Domestic Medicine*, 71-72. Material on soldiers' and athletes' diets is drawn from Buchan, *New Domestic Medicine*, 19, 57, 65, 594.

55 Roy, "Meat-Eating." See also Sinha's important study *Colonial Masculinity*.

56 Buchan, *Domestic Medicine*, 74.

57 Roy, "Meat-Eating," 82.

58 These ideas are not limited to Western traditions: they have ancient provenance in India, for example, where Hindus viewed meat products as stimulating of the passions. See Roy, "Meat-Eating," 75-76. On eighteenth-century dietary therapy and meat's critics in Europe, see Guerrini, "Diet for a Sensitive Soul," 35-37. Buchan, *Domestic Medicine*, 70-72, and *New Domestic Medicine*, 57, 65.

59 For an interesting reflection on the perceived purifying properties of white foods, see Mintz, *Tasting Food, Tasting Freedom*, Chapter 6, "Color, Taste, and Purity: Some Speculations on the Meanings of Marzipan."

60 The vast majority of Columbia traders whose records remain were Scots, more than half of whom were raised in Scotland. Several more were of Scottish heritage but were born in eastern North America. Two were Irish, and one had Welsh parents and had been raised in London. For fuller detail, see Vibert, *Traders' Tales*, Chapter 1.

61 Harris, *The Resettlement of British Columbia*, 43.

62 For the ethnic mix in the Columbia Department, see Vibert, *Traders' Tales*, Chapter 1.

63 Quesnel to J.M. Lamothe, May 1809, in Fraser, *The Letters and Journals*, 262; Dears quoted in Edward Ermatinger Papers, 1820-74 (transcript), 288-90, University of British Columbia (UBC) Special Collections; McLean, *Notes of a Twenty-Five Years' Service*, 186.

64 Buchan, *Domestic Medicine*, 71, 308, 393, 426.

65 One Shetlander in the early nineteenth century described the daily diet as coalfish for breakfast, coalfish and cabbage for the midday meal, and coalfish for supper. A fur trade observer of the same period noted that young men recruited from the Scottish Isles "seldom, if Ever, Eat Any thing better than Pease or Barley Bread with Salt Sellocks [fish] and Kale." Chief Trader Ferdinand Jacobs, quoted in Payne, "Daily Life," 475, 479.

66 Greer, "Fur Trade Labour," 197-214; and Payne, "Daily Life," 471.

67 Thompson, *David Thompson's Narrative*, 487, 476, 483-84; and Thompson, *David Thompson's Journals*, 97.

68 Spokane, Report on District, HBCA, B.208/e/1, folios 2, 3; and Sir George Simpson's Journals, 1841, HBCA, D.3/2, folio 88.

69 HBCA, B.208/e/1, folio 2.

70 For useful insights, see especially Hunn, with James Selam and family, *Nch'i-Wana, "The Big River"*; and Turner, Bouchard, and Kennedy, *Ethnobotany of the Okanagan-Colville Indians*.

71 Black-Rogers, "Varieties of 'Starving'"; Fort Nez Perces Post Journal, 1831-32, HBCA, B.146/a/2, entries for 20 February and 17 March 1832; and White, "Give Us a Little Milk."

72 Hunn, with Selam and family, *Nch'i-Wana*, 132-34.
73 The quotation is from Stuart, "Robert Stuart's Narratives," 62.
74 John McLeod Papers, folio 53, Library and Archives Canada. For similar remarks, see HBCA, B.208/e/1, folio 7; and Kamloops Report on District, 1827, HBCA, B.97/e/1, folio 4.
75 The middle-class element here is key. A commonplace middle-class critique of aristocratic culture held that the rich were decadent and careless – the view had transnational signifi- cance. Sarasúa, "Upholding Status," 56.
76 Thompson, *David Thompson's Narrative*, 417. See Malthus, *On Population*; Himmelfarb, *The Idea of Poverty*, Chapter 4; and Porter, "Mixed Feelings," 16.
77 See, for example, Tobin, "And there raise yams"; and Carlyle, "Occasional Discourse on the Negro Question." For reflections on the supposed laziness of First Nations peoples in British Columbia, see Lutz, *Makúk*.
78 Vibert, "Real Men Hunt Buffalo."
79 See Simpson, "Journal 1824-25."
80 Hall, *Civilising Subjects*, 27. See also the classic portrayal of solidifying middle-class gender identities in Britain in this era in Davidoff and Hall, *Family Fortunes*, especially 108-18 for manhood.
81 John McLoughlin to Edward Ermatinger, 1 February 1836, Edward Ermatinger Papers, 237- 38, UBC Special Collections.
82 Ross, *Fur Hunters of the Far West*, 19-20. Ross's claims are supported by NWC documents from 1806 that regulate rations of coffee and chocolate within the officer ranks: proprietors were to get six pounds of tea, four pounds of coffee, and four pounds of chocolate per winter. Principal clerks in charge of posts got somewhat less, and inferior clerks merited but a pound of tea and no coffee or chocolate. Interpreters and guides, who were at the top of the servant hierarchy, were entitled to none of these rations. See Ritchie, "Expecta- tions of Grease and Provisions," 124. For more on the disciplines of social sorting and labour force control, see Podruchny, "Unfair Masters and Rascally Servants?"
83 Mintz, *Sweetness and Power*, 185.
84 North West Company practice at headquarters allowed high-ranking servants to dine in the same hall as their superiors; they sat, however, at pine trestle tables and benches as opposed to the Hepplewhite table and Chippendale chairs of the bourgeois (officers). See Ritchie, "Expectations of Grease and Provisions," 131. Also see Fleming, ed., *Minutes of Council*, 25-26; and Fort Vancouver, Correspondence Book, 1825-33, HBCA, B.223/b/4, folio 31.
85 Ritchie, "Expectations of Grease and Provisions," 131. The foodstuffs in this example were consumed at Fort William; similar imports found their way to Columbia headquarters at Fort Vancouver.
86 HBCA, B.97/e/1, folio 3.
87 Thomas Farnham Jefferson, quoted in Loo, *Making Law, Order, and Authority*, 29.
88 Harris, *Resettlement of British Columbia*, 57.
89 On physical cues, see Hamilton, "Fur Trade Social Inequality," 74. See also Loo, *Making Law, Order, and Authority*, Chapter 1; and Harris, *Resettlement of British Columbia*, 43.
90 Ross, *Fur Hunters*, 72. This passage draws closely on *Traders' Tales*, 113-17.
91 Ross, *Fur Hunters*, 180.
92 As the decades wore on, the discourse became increasingly inflected with the language of racial contagion, the fear that white men would be deracinated by their attachments to First Nations women. Perry, "Reproducing Colonialism in British Columbia." See also Young, *Colonial Desire*; and Van Kirk, *"Many Tender Ties."* For parallel shifts in other imperial domains, see Hall, *Civilising Subjects*.

93 For the importance of domestic practice to cultural identity in a later period, see Raibmon, "Living on Display"; on the often-unfulfilled promise of white women, see Perry, *On the Edge of Empire*.
94 Comaroff and Comaroff, "Homemade Hegemony," 293.

Bibliography

Archival Sources

Hudson's Bay Company Archives (HBCA)
B.97/a/1, folio 5. Kamloops Post Journal, 1822-46.
B.97/e/1, folios 3, 4. Kamloops Report on District, 1827.
B.146/a/2. Fort Nez Perces Post Journal, 1831-32.
B.208/e/1, folios 2, 3, 7. Spokane, Report on District, 1822-23.
B.223/b/4, folio 31. Fort Vancouver, Correspondence Book, 1825-33.
D.3/1, folios 61-62. Sir George Simpson's Journals, 1824-41.
D.3/2, folio 88. Sir George Simpson's Journals, 1841.
D.4/92, folios 88-90d. Sir George Simpson's Official Reports to the Governor and Committee, "Standing Rules and Regulations," 1829-32.
D.5/19, folio 299. Sir George Simpson's Correspondence Inward, 1846-47.
PP 2035, Queries Connected with Natural History.

Library and Archives Canada
John McLeod Papers. Folio 53. Microfilm in British Columbia Archives and Records Service, A 1656.

University of British Columbia (UBC) Special Collections
Edward Ermatinger Papers, 1820-74.

Published Sources
Anderson, Benedict. *Imagined Communities: Reflections on the Origin and Spread of Nationalism.* London: Verso, 1983.
Auslander, Leora. "Beyond Words." *American Historical Review* 110, 4 (2005): 227-47.
Ballantyne, Tony, and Antoinette Burton, eds. *Moving Subjects: Gender, Mobility and Intimacy in an Age of Global Empire.* Champagne/Urbana: University of Illinois Press, 2009.
Bentley, Amy. "Reading Food Riots: Scarcity, Abundance and National Identity." In *Food, Drink and Identity: Cooking, Eating and Drinking in Europe since the Middle Ages,* edited by Peter Scholliers, 179-93. Oxford: Berg, 2002.
Black-Rogers, Mary. "Varieties of 'Starving': Semantics and Survival in the Subarctic Fur Trade." *Ethnohistory* 33, 4 (1986): 353-83.
Bourdieu, Pierre. *Outline of a Theory of Practice.* Cambridge: Cambridge University Press, 1977.
Brown, Jennifer S.H. *Strangers in Blood: Fur Trade Company Families in Indian Country.* Vancouver: UBC Press, 1980.
Buchan, William. *Domestic Medicine: Or, a Treatise on the Prevention and Cure of Diseases by Regimen and Simple Medicines.* 14th edition. London: A. Strahan and T. Cadell, 1794.
–. *The New Domestic Medicine: Or a Treatise on the Prevention and Cure of Diseases, by Regimen and Simple Medicines.* London: Thomas Kelly, 1827.
Burnett, John. *A History of the Cost of Living.* London: Pelican Books, 1969.

Butler, Judith. *Gender Trouble: Feminism and the Subversion of Identity*. London: Routledge, 1990.

Carlyle, Thomas. "Occasional Discourse on the Negro Question." *Fraser's Magazine* (1849). Reprinted in Thomas Carlyle, *English and Other Critical Essays*. Vol. 2. London: Dent, 1964.

Cartier, Jacques. "First Account of the New Land, Called New France, Discovered in the Year 1534." In *The Voyages of Jacques Cartier*, edited and translated by Ramsay Cook. Toronto: University of Toronto Press, 1993.

Certeau, Michel de. *The Practice of Everyday Life*. Berkeley: University of California Press, 1984.

Colley, Linda. *Britons: Forging the Nation, 1707-1837*. New Haven, CT: Yale University Press, 1992.

–. *Captives: Britain, Empire and the World 1600-1850*. London: Jonathan Cape, 2002.

Colpitts, George. *Game in the Garden: A Human History of Wildlife in Western Canada to 1940*. Vancouver: UBC Press, 2002.

Comaroff, John, and Jean Comaroff. "Homemade Hegemony." In *Ethnography and the Historical Imagination*, 265-96. Boulder, CO: Westview, 1992.

Cooper, Frederick, and Ann Laura Stoler. "Between Colony and Metropole: Rethinking a Research Agenda." In *Tensions of Empire: Colonial Cultures in a Bourgeois World*, edited by Frederick Cooper and Ann Laura Stoler, 198-237. Berkeley: University of California Press, 1997.

Davidoff, Leonore, and Catherine Hall. *Family Fortunes: Men and Women of the English Middle Class, 1780-1850*. London: Hutchinson, 1987.

Dickason, Olive. "Europeans and a New World Cosmography in the 1500s." In *Reading beyond Words: Contexts for Native History*, edited by Jennifer S.H. Brown and Elizabeth Vibert, 4-20. Peterborough, ON: Broadview Press, 1996.

Diner, Hasia. *Hungering for America: Italian, Irish, and Jewish Foodways in the Age of Immigration*. Cambridge, MA: Harvard University Press, 2001.

Douglas, Mary. *Implicit Meanings: Essays in Anthropology*. London: Routledge, 1975.

–. "Standard Social Uses of Food: Introduction." In *Food in the Social Order*, edited by Mary Douglas, 1-39. New York: Russell Sage Foundation, 1984.

Eidinger, Andrea. "Gefilte Fish and Roast Duck with Orange Slices: *A Treasure for My Daughter* and the Creation of a Jewish Cultural Orthodoxy in Postwar Montreal." Unpublished paper in possession of the author.

Ferguson, Priscilla Parkhurst. *Accounting for Taste: The Triumph of French Cuisine*. Chicago: University of Chicago Press, 2004.

Fiddes, Nick. *Meat: A Natural Symbol*. London: Routledge, 1991.

Flandrin, Jean-Louis. "Dietary Choices and Culinary Technique, 1500-1800." In *Food: A Culinary History from Antiquity to the Present*, edited by Jean-Louis Flandrin and Massimo Montanari, 403-17. New York: Columbia University Press, 1999.

–. "Introduction: The Early Modern Period." In *Food: A Culinary History from Antiquity to the Present*, edited by Jean-Louis Flandrin and Massimo Montanari, 1-9. New York: Columbia University Press, 1999.

Fleming, R. Harvey, ed. *Minutes of Council, Northern Department of Rupert Land, 1821-31*. Toronto: Champlain Society, 1940.

Foucault, Michel. *Discipline and Punish: The Birth of the Prison*. Translated by Alan Sheridan. New York: Vintage, 1979.

Fraser, Simon. *The Letters and Journals of Simon Fraser, 1806-1808*. Edited by W. Kaye Lamb. Toronto: Macmillan, 1960.

Gabaccia, Donna. *We Are What We Eat: Ethnic Food and the Making of Americans.* Cambridge, MA: Harvard University Press, 1998.

Gallagher, Catherine, and Stephen Greenblatt. "Introduction." In *Practicing New Historicism*, 1-19. Chicago: University of Chicago Press, 2000.

–. "The Potato in the Materialist Imagination." In *Practicing New Historicism*, 100-35. Chicago: University of Chicago Press, 2000.

Greer, Allan. "Fur Trade Labour and Lower Canadian Agricultural Structures." *Historical Papers,* Canadian Historical Association (1981): 197-214.

Grieco, Allen. "Food and Social Classes in Late Medieval and Renaissance Italy." In *Food: A Culinary History from Antiquity to the Present,* edited by Jean-Louis Flandrin and Massimo Montanari, 302-12. New York: Columbia University Press, 1999.

Grignon, Claude. "Commensality and Social Morphology: An Essay of Typology." In *Food, Drink and Identity: Cooking, Eating and Drinking in Europe since the Middle Ages,* edited by Peter Scholliers, 23-35. Oxford: Berg, 2001.

Guerrini, Anita. "A Diet for a Sensitive Soul: Vegetarianism in Eighteenth-Century Britain." *Eighteenth-Century Life* 23, 2 (1999): 34-42.

Hall, Catherine. *Civilising Subjects: Metropole and Colony in the English Imagination, 1830-1867.* Chicago: University of Chicago Press, 2002.

–. "Introduction: Thinking the Postcolonial, Thinking the Empire." In *Cultures of Empire: A Reader,* edited by Catherine Hall, 1-36. London: Routledge, 2000.

–. "The Rule of Difference: Gender, Class and Empire in the Making of the 1832 Reform Act." In *Gendered Nations: Nationalisms and Gender Order in the Long Nineteenth Century,* edited by Ida Blom, Karen Hagemann, and Catherine Hall, 107-36. Oxford: Berg, 2000.

–. "William Knibb and the Constitution of the New Black Subject." In *Empire and Others: British Encounters with Indigenous Peoples, 1600-1850,* edited by Martin Daunton and Rick Halpern, 303-24. Philadelphia: University of Pennsylvania Press, 1999.

Hall, Stuart. "Conclusion: The Multi-Cultural Question." In *Un/Settled Multiculturalisms: Diasporas, Entanglements, Disruptions,* edited by Barnor Hesse, 209-40. London: Zed, 2001.

–. "Cultural Identity and Diaspora." In *Diaspora and Visual Culture: Representing Africans and Jews,* edited by Nicholas Mirzoeff, 21-33. London: Routledge, 2000.

–. *Race: The Floating Signifier.* Northampton, MA: Media Education Foundation, 1996.

Hamilton, James Scott. "Fur Trade Social Inequality and the Role of Non-Verbal Communication." PhD diss., Simon Fraser University, 1990.

Harris, Cole. *The Resettlement of British Columbia: Essays on Colonialism and Geographical Change.* Vancouver: UBC Press, 1997.

Himmelfarb, Gertrude. *The Idea of Poverty: England in the Early Industrial Age.* New York: Knopf, 1984.

Holt, Thomas. "Marking: Race, Race-Making and the Writing of History." *American Historical Review* 100, 1 (1995): 1-17.

Hulme, Peter. *Colonial Encounters: Europe and the Native Caribbean, 1492-1797.* London: Methuen, 1986.

Hunn, Eugene, with James Selam and family. *Nch'i-Wana, "The Big River": Middle Columbia Indians and Their Land.* Seattle: University of Washington Press, 1990.

Jahoda, Gustav. *Images of Savages: Ancient Roots of Modern Prejudice in Western Culture.* London: Routledge, 1999.

Kelm, Mary-Ellen. *Colonizing Bodies: Aboriginal Health and Healing in British Columbia, 1900-50.* Vancouver: UBC Press, 1998.

Kidd, Colin. *The Forging of Races: Race and Scripture in the Protestant Atlantic World.* Cambridge: Cambridge University Press, 2006.

Kupperman, Karen. "Reading Indian Bodies." Chapter 2 in *Indians and English: Facing Off in Early America*. Ithaca, NY: Cornell University Press, 2000.

Lawrence, C.J. "William Buchan: Medicine Laid Open." *Medical History* 19 (1975): 20-35.

Lefebvre, Henri. *Critique of Everyday Life*. 3 vols. Edited by John Moore. London: Verso, 1991-2005.

Lehmann, Gilly. *The British Housewife: Cookery Books, Cooking and Society in Eighteenth-Century Britain*. Totnes: Prospect, 2003.

Loo, Tina. *Making Law, Order, and Authority in British Columbia, 1821-1871*. Toronto: University of Toronto Press, 1994.

Lutz, John. *Makúk: A New History of Aboriginal-White Relations*. Vancouver: UBC Press, 2008.

Malthus, Thomas. *On Population*. Edited by Gertrude Himmelfarb. New York: Modern Library, 1960.

Marshall, P.J., and Glyndwr Williams. *The Great Map of Mankind: British Perceptions of the World in the Age of Enlightenment*. London: Dent, 1982.

McLean, John. *Notes of a Twenty-Five Years' Service in the Hudson's Bay Territories*. Edited by W.S. Wallace. Toronto: Champlain Society, 1932 [1849].

Meek, R.L. *Social Science and the Ignoble Savage*. Cambridge: Cambridge University Press, 1976.

Mennell, Stephen. *All Manners of Food: Eating and Taste in England and France from the Middle Ages to the Present*. Oxford: Basil Blackwell, 1985.

Milanovic, Branko. *Worlds Apart: Measuring International and Global Inequality*. Princeton, NJ: Princeton University Press, 2005.

Mintz, Sidney W. *Sweetness and Power: The Place of Sugar in Modern History*. New York: Viking, 1985.

–. *Tasting Food, Tasting Freedom*. Boston: Beacon Press, 1996.

Montaigne, Michel de. "Of Cannibals." In *The Complete Essays of Montaigne*. Vol. 1. Translated by Donald Frame. New York: Doubleday, 1960 [1580].

Pagden, Anthony. *The Fall of Natural Man*. Cambridge: Cambridge University Press, 1982.

Payne, Michael. "Daily Life on Western Hudson Bay, 1714 to 1870: A Social History of York Factory and Churchill." PhD diss., Carleton University, 1989.

Perry, Adele. *On the Edge of Empire: Gender, Race and the Making of British Columbia*. Toronto: University of Toronto Press, 2001.

–. "Reproducing Colonialism in British Columbia, 1849-1871." In *Bodies in Contact: Rethinking Colonial Encounters in World History*, edited by Tony Ballantyne and Antoinette Burton, 143-63. Durham: Duke University Press, 2005.

Podruchny, Carolyn. "Unfair Masters and Rascally Servants? Labour Relations among Bourgeois, Clerks, and Voyageurs in the Montreal Fur Trade, 1780-1821." *Labour/Le Travail* 43 (Spring 1999): 43-70.

Porter, Roy. "Mixed Feelings: The Enlightenment and Sexuality in Eighteenth-Century Britain." *Sexuality in Eighteenth-Century Britain*, edited by Paul-Gabriel Bouc, 1-27. Manchester: Manchester University Press, 1982.

Pratt, Mary Louise. *Imperial Eyes: Travel Writing and Transculturation*. London: Routledge, 1992.

Purchas, Samuel. "North Virginia Voyages, 1606-1608." In *The English New England Voyages, 1602-1608*, edited by D.B. Quinn and A.M. Quinn. London: Hakluyt Society, 1983.

Raibmon, Paige. "Living on Display: Colonial Visions of Aboriginal Domestic Spaces." In *Home, Work, and Play: Situating Canadian Social History, 1840-1980*, edited by James Opp and John Walsh, 18-32. Don Mills, ON: Oxford University Press, 2006.

Ritchie, Leslie. "'Expectations of Grease and Provisions': The Circulation and Regulation of Fur Trade Foodstuffs." *Eighteenth-Century Life* 23, 2 (1999): 124-42.

Ross, Alexander. *Fur Hunters of the Far West.* Edited by Kenneth A. Spaulding. Norman: University of Oklahoma Press, 1956 [1855].

Roy, Parama. "Meat-Eating, Masculinity, and Renunciation in India: A Gandhian Grammar of Diet." *Gender and History* 14, 1 (2002): 62-91.

–. "Reading Communities and Culinary Communities: The Gastropoetics of the South Asian Diaspora." *Positions: East Asia Cultures Critique* 10, 2 (2002): 471-502.

Said, Edward. *Orientalism.* New York: Vintage, 1979.

Sarasúa, Carmen. "Upholding Status: The Diet of a Noble Family in Early Nineteenth-Century La Mancha." In *Food, Drink and Identity: Cooking, Eating and Drinking in Europe since the Middle Ages,* edited by Peter Scholliers, 37-62. Oxford: Berg, 2002.

Scholliers, Peter. "Meals, Food Narratives, and Sentiments of Belonging in Past and Present." In *Food, Drink and Identity: Cooking, Eating and Drinking in Europe since the Middle Ages,* edited by Peter Scholliers, 3-22. Oxford: Berg, 2002.

Sen, Amartya. *Poverty and Famines: An Essay on Entitlement and Deprivation.* Oxford: Clarendon Press, 1982.

Simpson, George. "Journal, 1824-25: Remarks Connected with the Fur Trade ..." In *Fur Trade and Empire: George Simpson's Journal,* edited by Frederick Merck. Cambridge, MA: Harvard University Press, 1968.

Sinha, Mrinalini. *Colonial Masculinity: The "Manly Englishman" and the "Effeminate Bengali" in the Late Nineteenth Century.* Manchester: Manchester University Press, 1995.

Smith, Adam. *Lectures on Jurisprudence.* Edited by R.L. Meek. Oxford: Clarendon Press, 1978.

Stoler, Ann Laura. "Tense and Tender Ties: The Politics of Comparison in North American History and (Post) Colonial Studies." *Journal of American History* 88, 3 (2001): 829-65.

Stuart, Robert. "Robert Stuart's Narratives." In *The Discovery of the Oregon Trail,* edited by Phillip A. Rollins. New York: Edward Eberstadt, 1935.

Suleri, Sara. *Meatless Days.* Chicago: University of Chicago Press, 1991.

Tarlo, Emma. *Clothing Matters: Dress and Identity in India.* Chicago: University of Chicago Press, 1996.

Thompson, David. *David Thompson's Journals Relating to Montana and Adjacent Regions, 1808-1812.* Edited by M. Catherine White. Missoula: Montana State University Press, 1950.

–. *David Thompson's Narrative of His Explorations in Western America, 1784-1812.* Edited by J.B. Tyrrell. Toronto: Champlain Society, 1916.

Thompson, E.P. *The Making of the English Working Class.* London: Victor Gollancz, 1963.

–. "The Moral Economy of the English Crowd in the Eighteenth Century." *Past and Present* 50 (1971): 76-136.

Tobin, Beth Fowkes. "'And there raise yams': Slaves' Gardens in the Writings of West Indian Plantocrats." *Eighteenth-Century Life* 23, 2 (1999): 164-76.

Turner, Nancy, Randy Bouchard, and Dorothy Kennedy. *Ethnobotany of the Okanagan-Colville Indians.* Victoria: Royal British Columbia Museum, 1980.

Van Kirk, Sylvia. *"Many Tender Ties": Women in Fur-Trade Society in Western Canada.* Winnipeg: Watson and Dwyer, 1980.

Vibert, Elizabeth. "Real Men Hunt Buffalo: Masculinity, Race and Class in British Fur Traders' Narratives." In *Cultures of Empire: A Reader,* edited by Catherine Hall, 281-97. London: Routledge, 2000.

–. *Traders' Tales: Narratives of Cultural Encounters in the Columbia Plateau.* Norman: University of Oklahoma Press, 1997.

Wheeler, Roxann. *The Complexion of Race: Categories of Difference in Eighteenth-Century British Culture.* Philadelphia: University of Pennsylvania Press, 2000.

White, Bruce. "'Give Us a Little Milk': The Social and Cultural Significance of Gift Giving in the Lake Superior Fur Trade." *Minnesota History* 48, 2 (1982): 60-71.

Williams, Raymond. *Keywords: A Vocabulary of Culture and Society.* London: Croom Helm, 1976.

Wilson, Kathleen. *The Island Race: Englishness, Empire and Gender in the Eighteenth Century.* London: Routledge, 2003.

Wrigley, Richard. *The Politics of Appearances: Representations of Dress in Revolutionary France.* Oxford: Berg, 2002.

Young, Robert. *Colonial Desire: Hybridity in Theory, Culture, and Race.* London: Routledge, 1995.

6

"Make it last forever as it is": John McDonald of Garth's Vision of a Native Kingdom in the Northwest

Germaine Warkentin

"I AM AS WELL ACQUAINTED with Red River and Saskatchewan – their sources and tributaries in all their length and breadth until they empty themselves into Lake Winnipeg as I was with the deck of the miserable Isaac Todd before we got to the Brazils – where I alone quelled a mutiny amongst the sailors in five minutes."[1] So wrote the eighty-six-year-old North West Company (NWC) trader John McDonald of Garth to Edward Ellice, an influential stockholder in the Hudson's Bay Company (HBC), on 16 July 1857. It was on the *Isaac Todd* that McDonald had rounded Cape Horn in 1813, and the incident of the mutiny is recounted with characteristic relish in his still-unedited "Autobiographical Notes."[2] Born of minor gentry in Scotland around 1771 and handicapped by a withered right arm (his nickname was "le bras croche"), McDonald arrived in the Northwest in 1791, where he traded on behalf of the NWC for two decades. In 1814, he retired near Cornwall, Upper Canada, where other fur trade men were settling, among them his brother-in-law, the explorer David Thompson. In 1816, he built a fine Regency cottage, Inverarden, and furnished it elegantly.[3] But he abandoned it to his metis wife, Nancy Small, in 1823, when he married Amelia, niece of another prosperous Nor'Wester, Hugh McGillis. With his second wife, he settled close by at Garth, Gray's Creek, where he served as justice of the peace and judge, supervised his tenants, and observed Canadian politics with sardonic interest.

John McDonald of Garth is remembered chiefly for his bravado, his mischievous account of rescuing David Thompson from the Blackfoot in 1808, and the letter to posterity he co-signed with Simon Fraser in August 1859. "We are the last of the old North West partners," McDonald and Fraser wrote, and their words have been quoted many times: "We have braved many dangers, run many risks." They had done no wrong, they claimed; they had been feared and respected by the Natives and had kept their men under subordination. "We have both crossed this continent ... We have met many new Tribes, We have run our Race, & as this is probably the last time we meet on earth, we part as we have lived in sincere friendship and mutual good will."[4] In April 1859, Sir George Simpson, governor of the HBC, sent a few cordial lines to the old gentleman for inclusion in his "Autobiographical Notes." Simpson's sharp tongue was perhaps reined in on this occasion, for, as he admitted, he had not been personally acquainted with McDonald. Simpson praised McDonald as one of the leading men of his day and went on to note his general popularity, "itself evidence of many good qualities ... your influence over the Indians, both by your kindness and firmness, the admirable discipline maintained among the servants under your command: your knowledge of the arts most useful in the Indian country; your dexterity as a canoe man, huntsman and horseman; your courage and enterprise ... your past useful and active life."[5] Two images reflect the contrasts between this earlier, active McDonald and the old man Simpson was addressing: Donald Hill's romantic portrait of McDonald around 1800, when the explorer was in his prime, and William Notman's photograph of a grim ninety-one-year-old McDonald taken in 1862 (see Figures 6.1 and 6.2).

McDonald had served a useful and active life – as Simpson acknowledged – but in the old man's view, at least, his usefulness had not yet come to an end. In 1936, the explorer's grandson, DeLery Macdonald, wrote to the Montreal *Gazette* that McDonald had "furnished, in his 90th year, much valuable information to the Government, when the purchase of the Hudson Bay Territories was being debated."[6] In his last decade, the old trader not only wrote an account of his experiences in the West, but he also attempted, whenever he could, to engage men in public life in a program to protect what he viewed as the finest country in the world from policies he was certain would ruin its greatest resources. To him, these resources were not only the animals sought by the fur trade but also the region's people, the Native peoples and metis (in the fashion of the day, he called them halfbreeds), who were so superlatively adapted to life there. As the decade passed, he came to terms with the idea of settlement, but he never gave up the dream of a great kingdom in the West, one that would be populated with hunters and defended by a Native militia, which would keep the region safe from petty traders and blind politicians on the other side of a carefully drawn boundary.

Using the almost unknown trove of unpublished letters McDonald wrote to circulate his ideas, this chapter shows how an elderly man who was fated to become a minor character in fur trade history sought to contribute to the resolution of an essentially modern geopolitical issue: the Native presence in North America.[7] Unhappily, to the men he was addressing, that presence was merely an obstacle to economic expansion. Furthermore, McDonald's own understanding of the geopolitics of the Native presence in North America was deeply flawed, first by his pre-modern, and thus primarily hierarchical understanding of the internal and external governance of nations, and second by his failure to consider what Native peoples themselves might have had to say about his proposals. Nevertheless, if we dig deeper, we see in McDonald's frustrated

Figure 6.1 The young John McDonald of Garth, painted in the late eighteenth or early nineteenth century by Donald Hill. McCord Museum, Montreal, M1594.

Figure 6.2 John McDonald of Garth, 1862, photographed by William Notman.
McCord Museum, Montreal, I-3554.1.

but ever optimistic project a perception of the West as an organic entity more evolved by far than that of the easterners he was trying to persuade and well worth our attention today, not for its specific (unworkable) recommendations but for its wider conceptual power, which, as the documents in this case show, was exceptional in the milieu in which he lived.

Although Robert J. Burns writes that McDonald's letters "displayed an amazing grasp of the economy and ecology of the west,"[8] what the old man actually said, and why he said it, are still almost unknown. Larry Green, author of the only intensive study of McDonald's autobiographical notes, blames this neglect on A.S. Morton's dismissive attitude to "that blusterer" and on the crudely excerpted version of the autobiography published by L.R. Masson.[9] To Green, McDonald's memoir of the old Northwest contains "some of the most vibrant, picturesque writing to be found in the fur-trade literature."[10] McDonald's twenty-odd years in the Northwest took him, over one decade, from the position of clerk under Angus Shaw at Moose Lake (in present-day Manitoba) to wintering partner to partner in charge of Fort des Prairies (in present-day Alberta), the largest of the NWC's departments. His autobiographical notes are rich both in the anecdotes of a trader and partner's life and in the insight accumulated during a professional lifetime of trading with and employing Native people. And given McDonald's doughty reputation – amply confirmed by his cheerfully egotistical prose – his notes reveal both a forthright acceptance of the Natives as they were and an unexpected openness to the delights of the place. "This we thought the most pleasant part of our lives," he writes of trailing his canoe brigade on horseback, "the riding a swift horse in the fine valley of the Saskatchewan – abounding [with] buffalo, and deers and all game – we rode all day, following the progress of the brigade against a current of four knots."[11] In the appeals that he wrote in his dotage, as he called it, the same wonder is expressed several times as he tries to explain why the Northwest should be treated as a different kind of colony.[12] What was the relationship in the mind of this acute old explorer-trader between his rich experience in the West, his urgent desire to shape current policy, and his private imaginings?

Irene Spry writes that, when Rupert's Land and the Native territories were transferred to Canada in 1870,

> nearly all the inhabitants (apart from the people of Red River Settlement) were wandering bands of Indians and groups of Metis hunters. The few settled communities consisted of fur trade personnel at the scattered Hudson's Bay Company posts; a handful of mission-based settlements ... [and] two or three semi-permanent clusters of cabins ... Even the inhabitants of such settlements spent much of their lives travelling in pursuit of buffalo or as tripmen and freighters

... Most of the population depended for its basic subsistence on the natural products of the countries over which they roamed and hunted. These products were open to use by the Indian bands that claimed the territory as their hunting grounds and by anyone else who could gain access to that territory ... Within their own hunting grounds each tribe lived off the land, using space, shelter, water, game, fish, timber and wild plants in accordance with customary patterns, well understood and respected by all the members of the tribe.[13]

By the 1850s, however, conflict had escalated between Native peoples and metis over control of the hunt and between Cree and Blackfoot over the food supply. American whisky traders pressed hard to sell alcohol to the Native peoples, and epidemic disease was a constant threat.[14] Debate about the future of the HBC charter, the expansionist H.Y. Hind's explorations on behalf of the Canadian legislature (1857-58), and Captain John Palliser's explorations on behalf of England's Colonial Office (1857-59) all showed that Native peoples' dominion in the West was passing away.

In 1857, McDonald told Edward Ellice that "I know more of the country than any others but I am no writer to write a book on the subject."[15] But that is precisely what he did two years later, during a hiatus between the two groups of letters examined below. In a sense, the letters and the autobiographical notes form a seamless whole. The first group of letters was written in 1857 and 1858 in response to the establishment in Britain of the House of Commons' select committee to review the charter of the HBC. William Henry Draper, chief justice of the Court of Common Pleas, Canada West, had been appointed as observer by Attorney General John A. Macdonald. He set sail for England amidst a hail of imprecations from the Toronto *Globe,* the organ of the expansionist policies of the Reform Party, for whom the appointment of "Sweet William" was a rank piece of political jobbery. Nevertheless, although he had been ill-briefed, Draper's performance in London would prove to be exemplary.[16] McDonald wrote several times both to Draper and to Ellice; the latter, because of his investments in the HBC, was the only British MP appointed to the select committee who could pretend to much knowledge of North America.

The main impetus behind the second group of letters (written in 1864-65) was probably the formation of the Great Coalition that produced the discussions at Charlottetown in 1864 and the seventy-two resolutions devised at Quebec and presented to the legislature in February 1865. In a prefatory epistle to the "Autobiographical Notes," McDonald explains to his son De Bellefeuille that he had written about his life in response to his son's insistence, but it is likely that the impulse to set down the record of his experience in the West was also related to his intense preoccupation throughout this crucial period with the political future of the territory.

McDonald put forward his 1857 proposals at a critical moment. The immediate issue was not simply the renewal of the Hudson's Bay Company's monopoly licence to trade, which had been awarded in 1838 and was due to expire in 1859. The United States – moving steadily westward, and shortly to become an intimidating military power – was emerging as a serious threat to British North America. What was to become of the Northwest if these opposing forces – one in colonial infancy and the other already more industrialized than many a European power – were to duel over this vast territory? Early British policy in North America was exemplified by the Proclamation Line, drawn in 1763 between the old and new colonies and Native territory. It was based on the assumption that Natives were self-governing peoples to be approached, as had been the practice, through diplomacy and prevented from exploitation by Europeans, whether the defeated French or the westward-looking Americans. But by the 1840s, as a result of propaganda by religious groups, a movement to "civilize" Native peoples had evolved and had been codified in the Indian Acts of 1857 and 1869. These acts substituted European ideals of individual responsibility and property tenure for the Native concept of common property; their goal was not the protection of Native peoples, but rather their assimilation.[17] Significantly, when the establishment of a confederated northern nation that would stretch from sea to sea was debated at Quebec in 1865, little was said about the Northwest or, shockingly, the Native peoples who lived there.[18]

McDonald's proposal was based on his western experience of five decades earlier, rather than on the unstable conditions of the 1850s, and on his assumption – unstated but evident – that the Crown would continue to protect Native peoples from exploitation. But he also took into consideration the future of the Oregon Territory (to be secured to the British) and California (to be secured to the Mexicans) and appealed to all the crowned heads of Europe to unite behind the notion of a new independent nation west of the Mississippi. In his letters, we can trace how the grand scheme he was proposing met first with practical obstacles then slowly adapted to changing circumstances but somehow retained its initial visionary hopes. The letters reveal the old trader combining the sagacity, impulse to action, and shrewd assessment of power relations evident in his autobiographical notes with an imaginative, though by the late 1850s utterly unrealizable, geopolitical vision.

McDonald's scheme appears in what is evidently a draft prospectus that was to be sent to interested parties and is now included with his letters in McGill University Library. The document is undated, and there is no evidence indicating to whom it was sent – or if it was sent at all. But the restatement of several points made in the single letter that remains of several written to Draper shows that the ideas the prospectus set forth were the basis on which he began. I reproduce it here in full:

My [— —]

In order to preserve the natives of North America from destruction, in order to prevent the farther aggression of the American republic, in order to secure the Oregon Territory to the British Government as well as California to the Mexican Government, in order to secure the Canadas to the British Government, in order to prevent a continual state of warfare amongst the different tribes of natives and to secure peace and amity amongst them:

It is necessary to organize all the different tribes under one head – as Chief – or crowned head, i.e. to form a federal union of all the natives under one general government and to make the Mississippi River the fixed boundary between that government and the American republic.

For this purpose all the crowned heads of Europe should combine to accomplish this object, viz: to form a new independent nation west of the Mississippi River.

The way to accomplish this vital Object is plain and easy, viz:

Firstly, a wise chief to be selected, under whatever name might be deemed best to give him.

Secondly, a stronghold in a fertile part of the country – suitable, and central – to be built as a place of resistance for this head.

Thirdly, a certain number of the principal chiefs of every tribe to be selected as ministers and counsellors to this head.

Fourthly, a body of five hundred horse, and five hundred infantry of chosen young warriors drafted from all the tribes in equal proportion to be formed, to enable this head to support his authority and obey the laws.

["Fifthly" omitted accidentally in original draft.]

Sixthly, agriculture encouraged, also manufactures and mills, etc.

Seventhly, missionaries and schoolmasters sent among the tribes.

Eighthly, limits and boundaries fixed between the tribes alloting to each tribe certain grounds as hunting grounds, etc.

Ninthly, all the tribes now residing within the limits of the United Canadas to be sent west of the Mississippi as part of this confederacy, the property now belonging to them to be purchased by government and paid by yearly instalments in presents and part in paying the expenses of their removal.

Tenthly, all the expenses in this undertaking to be paid by the sovereigns of Europe and their independence declared. Consuls from each power appointed to reside at the seat of Government and an annual allowance made by each European government to support this power for a limited number of years, until everything was fully settled and the different tribes reconciled to the change and subjected to this one Power. All which is submitted to — —.

N.B. An independent confederacy of this kind is the only barrier against the unbounded wish of the American republic to possess all North America, the only way to limit their territory and prevent them getting the Oregon Territory and California, the only safety to Canada, and much better than a dozen regiments and strong fortresses or allies offensive and defensive. The tribes west and north west of the Mississippi may be computed at 50,000 Warriors.[19]

It is easy at this late date, when there are few crowned heads left in Europe, to mock McDonald's proposal, but if we turn from his specific recommendations to the problems they were intended to remedy and the ideas he brought to bear on them, another picture emerges.

First, McDonald was obviously concerned with, and had sympathy for, Native peoples and their way of life as he had witnessed it on the Prairies. Second, McDonald assumed that the form of Native society was intelligible to minds shaped by the British experience rather than the aggressiveness of the American republic. "Republic" is a key word, for the prospectus sets out a fundamentally hierarchical – that is, pre-democratic – view of social organization. Third, McDonald pointed to the Mississippi River as the obvious geographical boundary line between a Native state and a white one, because, as Chief Justice Draper would later tell the Select Committee on the Hudson's Bay Company, at that time the headwaters of the Mississippi formed the presumed western boundary of the Province of Canada.[20] Fourth, he unrealistically believed that all Native peoples in the Canadas could be moved west, though he insisted that they should be reimbursed for the property they left behind. Finally, as one would expect of a man of his times, McDonald assumed that war was the natural political condition between peoples. However, he saw war as primarily defensive rather than acquisitive. That the sovereigns of Europe would be willing to unite to accomplish his scheme must have seemed perfectly obvious to someone who was equally certain that the diverse Native peoples of this new West would be willing to unite under "one head as Chief or crowned head."

McDonald nowhere mentions the most obvious analogies for his plan: the Proclamation Line of 1763, which divided settlers from Indian Territory in British North America, and the American legislative process after 1804, which was used to move US tribes west and culminated in the Indian Removal Act of 1834, the act that established much of present-day Oklahoma as Indian Territory.

Andrew Jackson's proposed Western Territory Bill of 1834, which embodied the concept of a tribal confederacy, was never passed, and by the 1850s the land was being opened for white settlement.[21] Although McDonald was an unusually energetic, experienced, and well-informed man, his mind, like that of the contemporaries he had outlasted, had been shaped not by the territorial and economic imperatives of modern American legislators but by the political mentality of a time before Waterloo, when it was assumed that the normal actor in a geopolitical situation was the warlike nation-state, headed by a monarch. McDonald therefore wanted to manoeuvre Native peoples into position to act as a buffer for British North America. He saw them as potentially independent geopolitical actors who would participate in a warlike state like those that had dominated European history during his youth in the Napoleonic period.

McDonald's essentially eighteenth-century project, however, had to take shape in mid-nineteenth-century Canada. Reading the Montreal *Gazette* and the Toronto *Globe* in their rural homes, he and his friends would have been well informed about current European affairs, because news brought by swift Atlantic steamers was reported quickly by telegraph from New York.[22] Like the men he was trying to persuade and whose background he shared, McDonald was confronted by an essential issue of modernity: what ought to be the relationship between the nations of Europe and the Native peoples of the Americas? Unfortunately, although the men to whom he addressed his letters were all influential, none had effective power. Chief Justice Draper was in London and had confessed to being ill-briefed to observe the British parliamentary committee. Edward Ellice had narrow and outdated views of Canada. Ronald Harwood's hands were tied in Toronto. John Sandfield Macdonald was out of office. And Sir Étienne-Pascal Taché was dying. McDonald's choice of whom to write to nevertheless sketches an important social scene that comprised Glengarry County, family connections, the HBC, and aging political friends. Draper was by far the most important of his correspondents: he spoke for Canada, he was in a position to act and, as we shall see, he recognized McDonald's knowledge and apparently put it to good use.

The 1857-58 Letters

In the first of the extant letters (25 July 1857), McDonald addresses Chief Justice Draper, apparently not for the first time.[23] Although Draper had been sent to London as an observer, he was eventually persuaded to testify before the select committee, which he did on 28 May and again on 4 June 1857.[24] McDonald's late-July plea to Draper was therefore futile, but the letter shows that he was giving practical shape to ideas he had mused about:

It is my humble opinion, Honorable Sir, though the short-sighted mass may think otherwise, that you will gain immortal honour by getting the territories beyond the Height of Land which I have described set apart as a reserve for generations of natives yet unborn and the H.B.Co. appointed – at least for a definite time – as trustees for them – under certain rules and restrictions.

I appeal to your own sense of justice to these poor Indians – Look what a poor set they are amongst whites. Endeavour then to keep them in their primitive state – *else the day will come when the British or Canadian Government must support them.* All the natives north of the Saskatchewan are what we call the Strong Wood Indians. The bow and arrow is of little use to them. They must have support. South of that river are what we call the Plain and Prairie Indians and can live independent of whites – they are here today and 100 miles off tomorrow towards the Miss[ouri?].

What advantage will it be to Canada if the whole country is laid open to all the interlopers in the world in less than ten years. Furs and all the animal tribe would be gone for ever – is it not better to make it last forever as it is – and allow the Natives to support themselves rather than to become a burden to government.

This arrangement I am sure the HBC will readily come into – for a limited time more or less.

It is a very great error to think that Furs are very plentiful – This Silver or Black Fox spoken of is rare. I do not think in 20 years I ever saw 20 such foxes and the annual H.B.Co. returns may show how many they annually get from the whole country.

By the Crown setting apart the country as a reserve, would not that settle the point in dispute at once?

If I suggest anything to your better judgement I shall be glad of it.

Within the limits I have described we have room enough for all the Population of Great Britain.[25]

In his testimony to the select committee, the chief justice twice noted that he had received valuable information from "le bras croche." But from Draper's letter of 31 August 1857 (see below), it is apparent that not all of McDonald's letters had reached him.

Draper had no easy task. In his letters to John A. Macdonald, he complains bitterly about how hard it is to obtain advice from the government he was supposed to be representing.[26] On his own, he had not only searched for relevant legal cases but also visited Britain's State Paper Office to find documentary evidence of the HBC's charter claims. In his lengthy testimony to the committee, he admitted freely that he had never travelled beyond the eastern shore of Lake

Superior. He nevertheless stressed three points: the need to establish the true boundaries of Canada, the strategic necessity of maintaining the West as a British possession, and the Canadian desire to extend settlement westward. The interests of a trading company such as the HBC, he argued, were incompatible with the encouragement of settlement. He then outlined a northern boundary line beyond which settlement was unlikely and marked a territory that could be left – on suitable terms – in the hands of the HBC. The line would run from Cape Perdrix in Labrador south through Lake Mistassini and then across the western interior at the same latitude as Norway House.[27] Sir John Pakington asked Draper, "Is it your opinion that the whole of that district which you have described, lying between the present boundary between the United States and the British Territory, and a line striking across the north of Lake Winnipeg, is fit for settlement?" Draper responded,

> I can only form an opinion founded upon the testimony of others. Before I left Canada, knowing that there was a gentleman of the name of Macdonald, whose name will be found in the Parliamentary Papers of 1849 as "*bras croche,*" who had been twenty-five years employed in the North-West Company. I corresponded with him, and I obtained a great deal of information which I thought exceedingly valuable, and upon which my opinion of the facility of that country is founded, together with other papers of a similar kind which I have read, but I have no personal knowledge of it whatever.[28]

Throughout Judge Draper's testimony, distinctive themes recur that also appear in McDonald's letters: a northern boundary for settlement beyond which there would be a Native preserve held for the time being by the HBC, just compensation for Native peoples, and the practicality of the historic Lake Superior route west. On the feasibility of the Lake Superior route, one senses that Draper drew on the experience of old Nor'Westers and not from that of the post-union HBC, of which the *Globe* accused him of being a supine tool. One MP, Charles Fitzwilliam, said he had heard that a committee of the Provincial House was currently sitting on the vexed question of access to the Red River settlement (which was also being debated furiously in the pages of the *Globe*). Draper acknowledged this, and to the question, who are the witnesses? he replied, "Many people who have retired, after having spent a number of years in that part of the country. I have heard the names of some few; but they are people who have resided in that part of the country, and who are living now in Canada, and whose testimony can be got at ... One of them, I dare say, would be the gentleman to whom I have referred, with whom I have corresponded on that subject, namely Mr. Macdonald."[29] McDonald wrote to Draper immediately on the latter's return to Toronto in August 1857, and Draper responded warmly: "I take this occasion of heartily thanking you for the very great trouble you have taken and for the very valuable information you gave me. I made frequent use of it as well in my conversation with individuals as in my evidence and correspondence."[30] Draper had had his fill of "parties who were interested in keeping things as they are or had even more sinister views"; their representations, he said stoutly, "were not founded in fact." But it is clear that in the end the chief justice, whose prime object was "to secure to Great Britain the whole territory bordering on the United States," had concluded that settlement, cautiously and knowledgeably pursued in the face of near-insuperable problems of communication, was the only way to establish sovereignty in the region. McDonald's information served Draper well, but it did not alter the judge's opinions.

John McDonald of Garth had a much harder time with Edward Ellice, whose questioning of Draper displayed the defensive posture – "it is we who can best protect the Indians" and "the area is unfit for settlement" – of the HBC at the time. Ellice was undoubtedly the unnamed party who held "sinister views" of Draper's letter. McDonald knew Ellice from their early days in the NWC and, prompted by the *Globe*'s report of Ellice's testimony of 23 June 1857, wrote to him twice on 16 July and once on 19 July.[31] McDonald was trying to engage the interest of a powerful man with heavy financial investments in North America and a long-standing involvement in the fur trade. Ellice, however, had not visited Canada for some years, though he would return briefly in 1858. Like Draper, he had never been west of Lake Superior, but as a member of Parliament he had been appointed to the select committee.[32] Ellice made his presence felt through the questions he asked, but he was also questioned sharply himself. His resolutely anti-historical testimony, based on strict mercantile thinking, contrasts acutely with Draper's careful research and long historical perspective.[33]

McDonald respected Draper's office, but with Ellice he took a more aggressive stance. Writing vigorously, as if to a fellow Scots merchant, he states, "I must pronounce you in error regarding the country east of the mountains; you never saw such a fine country and what I should say a more eligible country for immigration than the valleys of those two rivers [the Red and the Saskatchewan] and the intermediate space."[34] And he sturdily denies Ellice's contention that the land was marshy beyond the fertile river banks and inhospitable in general.[35] "While I thus express myself in regard to the beauties of the country I am far from wishing that it should be laid open for competition in the fur trade I can emphatically say no. The country in five years would be ruined as well as the Natives by a flood of petty traders from the south side of 45°–49E as well as from the Canadas. I know the evils of opposition and you yourself felt the effects."[36] McDonald does not advocate the long-term continuance of the charter but suggests that it should be extended for twenty-five years, when immigration will take over, and he proposes a boundary between settlement and a hunting preserve that is roughly the same as the one Draper described to the select committee. Furthermore, he insists that, if boundaries are to be drawn, they cannot be laid down mechanically in terms of latitude; instead, the boundaries need to follow the height of land because they could be more easily maintained by a suitable militia. His conception of the West is thus organic and functional, as opposed to the severely rational vision that would be imposed after 1869 by the orthogonal survey.

In his first letter, McDonald appeals to Ellice as an investor in the fur trade. If free trade is instituted, he argues, "Americans will infest the country and undersell all traders from the Canadas. True in a very few years like the Kilkenny Cats they would all eat themselves up but the tails, but they would ruin the country for ever." In his second letter, written the same day, he turns to the situation of Native people:

> The country would be ruined also beyond redemption. What then would become of the poor Natives for generations yet to come; the deer as well as the fur trade would be destroyed (their only support) ... Both Red River and the Saskatchewan Rivers are the only provision posts or departments. Without the pemmican from those departments the trade can be scarcely carried on by any one. It is a more portable food than any others that can be supplied & that will be cut off – by a free trade & the animals (the buffaloes) which supply it will be driven off by bad management out of the reach of the Indians who hunt them. Generations of Indians yet unborn will regret the day that free trade is introduced amongst them. Some of the present race may think it a fine thing for a short time."[37]

In the days of the NWC, furs had been abundant, but today "there is not a foot of the country unexplored from the Atlantic to the Pacific." "Had the country been under one rule," he continued, "the fur animals in general could have been husbanded and it would still have been a fine country."[38]

These are far from the nostalgic thoughts of a very old man, for McDonald proceeds to argue energetically for the immediate development of a railway or ship canal from Canada. He asserts that the HBC could retain its trade and then gradually recede ("recede" was the word then in use by all parties for a gradual withdrawal) from the more fertile territory as immigration increased. In his third letter (dated 19 July), McDonald stresses the importance of provisioning, for which all parties, whether those of the HBC or other "intruders or adventurers," would have to maintain posts, and he continues to ponder the problems of immigration and agriculture. "The valleys of those two rivers and the inter-vening country lying between them are the most eligible for immigration. These are parts of the country more fit for tillage than other parts but all parts – the High Prairies are as fit for pasture as any part of the world, witness the innumer-able herds of the Bison which graze upon them."[39] As before, McDonald wants limits (here unspecified) laid down to separate the area to be filled up "with a dense population" from the area within which the HBC would retain, though only for a limited period, its historical role. The letter, however, concludes firmly and prophetically: "Of course we will govern Red River and establish there what government we please in accordance with our laws in Canada."

Ellice offered three closely argued responses that illustrate the very limitations McDonald was trying to combat. Ellice's letters, like his testimony, reflect both a patronizing attitude and the reluctance to recognize settlement possibilities that infuriated the Reformers. He maintains he is "the only person left of those who could have protected the interests of your old associates, the factors and traders in the interior ... I have felt it my duty to stand by them."[40] Ellice doubts whether Canada can afford to take on responsibility for the HBC territory (McDonald seems to have been in agreement) and writes, "and your experience will tell you in what a precarious position the peace of the whole frontier will be placed, if while our authority was superseded no other efficient one was substituted for it." According to Ellice, when the disposition of the territory is settled, all agitation will cease, and the governors of the HBC will be only too happy to consult the wishes of the people of Canada, whose goodwill they will need to retain.[41] Ellice, however, defends his view of the country as fundamentally inhospitable to immigration and points out that without a population there would be no taxes to support a government. He makes no mention of the Native population in this, his first letter to McDonald (31 July 1857), or in his second (6 August 1857), though in the latter he observes patronizingly of the metis, "there is no reason to fear any serious danger from any bad feeling on the part of the half breeds towards the Company's curtailments. On the contrary, they are too much dependent upon them for employment and supplies; and I have also understood, too sensible of the good treatment they have received and the advantages of this connection, to wish to change masters for the mixed races of American and Canadian speculators, who alone could succeed to the Hudson's Bay Company."[42] Ellice then returns to the question that for him is clearly most pressing: who is to maintain law and order when and if the territory is trans-ferred from the HBC to Canada? In his third letter (14 September 1857), he stresses again that a decision must be made; the company "will not accept the condition of being placed between two stools." But his view of the wider picture was less sanguine than McDonald's:

You and I, at all events, shall never live to see railroads made from Canada to the Red River or Saskatchewan to connect the prairie with these flourishing settlements which are foretold in both! When I see even a road made between Lake Superior and Lake Winnipeg by which a wagon can travel – or a boat and a wagon can convey goods on reasonable terms to the interior – I shall begin to believe the further speculations of a visionary. And even in this case, unless all things in America are marvellously changed since I knew them, no such road could be maintained, or kept in repair, without sufficient settlements on the whole line.

And he concludes, "Here I must beg leave to close our correspondence. I do so with great feelings of respect for you and some admiration, at your age, with your aspirations for progress, more required even than the progress we have witnessed in America."[43]

Once Draper returned to Canada in August 1857, McDonald had to turn to the local political scene in search of supporters, a difficult task since the Reformers preached at every opportunity the mercantile and religious gospel of settlement and the need to civilize Native people. In January 1858, McDonald's relative by marriage, Ronald U. Harwood, was elected to the Legislative Council as the member for Vaudreuil, near Montreal.[44] Discussion of the Red River settlement and the problem of a practical route to the West continued, and McDonald must have thought an appeal to Harwood would have some effect. Harwood wrote to McDonald on 20 March 1858, "I have received this morning two letters from you which I assure you give me great pleasure, and I read them over carefully and shall endeavour to make myself master of the subject before it comes to the House for discussion."[45] Harwood said that he filed away McDonald's letters and intended to show them to his friends and perhaps use them in the House, but the subject would not come up for consideration for some time, when "it may be referred to a Committee to report upon, when my dear sir I think your personal evidence before that Committee might be the most effective way of carrying your views." Genially, Harwood also reported a new addition to the family: "By the time he grows up we may want him as Governor General in this new North West province we talk of forming." But he concluded, "I have a great many letters to write so that you must excuse me writing you often, but am always honoured and pleased when I receive one of your communications."[46]

The following July, however, Harwood wrote in haste, apologizing for not having answered McDonald's last letter and anxious to get his opinion on the proposed bill to incorporate the North West Transportation and Trade Company, a railway that had been projected by Toronto supporters of settlement at Red

River but was seriously undercapitalized.[47] "The parties say it is only the opening out of the old North West route, as used by the old Company. I fear there may be found great danger in giving powers there sought to a set of speculators without much capital." The enterprise, he continues, "may forestall a better regulated company when the time comes, and that in the mean time we run the risk of embroiling the country in a war with the Indians." The proposed company would expect protection from the province "in perhaps their unjust overreaching of the Indians." It would come into conflict with the HBC posts and "perhaps within a few years ruin the Indians by inciting them to kill off all the Buffalo for the hide and tallow ... Will you please at your earliest convenience to give me your opinion."[48]

The result of Harwood's letter, of course, was a long and detailed letter from McDonald. Its first paragraph shows both the enthusiasm and forward-looking attitude of the old man and his ability to adapt to new information, such as the discovery of gold in British Columbia:

> That there are fine countries west of us, at present as it were useless, there is no doubt of, particularly no doubt as far as regards my own observation, because I have seen most parts of the territory fit for agricultural purposes. To make that country available there must be a suitable, expeditious, and easy communication. This must be the Grand point in view for the consideration of a Grand Nation. That there is gold on the western coast, as well as coal and other minerals on the whole route, there is little doubt of. The communication, therefore, ought to be commensurate with the object in prospect – namely, upon a grand scale worthy of a great Nation. Consider for a moment the result – the riches of Asia [taken?] in a few weeks to Fraser's River, and from steamer in as many days to Montreal, and from steamer [he is still thinking of some sort of canal] in ten days to the London market."

McDonald believed that a small company with insufficient capital could not achieve this; it "would only be throwing obstacles in the way of a great scheme."[49]

McDonald then offers an overview of the problem of communication within the territory as a whole and suggests that there are several easily accessible points of entry to the Red River settlement: from Hudson Bay, either by the present Nelson River route used once a year by the "lazy H.B.Co.'s ships" or from James Bay to the southeast end of Lake Winnipeg and then to Red River. Steam vessels, he writes, could make at least three trips a year: "The distance cannot be much more than to Quebec." However, the Lake Superior route via the height of land from Fort William would probably be chosen unless one with less ascent were found.[50]

Apparently, McDonald's earlier letters to Harwood had laid out in more detail a plan for Native peoples (perhaps a copy of the prospectus was included), and McDonald returns to the idea in the letter of 9 July. The Indians must be paid for a right of way, he argues, because "they never exacted such from the Traders, as their object was different. There will be no great danger from any difficulties with them, at least until getting into the Prairies as they are there more in numbers and entirely independent. The route will still lie within the limits I have in my former letters to you described as a boundary between the Canadas and the Territory which I thought necessary to retain by the Crown as a reserve, north of what I should call all that was required for emigration." He proposes some changes to the boundary in the West he had described earlier, drawing it from the former Fort George to a northerly pass through the Rockies. What is important, however, is not the boundary itself but the concept, which puts into practical form the visionary project McDonald had outlined in the draft prospectus. By July 1858, McDonald envisages the whole territory as being filled with settlers to the south and with an immense Native reserve, characterized by Native social practices, to the north. McDonald believes that a railway or canal must surely be built, and quickly, but he recognizes that the proposed company's capital is inadequate to carry out a scheme that "will be the greatest one undertaken by any nation on earth and worthy of the nineteenth century."[51]

The same sense of impending grand possibilities illuminates McDonald's later letters. On 15 April 1858, McDonald had written to an unnamed "Honourable and Dear Sir" (possibly John A. Macdonald, who was by now the coalition premier), with whom he had been corresponding. He had already been reading H.Y. Hind's 1857 report, and his letter is chiefly concerned with the possibilities of settlement.[52] It recommends the formation of three colonies: two in the far west (the British Columbia mainland and Vancouver Island) and a third that would stretch across the north from the straits of Belle Isle to the Rockies, with an entry point at Fort William. To the south would lie the "20,000 acres fit for settlement mentioned by Mr. Hind," but a line would run "due north to the height of land already mentioned to you as forming the boundary between a reservation to the H.B.Co. and the Canadas. Thus we have the colony or province of Red River circumscribed and of itself extensive enough to contain the population of Europe." McDonald then proceeds to discuss the particulars of such a settlement, including its extension to the North Saskatchewan River, but most importantly he writes that "the Home Government is to have the sole management of this new province but it would be at the cost and under the rule of the British government and its colonists and at no costs to Canada."[53] The question of who would finance the government of the new colony clearly remained a concern for McDonald, as it had for Ellice.

McDonald's letter continues, "It is not required that the H.B.Co. should vacate the country all at once or at all. What is required is to recede as population advances and that the H.B.Co. should renounce all control or sovereignty over any part of the country south of a fixed boundary." McDonald does agree, however, that the HBC should be compensated if it withdraws from Vancouver Island (and the Northwest Coast). Farther east, however, the company should have no claim for compensation; at Fort William, he argues, "the North West Company were squatters, and the H.B.Co. has no better title." Although McDonald believes the HBC should retain the right to defend its own territory, he is contemptuous of the military potential of the stone forts at Red River and outlines what he believes would be a more effective system of military posts roughly from Pembina to a line along the Bow River. And he opposes a commercial fishery because the Natives "solely depend on fish in some parts."[54]

Native people did indeed depend on fish, as struggles over the danger of commercial fishing in the decades that followed would make clear. But by the time McDonald wrote this letter, much else that they depended on was also disappearing, including the great herds of buffalo, which were gone by 1879. The Prairies described by Irene Spry and so vividly evoked in McDonald's autobiographical notes were disappearing quickly, and the rationale for the solutions put forward by McDonald was disappearing with them. McDonald would die in 1866, before the West became Canada's responsibility, and it is perhaps as well that he was spared news of the final exhaustion of the buffalo herds. But as his letters show, he clearly recognized the organic relationship between territory and social use, was dismissive of according overgenerous rights to trading empires, and constantly expressed an understanding of Native people's needs. Today we would call someone with McDonald's views a Red Tory. The deep philosophical bases of his conservatism were rooted not in issues of property and hierarchy but in a concept of inclusive justice based on first-hand leadership experience. Within the limited terms permitted him by his advanced age and cultural formation, McDonald was thinking, and thinking broadly.

The 1864-65 Letters

Six years intervened between the 1857-58 letters and McDonald's final attempt to influence the course of affairs in the West. The 1864-65 letters might have been prompted by meetings in Charlottetown in September 1864 to consider the possibility of confederation; however, McDonald's concerns about defence show that he must also have had in mind Sioux warriors who had twice camped north of Fort Garry to keep out of the reach of American troops and were settling on the White Horse Plain to the west.[55] On 27 October 1864, McDonald sent a list of what, in his view, were essential facts to John Sandfield Macdonald. He hoped to get someone to write about these facts and warned him that an article in the Cornwall *Freeholder,* of which Sandfield was proprietor, would be no use because "it is not read beyond these counties."[56] Although Sandfield was a mighty figure in Glengarry, at that time he was out of political office, a victim of the hopelessly schismatic politics that characterized the months before the formation of the Great Coalition. Given that McDonald's own political vision was also turned eastward to Montreal, it is not clear what influence he thought he could or would wield.[57]

In McDonald's view, a regular military force would be of no use to defend Red River (presumably against a Sioux attack). In his letter to Sandfield, he writes that, because Native people will not attack a fortified position, a cavalry troop made up of "Half Breeds" (metis) on unshod horses, lightly armed, "with saddle and bridle such as are made in the country and used by the Indians" would be necessary. Touchingly, he argues that the troop could be supported wherever it would be needed by log blockhouses "on a scale that a small family might occupy."[58] No colony could be established, he concludes, without this measure. He then proceeds to consider a range of punishments for the kinds of Native depredations that might be encountered and points out, with insight that came directly from the old Northwest, that in Native cultures the whole tribe is answerable for the deeds of its members. It is clear that McDonald viewed the protection of Red River entirely in terms of the customary practices of the country, not from the point of view of Europeans.

It was frustrating to persuade Euro-Canadians of the special situation of the West. In a letter dated 28 October 1864, perhaps with the fractured political scene in mind, McDonald grumbles apocalyptically to Sandfield, "I think it is time to draw the sword and prepare ourselves for mortal combat." But he continues more temperately, "I would wish that someone would take up the cudgel in defence of a country interesting to me – a country much superior to what the Canadas are, and that in your seat in parliament, you should be *that one,* and all information I have in my brain you should have."[59] In February 1865, he wrote to the minister of militia, Sir Étienne-Pascal Taché, "offering certain suggestions for the defence of the far west and for the transportation of material."[60] Taché's secretary, J.G. Vansittart, thanked him on the minister's behalf and wrote that his suggestions "will receive his consideration when the subject comes up." Vansittart also replied to another missive from McDonald, written on 15 March 1865, but by this time Taché was very ill (he died on 30 July 1864). He said only that the minister had transferred the letter to the commissioner of Crown lands. Neither letter has been located.[61]

An article in the Montreal *Gazette* of 20 March 1865 initiated the last chapter in the continuing attempt of this ninety-two year old, only months from his own death in January 1866, to influence affairs. The article reports a debate in the House of Lords on the question of establishing a Crown colony in the North-Western Territory of British North America.[62] There is no evidence that McDonald's arguments had made their way to these heights, but Lord Wharncliffe's case for establishing a separate colony, one not dependent on Canada, would have appealed strongly to McDonald. As the debate shows, however, Wharncliffe's case did not persuade his fellow noblemen. The claims of the HBC had to be dealt with as did the expense of defending such an immense area. On 21 March 1865, McDonald, making reference to the *Gazette* article, issued his last plea to a person he addresses with marked respect but who remains unidentified, perhaps a British member of Parliament (the phrase "what we call the Saskatchewan" suggests someone unfamiliar with Canada). The letter not only sums up the case he had been making but also illustrates the transformation of McDonald's ideas since he drafted the prospectus and wrote to Chief Justice Draper in 1857. The letter also reveals that McDonald finally recognized his own waning powers.

Gray's Creek, Cornwall,
21st March, 1865

Honourable Sir:

In the *Gazette* of the 20th instant I see some remarks regarding the North West Territory. Without any preface, I wish to convey to you my ideas of the several points in argument. You may in the situation you hold and from your natural talents have a word to say on the subject.

Was the boundary between the Canadas and the Hudson's Bay territory left to my decision – and I may say I have seen every bit of it – I would begin at the Straits of Belle Isle and follow the height of land from that beginning to Jasper House in the Rocky Mountains where I have been when I last crossed the mountains, i.e. I would divide the waters flowing south and west, on the whole route from those falling northwards into Hudson's Bay. I would add the whole tract watered by those rivers and lakes southward to the Canadas. I would leave those regions watered northwards to the Hudson's Bay Co. for hunting grounds.

There is a ridge dividing those waters from the place of beginning to Lake Winnipeg. I would follow the east coast of that lake to the north end, then ascend what we call the Saskatchewan to Lac Bourbon (sometimes called Cedar Lake) crossing that lake and enter the real Saskatchewan, following it until I left it for Cumberland Lake to the north end of that Lake, to the height of land dividing the waters falling south into the Saskatchewan from those falling into the English River to the Beaver River at its entrance into Isle a la Crosse Lake, then ascending that river to Lac La Biche, then ascend Rivière La Biche to Athabascan River and ascend that river to Jasper House as I have said. This route I would make the division line between Canada and the Hudson's Bay hunting grounds. Within this boundary line I may safely say that the soil is fit for cultivation to the American lines, including Red River, etc.

Having thus roughly defined the boundary between Canada and the H.B.Co. I must add that I think Lord Wharncliffe's argument very good.

I do not think that the Canadas could ever manage such an extensive and complicated undertaking. It would form of itself a kingdom, and ought to be undertaken by the British government as a separate government supported by British capital in all its requirements and necessities. Its agricultural purposes, its smelting of ores, etc. The route, as I have already said, to [pass?] by an improved highway by Hudson's Bay, for all purposes, to and from. In the course of time it would become one of the first countries in the world, to the Pacific Ocean, and I may add one of the richest. The distance from Hudson's Bay to Lake Winnipeg being so short a distance, and then the difficulties to the Red River, Fort Dauphin River, and Saskatchewan being but little in the whole scale.

My first position is that adding it to the Canadas would only make it a piddling affair. My second is that if undertaken by Great Britain it would soon become a vast kingdom, and if the H.B.Co. should give it up totally, that there is space for the whole population of Europe, and capital. There are water privileges, the soil is good – forest and timber, abundance of fish – pasture ready by nature for any extent in cattle, sheep, horses, etc. True, the season is short for navigation by Hudson's Bay, but where one steamer can go one thousand may.

By this scrawl, if I could give you an idea of facts I should be happy in giving it to you as a legacy, to enable you to have a voice in any circumstances which may take place.

> I have the honour to be
> Honorable Sir, your obedient servant,
> John McDonald

P.S. I consider that there would be little required in the defensive way as the natives and Half Breeds would do that part. No enemy could invade their lands. A few hundreds of Half Breeds might, however, be trained as Home Guards, as the Natives themselves have in their camps.

Now, Honourable Sir, if you reflect upon all this, or make it a subject of your actions, I beg you to take a clear and correct copy of it, and by no means expose my dotage to others at 92.

Let Fort William be a Port of Entry to this new colony, and the route from Fort William to Red River and Lake Winnipeg partially improved.

Emigration sent from Europe the half of them would go to the States, but by Hudson's Bay none.

The object would be by forming a new colony; to make it self-existing, everything within itself.

The country between Lake Superior and Lake Winnipeg is a poor rugged country. Lands might be given gratis to anyone who would settle them, as there are good spots, however.

J. McD.[63]

Over the decade during which he argued for his dream, McDonald had to adjust his thinking. No longer did a Native territory in the West seem possible, though the concept of an HBC hunting territory, governed according to country custom and separate from the great kingdom yet to be developed, would preserve its essence. Nevertheless, the various expressions of what McDonald termed his legacy articulated a single theme: the West was a single coherent entity that needed to be treated as such.

McDonald wrote a last, jocular letter to Sandfield Macdonald in July 1865, after the Confederation debates of February and March had taken place in Quebec. In it, he rejoices that the British government has at last recognized the HBC's title to its territory, a recognition that makes it possible for the Canadas to buy the land when financial means become available: "They have laid the foundations of a mighty empire when the confederation is fully accomplished."[64] But despite his conviction that settlement should and will take place, McDonald still imagines the empire not in terms of railways and steamships but from the viewpoint of the Native militia he had championed for so long: "It is said that we will have a long frontier to defend. So have we a long backbone to fall back upon with our effects where no enemy can penetrate, and leave only bare walls and smoking ruins behind us. Seasons are too short and winters too long for any enemy to expect conquest. Would an enemy expect to winter in the country, could they expect warm and comfortable quarters or burning ruins? I guess they would not try a second time." Sandfield, however, out of office and an opponent of federalism, had played no role in the events of 1864-65, though he would one day take his place as the first premier of Ontario. "Such and such have been accomplished and hang yourself Sandfield, you were not there," mocks

McDonald, quoting the famous rebuke of Henry IV of France to his dilatory captain, Crillon, known as "le brave." "Hang yourself, brave Crillon; we fought at Arquìs and you were not there."[65]

Understanding the West as a Coherent Social Entity

Six years after McDonald's death, George M. Grant travelled west with Sanford Fleming and wrote a famous book, *Ocean to Ocean* (1873), that recorded their journey. Grant had no doubt that railways, the resulting onrush of settlement, and the markets that the new immigrants would provide represented the future of Canada. Like the United States, "the Dominion also aspires to greatness, and believes that it has within its borders all that is required to make a nation materially great." There are three ways, he continues, of dealing "with the less than half-million of red men still to be found on the continent of America": first, extermination, which "no Christian nation would now tolerate ... for an instant"; second, the cruel insistence that there is no "Indian Question," which abandons Native peoples to the exploiters; and third, a paternal way, which assumes that gentle assimilation will take place. "At all events," he writes confidently, "there are no Indian difficulties in our North-west." Indigenous resistance to colonialism has been proving him wrong ever since.[66]

It is easy now to dismiss John McDonald of Garth as a garrulous old gentleman whose antiquated proposals could not possibly envisage the West of 1872 as George M. Grant saw it, or perhaps failed to see it, with Native peoples confined to their miserable reserves as the common lands disappeared before the onslaught not only of the settler but also of the settler's concept of private property.[67] The Confederation debates over which McDonald rejoiced to Sandfield Macdonald made scant mention of Native peoples, to say nothing of their very different concept of property, and members of the British Select Committee on the Hudson's Bay Company of 1857 had even argued about whether their report should include a passage on the fatal effect to the Native population of open competition in the fur trade and yet more exploitation of alcohol.[68] Whatever the limits of his ideas, McDonald, like others who had lived long in the West, would not have made such mistakes. Today it is the scope and cohesiveness of his understanding of the West that impresses us. A.S. Morton might have called him a blusterer, but he also recognized that McDonald's response to the West could rightly be compared with that of the great geographer David Thompson: "His *Autobiographical Notes* ... show a sensitiveness to the beauties of the scene such as is to be found in no other document ... None, except perhaps John McDonald of Garth, saw the beauties of the North-West landscapes as he [Thompson] did."[69] Indeed, buried in these little-known letters, with their vast and unrealizable design, is an understanding of the West as a coherent social entity worthy to be set alongside Thompson's much-praised depiction of the region as a coherent geographical and natural entity. The methods of counter-factual history invite us to speculate. What if McDonald had reached the minds of the men he sought to persuade? What if a Native preserve north of the height of land had been created? What if the social life of Native people as they lived when all was held in common had continued into the twenty-first century? What, then, would it be like to write the history of Canada today?

Notes

Most of McDonald's letters and his "Autobiographical Notes" are housed in McGill University Library's Rare Books and Special Collections. I am indebted to Richard Virr for making access possible during the department's temporary closure in 2004. I am also indebted to Glenn Wright, Patricia Kennedy, and Martin Ruddy of Library and Archives Canada for assistance with McDonald's letters in the LAC's collection. I am grateful also for access to materials at the Archives of Ontario. Johan Draper kindly copied a letter in his possession written by his great-great-grandfather. Larry Green's kind gift of his thesis on McDonald is referred to in the notes. David Anderson, Lorne Hammond, James Mochoruk, and Laura Peers assisted with crucial references. Carolyn Podruchny, William E. Moreau, and John Warkentin read the chapter in draft form and commented on it. Any errors or omissions are entirely my responsibility.

1 John McDonald of Garth to Edward Ellice, 16 July 1857 (first letter of two with that date), Library and Archives Canada (hereafter LAC), MG 24 A 58, vol. 2, folios 25-34.
2 "Autobiographical Notes of John McDonald of Garth," John McDonald Collection, McGill University Library, Rare Books and Special Collections (hereafter MRBSC), MS 406/8-9. The "Autobiographical Notes" have been printed only once, in six instalments, in the *Cornwall Freeholder*, 2 March-6 April 1866. The version in Masson, *Les bourgeois*, 2:1-59, is badly excerpted and inaccurately transcribed. Stimulated by references in my anthology *Canadian Exploration Literature*, Larry Green wrote an important master's thesis on McDonald (see Green, "An Analysis of the Autobiographical Notes of John McDonald of Garth") and, when it was completed, graciously sent me a hard copy and microfilms. An authoritative transcription of the original document is being made, and Carolyn Podruchny and I are preparing a critical edition.
3 See Bowering, *Inverarden Regency Cottage Museum*. The museum was closed in 1999, but the McDonald artifacts associated with it have been stored by the Stormont, Dundas and Glengarry Historical Society.
4 Simon Fraser and John McDonald of Garth, 1 August 1859, in Fraser, *Letters and Journals of Simon Fraser*, 271. The memorandum is located in the McCord Museum, Montreal, MS M18638.
5 Sir George Simpson to John McDonald of Garth, 21 April 1859, John McDonald Collection, MRBSC MS 406/4.
6 DeLery Macdonald to Montreal *Gazette*, 27 January 1936. The letter is of interest in itself, for it describes Macdonald's efforts to collect the memorabilia of the old NWC partners. He suggests housing them in a "Room of the Old Nor'Westers" in the Château Ramezay Museum or the McCord Museum.
7 The extant letters relating to McDonald's project were written between July 1857 and July 1865. Some of the copies of letters from McDonald may simply be drafts or letters that were never sent, and some letters in the chronological sequence may be missing. The first

dated letter, to Justice Draper, continues a discussion initiated earlier, and Draper's letter of 31 August 1857 (see below) mentions two letters from McDonald that had missed him in London but had been forwarded to him in Toronto. Letters to others might have been lost or have yet to be uncovered. In quotations from the documents cited below, spellings and punctuation have been normalized, and scribal abbreviations are silently expanded. McDonald often uses the French "Lac" instead of the English "Lake," but he does so inconsistently; therefore, that, too, has been normalized, except in the obvious case of French names. McDonald's rapid, sloping hand is extremely difficult to decipher, even for someone who knows it well. I am grateful for the aid provided by the typed transcriptions of these letters made early in the twentieth century and filed with the documents (John McDonald Collection, MRBSC 406/7). A few inaccuracies in those transcriptions have been corrected. Some of the readings in the letters located at LAC are uncertain; the manuscripts are fragile, and they can only be accessed on microfilm.

8   Burns, *Inverarden*, 168.

9   Morton, *A History of the Canadian West*, 461; Masson, *Les bourgeois*, 2:1-59.

10 Green, "John McDonald of Garth," 4.

11 McDonald, "Autobiographical Notes," John McDonald Collection, MRBSC, MS 406/8, folio 58.

12 For "dotage," see McDonald to "Hon'ble Sir" [identity unknown], 21 March 1865, John McDonald Collection, MRBSC, MS 406/5, folio 3.

13 Spry, "The Tragedy of the Loss of the Commons," 203-4.

14 Friesen, *The Canadian Prairies*, 130-31.

15 McDonald to Ellice, 16 July 1857 (second letter of two with that date), LAC, MG 24 A 58, vol. 2, folios 25-34.

16 See *Correspondence of Chief Justice Draper* (hereafter *Correspondence*) and the letters concerning his mission, Archives of Ontario (hereafter AO), F1027-1, MS 6460, 37c-5(1)-(2).

17 For the development of British and Canadian policy toward Native peoples before Confederation, see Tobias, "Protection, Civilization, Assimilation," and Milloy, "The Early Indian Acts."

18 John Warkentin observes that in the thousand pages of the Confederation debates there are only two incidental references to Aboriginal peoples (601 and 774): "To the legislators, completely engrossed as they were with other matters, aboriginal peoples seemed not to exist. Even when a phrase such as 'a native population' was used, it referred to the population of European origins that had been in North America for three, four or more generations, not to the aboriginal population." Warkentin, "Geography of Confederation," 17, citing the debates, 139. The debates were published as Canada, *Parliamentary Debates on the Subject of the Confederation of the British North American Provinces*.

19 Prospectus? undated, John McDonald Collection, MRBSC MS 406/6.

20 Select Committee of the Hudson's Bay Company, *Report* (hereafter *Report*), 222. The boundaries of early Canada are discussed by Nicholson, *The Boundaries of Canada*; for the issues debated here, see 11-16.

21 For the development of American policy with respect to Native territory in the West, see Bailey and Bailey, "Indian Territory," 271-73.

22 See Goheen, "The Impact of the Telegraph on the Newspaper," 107-29.

23 The postscript of the first of McDonald's letters to Edward Ellice on 16 July 1857 says that McDonald had sent the same sentiments to Justice Draper, "if he got my letters." LAC, MG 24 A 58 vol. 2, folios 25-34.

24 The committee would issue its report on 31 July.

25 McDonald to Draper, 25 July 1857, John McDonald Collection, MRBSC, MS 406/4 (in my view, probably a draft).

26 Draper said as much to the select committee itself (*Report*, 211), and a private letter to John A. Macdonald makes his misery evident (draft letter dated 12 June 1857, in the possession of Johan Draper, Toronto).

27 *Report*, 217.

28 Ibid., 221-22.

29 Ibid., 229-30.

30 Draper to McDonald, 31 August 1857 (draft copy?), Masson Collection, LAC, R2155-0-7-E (formerly MG19, C1), vol. 36. In an earlier finding aid, this letter is described as being addressed to John A. Macdonald; however, the contents indicate that it was sent to John McDonald of Garth. In addition, Draper usually addressed letters to John A. Macdonald with "My dear Attorney General," and this letter begins more formally with "My dear Sir."

31 Ellice was present at the tumultuous sailing of the *Isaac Todd* from Portsmouth in 1813 and approved with a wink McDonald's handling of difficulties with the crew; see "Autobiographical Notes," John McDonald Collection, MRBSC, MS 406/9, folio 152. *Globe*, 13 July 1857.

32 *Report*, 343.

33 Contrast, for example, Ellice's refusal to even discuss the pre-union affairs of the HBC (*Report*, 343-44) and Draper's shrewd use of evidence gleaned during his visit to the State Paper Office (*Report*, 212, 217, and *Correspondence*, 8).

34 McDonald to Ellice, 16 July 1857 (first letter); *Report*, 332.

35 *Report*, 350.

36 McDonald to Ellice, 16 July 1857 (first letter); *Report*, 332.

37 McDonald to Ellice, 16 July 1857 (second letter), LAC, MG 24 A 58, vol. 2, folios 25-34.

38 Ibid.

39 McDonald to Ellice, 19 July 1857, John McDonald of Garth fonds, LAC, MG 24 A 58, folios 25-34.

40 Ellice to McDonald, 31 July 1857, John McDonald Collection, MRBSC, MS 406/4.

41 For information on William Kennedy (mentioned specifically by Ellice in his letter of 6 August) and other vociferous opponents of HBC hegemony in Red River in the context of the debate over the West, see Swainson, "The North-West Transportation Company."

42 Ellice to McDonald, 6 August 1857, John McDonald Collection, MRBSC, MS 406/4.

43 Ellice to McDonald, 14 Sept. 1857, MRBSC, MS 406/4.

44 McDonald's son, De Bellefeuille Macdonald (the spelling varies), to whom he addressed "Autobiographical Notes," had married Harwood's daughter Louise. Because Harwood himself had married a Lotbinière, the marriage linked several notable fur trade families with a Quebec connection of historic distinction. The genealogy of this unusual pair is full of McGillivrays, Campbells, Le Gardeurs, Lotbinières, and Taschereaus. Their descendants remained significant in "correct" Montreal society well into the twentieth century, as clippings in the Archives of Ontario collected by a Calgary descendant show: see AO, John McDonald of Garth Collection, series 5 and 6.

45 Harwood to McDonald, 20 March 1858, John McDonald Collection, MRBSC, MS 406/4.

46 Ibid.

47 For details of the company and its investors, see Swainson, "The North-West Transportation Company."

48 Harwood to McDonald, 8 July 1858, John McDonald Collection, MRBSC, MS 406/4.

49 McDonald to Harwood, 9 July 1858, John McDonald Collection, MRBSC, MS 406/4.

50 Ibid.

51 Ibid.
52 Province of Canada, Provincial Secretary's Office [S.J. Dawson, George Gladman, and H.Y. Hind], *Report on the Exploration*. Hind's report occupies pages 136-425.
53 McDonald to unknown correspondent ["Dear and Honorable Sir"], 15 April 1858, John McDonald Collection, MRBSC, MS 406/4.
54 Ibid.
55 Rich, *The History of the Hudson's Bay Company,* 2:850, 856-57.
56 McDonald to Sandfield Macdonald [addressee surmised from contents], 27 October 1864, John McDonald Collection, MRBSC, MS 406/6. The list of talking points appears in rough draft on a conjunct leaf of the letter, which is either a copy or was never sent.
57 For Sandfield's career at this time, see Hodgins, *John Sandfield Macdonald,* 71-76.
58 Ibid.
59 McDonald to Sandfield Macdonald, 28 October 1864, John McDonald Collection, MRBSC, MS 406/5 (emphasis in original).
60 J.G. Vansittart to McDonald, 23 February 1865, John McDonald Collection, MRBSC, MS 406/5.
61 J.G. Vansittart to McDonald, 25 March 1865, John McDonald Collection, MRBSC, MS 406/5. The letter concludes that the commissioner of Crown lands "will not fail to notice your remarks in your son's favour." Evidently, McDonald had also appealed to Taché for patronage on behalf of his son.
62 There is a typed copy of the article among the transcriptions of McDonald's letters at McGill, which would suggest that the original (no longer in the file) was a copy in his own (difficult) hand.
63 McDonald to [unknown], 21 March 1865, John McDonald Collection, MRBSC, MS 406/5. Possibly a draft of a letter never sent.
64 McDonald to Sandfield Macdonald, 18 July 1865, John McDonald Collection, MRBSC, MS 406/5.
65 Ibid.
66 Grant, *Ocean to Ocean,* 88, 93, 94, 97.
67 Irene Spry's distinguished article on the "Tragedy of the Loss of the Commons in Western Canada" narrates this melancholy story in detail.
68 To their credit, the passage made it into the report. Nine committee members voted in favour; two were opposed. See *Report,* xv.
69 Morton, *A History of the Canadian West,* 458, 495.

Bibliography

Archival Sources

Archives of Ontario (AO)
Correspondence of Chief Justice Draper, F 1027-1.
John McDonald of Garth Collection.

Library and Archives Canada (LAC)
John McDonald of Garth fonds.
Masson Collection.

McGill University Library, Rare Books and Special Collections (MRBSC)
John McDonald Collection, MS 406/1-10

Published Sources

Bailey, Garrick, and Roberta Glenn Bailey. "Indian Territory." *Encyclopedia of North American Indians,* edited by Frederick E. Hoxie, 271-73. New York: Houghton Mifflin, 1996.

Bowering, Ian. *Inverarden Regency Cottage Museum: A History, 1816-1984.* Cornwall: Stormont, Dundas and Glengarry Historical Society, 1984.

Burns, Robert J. *Inverarden: Retirement Home of Fur Trader John McDonald of Garth.* History and Archaeology 25. Ottawa: Parks Canada, 1979.

Canada. *Parliamentary Debates on the Subject of the Confederation of the British North American Provinces ... etc.* Quebec: Hunter Rose and Co., 1865.

Correspondence of Chief Justice Draper ... as to the Proceedings of the Committee of the House of Commons. Toronto: John Notman, 1884.

Fraser, Simon. *The Letters and Journals of Simon Fraser, 1806-1808.* Edited by W. Kaye Lamb. Toronto: Macmillan Company of Canada, 1960.

Friesen, Gerald. *The Canadian Prairies: A History.* Toronto: University of Toronto Press, 1984.

Goheen, Peter. "The Impact of the Telegraph on the Newspaper in Mid-Nineteenth-Century British North America." *Urban Geography* 11, 2 (1990): 107-29.

Grant, George M. *Ocean to Ocean.* Toronto/London: James Campbell and Son/Sampson Low, Marston, Low, and Searle, 1873.

Green, Larry. "An Analysis of the Autobiographical Notes of John McDonald of Garth." Master's thesis, University of Saskatchewan, 1999.

–. "John McDonald of Garth: The Last Nor'Wester." *Alberta History* 47, 4 (1999): 2-12.

Hodgins, Bruce W. *John Sandfield Macdonald, 1812-1872.* Toronto: University of Toronto Press, 1971.

Masson, L.R., ed. *Les bourgeois de la Compagnie du Nord-Ouest.* 2 vols. Québec: Coté et Cie., 1889-90.

Milloy, John S. "The Early Indian Acts: Developmental Strategy and Constitutional Change." In *As Long as the Sun Shines and the Water Flows,* edited by Ian A.L. Getty and Antoine S. Lussier, 56-64. Vancouver: UBC Press, 1983.

Morton, A.S. *A History of the Canadian West to 1870-71.* London: Thomas Nelson and Sons, 1939.

Nicholson, Norman L. *The Boundaries of Canada, Its Provinces and Territories.* Canada, Department of Mines and Technical Surveys, Geographical Branch, Memoir 2. Ottawa: Queen's Printer, 1954.

Province of Canada. Provincial Secretary's Office [S.J. Dawson, George Gladman, and H.Y. Hind]. *Report on the Exploration of the Country between Lake Superior and the Red River Settlement.* Toronto: J. Lovell, 1858.

Rich, E.E. *The History of the Hudson's Bay Company, 1670-1870.* Vol. 2, *1763-1870.* London: Hudson's Bay Record Society, 1959.

Select Committee on the Hudson's Bay Company. *Report of the Select Committee on the Hudson's Bay Company Together with the Proceedings of the Committee, Minutes of Evidence, Appendix and Index.* London: HMSO, 1858.

Spry, Irene. "The Tragedy of the Loss of the Commons in Western Canada" (revised edition), in *As Long as the Sun Shines and the Water Flows,* edited by Ian A.L. Getty and Antoine S. Lussier, 203-28. Vancouver: UBC Press, 1983.

Swainson, Donald. "The North-West Transportation Company: Personnel and Attitudes." *Transactions of the Manitoba Historical Society,* Series 3, 26 (1969-70). http://www.mhs.mb.ca/docs/transactions/3/nwtransport.shtml.

Tobias, John L. "Protection, Civilization, Assimilation: An Outline History of Canada's Indian Policy." In *As Long as the Sun Shines and the Water Flows,* edited by Ian A.L. Getty and Antoine S. Lussier, 39-55. Vancouver: UBC Press, 1983.

Warkentin, Germaine. *Canadian Exploration Literature.* Toronto: Oxford University Press, 1993.

Warkentin, John. "Geography of Confederation." Department of Geography Discussion Paper No. 57, York University, 2004.

Part 3

Ways of Knowing

This section explores how scholars know what they come to know and how the personal lives and relationships scholars engage in with Aboriginal people can shape their understandings and analyses. The chapters are different in approach to most scholarly historical writing on Aboriginal and fur trade history. They reflect developments across the social sciences in which the authorial presence and role in the construction of knowledge is highlighted; like recent scholarship, they also acknowledge scholarship's political contexts and processes and question the concept of objectivity. The personal and sometimes emotional stance of the chapters demonstrates ways of coming to know that incorporate these developments, but the stance also builds on traditional scholarly approaches. Heather Devine's autobiographical account, "Being and Becoming Métis," describes her discovery of personal identity and how learning about her Metis heritage has informed her scholarship. Like many Metis families who did not want their children and grandchildren to face racism and prejudice, Devine's family downplayed their Metis origins over several generations, producing confusion between what people were told and what they experienced. Devine's honest account of her personal and scholarly journey toward understanding is rare and all the more valuable for showing how powerful the knowledge of one's cultural identity can be and what special perspectives Aboriginal scholars can bring to the study of their ancestors' lives. Devine became a historian by working on her own family history and by completing her doctorate under the supervision of John Foster and Jennifer S.H. Brown. She now researches Canadian Native history, western Canadian ethnicity, museum and archival studies, and public history while teaching in the Department of History at the University of Calgary.

In "Historical Research and the Place of Oral History," Susan Elaine Gray shows how important it can be for non-Aboriginal scholars to spend time with Aboriginal people to learn from them (including culturally appropriate ways of learning) and to develop relationships within which they can come to understand Aboriginal perspectives. Gray completed her doctorate at the University of Manitoba under the supervision of Jennifer S.H. Brown and has continued her research on Aboriginal history in western Canada as a postdoctoral fellow who works with Brown at the Centre for Rupert's Land Studies. Gray's example of embodied learning within the context of respectful relationships is a crucial methodological practice. It can restore relations of trust between university-based scholars and Aboriginal community members after a long period during which Aboriginal people felt that, despite being studied to death, as they often say, few benefits flowed back to communities. Learning through living, learning to respect cultural protocols about how to ask questions, and learning to give as much as Aboriginal interviewees open doors for understanding. Culturally based perceptions in the present shed light on important historical issues and on the reading of historical documents. Learning the realities that Aboriginal people face in the present can be an important basis for understanding the realities they faced in the past.

7

Being and Becoming Métis: A Personal Reflection

Heather Devine

WHEN I WAS FIRST approached to write a paper on Métis identity formation, I agreed because I thought that perhaps a personal reflection on the topic might resonate with others with similar experiences and offer some explanations to those who did not understand the phenomenology of becoming Métis.[1] This reflection has been much more difficult, personally, than I could have anticipated. On the one hand, it is difficult to articulate what is essentially my private experience and that of my immediate family and package it for public scrutiny. I feel vulnerable in such a situation. On the other hand, from an academic perspective, I have always had a problem with the uncritical acceptance of autobiographical sources to understand the experiences of a group of people, whether they be Aboriginal, homosexuals, war veterans, politicians, or any other collective. I am also concerned with the recent tendency of some publishers (and readers) to uncritically privilege autobiographical accounts created by members of marginalized groups over mainstream ethnohistory.[2]

Although the embrace of autobiography may be an expedient way to correct the paucity of minority voices in academia, it has shortcomings.[3] In a review essay some years ago, I presented the following perspective on the subject:

> In its favour, autobiography has an important role to play in understanding the lived experiences of ethnocultural groups, both historical and contemporary. For those racial, religious, and cultural minorities estranged from the mainstream institutions responsible for shaping – and suppressing – cultural identity, autobiography offers freedom of expression without the editorial contamination of mainstream "experts." At its best, autobiographical writing provides an insider's perspective on identity that is intrinsically superior to the analyses of even the most sensitive observer. The best autobiographies offer a window into an area of ethnicity that is imperfectly understood – this being the existential, psychological dimensions of living as a person of a particular ethnic identity.
>
> Autobiography has its own shortcomings, however. For example, autobiography, by its very nature, is intrinsically biased. One can never assume that the entire life story is being provided, that the facts are entirely accurate, or that the chronicler is neutral in his or her assessment of past personalities or events. Autobiographies are also very particularistic. Making broad generalizations about

ethnic identity based on one or two autobiographical assessments is a risky undertaking at best. At their worst, when produced by individuals with social, political, or economic agendas, autobiographies can devolve into thinly disguised propaganda pieces.[4]

I have not diverged from this view of autobiography, yet I found myself writing what is essentially an autobiographical essay. So how did I approach this task?

Certainly, there is no shortage of critical literature on the subject. One volume I found particularly helpful for coming to terms with autobiography was Paul John Eakin's collection *The Ethics of Life Writing* (2004). The essays in this volume address a number of the issues that bedevil writers of life narratives. A primary focus (alluded to previously in the context of Aboriginal biography) concerns the authenticity or representativeness of a person's life history in relation to group experience. Ethical issues abound, including one's obligations when exposing the private lives of relatives and friends in the context of life writing and the aesthetic and factual choices involved in revealing or concealing information. For example, when does the inclusion of too much detail – or giving the narrative a literary treatment – become self-indulgent, prurient, or even dishonest rather than informative? Predictably enough, the writers of the essays and the editors of the volume did not come to any satisfying or definitive answers to the questions raised. What was suggested, however, is that "identity and morality are inextricably connected" and that life writing can serve as a form of moral deliberation, "with the goal of establishing ethical relationships to the past, present, and future, all conditioned by a clear-eyed examination of causes, extenuations, weaknesses, emotional crimes, and gifts."[5]

On reflection, it occurred to me that the practice of history, like life writing, is also a form of moral deliberation intended to establish ethical relationships to the past, present, and future. Maybe that is why I gravitated to history as a way to explore issues of personal and collective identity in the first place, because history is about trying to understand why past events transpired as they did, how the course of the past has affected our lives in the present, and how the past might influence our decision making in the future.

It was also necessary to situate myself ethically within the larger context of Aboriginal scholarship, in particular as an Aboriginal scholar of Métis ancestry. What social and cultural baggage do I bring to the table when I discuss the controversial topic of Aboriginal identity? Is it possible for an urban mixed-blood to possess an authentic Aboriginal voice?

Much of the recent scholarship on the subject of Aboriginal identity is contentious, particularly the debates over mixed-race scholars who claim distant Aboriginal ancestry and are hired, subsequently, by Native Studies departments as Aboriginal academics. The critics maintain that these individuals are ethnic frauds who bring inaccurate (even fabricated) Aboriginal life experiences into the classroom. They also argue that the presence of these scholars serves merely to maintain the academic status quo, thereby undermining the efforts of "real" Indian academics to get hired or to effect change in the academy.[6] Not all literature on the subject is quite so heated, however. As Linda Tuhiwai Smith notes, the sheer brutality of residential schools and government legislation was intended to obliterate collective indigenous identities and impose a new order. She goes on to state that "the effect of such discipline was to silence (forever in some cases) or to suppress the ways of knowing, and the languages for knowing, of *many different indigenous peoples*. Reclaiming a voice in this context has also been about reclaiming, reconnecting, and reordering those ways of knowing which were submerged, hidden, or driven underground."[7]

Certainly, the lived experiences of most indigenous people reflect this reality. This is the case for the Canadian Métis, who have spent most of the past few decades reasserting their long-submerged collective and individual identities. The Canadian Métis are unique among North American peoples of mixed race. Unlike our metis relations elsewhere, we were able to develop a distinct and separate ethnic identity on the North American continent, despite the assimilative pressures of both our Aboriginal and non-Aboriginal parent cultures. The process of "reclaiming, reconnecting, and reordering" one's Métis identity remains poorly understood, largely because we have had to depend on the willingness of individual Métis to take on the task of articulating this process of ethnogenesis in a manner accessible to academics and members of the public.

And in that spirit, I offer you my personal journey.

My Story

When I was a small child growing up in central Alberta in the 1950s, I had absolutely no concept of what "Native" meant. I certainly didn't realize that my own mother might possibly be Native. All I knew was that my mother had thick black hair and brown skin and brown eyes and didn't look anything like the other moms on the block where we lived. I liked to brush my mother's hair because it was so thick and black and shiny. When I asked her why she had black hair and brown skin, she would say that she was adopted and didn't know who her real family was.

It was all a big mystery, which really didn't seem to matter at the time. In the little town where our family lived, I was unaware of any sense of possibly being different. Our world was a quiet rural cocoon made up of old folks, vegetable gardens, caring neighbours, Sunday school, and birthday parties.

Figure 7.1   Heather Devine with her mother and sister, October 1959. Personal collection of Heather Devine.

When I was eight years old, my parents moved our family to a large town in northern Alberta. Our first home was in a trailer park situated down the hill and across a creek from a Native shanty town, known unofficially as Moccasin Flats and sometimes as Little Vietnam. Day in and day out, I watched the residents of Little Vietnam trudge slowly up and down the hill, in various stages of drunkenness, while the local kids in the trailer park yelled at them. Invariably, it was "the Indians" or "the half-breeds" who were accused of stealing meat from people's freezers, which were located in the wooden porches attached to their trailers.

With my friends, I would sneak up the banks of the creek to spy on the Native residents of Moccasin Flats. Once, I can remember running away in terror when an old Kokom, her eyes a-twinkle, knelt down where my friend and I were hiding in some bushes near the creek where she was washing clothes and said, "I see you."

In the fall of 1964, I went to school, where I got to know a resident of Moccasin Flats. Her name was Rosalie. She was poor and wore dirty, threadbare clothes to school. I was the new kid in Grade Four. We were both shunned as outsiders, so we ended up sharing a locker.

Rosalie was shy and quiet. When winter came, she still arrived at school with bare legs, shoes with holes, and no socks. I asked her if she was cold, and she claimed she wasn't. I didn't believe her. By the end of the school year, she was gone. I don't know what happened to her.

By the time I reached Grades Five and Six, I was fairly familiar with the racial pecking order in our town, a hierarchy that I did not question and that had little to do with me – or so I thought. Whites were on top, Métis (at least those with jobs) were in the middle, and Indians were at the bottom. Native kids got hassled a lot by the teachers – for absenteeism, for poor hygiene, and for inappropriate dress. One Métis kid in my class regularly got singled out by my Grade Six teacher for poor hygiene because his fingernails were dirty and he didn't bathe. Of course, he had no access to running water at home, but this didn't seem to make much of a difference to the teachers in our school. Most Native kids in the school had mukluks to wear on their feet in the winter, but they then had to put up with being lined up with their faces against the wall of the school for wearing rags on their feet, not "proper footwear." Another crude diagnostic of Aboriginal identity in our community was the eyeglasses worn by Native students. Welfare recipients who required vision care were issued plain glasses with solid black frames – cat's eyes for the girls and square frames for the boys. The glasses were so ugly that no one with a choice (i.e., money) would ever buy them. Those black glasses were like having the words "welfare recipient" painted in large letters across your face.

Needless to say, the Native kids in town were pretty tough. I learned early on to watch my *p*'s and *q*'s around certain kids with a chip on their shoulders. I also learned, in a streetwise sort of way, the significance of kinship in the Native community. I observed, very early on, that anyone who got into a fight with a Native kid would eventually be fighting the brothers, sisters, and cousins as well.

There was another group of Native families in the community who were, for all intents and purposes, invisible from an "Aboriginal identity" point of view. These were the families whom Commissioner A.E. Ewing in the 1930s might have described as "respectable" Métis.[8] Generally, these families were headed by one Native parent and one white parent, one or both of whom were gainfully employed, and were housed and conducted themselves in accordance with the mainstream. A discreet silence was maintained about their Native ancestry, though most long-term residents knew who was, and who was not, Native.

When outsiders who looked Native moved into the community, subtle, and not so subtle, inquiries were made by white acquaintances: Do you speak French? Do you speak Cree? Métis ancestry was simply not discussed in the open in our town. Instead, the local whites arrived at their own conclusions and acted accordingly.

These oblique questions and other not-so-subtle occurrences were the first incidents that alerted my mother and the rest of our family to the possibility that her hidden ancestry might possibly be Native. First there were the questions about speaking French or Cree. Then there was the behaviour of local storekeepers. My mother stopped shopping at one local grocery because the owners treated her like a thief every time she and my younger sister entered the premises.

The local Métis were also not shy about discussing Mom's ancestry. "Mary, you're Métis!" they would tell her, despite her protestations that she was adopted and really didn't know what she was. On another occasion, my mother was accused by another Métis woman, a complete stranger, of being uppity because she was married to a white man. For my mom, it was all very confusing, given that she had no real knowledge of having a Métis background at the time.

Finally, there was the bullying and name calling that seemed to come from nowhere. Although in the past my older sister and I had experienced bullying, we did not attribute it to any sense of being different – certainly not because of skin colour. Like many families of mixed race, not everyone in our family looked Native. My mother and two of my sisters were dark, but my skin and hair were lighter because I resembled my father more than my mother. We also didn't have the characteristic accent that marked the spoken English of people raised in Native households. But when my sisters and I were together, physical intimidation came with racial slurs. I can remember on one occasion being forced to either kiss the ground or get beaten up. On another occasion outside the local swimming pool, my older sister was called a dirty Indian. I defended her forcefully by saying that we were Irish and German, the only ethnicity that we knew about in our family at the time.

Given the attitudes prevalent in town, it is small wonder that those with mixed ancestry tended to hide it whenever possible. But those Métis who were poor and the Non-Status Indians who came into town with their welfare cheques at the end of the month were not so fortunate.

Two communities existed side by side in our town. One was Native, and the other was white. It was only in later years, in the 1970s and '80s, that the oppressive living conditions of local Native people appeared to improve. Low-rental housing was provided for poor families, social services for Aboriginal people were introduced into the community, and the poverty of those less fortunate eased somewhat.

When I was growing up, I did not understand the roots of Aboriginal poverty. I did not understand what made a person Indian and what made a person Métis.

I certainly did not understand why Treaty Indians had benefits and rights while Non-Status Indians who were culturally identical to their treaty cousins had no rights and no protection. Like most young people raised in a working-class environment, I had my own money problems to deal with. There were very few well-paying jobs for teenagers: in my town, most decent jobs were taken by adults who truly needed them.

Most teens took one of two paths after high school – they either stayed in town or moved away. If you wanted more education or wanted to see the world, you left. I left. Over the ensuing years, I returned sporadically to work during the summers and, later, to teach. During this period, I remained ignorant of any Native heritage in my family. In the 1970s, however, a significant event turned my worldview upside down.

My mother discovered her biological family.

Apparently, my adoptive grandparents had given my mother some rather sketchy details regarding her birth and adoption before they passed away, including her original given name and surname. Armed with this rather scanty information, my mother began her search, telephoning people with the same surname, which was fairly uncommon. Eventually, my mom and dad found themselves in a small town north of the Qu'Appelle Valley in Saskatchewan, where my mother made inquiries at the municipal office regarding the family that had her surname. After several referrals, telephone calls, and letters of inquiry, my mother received a telephone call from a woman who had heard of her visit and told her that she could help her find her mother. My mother, however, had to give her time. Some time later, my mother received a second telephone call, from yet another woman, who asked if she was the woman searching for her mother. When my mom answered in the affirmative, the voice on the other end of the line said, "I'm your mother."

My mom eventually reunited with her biological mother, and she was able to ask her about the source of her dark skin, hair, and eyes. Her mother replied with the rather interesting information that her father was of Syrian extraction. Because her biological father had apparently passed away, my mother was not able to confirm this. So, for a few more years, my mother, my sisters, and I operated under the assumption that our unknown grandfather was Syrian, an ancestry that made absolutely no sense to us in the context of rural Saskatchewan and served to further deepen the mystery of our shared past.

It took a few years for my biological grandmother to reveal the name of my mother's father and even more time for my mother to track down her father's family and make discreet inquiries by mail. As it turned out, my mother's father was of Syrian and Métis extraction. Although her father had passed away before she could meet him, she was able to meet his three sisters, who lived in Regina.

Figure 7.2   Heather Devine's mother with her adoptive family, Saskatchewan, 1943.
Personal collection of Heather Devine.

They graciously welcomed her into their homes and shared with her information about her father. Apparently, my mother's father had known of her existence
and had expressed a desire to search for her but did not know where to start.
Mom's aunts also directed her to the tiny village of Lebret, about an hour's drive
away, where she could look at the parish records of their Métis mother's family,
the Desjarlais.

It is hard to explain what happens to a person who discovers previously hidden ancestral roots. Often the knowledge comes with a feeling of elation and
relief because, for the first time, isolated events in the past can be understood
in light of the new information and begin to make some sense. Certainly, our
experience of discrimination and our isolated, puzzling encounters with other
Native people in northern Alberta could be placed in some kind of context.
Unbeknownst to my mom, my sisters, and me, our ethnicity was physically
obvious to other people long before we were aware of it ourselves. Because we
had all been socialized as mainstream Euro-Canadians, we were completely
oblivious to the social ramifications of our physical appearance until we moved
to a community with a large population of Native people. Both Natives and
whites expected us to have a specific tool kit of values, attitudes, behaviours,

and skills to match our physical appearance. When we did not respond appropriately, confusion resulted on both sides.

I am sure that people who become born-again Christians or gays who come out of the closet experience a similar epiphany in terms of their sense of self. But I can only speak of my own personal experience, which, to borrow a book title, became for me the experience of being and becoming Métis.[9]

After the initial sense of relief subsided, it was replaced with an intense desire to find out everything I could about my Métis ancestry. I started my search when my mother phoned to tell me about her visit to the Roman Catholic church at Lebret, where she was able to see my great-grandmother's baptismal records. Mom gave me the names of Rosine Desjarlais' parents (Thomas Desjarlais and Madeleine Klyne), the sponsors at her baptism (Veronique Klyne and Joseph Bellegarde), and the officiating priest (Father Joseph Hugonard, O.M.I.). My cousin in northern Saskatchewan also provided me with all sorts of family information – baptismal records, reminiscences, and a limited family tree. During the mid-1980s, I became preoccupied with the genealogy of my mother's family, which had miraculously revealed itself. A small handful of names and a healthy curiosity and interest in the past started me on a quest that soon became an obsession that occupied most of my free moments and caused my family no end of puzzlement and, at times, consternation.

As it turned out, there was a local chapter of the Alberta Genealogical Society (AGS) in the city of Edmonton, where I lived. Edmonton was also the home of the founder of the AGS, Charles Denney. Denney, now deceased, was a former provincial archivist of Alberta. In his younger years, he had begun the task of researching the ancestry of his first wife, who was descended from some of the earliest Scots and Métis settlers at Red River. His initial interest in his wife's ancestry blossomed into a consuming interest in the genealogy of the Métis people of western Canada. Denney donated his extensive collection of genealogical records – compiled from parish records, scrip affidavits, and correspondence from descendants throughout western Canada – to the Glenbow Archives in the 1980s. Denney continued to work on Métis genealogy after the bulk of his collection moved to Calgary, however, and he kept the working copies of the collection at the Edmonton Branch Library of the AGS. I became a regular visitor to that library, where I meticulously compiled the family tree of Rosine Desjarlais and her numerous ancestors and learned a great deal of early western Canadian history along the way from Denney's huge collection of history books.

The Edmonton Branch of the AGS holds monthly meetings with featured guest speakers. On one occasion, a history professor from the University of Alberta, John Foster, came to speak about the fur trade and the Métis. During the coffee break that followed, I approached Professor Foster with a list of names of North West Company voyageurs who figured in my genealogy. I asked him politely if he could tell me anything about these people.

To his credit, Professor Foster did not laugh at me, tell me he was too busy, or simply suggest some books to read. Instead, he invited me to stop by his office at the University of Alberta. At that time, I was working for the government of Alberta in a building on campus, and it was a five-minute walk from my office to his. I agreed to meet with him the following week.

Armed with my list and a series of additional questions, I went to see Foster the next week. As it turned out, he did not answer any of my questions. But that didn't stop us from having a wonderful conversation about the fur trade, the Métis, and genealogy. This was the first of a series of informal conversations in which I learned from him and he learned about me. During these sessions, Foster sought to channel my interest in genealogy toward academic work by suggesting that I take his undergraduate course on the pre-settlement West, which I subsequently did. I used that course to investigate the origins of one of my fur trade ancestors, a Canadien voyageur of Hessian extraction by the name of Klein.[10] When I completed the course successfully, Foster suggested that I consider graduate school. But since I was employed full time with the Alberta government, it was not a proposal I was prepared to take seriously.

Instead, I agreed to take a directed study course as an unclassified student under Professor Foster's guidance. During the course, I investigated a number of seemingly esoteric topics, such as patronage in pre-industrial societies and the structure and ethos of Highland Scottish clans. My research culminated in a paper devoted to expatriate Scots in North America, their military and commercial experiences under Sir William Johnson, and their eventual formation of the North West Company.[11]

In retrospect, I realize that my preoccupation with the historical aspects of my ancestry was a safety mechanism of sorts. By 1990, my job involved close work with Aboriginal communities interested in preserving and interpreting their heritage. I found myself dealing with contemporary Native issues on a daily basis. Keeping my ancestry to myself was a way of maintaining some distance between my personal investigations into Aboriginality and my day-to-day work, a stance that grew harder to maintain as time went on. I found myself increasingly conflicted about my role as a government worker and my evolving perceptions of Native issues, and I was influenced not a little by the unanswered questions about my own heritage.

I had started a correspondence with my mother's cousin, who was teaching in northern Saskatchewan on an Indian reserve at the time. We soon found that we shared a common interest in our family history and swapped information,

Figure 7.3   Heather Devine with her great-aunt Rachel in the 1990s, Regina.
Personal collection of Heather Devine.

recipes, and observations about the world in general and the Native world in
particular. The events at Oka were particularly disturbing. When we were discussing the stoning of women, children, and old people on the Mercier Bridge,
my cousin said, "I felt like they were throwing rocks at *me*."[12]

It was not until I found myself at a national treaty conference in Edmonton that I began to feel, in some measure, what my cousin was experiencing. A Mohawk chief who addressed the crowd displayed the famous Two-Row Wampum and discussed its significance in the context of treaty rights. The chief also took the opportunity to address a scattering of Métis representatives in the audience: "You may have your jig and your Red River Cart, but you're not really Aboriginal." My initial reaction was anger, which was obviously shared by the Métis in the audience, many of whom pointedly walked out in protest. My second reaction was frustration – I wanted to leave the room as well, but I was present at the conference in a professional capacity, as a government technician working with Indian bands.

It was my first encounter with the political reality that Métis people across Canada face as they struggle to find a place in either the Treaty Indian or mainstream community, only to be rejected by both. Depending on where they live, they respond as best they can; they try to access the patchwork of government services provided as almost an afterthought to the Métis. Some try to achieve recognition or status as Indians, a zero-sum game. At what point do Métis people throw in the towel and suppress their dual heritage for the good of their children? Do they try to become white? Why, for example, did my great-grandmother not teach Cree and Saulteaux (Ojibwe) to her children, for she spoke those languages herself? Why did she seek to distance herself from her own background during much of her life? These questions nagged at me.

Eventually, fate intervened. My job ended with the Alberta government in the spring of 1993. A week later, I applied for and received my Métis card from the Métis Nation of Alberta and was invited to join a Métis women's organization around the same time.

It was at this point that I left what could be called the safe or honeymoon period of my explorations into my Métis identity to come face to face with contemporary reality. As I mentioned earlier, I was careful not to bring up the topic of ancestry, ostensibly to maintain neutrality at work. In reality, I was being dishonest with myself. The real reason that I kept my ancestry to myself was because I was afraid of how people would react.

I was not ashamed of my Métis roots. Far from it. I was very proud of my newly discovered heritage. What I was afraid of was being rejected by other Métis people. One of the realities of discovering one's Aboriginal ancestry is that new Métis (i.e., people who discover their Métis heritage later in life rather than being raised within their heritage) are often lumped in the same category as "the wannabe."[13] The wannabe is primarily an American phenomenon, though Europe has its own unique subculture of European re-enactors. Wannabes are non-Native people who are fascinated with the trappings and spirituality of traditional Aboriginal culture and want to become Native. They can be found at powwows, they may be employed in government agencies working for and with Native people, they immerse themselves in Aboriginal spirituality, and they try desperately for acceptance. Some of them marry into the Native community as a means of entrance. Because there is a real problem with wannabes appropriating and distorting Aboriginal cultural and spiritual practices and marketing artwork, clothing, and other commercial items as Indian, there has been a violent backlash against these people by Native American organizations and individuals.

During the nineteenth century, non-Natives who intermarried with Indians were often viewed as economic and political threats by full-bloods on American reservations because their bicultural backgrounds enabled them to exploit the existing commercial and governing networks – usually at the expense of their fellow tribespeople.[14]

As the ravages of removal, allotment, and, later, termination and relocation were visited on American indigenous communities, it became far more difficult to maintain a sense of cultural and spiritual separateness. Race became the key to maintaining indigenous distinctiveness and became the basis for government policy when it came to determining membership in Native American tribal communities. Racial dilution is seen as an even greater threat today, even though race has been discredited as a useful determiner of ethnicity. As a result, any individual perceived as non-Indian who tries to join a Native American tribal community is viewed as a threat to the genetic and cultural integrity of the entire tribe. The failure of individual communities to maintain this form of isolation, in turn, is viewed as a threat to the survival of all indigenous communities as separate and distinct corporate entities. How can an individual claim to be an Indian, they argue, if he or she differs little, racially or culturally, from the mainstream society that surrounds the reservation?

The Métis as a group are notable for their absence as a defined tribal category among indigenous groups recognized by the United States government. This omission is curious, especially given that the US government closely monitored the activities of mixed-bloods in the American Southeast and Midwest and eventually established a series of halfbreed tracts beginning in the 1820s to accommodate mixed-blood members of tribal groups. Moreover, there are several mixed-race communities in the United States that share long-standing historical and kin connections with Métis communities in Canada. Notwithstanding the efforts of several of these American mixed-race groups to arrive at some form of accommodation with incoming settlers while maintaining their kinship links with tribal cousins, they were generally unsuccessful in the long run. In the struggles over land and political influence that invariably ensued, most of these American biracial populations were disenfranchised from their Aboriginal communities of origin.[15]

In recent years, debates about the racial makeup of Native American tribal communities have taken an interesting turn. In the American southeast, the home of the Five Civilized Tribes, the pressure to exclude racially mixed people has been directed at those tribal members with African American rather than Euro-American ancestry.[16] The tribal group most affected by this controversy is the Cherokee. The reasons for exclusion are complex, but they can be traced to an upsurge in applications for tribal membership as Native American communities involved in casino gambling became prosperous. The American South has traditionally been the most poverty-stricken of US regions; not surprisingly, it also has the largest concentrations of poor African Americans.[17]

In Canada, the Métis have been a historical and political reality for at least two hundred years, and communities of culturally distinct Métis people continue to function in a Métis cultural context today. Although there was a fifty-year hiatus after 1885 when Métis political organizations were powerless if not invisible, today there is a very strong network of provincial and national Métis organizations that lobbies for the political, social, and economic well-being of its constituents.[18]

There has always been tacit recognition among Métis politicians that a combination of government policy and discrimination has resulted in large numbers of Métis people losing their heritage over succeeding generations. However, until recently, there has been some resistance to accepting new Métis back into the fold, despite the political capital that large numbers of Métis would provide the provincial and federal organizations seeking program funds. There have been many reasons for this reluctance. The presence of uncomfortable cultural and economic differences between new and established Métis sometimes made it difficult to integrate new arrivals. Like other Canadian Native groups, Métis politicians have also been concerned with the question of social optics, that is, the need to establish distinctive cultural and racial boundaries between themselves and non-Native Canadians. This task has been made much more difficult by the amount of intermarriage and cultural effacement that occurred in the decades after 1885. Although Métis have always had formal and informal mechanisms for identifying their own people at the community level, the constitutional recognition of Métis hunting rights resulting from the *Powley* ruling of 2003 has now made it imperative to establish a visible, recognizable corporate identity for the eyes of skeptical government officials and the Canadian public at large.[19] Métis politicians have also had to fight for political recognition in the face of opposition from First Nations groups who resent the emergence of another Aboriginal group competing for scarce government resources.

Most governments keep detailed statistical records of their populations to create, deliver, and adjust programs and services to meet changing economic and social needs. Since the 1982 changes to the Canadian Constitution, which identified Métis as one of three constitutionally distinct Aboriginal identities in the nation, Statistics Canada has been increasingly active in monitoring and analyzing census data on Métis populations. In recent years, for example, it has noted that the number of people self-identifying as Métis has skyrocketed across Canada. Métis sociologist Chris Anderson has recently observed that the increase in Canadian Métis during this period has been an "astonishing and demographically improbable increase of 43 percent."[20] There are a number of explanations for this population explosion, but to the cynical observer, the sudden increase in Métis people through self-declaration can only be attributed to some economic or social advantage.

In recent years, "identity politics" has become a mode of expressive self-affirmation as well as instrumental self-advancement. This is in part because ethnic categories have become a critical tool of the state apparatus. Nation-states create categories for various reasons, such as to count people for census, taxation, and apportionment for political representation. Ethnic categories as generated by state policy are relevant to a variety of civic and political matters; furthermore, they are appropriated and used by various groups for their own strategic needs.[21]

It is clear that in recent years instrumental ethnicity, that is, the tactical use of ethnicity for personal or group gain, has influenced the establishment, membership, and policies of Métis organizations across Canada. When organizations such as the Métis Association of Alberta were first established, however, the initial impetus was the alleviation of the desperate circumstances facing many Non-Status Indians and Métis in northern Alberta.

By the 1930s, the living conditions of the northern Alberta Métis had deteriorated seriously. Because of problems with the implementation of Métis scrip after Treaties 6 and 8, most of the Alberta Métis did not have title to their own land. Instead, they subsisted as squatters. Crown land – upon which the northern Métis relied for hunting, fishing, and gathering – was about to be opened for homesteading after the federal government transferred responsibility for the management of natural resources to provincial governments in 1930.[22] Because many northern Métis lived outside of large communities in the bush, they and their children had little access to medical services, schools, or permanent employment. The onset of the Depression made life even more difficult for a people already impoverished. In response to their desperate plight, the Alberta government established the Ewing Commission in 1934 to examine the social conditions of the Métis and develop strategies for assisting those in need.

The terms of reference that governed the commission's research were strictly defined. Chairman A.E. Ewing was explicit in his view regarding the role of historical, political, and economic evidence:

> I do not see much good in raking up any mistakes that were made (or at least what some people may think were mistakes) years ago. If you want to go into the history of the whole situation from early times and show that there is a moral responsibility resting upon the State to care for these people, not only a moral, but perhaps a legal responsibility, that is one matter; to say that their condition is such at the moment the State must act upon these conditions is another matter. Do you wish to establish that there is a moral responsibility on past governments for the condition of the half-breed population today? ... I am simply saying that it will not get us far to harp on what has happened in the past.[23]

Having dispensed with the historical context that could have helped to identify the social, political, and economic origins of Métis destitution, the commission proceeded to focus on the contemporary health, education, and overall welfare of Alberta's Métis.[24]

One of the initial tasks of the commission was to define who was and who was not a halfbreed to determine which Aboriginal people would receive benefits from any future government assistance intended for Métis people. Although they invited Métis representatives and other knowledgeable individuals to participate in the hearings, the committee members had their own ideas about what constituted the Métis identity. Métis representative Malcolm Norris – an educated, middle-class intellectual – found it particularly difficult to communicate an inclusive definition of Métis identity to a committee unable, or unwilling, to hear it:

Hearings, Feb. 25, 1935

> MR. NORRIS: ... We would put the half-breed population, men, women, and children as from eight to ten thousand, or even in excess of that. I would say that from ten to thirteen thousand is the more accurate figure. Of course I should say this, there are a number of Métis people who do not wish to be classed as Métis, they are camouflaged as white men.

THE CHAIRMAN: Arising from a remark you have just made, there is rather an important matter, "how do you define a half-breed or a metis?"

MR. NORRIS: Well, that is rather a delicate question and I have not met a man yet who could fully define or explain to me just what is meant by the term "half-breed." As to the definition of half-breed or metis, personally I hold this opinion, anyone who is not qualified unless, well in other words, if he couldn't pass a grade four examination, who might be really one-sixteenth [sic] breed and who has not been assimilated in the social fabric of our civilization is a metis, or put it this way, if he had a drop of Indian blood in his veins and has not been assimilated in the social fabric of our civilization is a metis –

THE CHAIRMAN: Is your view this, correct me if I'm wrong, that anyone who has the slightest strain of Indian blood and who lives the life ordinarily lived by the metis population, not differing from them in the standpoint of education and ordinary life, should be treated as a half-breed, for the purposes of this Commission?

MR. NORRIS: Yes, sir that is so, maybe I can make it clearer, you will find this in the North West Territories regulations as to camping and trapping. That any half-breed living the life of an Indian would be qualified to trap in certain reserves that were restricted from other people.

MR. DOUGLAS: What you mean is, that he would be able to get a license to trap?

MR. NORRIS: I am trying to give you some definition of what I mean by the term half-breed. A man might have more white blood in his veins than Indian, a red moustache, blonde hair, and he might be living absolutely the life of an Indian, but he would be given the name and come within the category of a half-breed. In dealing with a man of that type, with only a small proportion of Indian blood in his veins, yet he would be in the category of the half-breed.

MR. DOUGLAS: That is where he belongs?

MR. NORRIS: Yes ... More or less, yes. Of course we have to remain, or try to remain in the region of logic, certainly there would be some who would have to be eliminated, a certain number whom we could not expect to receive any consideration from any Government.

MR. DOUGLAS: Stay with that a moment, as a general rule in compiling a statement as to the number of half-breeds you would say that anyone with Indian blood in their veins, living the life of a half-breed, should be treated as a half-breed, that is how I understand your definition?

MR. NORRIS: Yes, sir, that is so.[25]

Although Malcolm Norris tried to keep the concept of identity definition separate and distinct from the task of identifying needy Métis people for government assistance, he was ultimately unsuccessful. In the end, the government commissioners arrived at a definition of Métis identity that was teleological in nature. If you were poor, diseased, uneducated, and primarily Indian in your genetic makeup, you were Métis. The definition served to identify the most destitute and needy members of the Non-Status Indian population, but it failed to incorporate the diversity of subsistence patterns, social classes, geographical locales, languages, religions, Aboriginal ancestries, and political sentiments that were, and are, the cultural reality of the Métis people.

The commissioners chose, in effect, to develop a pathological definition of Métis identity that excluded all Métis who were economically prosperous, urban dwellers, businesspeople or professionals, or had less than 25 percent Aboriginal blood quantum.[26] The respectable Métis, as these individuals were called, were arbitrarily stripped of their Aboriginal rights and heritage, an act that widened the social and economic gap between themselves and their less fortunate kin. For the respectable Métis, the only path was complete assimilation.

The Métis people, as defined by the Ewing Commission, were people who were destitute, unskilled, uneducated, and incapable of helping themselves. In return for accepting this pathological definition, they were allowed to retain remnants of their Aboriginal identities, to become quasi-Indians who lived on quasi-reserves. What they gave up, in return, were broad networks of kinship with both their Native and Euro-Canadian relatives – the linkages that, in the past, had always been essential to maintaining their freedom and special identity in a hostile world.

It is the children of the "respectable" Métis, as well as the offspring of those Métis forced to make their living in the mainstream towns and cities of the non-boreal south, who met a wall of silence from their parents and grandparents when they asked questions about their Aboriginal past. It is these lost generations of Métis children and grandchildren, along with a motley collection of Métis adoptees and foster children, who now find themselves at the doors of Métis locals in western Canada, trying to reconnect with their long-lost heritage.

As noted earlier, the Métis politicians and bureaucrats who control the levers of power in Métis organizations may be hesitant to welcome these lost birds into the nest because cultural differences that stem from assimilation can create unforeseen political difficulties within organizations. Although most Métis organizations normally welcome new members, they are not always eager to have these individuals active in the organization in any meaningful way – unless

Figure 7.4   Heather Devine's grandmothers: three generations, c. 1900. *Left to right:* Magdeleine Klyne, née Beauchemin; Marie Justine (b. 17 July 1884) and Rosine (b. 11 June 1880) Desjarlais; Magdeleine Desjarlais, née Klyne. Saskatchewan Archives Board R-8823.

they can keep them under control. Many of the new Métis are well educated; they have postsecondary training and a solid familiarity with the policies and procedures for administering mainstream organizations.

Unlike earlier Métis politicians who came from backgrounds more privileged than those of their followers, the cohort of Métis politicians that has been responsible for reviving Métis organizations from the 1960s onward is composed primarily of working-class activists.[27] Outsiders might be surprised at the hefty salaries that many of the officers in Métis organizations enjoy. Their compensation is often higher than individuals with similar qualifications would receive in mainstream organizations. The insiders who occupy these well-paying positions are keenly aware of the power that controlling the economic levers of the organization provides. They will do their utmost to marginalize anyone who might possibly threaten the economic status quo of the organization – whether it be through the introduction of professional qualifications for administrative positions, an insistence on strict financial controls, or a determination to seek a position of influence within the organization itself.

It is small wonder that politicians in Métis country have enjoyed a less than savoury reputation over the past three decades.[28] Stories of physical intimidation, financial malfeasance, political factionalism, and character assassination are not hearsay but rather a sad reality – not only in Métis political circles but also in some First Nations communities and organizations.

When I discussed a few of these scandals with my cousin in Saskatchewan, he merely laughed and said that educated people were a threat. Then he proceeded to tell me about his own adventures in Métis politics during the 1970s, which culminated in physical threats against him and my great-aunt Lulu. Their crime: starting a new Métis political organization in Regina and successfully applying for funds – at the expense of the main organization.

My personal baptism of fire came during my tenure on the board of a Métis women's organization. I served for two years on the board as a member at large, without signing privileges of any sort. By the end of my term, I was forced to mobilize the remaining board members to oust our president, who had managed to circumvent the administrative checks and balances in the operation of our organization to empty the bank accounts over a four-month period. For two months, I conducted what was essentially an audit of our finances. I investigated our non-profit status with the provincial government, contacted our elders to make the necessary decisions, called meetings, and contacted our funding agencies to advise them of what had taken place. At the end of it all, I thought long and hard about the brutal derailment of the organization. In retrospect, I realized that one of the reasons I had been welcomed to the organization, and to the board, by our president was because she saw me as a new Métis – someone eager to be accepted and, therefore, someone whom she could control. Even if I did ask questions, I could be lied to or otherwise diverted because I was naive and trusting.

What our president did not know was that I was not totally naive or totally insecure. First of all, I had the advice and moral support of my Métis cousin in Saskatchewan, who had warned me about political corruption of this sort. Because my cousin was born and raised Métis on both sides of his family, he had no insecurities regarding his identity. He had torn up his Métis card some time earlier (a common act among modern Saskatchewan Métis, as it turns out). As he pointed out to me, "I don't need a card to tell me who I am."

Also, unbeknownst to my colleagues, I had been doing a great deal of reading. At that time, the importance of historiography and theory was, for me, confined to my doctoral program in history, which Professor Foster had persuaded me to undertake in 1993. What I did not realize until much later was how instrumental the literature actually was in enabling me to make sense of Métis ethnicity – not just my own developing identity but the diversity of Métis social and political identities throughout history. For me, preparing for comprehensive exams while I participated in Métis political activities became an exercise in what Paulo Friere might call conscientization – a process of action and reflection that identifies contradictions in one's daily life and allows one to critically assess these discrepancies in a manner that results in personal and political liberation.[29] My own process of conscientization was aided and abetted by other Métis people who had experienced similar identity issues in the past and recognized that I was in the process of grappling with the inherent contradictions that are an essential part of becoming Métis. These people provided encouragement, support, and explanation along the way. I recognize now how important acceptance by other Métis is to the process of developing one's sense of self as a Métis person.

I realize now how fortunate my mother and I were to have frequent telephone calls, letters, and visits with our Métis relatives during those years when we were getting reacquainted with our Métis heritage. Part of the diagnostic criteria used by modern Métis organizations to assess one's fitness for membership is to be accepted by the Métis nation as Métis. According to the official definition, the Métis nation consists of those Métis people who live in the "historic Métis homeland."[30] For me, acceptance means being treated as kin by my Métis relatives – along with the privileges and obligations associated with that designation.

I would be dishonest if I said that the discovery of my Métis heritage did not affect how I approached my research. In fact, I realize now that I would not have become an academic at all had I not become so absorbed with trying to answer the numerous questions that arose as I delved deeper and deeper into the study of western Canada, the fur trade, and the social and political legacy of Louis Riel and the Indian Act on the experience of Métis people. Because I have been trained as an academic, I have tried to frame my inquiries so that the observations and the conclusions have historical and cultural relevance for a broad audience. At the same time, the process of researching and writing has become, for me, a way to reach a new understanding of my identity, which has been irrevocably altered by my mother's rediscovery of her family.

On a day-to-day basis, my identity affects me in more insidious ways. J.R. Miller's prescient comments in an article from the 1980s continue to be relevant today: "One major hurdle [to the successful pursuit of further studies of the Métis] that seems to be causing problems is politicization, which takes at least two forms: self-censorship and partisanship. Scholars who work with native communities frequently find themselves confronted with the question of whether or not to publish a scholarly opinion that might run counter to the current political objectives of the community they are studying. Examples abound."[31] For several years, I studiously avoided research outside of the academy that might eventually involve legal activity, whether it be land claims or other litigation. However, I soon realized that one's published work is open to public access – and subsequent utilization in court cases – whether one likes it or not. I had listened to enough colleagues relate their unpleasant and stressful court-room experiences as expert witnesses to know that I did not want to have these experiences myself. Other associates were horrified to discover that their research was being quoted out of context and used in a manner they considered contrary to their own personal philosophies.

But I eventually came to the opinion that if qualified researchers did not participate in outside research – whether it be for land claims or Aboriginal rights, cultural resource management or historical research for heritage agencies – then what use were academics to the community at large? With this in mind, I have taken on a limited number of research projects and have limited myself to historical topics. In doing so, I try to rely on a wide array of ethnohistorical documentation to shape my historical narrative.

Although I am a historian, I cannot avoid that I am Métis, even though I was ignorant of this fact for most of my childhood. I have tried to explain this to people through the use of a rather awkward analogy. It's like cooking a raw egg – once it's cooked, it can never be returned to its raw state. For me, my child-hood ignorance of my heritage was like an egg in its uncooked state. Once I discovered my background, I could never go back to being whoever I was before I learned about my ancestry. I guess I am "cooked" for all time.

Because I know I am Métis, it influences the topics on which I choose to work and the people and agencies with whom I choose to be associated, either as a researcher or as a private individual. This is not particularly unusual – all people make these choices, not just academics. But for many years, academics (particularly historians) laboured under the illusion that they were impartial in their role as researchers. What nonsense! Obviously, I have a soft spot for all things Métis, and I always will. And because of this innate partiality, I will always try to monitor my work to make sure that, to the best of my ability, it is as balanced from a documentation perspective as possible. And if I do not monitor myself, I know that my colleagues will be more than happy to do so in print and in public. Such is the beauty of peer review.

Holding oneself out as Métis in academia continues to be an awkward experience for me. I am well aware that I was not raised in a Métis tradition, so I have been largely reluctant to bring it up, lest I be accused of the dreaded instrumental ethnicity that follows so many newly minted Métis around. I have always made a point of being honest and transparent about my experience of being and becoming Métis, particularly to my students and colleagues, lest they make any incorrect assumptions about my lived experience.

Unfortunately, because there are so few people of Native ancestry teaching in universities, Native academics are constantly called upon to act in a variety of capacities – as role models, as mentors, as sponsors, as committee members, and as experts on all things Aboriginal. This has resulted in more than a few cases of burnout for Aboriginal academics. It also means that the ethnicity of Aboriginal academics – which should be private – has been commodified, regardless of the wishes of the individual. Perhaps the most obvious example of this trend is when an Aboriginal academic finds him- or herself as the token Aboriginal representative on a committee, regardless of whether his or her knowledge or training is relevant to the work at hand.

Of course, when I reflect on my activities as a Métis historian and as a historian of the Métis I cannot help but ponder the quality of my academic work in light of my status as an Aboriginal academic and all of the political and cultural baggage that this designation implies. Obviously, my interests have evolved over time. When I first started doing historical and genealogical research as a hobby, I gravitated toward topics related specifically to my own Métis ancestors simply because they provided a psychological comfort zone and because they provided common ground for my relatives and me. Later on, my academic training provided me with knowledge and understanding of the broader historical, cultural, and political issues affecting Métis people as a whole. As a result, I seek to frame my current investigations in a way that will give my research broader significance and utility to people beyond the members of my extended family.

Personally, I do not feel that I approach the task of research any differently from non-Métis scholars, with the possible exception of the initial choices I make regarding research topics. Many years ago, when I was in Edmonton studying for my comprehensive exams with the help of Olive Dickason, I suggested in passing that being Métis made a difference in how one approached research on Métis history. Dickason, always the critically trained historian, pounced. She demanded that I explain myself. I lamely replied that Métis historians probably choose topics that are more obscure or even more difficult or tedious to research because they have a stronger intrinsic interest in topics that other scholars might avoid.

I do believe that I choose topics in which I am emotionally and intellectually invested, but so does everyone else. However, I also believe that I have chosen Métis-oriented topics that other, more tactical researchers would have chosen to avoid. The most obvious example that comes to mind is my ongoing research on "The Buffalo Hunters of the Pembinah," an orphaned manuscript in North Dakota that has a murky provenance, which I have been studying for approximately sixteen years. This rather problematic project, which also has become a bit of an obsession, has earned me some unwelcome notoriety, not to mention several headaches. Had I not been entranced by the possibility of new primary source data on the Plains Métis, I would have sensibly left the document to languish in Bismarck.[32]

Epilogue

What does it mean to be Métis?

When I started to investigate my ancestry, I was not thinking about becoming anything. I was drawn toward investigating my mother's past – my own past – which had been hidden for so many years. Initially, I sought to investigate my heritage from the safe, impartial perspective of the historian. But as I came to know my extended Métis family, I realized that, for me, the question of identity has become increasingly irrelevant.

Ironically, I am presently faced with the prospect of having to renew my Métis membership card, even though I do not have the documented proof of Métis ancestry required by the Métis National Council. My mother's adoption records do not identify her Métis father by name because it was the practice in Saskatchewan long ago not to identify the fathers of illegitimate children. So, despite our reunion with our Métis family and our acceptance back into the family fold, the oral evidence of our kinship may not be enough to convince the Métis political organizations that we are, in fact, Métis.

I will always be an outsider, to some degree, in the Métis cultural and political community because the community is only now coming to terms with the legacy of separation from, and denial of, Métis heritage that has almost become a diagnostic trait for modern Métis ethnicity in Canada and the United States. The First Nations survivors of Indian residential schools are not stigmatized for their loss of culture because they are viewed, quite correctly, as having been forced to assimilate against their will. But what about Métis people forced to make pragmatic social and economic choices after 1885 to survive in a mainstream society that did not value their heritage? Were they not forced to assimilate?

I have concluded that as long as Métis people struggle to satisfy some nebulous, shifting standard of Métisness, Aboriginality, or other racially charged definition, there will always be the threat of not being Métis enough. In the old days, being and becoming Métis was not strictly a biological phenomenon: it was also a function of behaving like a relative – sharing what you had, living and working and worshipping alongside other Métis, and raising one's children as part of a larger Métis cultural community that you defended.

Because the assimilative pressures of participation in mainstream society will not go away, we have to accept that identity issues will always be with us and that the only way to deal with threats to identity is to learn our history and our culture and to be with our relatives. If Métis people persist in quietly assimilating because they or their children aren't Aboriginal enough to suit other Métis and Treaty Indians, they will apologize themselves out of existence. Métis must be willing to stand up and be counted, to draw a line in the sand, or there will be no Métis people left.

This is the reality of Métis identity in the new millennium.

Today, in the post-*Powley* world, the dominant society requires that the Métis define their ethnic separateness in a quantifiable fashion. Who will belong, and who will not? The challenge facing the Métis political community over the next decade will be how to reconcile the need to consolidate the collective identity and indigenous status of the Métis people without damaging the ability to be inclusive and adaptable in the wake of change.

And me? I will still be able to visit my Métis cousins in Regina, and together we will go to Lebret and visit our ancestors' graves, as we do on virtually all of my visits. I will still research and teach Métis history, and I will still be fascinated by all things Métis.

And sometimes I'll even get the chance to jig. At a Métis dance in Regina a few years ago, one of my extended cousins, a little girl of about six years old, told me all about her dancing lessons and proudly told me that she had learned how to do the Duck Dance. And when the fiddles started to play, she shyly said to me, "I'll dance if you come with me." We went hand in hand to join the crowd on the dance floor and started to jig, while the rest of our family laughed and clapped and cheered us on.

And that, for me, is what it means to be Métis.

Notes

1 The spelling of "Métis" that I use in this essay is the standard version used by the Métis National Council.

2 The issues of power and control over the depiction of Aboriginal history and culture continue to preoccupy indigenous writers, despite the emergence of a critical mass of Aboriginal scholars over the past two decades. For a succinct overview of Aboriginal concerns with mainstream scholarship on Indians, see Mihesuah, "Introduction."

3 The genre of Indian biography has no shortage of critics. See Cook-Lynn, "American Indian Intellectualism and the New Indian Story."

4 Devine, "Métis Lives, Past and Present," 86.

5 Howes, "Afterword," 246.

6 See Pewewardy, "So You Think You Hired an 'Indian' Faculty Member." For a literary variation on this theme, see Cook-Lynn's discussion of the urban mixed-blood Indian and American writing in "American Indian Intellectualism and the New Indian Story," 124-31.

7 Smith, *Decolonizing Methodologies,* 69, emphasis added.

8 Judge Albert Freeman Ewing was appointed by the provincial government of Alberta in 1934 to chair a commission charged with investigating the educational, health, and welfare needs of Alberta Métis people. The commission's eventual imposition of an arbitrary definition of Métis identity intended to limit the expense to government is discussed later in this chapter. For additional information, see Wall, *The Alberta Métis Letters.*

9 See Peterson and Brown, eds., *The New Peoples: Being and Becoming Metis.*

10 Michael Klein (also Klyne or Cline) was a voyageur in the Athabasca Department of the North West Company who eventually became an interpreter and then a postmaster for the Hudson's Bay Company. I have since written several papers on Klein and his descendants, including "A Fur Trade Patriarch" and "Métis or Country-Born?"

11 See Devine, "Roots in the Mohawk Valley."

12 The armed standoff at Oka, Quebec, which began on 11 July 1990 and ended on 26 September 1990, came about as a result of a centuries-old land claim dispute over a burial ground that belonged originally to the Kanesatake Mohawk community. These lands, which were acquired by the Roman Catholic Church in 1717 and sold in 1936, became the site of further protest when the nearby town of Oka built a golf course on a portion of the land in question. The situation became violent when local Mohawks constructed a barricade to block access to the land after the town of Oka approved an expansion of the golf course. When the Sûreté du Québec was called in to dismantle the barricade, one of their members was shot and killed. The situation escalated as other Aboriginal groups in Canada joined the protest, and the Canadian army was brought in to end the conflict. See York and Pindera, *People of the Pines,* and Obomsawin's film *Kanehsatake.*

13 An excellent historical and cultural overview of the various sociopolitical issues arising from the phenomenon can be found in Green, "The Tribe Called Wannabe."

14 For a comprehensive introduction to Indian removal, allotment, termination, and relocation, see Horsman, *The Origins of Indian Removal*; Foreman, *Indian Removal*; Carlson, *Indians, Bureaucrats, and Land*; Otis, *The Dawes Act*; Washburn, *The Assault on Indian Tribalism*; Deloria, ed., *American Indian Policy*; Prucha, *Americanizing the American Indian*; Hoxie, *A Final Promise*; Philp, *Termination Revisited*; and Fixico, *Termination and Relocation*.

15 For scholarly discussions of these issues, see Unrau, *Mixed-Bloods and Tribal Dissolution*; Meyer, *The White Earth Tragedy*; Thorne, *The Many Hands of My Relations*; Murphy, *A Gathering of Rivers*; Sleeper-Smith, *Indian Women and French Men*; Ingersoll, *To Intermix with Our White Brothers*; and Foster, *We Know Who We Are*.

16 For a comprehensive overview of the racial ideology that governs the relationship between African Americans and Native peoples of the American southeast, see Forbes, *Africans and Native Americans*.

17 For a demographic overview of the complex racial admixtures in the Cherokee population, see Thornton, *The Cherokees*, and Sider, *Lumbee Indian Histories*. For an in-depth examination of the movement to dispossess the Black Cherokees of Oklahoma, see Sturm, *Blood Politics*. For a recent article that examines the intersection of biology and politics in the removal of "black Indians" from the membership rolls of the Five Civilized Tribes of Oklahoma, see Koerner, "Blood Feud," 119-25, 145-46.

18 Two recent publications document the revival of Métis political activity in western Canada, particularly in Alberta. For a history of Métis political activism from the 1960s to the present day, see Weinstein, *Quiet Revolution West*. A detailed study of the Ewing Commission and the formation of the Métis Association of Alberta can be found in Wall, *The Alberta Métis Letters*.

19 For an online summary of this important constitutional case, see Indian and Northern Affairs Canada, "Métis Rights – Powley," and Métis National Council, "Métis Rights – Powley Information."

20 Between 1996 and 2001, the Métis population grew from 204,000 to 292,000. See Andersen, "From Nation to Population."

21 Suarez-Orozco, "Everything You Ever Wanted to Know," 12. See also Andersen, "From Nation to Population."

22 Sawchuk, Sawchuk, and Ferguson, "The Métis Settlements," 187.

23 Government of Alberta, *Reports, Evidence*, 442, quoted in Hatt, "Ethnic Discourse in Alberta," 70.

24 Ibid.

25 Government of Alberta, *Reports, Evidence*, "Transcript of the Commission Testimony of Malcolm Norris (Deponent), 25 February 1935," 449.

26 See Hatt, "Ethnic Discourse in Alberta," 70-72. This definition of Métis identity no longer exists because Métis organizations demanded that the definition be much more inclusive. As many Métis leaders have observed, Louis Riel himself would not have qualified for recognition as Métis because of his one-eighth Aboriginal ancestry. The contemporary definition of "Métis" endorsed today by local and national Métis organizations is one that incorporates biological and legal evidence of Aboriginal ancestry, self-definition as Métis, and Métis community recognition and acceptance.

27 Malcolm Norris and his colleague James Brady Jr., two of the founders of the Métis Association of Alberta, both came from middle-class backgrounds. Malcolm's father, John Norris, was a transplanted Scottish employee of the Hudson's Bay Company in Edmonton who eventually became one of the city's earliest and most successful businessmen. James

Brady's father, James Brady Sr., was born in Ireland, the son of a wealthy railway contractor and engineer. He studied law at Exeter College in England before emigrating to Canada to work for the Canadian Pacific Railway. See Dobbin, *The One-and-a-Half Men*, 28-33.

28 Almost every Métis political organization in western Canada has experienced some form of electoral or financial scandal. The Manitoba Métis Federation's legacy of internal corruption, electoral fraud, and violence was revealed in a controversial exposé written by former investigative journalist Sheila Morrison and titled *Rotten to the Core;* see also Smith, "Manitoba Métis President Suspended." In 2004, the Métis Nation of Saskatchewan held a general election that was plagued by fraud and voting irregularities. An investigation commissioned by the Government of Saskatchewan concluded that the 2004 election had been neither fair nor democratic. See Lampard, *A Study to Answer the Question.* Nine people eventually pleaded guilty to election fraud after the results of the election were suspended and the federal and provincial governments suspended operating funds to the organization. See also Adam, "Former MNS Official Goes to Jail for Election Fraud."

29 See Freire, "Cultural Action and Conscientization," 519n1, and "Cultural Action for Freedom."

30 Definitions of Métis identity are multifaceted and have evolved over the years. An excellent article on the subject is Giokas and Chartrand, "Who Are the Métis in Section 35?" See also Métis National Council, "Who Are the Métis?"

31 See Miller, "From Riel to the Métis," 19.

32 For additional information on this project, see Devine, "New Light on the Plains Métis."

Bibliography

Adam, Betty Ann. "Former MNS Official Goes to Jail for Election Fraud." *Saskatoon Star-Phoenix*, 6 November 2008.

Andersen, Chris. "From Nation to Population: The Racialization of 'Métis' in the Canadian Census." *Nations and Nationalism* 14, 2 (2008): 347-68.

Carlson, Leonard A. *Indians, Bureaucrats, and Land: The Dawes Act and the Decline of Indian Farming.* Westport, CT: Greenwood Press, 1981.

Cook-Lynn, Elizabeth. "American Indian Intellectualism and the New Indian Story." In *Natives and Academics: Researching and Writing about American Indians,* edited by Devon A. Mihesuah, 111-38. Lincoln: University of Nebraska Press, 1998.

Deloria, Vine, ed. *American Indian Policy in the Twentieth Century.* Norman: University of Oklahoma Press, 1985.

Devine, Heather. "A Fur Trade Patriarch: Michael Klyne of Jasper House." Paper presented at the 2008 Rupert's Land Colloquium, Rocky Mountain House, Alberta, 14-16 May 2008.

–. "Métis or Country-Born? The Case of the Klynes." Paper presented at the annual meeting of the Canadian Historical Association, St. John's, Newfoundland, 5-8 June 1997.

–. "Métis Lives, Past and Present: A Review Essay." *BC Studies,* 128 (2000-1): 85-90.

–. "New Light on the Plains Métis: *The Buffalo Hunters of Pembinah, 1870-71.*" In *The Long Journey of a Forgotten People: Métis Identities and Family Histories,* edited by Ute Lischke and David W. McNab, 197-218. Waterloo: Wilfrid Laurier University Press, 2007.

–. "Roots in the Mohawk Valley: Sir William Johnson's Legacy in the North West Company." In *The Fur Trade Revisited: Selected Papers of the Sixth North American Fur Trade Conference, Mackinac Island, Michigan, 1991,* edited by Jennifer S.H. Brown, W.J. Eccles, and Donald P. Heldman, 217-42. East Lansing: Michigan State University Press, 1994.

Dobbin, Murray. *The One-and-a-Half Men: The Story of Jim Brady and Malcolm Norris, Métis Patriots of the Twentieth Century*. Vancouver: New Star Books, 1981.

Eakin, Paul John, ed. *The Ethics of Life Writing*. Ithaca, NY: Cornell University Press, 2004.

Fixico, Donald L. *Termination and Relocation: Federal Indian Policy, 1945-1960*. Albuquerque: University of New Mexico Press, 1986.

Forbes, Jack D. *Africans and Native Americans: The Language of Race and the Evolution of Red-Black Peoples*. 2nd ed. Urbana: University of Illinois Press, 1993.

Foreman, Grant. *Indian Removal: The Emigration of the Five Civilized Tribes of Indians*. Norman: University of Oklahoma Press, 1932. Reprinted in 1953 and 1956.

Foster, Martha Harroun. *We Know Who We Are: Métis Identity in a Montana Community*. Norman: University of Oklahoma Press, 2006.

Freire, Paulo. "Cultural Action and Conscientization." *Harvard Education Review* 68, 4 (1998): 499-521.

–. "Cultural Action for Freedom: Editors' Introduction." *Harvard Education Review* 68, 4 (1998): 471-75.

Giokas, John, and Paul L.A.H. Chartrand. "Who Are the Métis in Section 35? A Review of the Law and Policy Relating to Métis and 'Mixed-Blood' People in Canada." In *Who Are Canada's Aboriginal Peoples? Recognition, Definition, and Jurisdiction*, edited by Paul L.A.H. Chartrand. Saskatoon: Purich Publishing, 2002.

Government of Alberta. *Reports, Evidence, etc. Re: The Report of the Royal Commission to Investigate the Conditions of the Half-Breed Population of Alberta*. Edmonton: Department of Lands and Forests, 1935.

Green, Rayna. "The Tribe Called Wannabe: Playing Indian in America and Europe." *Folklore* 99, 1 (1988): 30-57.

Hatt, Ken. "Ethnic Discourse in Alberta: Land and the Métis in the Ewing Commission." *Canadian Ethnic Studies* 17, 2 (1985): 64-79.

Horsman, Reginald. *The Origins of Indian Removal, 1815-1824*. East Lansing: Historical Society of Michigan, 1970.

Howes, Craig. "Afterword." In *The Ethics of Life Writing*, edited by Paul John Eakin, 244-64. Ithaca, NY: Cornell University Press, 2004.

Hoxie, Frederick E. *A Final Promise: The Campaign to Assimilate the Indians, 1880-1920*. Lincoln: University of Nebraska Press, 1984.

Indian and Northern Affairs Canada. "Powley – Frequently Asked Questions." Indian and Northern Affairs Canada. http://www.ainc-inac.gc.ca/ai/ofi/mrm/pwy/index-eng.asp.

Ingersoll, Thomas N. *To Intermix with Our White Brothers: Indian Mixed-Bloods in the United States from Earliest Times to the Indian Removals*. Albuquerque: University of New Mexico Press, 2005.

Koerner, Brendan L. "Blood Feud." *Wired* (September 2005): 119-46.

Lampard, Keith. *A Study to Answer the Question: Was the Métis Election of 2004 Run in a Fair and Democratic Manner Such that Its Results Can Be Relied upon by Métis People and the Government of Saskatchewan?* 2004. http://www.fnmr.gov.sk.ca/documents/metis/Lampard2004.pdf.

Métis National Council. "Métis Rights – Powley Information." Metisnation.ca. http://www.metisnation.ca/rights/powley.html.

–. "Who Are the Métis?" Metisnation.ca http://www.metisnation.ca/who/index.html.

Meyer, Melissa L. *The White Earth Tragedy: Ethnicity and Dispossession at a Minnesota Anishinaabe Reservation*. Lincoln: University of Nebraska Press, 1994.

Mihesuah, Devon A. "Introduction." In *Natives and Academics: Researching and Writing about American Indians*, edited by Devon A. Mihesuah, 1-22. Lincoln: University of Nebraska Press, 1998.

Miller, J.R. "From Riel to the Métis." *Canadian Historical Review* 69, 1 (1988): 1-20.

Morrison, Sheila Jones. *Rotten to the Core: The Politics of the Manitoba Métis Federation.* Winnipeg: J. Gordon Shillingford, 1995.

Murphy, Lucy Eldersfeld. *A Gathering of Rivers: Indians, Métis, and Mining in the Western Great Lakes, 1737-1832.* Lincoln: University of Nebraska Press, 2000.

Obomsawin, Alanis, director. *Kanehsatake: 270 Years of Resistance.* Ottawa: National Film Board of Canada, 1993.

Otis, Delos Sacket. *The Dawes Act and the Allotment of Indian Land.* Norman: University of Oklahoma Press, 1973.

Peterson, Jacqueline, and Jennifer S.H. Brown, eds. *The New Peoples: Being and Becoming Metis in North America.* Winnipeg/Lincoln: University of Manitoba Press/University of Nebraska Press, 1985.

Pewewardy, Cornel D. "So You Think You Hired an 'Indian' Faculty Member: The Ethnic Fraud Paradox in Higher Education." In *Indigenizing the Academy: Transforming Scholarship and Empowering Communities,* edited by Devon A. Mihesuah and Angela Cavender Wilson, 200-17. Lincoln: University of Nebraska Press, 2004.

Philp, Kenneth R. *Termination Revisited: American Indians on the Trail to Self-Determination, 1933-1953.* Lincoln: University of Nebraska Press, 1999.

Prucha, Francis Paul. *Americanizing the American Indian.* Lincoln: University of Nebraska Press, 1973.

Sawchuk, Joe, Patricia Sawchuk, and Theresa Ferguson. "The Metis Settlements." In *Métis Land Rights in Alberta: A Political History,* 187-215. Edmonton: Métis Association of Alberta, 1981.

Sider, Gerald M. *Lumbee Indian Histories: Race, Ethnicity, and Indian Identity in the Southern United States.* Cambridge: Cambridge University Press, 1993.

Sleeper-Smith, Susan. *Indian Women and French Men: Rethinking Cultural Encounter in the Western Great Lakes.* Amherst: University of Massachusetts Press, 2001.

Smith, Linda Tuhiwai. *Decolonizing Methodologies: Research and Indigenous Peoples.* London: Zed Books, 1999.

Smith, Michael. "Manitoba Métis President Suspended and Under Investigation." *Windspeaker,* 1 August 1996.

Sturm, Circe. *Blood Politics: Race, Culture, and Identity in the Cherokee Nation of Oklahoma.* Berkeley: University of California Press, 2002.

Suarez-Orozco, Marcelo M. "Everything You Ever Wanted to Know about Assimilation But Were Afraid to Ask." *Daedalus* (Fall 2000): 1-29.

Thorne, Tanis E. *The Many Hands of My Relations: French and Indians in the Lower Missouri.* Columbia: University of Missouri Press, 1996.

Thornton, Russell. *The Cherokees: A Population History.* Lincoln: University of Nebraska Press, 1990.

Unrau, William E. *Mixed-Bloods and Tribal Dissolution: Charles Curtis and the Quest for Indian Identity.* Lawrence: University of Kansas Press, 1989.

Wall, Denis. *The Alberta Métis Letters, 1930-1940: Policy Review and Annotations.* Edmonton: DWRG Press, 2008.

Washburn, Wilcomb E. *The Assault on Indian Tribalism: The General Allotment Law (Dawes Act) of 1887.* Philadelphia: Lippincott, 1975.

Weinstein, John. *Quiet Revolution West: The Rebirth of Métis Nationalism.* Calgary: Fifth House, 2007.

York, Geoffrey, and Loreen Pindera. *People of the Pines: The Warriors and the Legacy of Oka.* Toronto: Little, Brown 1991.

8

Historical Research and the Place of Oral History: Conversations from Berens River

Susan Elaine Gray

MUCH OF MY WORK has centred on the lives of people who lived along the Berens River of Manitoba and northwestern Ontario between 1875 and 1940.[1] Specifically, I have been interested in these people's complex responses to Christianity and the conversations (spoken and unspoken) that went on between Ojibwe people and missionaries (who were both Methodist and Roman Catholic). These conversions and the adoption of Christianity had multidimensional meanings and were interpreted in myriad ways by the Native players in these dramas. Christian rituals and practices were integrated into the Ojibwe worldview in ways that were controlled and meaningful to the participants. Over the past 150 years, both Christian and Ojibwe ideas have been interwoven in the lives of Berens River residents. Both strands hold meaning, power, and sincerity. Aspects of Christianity sustain many in their daily lives, even while many of these same people's beliefs remain grounded in Ojibwe concepts such as the Thunderbirds, the power of *midewag* and healers (persons still referred to as medicine men and conjurors when people in Berens River speak in English), and the use of dreams as vehicles of prediction, guidance, and foreshadowing.[2] Ojibwe people who lived along the Berens River experienced and still experience a deep, dynamic, and complex religion that is based on the power of belief and is adaptive and flexible. They were quick to welcome new ideas and practices into their midst, if they appeared to be helpful and valuable.

This chapter is, at heart, a look at the personal connections between researcher and community – connections that, if successfully made, can vastly augment understanding. It is challenging indeed to parachute oneself into a community and to seek collaborations and partnerships with Aboriginal people who, in some cases, have been exploited by academics who have damaged (or blown up) bridges between scholars and their "research subjects."

The process of developing connections cannot be forced, and no methodology can tell a researcher exactly how to make Aboriginal people (or anyone else for that matter) decide that they want to work with her. In his Foreword to my book *"I Will Fear No Evil": Ojibwa-Missionary Encounters along the Berens River, 1875-1940,* the Very Reverend Dr. Stan McKay wrote that he read with interest about my efforts to establish a personal connection with the people of Berens

River, including my initial failure and ultimate success: "Susan Gray had a plan in place before her visit to Berens River but it was not the 'People's plan.' The learned practice and the testing of motives explain the requirement for building right relationships with the Ojibwa of Berens River. The testing of intentions was part of treaty negotiations a century before Susan visited Berens River and it is a continuing tradition. [Her] project built momentum when it was understood that it would be a means of giving voice to the elders."[3]

Working collaboratively is not always successful, and successes can, at best, take a long time to achieve. In a recent article, Laura Peers discusses her efforts to build a bridge between the Pitt Rivers Museum, which holds hair samples taken by Beatrice Blackwood from Red Lake Ojibwe people in 1925, and the members of this community. Peers consulted with the Red Lake people and discovered that they did not realize that the Oxford museum held their ancestors' hair samples. She describes the emotive experience involved in discovering the meanings surrounding the hair. Caught between trying to explain Blackwood's actions and her own need to build personal communication and trust with community members, she tells the story of the ups and downs of a journey that went from negativity and anger to a "defusi[on] of the tension which sometimes resulted from the gaps we were attempting to bridge" to silence.[4] At the end of the article, the jury remains out regarding the success of her committed attempts to establish ties. She writes, "Since criticism of the past can be articulated towards contemporary representatives of an institution ... and since criticism is never supposed to be expressed directly in Ojibwe culture, it is ... possible that the silence from Red Lake is a form of criticism of Blackwood's actions in the past. I hope it is also a reflective pause before further communication and action."[5]

This chapter relies on the crucial role of emotion and the senses in the scholarly construction of knowledge and the authenticity and dynamism of relationships that can occur between Aboriginal people and non-Aboriginal researchers. The extent to which scholars are cognizant of the importance of these issues – and the extent to which they elevate their research from a pure concentration on factual quests to the mystery and depths involved in forming ties with their Aboriginal partners – shape whether their work will be lifted from the mundane to the inspiring. Many academics remove themselves from their narratives and do not discuss the real-life scholarly processes they employ to create knowledge; as a consequence, their prose is impersonal and antiseptic. By intertwining the personal and the scholarly, I seek to expose the extent to which scholarship is a joint creation of the researcher and those whose lives he or she wishes to understand.

Forming Personal Connections in Berens River

In 1994, in the midst of my archival research into Ojibwe-missionary encounters, I talked to elders at Berens River about their beliefs. Their voices gave life and resonance to my work, and I found that I could best illustrate syncretic blendings and integrative philosophies (as well as negative reactions to Christianity and individual missionaries) through the stories and thoughts that they shared. People told me stories only after I had established trusting relationships with them. In every case, our early discussions were stilted and formal; for example, one man at first would do nothing but recite lines he had been taught by Euro-Canadian educators who wanted him to speak to gatherings of schoolchildren. At some point during each meeting, however, the elders decided they wanted to talk to me. I could never figure out how they made these decisions, but they opened the way to real dialogue. All became passionate, in their own ways, about what they were saying and about communicating their stories to the wider world. By the time I finished my visits, I realized that these elders had added nuance, depth, new levels of meaning, and a world of animation to my archival findings.

Life along the Berens River between 1875 and 1940 has been relatively well documented. Several archives hold missionary writings, government records, and other primary sources, and anthropologist A. Irving Hallowell published a wealth of material detailing the time he spent among the Ojibwe people who lived along the Berens River in the 1930s. Hallowell was a close friend of William Berens, who was chief of Berens River from 1916 until his death in 1947.[6] There were ample sources for me to do a study. What I did not know then, however, was that my work would be given real resonance and depth through a very different kind of source material.

It was the Ojibwe people who live in Berens River who breathed life into my work and, in so doing, turned my work about the past into living, passionate, and humane stories. It was one thing to read and think, for example, about how the Ojibwe incorporated new ideas or rituals, but a multitude of meanings and a rush of vitality were transfused into the study when I sat with the people of Berens River who opened their hearts and minds to me. They blew off academic dust and turned on lights. They were the prisms through which light shone and refracted into nuance and clarity. I realized that their voices were central to this story and that I needed to do justice to their passions and convictions.

Interweaving Ojibwe and Christian Worldviews

When the first missionaries began to visit in the 1840s, Native people along the Berens River brought many concerns to their encounters with Christianity. The

Ojibwe who met with and heard about these newcomers saw value in literacy, Western education, and technical resources. The Bible appeared to be a source of potentially helpful and beneficial messages, spiritual protection from illness and other crises, and defence against bad medicine.

The people at Berens River did not, however, accept Christianity out of hand. They sometimes disagreed with the lessons taught to children in schools and saw no need to adopt all aspects of teachers' methods or the new religion. They were unreceptive to missionaries who did not show respect for Ojibwe rituals. For example, in 1927 sixteen-year-old Mary Boucher was dying of consumption at Little Grand Rapids. Although her father, George, invited Brother Frederick Leach to visit, he would not allow Leach to baptize his daughter. Leach was upset and frustrated by the idea that "George [was] as obstinate as a mule ... Poor little kid it made my heart ache to see her ... Geo. Boucher refuses religious consolation to Mary."[7] Clearly, Native people were making choices – it was they who decided when, to what extent, and with what meanings they would accept Christianity.

John Edward Everett, when I visited him in his kitchen at Berens River, was clear about the importance of Catholicism in his life: "Today, I'm a Catholic – cross, water – God, there is only one God. The holy water is good ... When I was born, they baptized me as a Catholic. I'll stay that way 'til I die." Yet this same man's interpretations and ideas were unique, and he had developed his thinking so that his spirituality had particular resonance to him. For example, he did not place great store in the Virgin Mary. When I asked him to tell me about his thoughts on her, he said, "I can say this: in the name of the Father, the Son, and the Holy Ghost, amen. Why? Because she's a statue, eh? Virgin Mary – she's a statue. I don't want to kneel down there and ask Virgin Mary to forgive my sins. Well, I used to do it, you know – just because I was taught to be that way. But now, who am I asking today? *Lord*, I say, forgive me my sins ... I got a cross – beads – rosary beads for saying that prayer. But not now ... There is only one. He died for us. Okay, he died for us on the cross."[8]

One of the most fascinating aspects of my conversations with the people of the Berens River community was learning about the complex ways they had interwoven the Ojibwe and Christian worldviews. The power and meaning and sincerity of those beliefs are resounding. Many older people were eloquent about how their faith in biblical scriptures and prayer sustained them. And yet it was equally true that their beliefs were grounded in concepts such as Thunderbirds, the power of medicine men and conjuring, and the use of dreams as the vehicles of prediction, guidance, and foreshadowing. Their religion was a dynamic and complex combination of deep belief on one hand and adaptability and flexibility of thought on the other.

Missionaries, notably Methodists, first visited Berens River in the 1840s and 1850s. A Methodist outpost was established there in 1873. Two years later, the Berens River Ojibwe were brought into Treaty 5. William Berens became chief in 1916. He succeeded his father, Jacob Berens, who had signed Treaty 5 in 1875 and was the second elected chief of Berens River.[9] By 1916, the Methodists had established a strong presence in the community (supported by the Berens family), and the Roman Catholics would become another strong presence two years later. In the Methodist corner of the arena was Reverend John Niddrie, who arrived in 1916 and stayed until his death in 1940 (he retired in 1938). In the Oblate corner was Brother Frederick Leach, who took his perpetual vows at Berens River in March 1920 and retired in that community in 1978 (he died in St. Boniface, Manitoba, in 1982).[10] These were the missionaries whom my friends and informants remembered most vividly.

Ojibwe Flexibility and Adaptability

Between 1916 and 1940, the community at Berens River was rocked by transformation. Increasing involvement in commercial fishing, the erection of new permanent buildings, participation in agricultural pursuits, day school attendance, floatplanes, outboard motors, and tractor trailers were some of the phenomena that marked the landscape and changed the social and economic climate.

By 1940, the families of the Ojibwe women and men with whom I spoke had been wards of the Dominion government for sixty-five years and had been part of many changes. Missionaries and day school teachers, both Catholic and Protestant, had come and gone, and the community included churches, schools, and commercial operations. The families responded to those changes in their own ways and took in stride those aspects of Euro-Canadian institutions that were unavoidable (such as compulsory school attendance) or that they believed were of use to them (such as incorporating aspects of Christianity into their worldview) as they moved through life. They coped with change and growth within a framework that remained clearly Ojibwe.

By the 1990s, when I met with members of the older generation of that decade, age had brought wisdom and a certain peace, and the elders were in a position to look backward and forward with a perspective born of experience. As a doctoral student working on a dissertation, I began by examining a plethora of written records and then made arrangements for a research trip to Berens River. A good month before I planned to arrive in the community, I spoke several times on the phone to a pleasant, helpful man who worked in the band office. He assured me that he would arrange for me to interview some of the elders in the community and that he would meet my plane at the airport. But when my small plane landed in Berens River on a freezing cold, grey December morning, my friend was conspicuously absent.

Through some lucky encounters and the kindness of the owner of the Berens River Hotel, I finally made it to the band office. I felt vulnerable but hopeful. My stomach literally turned over, however, when my inquiry was answered at the front desk with "Percy? Percy's in the bush!" Vulnerability shifted to panic. I had limited time to do some interviews, and my sole contact was in the bush. Not one person in the office seemed to care a wit about my agenda. Someone told me to sit down on a bench, and so I did. I sat and sat in mute misery and tried to imagine what I would say to my advisor when I returned with blank tapes.

But something *was* happening, although I didn't realize it at the time. I was being observed carefully. After an hour and a half, I was frantic and becoming quite bitter. Just then, someone came over and invited me into one of the offices. A group of Ojibwe men were gathered there, and they surveyed me calmly. They asked what I wanted and what I was doing in Berens River. I, somewhat less calmly, explained why I wanted to speak to people in the community. Their expressions were impassive except for one man who introduced himself as Andrew Bittern and smiled once when I explained how much this work meant to me and how worried I was. They went away for a while and came back. Within minutes, they made a list of some of the oldest and accessible people in the community. It was Andrew Bittern who volunteered to drive me everywhere I would need to go during my stay in Berens River.

I had read a great deal about Ojibwe adaptability and flexibility. It was amazing to see in action what I had read in the abstract. Here was a clear example of people choosing to participate and facilitating events on their own terms. As it turned out, I would have been lost without their support. Because he had decided that my work was interesting and worthy of his effort and attention, Andrew faithfully picked me up, dropped me off, and picked me up again from many homes within a fairly wide geographic radius. And he took me back to my hotel to eat or to pass the time between appointments. It was Andrew who went first to the doors of the people's houses and spoke to them in Ojibwe, telling them what I wanted and asking them if they wanted to see me. They did. It was Andrew who got people to take their big dogs away (even though I know that a couple of times he was almost as intimidated by them as I was).

Meanwhile, the people in the band office spread the word. Within a short time, one young man approached me and suggested I talk to his grand-uncle. At breakfast in the hotel, another man told me I should speak to his mother, to whom he drove me to meet. Somehow, I was becoming as flexible as they all were, and this was key to the trip's success. I was open to any and all shifts and encounters. Word spread with remarkable speed, and it was not long before people were saying on my arrival, "I heard you were around! I'm surprised you took so long to get here!" The people had decided they wanted to talk to me, and so they did.

The Process of Connecting

Another important phenomenon occurred in each interview, and it illustrated how the older people I met set conversational trajectories. Each person listened politely while I explained what I was doing. Each person spent the first hour answering my questions pleasantly and with reserve, along fairly standard lines. They related the names of their ministers or priests and told me about attending Sunday school as children. In many cases, outsiders had talked to them before, and they had some stock responses in hand. The tone was always polite, impersonal, and guarded. In each case, I began to wonder if the person would ever really talk to me and was afraid that I would not be able to make a connection. And then, a magic moment would arrive when the person would suddenly become full of animation and his or her guard would suddenly come down. I am still not sure what made the grey cloud cover blow away. Did they become satisfied that I honestly wanted to know what they thought? Did they decide that they simply liked me and wanted to help? Did they realize that this was a way for them to make their stories heard? Whatever it was, they became passionate and open and spoke from their hearts. Walter Green, for example, was used to making public appearances at many schools throughout the province of Manitoba, including Winnipeg.[11] It was remarkable to witness the moment when he stopped relating standard stories of Ojibwe lore and began talking to me about his own visions and fears and the deep loves of his life – his love for music and the beauty and power of some of his dreams.

Perhaps the fact that I am female was also significant, especially when I spoke with women. Although the man who drove me to meet his mother, Betsey Patrick, did not say so, it seemed that he believed his mother would enjoy talking with another woman. In the summers of the 1930s and 1940s, when he travelled to the communities along the Berens River to work with William Berens and other Ojibwe people, A. Irving Hallowell realized quickly that many women were reluctant to speak with him. In the summer of 1934, therefore, he brought a graduate student, Dorothy Spencer, with him, who, he hoped, would be able to interact with the women somewhat more closely and freely than he had and collect some of their stories. Because the woman who was to interpret for Spencer had moved away, however, Spencer was only able to collect a handful of stories.[12]

Perhaps the women with whom I spoke told me things they would have been less comfortable discussing with a man. For example, Ida Green was so shy at the beginning of our conversation that I began to fear she would never be comfortable enough to really talk about her thoughts and her life.[13] Yet, as with all the other elders in the community, she too reached a point in our visit when she simply, figuratively speaking, let down her hair and began to laugh uproariously at her memories of the girls getting the boys in trouble when she was a young student attending the Methodist day school under Colin Street. When she told me about these little schoolyard conflicts, it was as though they had happened only the day before:

> The boys were fighting the girls – the girls were fighting the boys *[laughter]*. So I always go out from there [the schoolhouse] – go outside [at lunch when the teacher went home] and stay in the bush with the other girls *[laughter]*. We were eating our lunch there – it was the boys chasing us, you know *[laughter]*. Then, when the teacher comes, we always just come in the schoolhouse *[laughter]* ... sometimes we'd tell him [the teacher], and he'd get after those boys because they were chasing us ... yeah, the boys were mad at us *[laughs]*. "When we catch you girls, we're going to give you a licking!" So then we always stays outside.[14]

Some of the memories that Ida chose to share with me were very personal – things she may not have disclosed had she been speaking with a male whom she had just met for the first time. I asked her, for example, what kinds of stories she remembered her father, William, telling at the dinner table when she was growing up. "Well," she responded, "he always told us not to chase around the boys and not to chase girls around. So he said, 'If you go with the boys at night, you might catch babies from them.'" Ida was twenty-seven years old when she married Gordon Green, and she felt comfortable enough to tell me about her elopement: "They didn't let us marry – but – we got married in the night. Because they doesn't let us to get married ... because they don't like that man – they don't like Gordon ... I don't know [why]! They told me I'd be starving when I got married to Gordon. I never starved when I got married. My cupboard was always full – and our fridge."[15]

Sometimes I had to have the courage to reveal a little of myself before the transformative moment. Fred Baptiste, for example, answered questions for an hour in a chant-like monotone. As I looked around the walls of his tiny house, I was suddenly struck by his many pictures, all of which illustrated biblical stories and themes. I told him I loved their brilliant, vivid colours. He sat quietly, looking at me for a long time. Then, abruptly, he asked me to interpret the meaning of a picture of Jesus knocking at the door of a house. "You know that's a picture of Jesus," he said, "can you make anything out of that?" I was mindful of creating bias and contaminating the conversation with too many of my own ideas. And so, a bit antiseptically, I answered, "Well, I see Jesus knocking at a door, and it's closed and it's night. What's *your* take on that?" Fred jumped up and leaned over the table, his nose in my face. "He's standing at the door, knocking at the door. He's knocking at the door to your heart. And would you let him in or not? I want you to answer that!" I froze. What if I said the wrong thing? Would this interview be held up, years later, by some academic as proof of my lack of a proper approach? "You want me to answer that?" I asked. He replied "Yes! Yes! If Jesus knocks at your door – that's your *heart's* door, eh? – are you going to let him in?" I said faintly that I thought I would.

And with that personal exposure, Fred went on to lay himself bare, "Sure! Sure! Nobody'd ever turn him down!" Then he told me that, for years, he had owned a wonderful feather. It was, he explained, the feather of a baby Thunderbird. This new and real Fred shared his response to the recent funeral of his friend, Alec McKay. Just before the funeral, Fred had been looking at one of his wall hangings. This particular one depicted the Last Supper. He told me, "I took a piece of cake in a piece of Kleenex and I got up. They were talking about Jesus with this Last Supper he had with the disciples before he goes to heaven. 'There's a piece of cake with this Kleenex,' says I, 'you're always talking about Jesus having the Last Supper. Now I'm going to put this cake where Alec can have it – inside his coffin.' I was having the last supper with Alec before he goes down into the grave. He said that when he goes home, he's going to tell other people that I did that." Fred explained that other people at the funeral had disapproved: "They said I shouldn't have put that in his casket, you know. They just say, 'Amen,' you know, and other people just say, 'Thank God!'"[16]

On one level, Fred's response represented a wonderful example of his blending of the Christian idea of the Last Supper with the Ojibwe concept of placing articles of food and tobacco with deceased persons to prepare their spirits for the journey to the afterlife. On another level, it was a heart-warming shared experience. Fred was talking to me as one human being to another rather than as an interviewee to an interviewer.

The Value of Oral History

Other concepts, relationships, and beliefs were likewise illuminated by the old people's discourse and remembrances. Historical documentary sources had told me about the animosity between Catholics and Protestants on the mission fields, and the contemporary published literature was illuminating. Joseph-Étienne Champagne, for example, wrote in his *Manual of Missionary Action* in 1948 that "the only Christian missionaries are the Catholic missionaries, because Christ has given the missionary mandate only to the Catholic Church ... [Protestant missionaries are] missionaries of a ... church which is not the Church of Christ."[17]

The Berens River missionaries included the Canadian Methodists in one camp and the Roman Catholic Oblates of Mary Immaculate in the other. The letters and other written sources generated by Reverend Niddrie, Brother Leach, and his superior, Father De Grandpré (who was sometimes at Berens River with Leach), bore out the idea that Protestant-Catholic dynamics were sometimes rather strained at Berens River. The Methodists had enjoyed a monopoly in the community since 1873, and it was with chagrin that they saw the Catholics build their first chapel at Berens River. By 1918, when Leach and De Grandpré opened the Roman Catholic day school under the auspices of Brother Leach, the Oblates were an active presence.[18] This tension took on an entirely new dimension, however, when I heard Percy Berens and Fred Baptiste roar with laughter as they remembered the struggles between the two.[19] Percy was especially vivid:

> PB: *[laughter]* Father De Grandpré was the priest's name, and Niddrie was the United Church minister – and they used to fight just like a cat and a dog *[laughter]*! *Really* ... I'm telling you the truth!
> SG: What would they fight about?
> PB: Their religion. Niddrie thought his religion was better than Father De Grandpré's religion *[laughter]*. Sure! They fought just like a cat and a dog.[20]

The letters of the missionaries told of strong denominational tensions, and I had the impression that this was a truly divided community. But, sitting around kitchen tables at Berens River, I realized that, despite the enmity between the clergy, the Ojibwe members of the churches generally got on very well with one another, and many attended services at both Catholic and Protestant churches on Sundays. When I asked people why they would do this, they said, a little surprised at the question, that they would learn more if they attended both churches. From the time of the earliest conversions at Berens River, Ojibwe had adapted their existing beliefs to make room for new ideas. Thus, to the chagrin of the missionaries, Christianity did not supplant but often complemented the Ojibwe worldview.

William Berens told Hallowell a story that beautifully illustrated the continuation of his belief in Ojibwe ideas. When he was a young man, Berens sustained a critical injury to his knee and spent a considerable amount of time in the Winnipeg General Hospital. The surgeon extracted two grains of shot and two pieces of metal from the wound, but the knee would not heal. Doctors did not know what to make of William's assertion that he had never been shot. Nor, he claimed, had his mother been shot while she was carrying him. They especially did not understand when William tried to explain that his knee had been damaged as a result of bad conjuring – punishment had been inflicted on him after he refused to give a drink of alcohol to an old but powerful man.

After the incident, William eventually grew worried. It was October, and, with freezing weather setting in, the boats would soon stop travelling to Berens River. William knew that medicine from home was the only hope he had for a cure. The doctor was concerned about discharging a patient in William's condition, but the young man was adamant. His father, Jacob, who had been a gifted and powerful conjuror, had given up his medicine bundles and stopped practising upon conversion. His Christianity prevented him from directly performing a cure, but the old man lost no time getting William to another powerful medicine man – Jacob's brother Albert. Jacob was clear when he spoke to his brother, "You are pretty good ... but I'll tell you what medicine to use."[21]

The continued substance and depth of the Ojibwe belief system in the lives of Berens River people were best conveyed to me through the stories and thoughts of the elders themselves. Walter Green, a dedicated United Church member, told me about the power of dreams. One of his stories was about an angel who had taught him to play the organ in a dream:

You know, when I was a little boy ... they used to ask my uncle to play the organ. *Boy,* did I wish I could play – many times I'd stand there watching him. But one night ... I had a dream. Somebody came over to me, like an angel, you know? A lady. So she took me and grabbed my hand and said, "Come on over this way." Her face was just beautiful, and there were flowers all around her. So she took me out, and we came to a great big building. It was a building like marble, you know? And she took me in[side] ... We walked for a long way and, while we were walking, she turned to one room and said, "This is the place." And I looked around and saw an organ – a pipe organ. So she said, "Is this what you want to play?" I said, "Yes, very much." And then she sat down, and I sat down beside her. And first she played *Jesus Loves Me* – do you know that song? Then she played it twice. Then she said, "Okay, you play." So I sat down, and I played for a long time. That's how I learned. When I was fourteen, I played the organ in the church, prayer meetings, wakes.[22]

It is one thing to read of Ojibwe people's beliefs regarding dreams and dream visitors, or *bawaaganag,* but quite another to hear a voice filled with warmth and awe say, "Oh, they're just so wonderful, they can do anything!"[23] I remember, at that moment, contrasting the light of Walter's eyes with the hours I spent in the archives struggling to read microfilm in the darkness.

Hallowell wrote about fears associated with bad conjuring.[24] Intellectually, I had what I thought was a grasp of this idea. Its power and reality, however, were lost on me until I heard the bitterness in Percy Berens' voice when he told me about the price his brother Jacob had paid for incurring the jealous wrath of a conjuror:

PB: One of my brothers *died* of that kind of thing.
SG: Which one?
PB: The oldest, Jacob was his name.
SG: Jacob died from bad conjuring?
PB: Yes, yes. Just because that man – when the Hudson's Bay Company used to have dog teams to take the fur in, dogs from Island Lakes and Oxford House, that's called a fur train. And they used to get a train of dogs and a guy from Poplar River, maybe. And that's where my brother – he beat them guys from Island Lake and Oxford House and Nelson House. Because they were jealous of him, they thought my brother was using medicine for his dog team to be so good.[25]

It was the elders who made clear the difference between good and bad medicine. Walter Green used two examples to explain the difference. He selected the positive example of the shaking tent to show how beneficial a good conjuror could be to people who availed themselves of his services.

Nobody else [can] do it – [the shaking tent ceremony] – just like one who, as I said, is blessed. There was an old man and his wife way back to Pikangikum – that's in Ontario. And then he wanted to know about his daughter – if she's well – if she's doing good. So he asked one of those shaking tent guys – something like what we have here with the telephone – so they made a shaking tent with willows ... and they covered it with canvas ... and spirits started to sing or started to talk. All of a sudden ... there was this guy inside the shaking tent – all of a sudden! How did he get in? That's one of the magical and blessed things. And then he talks to this old turtle. Mikinak ... So he sends out this turtle, and in about half an hour or less he came back. All the way to Pikangikum! And he said, "Your daughter's fine. She's doing good." It's one of the most wonderful things in the old days. Some of them are blessed with visits – some of them are blessed so they can do anything. But they have to do right with it. Some of them did it in the wrong way.

The negative example was as follows:

The wrong way is, like, for instance, suppose someone goes trapping and gets everything he wants, and then someone gets jealous and [the jealous person causes something bad to happen to him by dreaming about revenge]. Now this trapper doesn't get anything as good as he did. Some of those people use dreams – like one old man. There was a conjuror, and what they used to do was come out here with them great York boats to get some groceries. And they'd go to the Hudson's Bay, and there was an old man – he was a very good medicine man – but he went out sitting on the lake with his grandson. And they came to an island out there, they call it Spruce Island. And on the second night he met these guys, and they were having a good time, having a lunch or something, and they were ready to sail to Norway House. That old man got out of his boat, and he was sitting on a rock, and those guys were having a great time eating and getting ready to go. They didn't even offer him a cup of tea or anything. You know, I don't even think they looked at him! So he said to his grandson, "Come on, let's go!" And he turned to them and said, "You guys from Norway House, you're going to have quite a time here – you're going to be here for quite a while." *[laughter]* And then the north wind started to blow – it blowed and blowed, they said, for about four days. They couldn't get going. So after about four days, he went to them – these were the same guys who had left him alone. They didn't have any food or grub. So he said, "Look, you guys, you didn't even offer me a cup of tea. So you have to stay here for a few days." So that's how the medicines work.[26]

The esteem for the good that medicine men could do was conveyed clearly and passionately by the same people who spoke with passion about the contributions of churches and schools in their community. When I asked Percy Berens about Leach's and Niddrie's abhorrence of medicine men, he explained vehemently, "Because they didn't believe in it. That was what was wrong. That's the trouble. They didn't *really* have it explained to them what it means for an Indian to be a medicine man. They should have known better. That man there, that medicine man, he's going to save lives! For other people! It's a good thing! I very appreciate your bringing this whole thing up, this medicine thing. The old people lived long in my time, no babies died that much as what they do now because the Indians knew the medicine."[27] Other elders explained that it was unfortunate that the missionaries had not realized that the power of medicine men and women had come from God and that older people had once used that medicine to accomplish wonderful things.

The Thunderbirds also came alive for me in these homes. When I asked Percy Berens if he believed in these beings, he was passionate: "Oh yeah! It's a bird! It's a bird. You should go to Poplar River [to see their nest of boulders]. White people don't believe it's a bird, a Thunderbird, they don't believe in that. But we Indians absolutely believe it's a bird." Without the Thunderbirds, he explained, there would never have been rain, and everything would have long dried up.[28] Equally impassioned on this subject was John Edward Everett, who, as discussed above, was a practising Roman Catholic. Yet, about Thunderbirds, he explained, "We smoke our pipes west – all the directions – north, east – because we see a big cloud, and where's it coming up from? This moving cloud! What's going to happen? All of a sudden it's like a *bomb*, eh? If you smoke, the thunder cloud will go past. The Thunderbirds. Many moons. Love your neighbour as you love yourself. Listening to the white people today, you hear Thunderbirds come when there's cold air with hot air. No way. Young Thunderbirds in the fall, they're just like ... Oh! They make a really loud noise!"[29]

Oral history vastly enhanced my understanding of the power of belief and Ojibwe flexibility, or give and take, regarding choice of belief. Percy Berens probably summed it up best. "You say you don't believe in spirits at all," I said to him. "No, I don't," he replied, "I've got only one belief and only one spirit." I asked him if he was saying that spirits do not exist at all or if he was simply saying that he did not choose to believe in them. He was clear, "I don't *choose* to believe in them spirits ... But they can exist for other people. If you believe strong enough to believe that there's spirits there, then they're there. And that's what those old-time Indians had. They strongly *believed* in them spirits of evil and righteousness. That was their belief, see? Evil and righteous spirits." I pressed him a little about how he integrated aspects of two different worldviews – a practice so foreign to Christian missionaries. "Percy," I asked, "some white people say you should believe in the Bible but that you shouldn't believe in the ability to conjure or in Thunderbirds. So how come the Indians are different from the white people that way?" I will never forget the laughter that filled the sunny room on that winter afternoon. He replied, "That's very easy to answer that question! Because the Indians are smart, clever – but the white man is stupid, ignorant. Isn't that correct enough? Sure! *We* believe."[30]

The Integration of Ojibwe and Christian Beliefs

Although scholars are divided on the question of whether a Supreme Being was a pre- or post-contact phenomenon, by the mid-nineteenth century, Ojibwe people generally believed in some form of Supreme Being. There are two ways to say "God" in Ojibwe: "Gaa-dibenjid" or "Gaa-dibendang" (the all-encompassing power of life). These words are generally never spoken but might have been linked to thoughts about the genesis of metaphysical gifts. The Ojibwe concept of a spirit or *manidoo* (Manitou) refers to more accessible spirits such as the Thunderbirds. The concept of a superior being was not likely missionary-induced: the idea of an intimate and personal relationship with God is a Christian one, and the Ojibwe relationship with a superior being was highly impersonal.[31] Even today, this difference is a real one. Betsey Patrick, for example, discussed her confusion over the two concepts: "I always grew up hearing about God the Father and praying to God the Father – but now I hear so much talk about God the Creator. How can people pray to God the Creator? Because this is Manitou?"[32] The statement shows the discrepancy between the personal relationship involved with one God and a more impersonal one with another God.

Percy Berens' stance differed from Betsey Patrick's. He had strong words regarding both Ojibwe belief in a superior being and the incorrect assumption, held by Euro-Canadians, that non-Natives had been the ones to introduce God to Native communities: "Sure! *We* believe. *We* Indians believe this world was created by one person. The Great Spirit. Manitou. You know, when the missionaries first came here, they thought that our ancestors that were Indians, they didn't know God. Yet everything they did, these ancestors – way back before they ever seen a missionary – they were talking about Manitou. What is Manitou? God."[33] The Ojibwe along the Berens River had varied in their responses to Christianity. However, grounded in the knowledge that power came from the strength of belief, they thoughtfully incorporated new concepts and elements into their own framework as they saw fit and applied empirical thought to their religious life. Their mental landscape was wide and inclusive, and it is from the vantage point of *this* truth that we need to take a new look at their religious history.

That most missionaries, settlers, and traders suffered a failure of understanding on all these fronts profoundly influenced missionary-Indian encounters, sculpted interactions between the two cultures, and coloured Euro-Canadian interpretations of the present and the past. The newcomers' sense of possessing an exclusive truth sustained both their convictions and their prejudices, although those who grew to truly like their parishioners – for instance, Reverend John Niddrie and Brother Leach at Berens River and Luther Schuetze at Little Grand Rapids – certainly came to a deeper understanding and judged their parishioners less harshly.

My encounters at Berens River had a formative impact on my work. As I suggested earlier, I realized the necessity of stepping out of the structure and order of archival research and into another kind of order. Historically, when I encountered new situations, especially those in which I had a limited time to accomplish a great deal of work, I had tried to control things by planning ahead. What the people at Berens River taught me is that the real way to ensure quality, of work and of life, is to embrace everything (the chance encounters, the unforeseen bends in the road), to be open, listening, and flexible – words truly reminiscent of the Ojibwe worldview. It was fascinating, as well, for me to not only read about but also experience Ojibwe people assessing a situation, deciding whether to participate, and initiating a gentle control over the events.

Although some scholars are reluctant to credit oral history as a valid methodology inherent to the pursuit of excellent historical research, scholars such as Julie Cruikshank have created deeply moving and illuminating works through skilled use of this medium. As Cruikshank observes, "Oral histories are more than just the spontaneous product of an encounter between an interviewer and a subject: the narrative has symbolic qualities – a kind of autonomous life that simultaneously reflects continuity with the past and passes on experience, stories, and guiding principles in the present."[34] Her comparison of oral and written accounts of the Klondike Gold Rush in 1896 shows most clearly the importance of using oral history to teach about cultural differences, not only differing interpretations of past events but also different values and attitudes. She concludes that examining both written and oral accounts directs us "away from a simple search ... and closer to an investigation of the social processes in which all narratives are embedded."[35]

The voices of the actors in the dramas that played out encounters between Ojibwe people and missionaries gave a meaning and added a dimension that I never could have experienced through written sources alone. These people did much more than simply fill in gaps: they breathed life into my work and made it sparkle. Indeed, in the end, oral history led me to begin to comprehend the depth of the Ojibwe capacity to integrate aspects of both Ojibwe and Christian worldviews. The only way for me to understand the Berens River elders' passionate feelings about the power of belief was to listen to them. Its effect on my work was transcendent – magical, really. I hope this chapter provides an example of the alchemy – the magic – that comes from the life and light that can infuse scholarly work when one makes a connection between written sources and the lived lives of the human beings who try to speak to us through these sources. For historians, these worlds are usually separated by a great chasm. If we do it well, oral history enables us as researchers to step easily across that gulf.

Notes

1 The dissertation evolved into the book *"I Will Fear No Evil."* Parts of this chapter have been taken from the Preface, xiii-xxx.
2 Thunderbirds *(binesiwag)* are other-than-human beings who take the form of giant birds who rule the sky and bring thunder and lightning. Midewag were members of the Midewiwin or Grand Medicine Society. This society worked to bring healing and a healthy life to Ojibwe people. It was composed of several levels. Membership in each level required training and special powers.

3   Gray, "*I Will Fear No Evil*," ix-x. Stan McKay is a former moderator of the United Church of Canada who has extensive family connections in Ojibwe communities throughout northern Manitoba. One of the most important Aboriginal spiritual leaders today, Stan is a descendant of the Berens family.

4   Peers, "Strands," 85.

5   Ibid., 91.

6   These records include, among others, sources from the Provincial Archives of Manitoba; the Archives Deschâtelets in Ottawa; the Oblate Archives, Manitoba Province, in Winnipeg; the United Church Archives, Conference of Manitoba and Northwestern Ontario, at the University of Winnipeg; the United Church Archives at Victoria University in Toronto; and the Department of Indian Affairs Records at Library and Archives Canada. The Hallowell records are held by the American Philosophical Society in Philadelphia. For more on the relationship between Hallowell and Berens, see Berens, *Memories, Myths, and Dreams.*

7   Journal of Brother Frederick Leach, Oblate Archives, Manitoba Province, Winnipeg.

8   John Edward Everett to Susan Gray, Berens River, Manitoba, 2 December 1994. Everett was born on 28 June 1920 at Berens River. His mother was Carrie Scott-Everett, and his father was Harry Darcy. He was adopted as a young boy by his aunt and uncle, Alice and John James Everett. John married Mary Jane (Ross), whose father, William Ross, was a medicine man.

9   As a young man, Jacob Berens was probably among the Ojibwe at Berens River who approached Rev. George McDougall in 1860 to ask for a missionary and express an interest in Christianity. McDougall baptized Berens, whose conversion led the Methodists to found the 1873 mission at Berens River. Berens, *Memories, Myths, and Dreams,* Part 1.

10 Gray, "They Fought Just Like a Cat and a Dog!"

11 Walter Green was born at Berens River on 31 October 1912. His mother, Elizabeth Keewatin, who came from Jack Head, died when Walter was four days old. His father was Cuthbert (Cubby) Green (a Methodist Ojibwe). Two of Elizabeth and Cubby's daughters, Alma and Sophia, on their mother's death, were adopted by Catholic women, Sarah Shaw and Marguerite McKay. Ultimately, there was a serious battle over the girls when the Methodist missionary Percy Jones tried in 1918 to have them taken away from their Catholic homes and sent to the Protestant school at Norway House. Brother Leach appealed to Indian Agent Carter, who ordered that the girls be returned to their guardians and attend the Catholic school at Berens River. Leach was very frustrated with William Berens, who involved himself in the struggle, working with Green and Jones. Berens told Leach that, as chief, he had a right to involve himself in matters concerning his band. See Gray, "*I Will Fear No Evil*," 56.

12 Berens, *Memories, Myths, and Dreams,* Part 4.

13 Ida Green was born at Berens River in 1918. She was adopted by her aunt and uncle, Nancy and William Berens, when her mother, Sarah Everett (Nancy's sister), died in the 1918 influenza epidemic. Ida married Gordon Green in 1935.

14 Personal communication, Ida Green to Susan Gray, Berens River, Manitoba, 1 December 1994.

15 Ibid.

16 Personal communication, Fred Baptiste to Susan Gray, Berens River, Manitoba, 1 December 1994.

17 Champagne, *Manual of Missionary Action,* 37.

18 Gray, "*I Will Fear No Evil*," 43-61.

19 Percy Earl Berens was born at Berens River in 1912. His parents, William and Nancy Berens, named their son after the Methodist missionary Percy Earl Jones. For discussion of Wil-

liam's and Nancy's family histories, see Berens, *Memories, Myths, and Dreams,* Part 1. Fred Baptiste was born at Berens River in March 1918. He was baptized by Rev. Percy Earl Jones and grew up in the United Church. His mother, Elizabeth (Bear), was born in Berens River, and his father, Alec, was from Norway House.

20 Personal communication, Percy Berens to Susan Gray, Winnipeg, Manitoba, 15 November 1994.
21 See Berens, *Memories, Myths, and Dreams,* Part 2. See also Gray, "I Will Fear No Evil," 76-77.
22 Personal communication, Walter Green to Susan Gray, Berens River, Manitoba, 1 December 1994. For more discussion, see Gray, "I Will Fear No Evil," 35-36.
23 Personal communication, Walter Green to Susan Gray, Berens River, Manitoba, 1 December 1994.
24 For Hallowell's work on this subject, see *Contributions to Ojibwe Studies.*
25 Personal communication, Percy Berens to Susan Gray, Winnipeg, Manitoba, 15 November 1994.
26 Personal communication, Walter Green to Susan Gray, Berens River, Manitoba, 1 December 1994.
27 Personal communication, Percy Berens to Susan Gray, Winnipeg, Manitoba, 15 November 1994.
28 Ibid.
29 Ibid.
30 Ibid.
31 See Hallowell, *Contributions to Ojibwe Studies,* "Spirits of the Dead in Saulteaux Life and Thought," 29-51. See also Long, Preston, and Oberholtzer, "Manitu Concepts of the Eastern Cree."
32 Personal communication, Betsey Patrick to Susan Gray, Berens River, Manitoba, 1 December 1994.
33 Personal communication, Percy Berens to Susan Gray, Winnipeg, Manitoba, 15 November 1994.
34 Cruikshank, *Life Lived Like a Story,* x.
35 Cruikshank, "Discovery of Gold on the Klondike."

Bibliography

Archival Sources

The Oblate Archives, Manitoba Province
Journal of Brother Frederick Leach.

Published Sources

Berens, William, as told to A. Irving Hallowell. *Memories, Myths, and Dreams of an Ojibwe Leader.* Edited with introductions by Jennifer S.H. Brown and Susan Elaine Gray. Montreal and Kingston: McGill-Queen's University Press, 2009.
Champagne, Joseph-Étienne, O.M.I. *Manual of Missionary Action.* Ottawa: University of Ottawa Press, 1948.
Cruikshank, Julie. "Discovery of Gold on the Klondike: Perspectives from Oral Tradition." In *Reading beyond Words: Contexts for Native History,* edited by Jennifer S.H. Brown and Elizabeth Vibert, 431-58. Peterborough, ON: Broadview Press, 2003.
–. *Life Lived Like a Story: Life Stories of Three Yukon Elders.* Vancouver: UBC Press, 1990.

Gray, Susan Elaine. *"I Will Fear No Evil"*: *Ojibwa-Missionary Encounters along the Berens River, 1875-1940.* Calgary: University of Calgary Press, 2006.

–. "'They Fought Just Like a Cat and a Dog!': Oblate-Methodist Relations at Berens River, Manitoba, 1920-1940." *Prairie Forum* 24, 1 (1999): 51-64.

Hallowell, A. Irving. *Contributions to Ojibwe Studies: Essays, 1934-1972,* edited with introductions by Jennifer S.H. Brown and Susan Elaine Gray. Lincoln: University of Nebraska Press, 2010.

Long, John S., Richard J. Preston, and Cath Oberholtzer. "Manitou Concepts of the Eastern Cree." In *Papers of the 37th Algonquian Conference,* edited by H.C. Wolfart, 451-92. Winnipeg: University of Manitoba Press, 2006.

Peers, Laura. "Strands Which Refuse to Be Braided: Hair Samples from Beatrice Blackwood's Ojibwe Collection at the Pitt Rivers Museum." *Journal of Material Culture* 8, 1 (2003): 75-96.

Part 4
Ways of Representing

Issues of representation and the relations of power that representations embody have been in the foreground of work in the social sciences since the late 1980s. These three chapters explore representations of Aboriginal people in three different realms: in personal and governmental identification, in ethnographic writings, and in public commemoration. Theresa Schenck's chapter, "Border Identities: Métis, Halfbreed, and Mixed-Blood," examines questions of identity among metis people affected by the international border. Schenck is of Ojibwe and Blackfoot descent and has ancestors who participated in the Great Lakes fur trade. A former teacher of French and Spanish, Schenck received her doctorate in anthropology from Rutgers University, studied with Jennifer S.H. Brown as a Native American Fulbright Scholar to Canada, and currently teaches in the Department of Life Sciences and Communication and the American Indian Studies Program at the University of Wisconsin-Madison. In her chapter on the Great Lakes and Upper Mississippi Ojibwe and their mixed-blood children, she examines how metis families south of the forty-ninth parallel struggled for recognition as Aboriginal people. In Canada, metis people have been recognized by the Constitution as a distinct people with rights, but the United States has never recognized the category of metis. Individuals, consequently, have had to make choices about allegiance and public versus private identity. These constitutional differences have led to vastly different metis societies on either side of the border.

In "Edward Ahenakew's Tutelage by Paul Wallace," historian David R. Miller, who teaches indigenous studies at First Nations University, describes the career and writings of Edward Ahenakew, a Cree from central Saskatchewan who became an Anglican missionary and worked with elders in his own community. Ahenakew collaborated for years with Paul Wallace, an English professor from Pennsylvania who shaped Ahenakew's writing on Cree culture and oral traditions and treated Ahenakew both as a student who needed professional mentoring within an academic setting and as an exotic Cree elder. The chapter carefully examines the nuances of their relationship, which was echoed in many relationships between Aboriginal people who sought to record their cultural traditions and non-Aboriginal scholars who sought to make the material accessible to university-based academics.

Finally, "Aboriginal History and Historic Sites," by anthropologist and historian Laura Peers and historian and heritage manager Robert Coutts, explores how Aboriginal peoples have been represented (and misrepresented) at public history sites and how developments within public history and scholarly history have combined with Aboriginal pressure to improve the nature of representations of Aboriginal histories and cultures in public settings to produce a series of experiments and shifts in the interpretation of Aboriginal history at historic sites. After completing a doctorate in anthropology at McMaster University, Peers studied with Jennifer S.H. Brown as a postdoctoral fellow before moving to Oxford University to lecture in anthropology and curate at the Pitt Rivers Museum. Coutts has worked with Brown for years on the advisory board of the Centre for Rupert's Land Studies and is currently a senior historian at Parks Canada.

9

Border Identities: Métis, Halfbreed, and Mixed-Blood

Theresa Schenck

THE ESTABLISHMENT OF A border on the Plains between Rupert's Land and the United States in 1818 created a myriad of problems for the Native peoples of the area, some of which still exist today. Not least among them was the issue of Aboriginal identity: whether people of mixed Caucasian and Amerindian descent are indeed a separate people and how they are viewed, especially on the American side of the border. In this chapter I discuss various issues of identity as they developed among the Ojibwe (Chippewa) of Lake Superior and the Mississippi in the nineteenth century and how the imposition of an artificial boundary affected conceptions of mixed-blood people, or métissage, as some prefer to call it.[1]

Identity, of course, can be understood in many ways. It is not only how one views oneself but also how one is viewed by others. Thus, a person can have more than one identity, for the way one views oneself is not always the way one is viewed by others. Identity is at the very core of being, yet it can depend on the perspective of the other. It can also be considered as the sum of all our experiences. The identity I want to discuss is Aboriginal identity: how the border influenced the way Native people viewed themselves and the way others viewed them.

Borderland People

At the time of the Treaty of Paris in 1783, certain geographical features of North America were unknown to the negotiators. This caused much confusion later as cartographers began to draw boundary lines. According to the treaty, the line between Rupert's Land and the United States was to run "through Lake Superior northward of the Isles Royal and Phelipeaux to the Long Lake in that region; thence through the middle of said Long Lake and the water communication between it and the Lake of the Woods, to the said Lake of the Woods; thence through the said Lake to the most northwesternmost point thereof, and from thence on a due west course to the river Mississippi."[2] There was not only no Isle Phelipeaux but also no Long Lake, and no line drawn due west from Lake of the Woods would ever intersect the Mississippi or any of its tributaries. The inhabitants of the area remained blissfully unaware that they lived in what would become a disputed zone. Their identities were secure: some were employees of two great fur-trading companies, or freemen who owed no allegiance to anyone; many more were Native people whose ancestors had lived in the region for generations. To them, there were no borders.

Throughout the late eighteenth and early nineteenth centuries, there was a great deal of movement across these undefined borderlands as traders and hunters followed the fur-rich sources of the Red River south from Rupert's Land but also as Canadians followed the age-old route to the West across Lake Superior through the area known today as the boundary waters and onto the Plains. Ojibwe, meanwhile, continued to move into the regions north and west of Lake Superior. The "Iche-poyes" were mentioned as early as 1726 in the Fort Albany journal, but by the latter part of the eighteenth century they had moved west along the Assiniboine River and included not only Sauteurs from Sault Ste. Marie but also Ojibwe hunters from Red Lake, south of Lake of the Woods.[3] Ojibwe are mentioned for the first time in the Brandon House journal in 1797, but we know they were in western Manitoba long before that date. (My grandfather's Ojibwe great-grandmother was born west of Brandon in the mid-1780s.) Odawa from Michilimackinac and farther south came too, joining their Ojibwe relatives and the Cree and Assiniboin who were already in the region. John Tanner's *Narrative* of life in this region attests to the rich diversity of the Native population and their ability to retain their tribal identity even as they lived, fought, and worked together.

From this great diversity of Native people and their association with the personnel of the fur trade was born a new people whose identity soon became entwined in border issues. The freemen, as they were then known, many of whom had Native wives and children, were the hunters who provided meat and furs for both the Hudson's Bay Company (HBC) and the North West Company (NWC). The prairie southwest of the forks of the Red and Assiniboine Rivers was their hunting ground, and as the fur trade expanded and as competition between the two companies reached a fever pitch they were singled out and designated as a new nation of Aboriginal people with the same rights to the soil as Indians. And the term *"métis,"* the French equivalent of "halfbreed," was applied to them.[4] According to the testimony of participants, the birth of the Métis took place not in Manitoba but at the freemen's camp on the Turtle River (in present-day North Dakota) in 1814.[5]

Although the Métis had long hunted in this disputed area, and had even wintered there, few had ever settled in the region. But when the arrival of HBC settlers at the forks of the Red and Assiniboine Rivers in 1812 led to several years of conflict between the two great trading companies, many Métis felt safer at a distance from the burgeoning colony and began to establish themselves near the old trading post at Pembina in present-day North Dakota.[6] After the disturbances of 1815-17, while discussions about the border were in progress, many believed that the Red River and its tributaries would be in British territory. Thus, when the Red River First Nations sold some of their land to Lord Selkirk in 1817, the sale included all the land along the river south to the Grand Forks. The following year, the border was proclaimed to be at the forty-ninth parallel, although it was still not certain just exactly where that parallel intersected with the Red River. The Métis of Pembina – fortified with a church, a school, and a priest from Quebec – decided to stay.

In 1823, Stephen Long determined that the forty-ninth parallel passed just north of the little settlement at Pembina, which he described as consisting of about sixty log houses. As for the inhabitants, he found them only slightly elevated above the rank of "savage" but noted that there were exceptions – those of Canadian or foreign extraction. "By far the greater proportion of the inhabitants are of mixed blood, the descendants of Canadians and Indians, or foreigners and Indians. In their manners they exhibit few traits indicative of a higher refinement than their savage neighbors ... Their style of living is very similar, except that their habitations are more comfortable and more skillfully constructed ... Some few of the more respectable of this community ... keep cows and cultivate small plantations."[7]

For a variety of reasons, the Pembina Métis began to return to the Red River Colony in 1823. According to Father Dumoulin, attacks by the Sioux (the rightful owners of the land) had increased, meat was scarce, and there was a threat of famine.[8] Rivalry with the American Fur Company prompted the HBC to call for the withdrawal of all settlers and traders from the American side of the border, threatening to cut off supplies if they failed to do so. Many of the Métis who returned settled either at White Horse Plain or St. Boniface. In the ensuing years, however, as Pembina became a major centre of trade with St. Paul, Métis gradually returned to the area, and a priest was restored to them in 1848.

A careful analysis of the information given in the Pembina census of 1850 reveals 177 families and a total population of 1,116. Because age and place of birth are given, it is easy to determine how many families were truly old Pembina families and how many were newcomers. It appears that about twenty-five families had never left Pembina, for all members of each family had been born there. The birthdates and birthplaces of individuals in other families indicate that they originated in Pembina, relocated to the Red River Colony, and returned to Pembina. The majority of families, however, were clearly composed of immigrants who arrived within the five years preceding the census. In fact, at least twenty-one families were entirely of Red River origin and had children born who had been born in Pembina after 1845. Finally, an amazing number of families, twenty-eight, had no members born in Pembina, and many of them had been in Pembina only since 1849.[9]

Mixed-Blood Identity in the United States

In the United States, there had been no special recognition of people of mixed Indian and European descent. This was not to deny their existence, but they did not develop as, nor were they seen as, a separate people. From the Indian viewpoint, identity was simply a matter of lifestyle. Those who lived as Indians were Indians; no distinction between Indian and halfbreed was made. Those who lived as whites were whites. There was no in-between category, because everyone in the frontier settlements lived in a similar manner.[10] But the government soon recognized that people of mixed descent, especially those who had been raised in part by their European fathers, might just be the answer to the "Indian problem." (In the United States, Indians were perceived as being in the way of Manifest Destiny, an obstacle to white settlement and progress. The government could keep moving Indians west for only so long until white settlement caught up with them.) Government officials hoped that, if mixed-bloods were granted land next to lands reserved for Indians, they would settle down in European fashion and devote themselves to agriculture. By doing so, it was hoped, they would encourage their Indian relatives to settle and farm also. Agriculture was, of course, seen as the only road to civilization.[11]

Beginning in 1817, many Indian treaties granted land to halfbreeds in the United States. A careful study of these treaties, however, reveals three important considerations. First, the grantees were not always mixed-bloods; they were often Indians who had shown in some way a proclivity for "civilized" life. Second, the mixed-bloods were not seen as having Aboriginal rights but as being dependent on the largesse of their Indian relatives, and Indians were strongly encouraged, perhaps even threatened, to share land or money with mixed-bloods. And third, it was believed that the example of the mixed-bloods would help elevate Indians toward civilized life. In 1826, in the Treaty of Fond du Lac, the Lake Superior traders who were married to Ojibwe women tried to get the Indians to grant to their "half breed relations" 640 acres of land, or one section each, around Lake Superior.[12] The Senate did not approve this article of the treaty, however, and no land was allotted. The names on the list included only the descendants of prominent and influential traders, not all children of mixed descent. The intent was clearly to recognize the traders' children but not all halfbreeds.

In 1836, Indian Agent Henry Schoolcraft, whose wife was half Ojibwe, negotiated a treaty with the Ojibwe and Ottawa of Michigan. This time traders asked for money rather than land for their children. But to ensure that their children would receive more money than ordinary mixed-bloods, they came up with a scheme that would divide mixed-bloods into three classes according to the esteem in which they were held by the Indians and their ability to take care of money. Those of the first class would get one half more than those of the second class, who would then get twice as much as those of the third class. The decision was made by Schoolcraft and his cohorts. By limiting the number of people considered to be held in esteem, they were able to ensure more money for their own relatives. Needless to say, members of Schoolcraft's and his wife's family were judged to be of the first class and came away with over $23,000, nearly one-sixth of the money allotted. There were many complaints from mixed-bloods about the apportionment of money and the division of mixed-bloods into classes.[13]

In the 1837 treaty with the Chippewa of Lake Superior and the Mississippi, the traders, most of whom were married to Ojibwe or mixed-blood women, persuaded the Indians to set aside $100,000 to be distributed among "the half-breeds of the Chippewa nation." This time the commissioner of Indian Affairs specified that there would be no classes and that all halfbreeds would receive equal allotments. (According to the terms of this treaty, Indians would receive only $190,000 over a period of twenty years and $510,000 in goods and services over the same period). In reality, the greatest portion of this money for goods and services went to traders who provided highly over-priced provisions.[14]

Before this article of the treaty could be implemented, the issue of Indian and mixed-blood identity arose. In December 1836, Alfred Aitken, eldest son of the trader William Aitkin and his Ojibwe wife, had been killed by an Ojibwe from Leech Lake on the Upper Mississippi. The old man demanded retribution in the Indian style, that is, he wanted the Indian to be killed. The Ojibwe, however, did not want to enter into what could become a long blood feud; at the request of the governor, they turned the accused over to the courts for a trial, which was held in Prairie du Chien in Wisconsin Territory. There were two basic issues to be decided. First, did a territorial court have jurisdiction over a crime committed in Indian Territory? And second, was the murdered man a white man or an Indian? Should the case be handled as one that involved an Indian who allegedly murdered a white man or an Indian who allegedly murdered another Indian? The documents related to this case reveal much about attitudes toward mixed-blood identity at the time.

In May 1838, the jury decided that an Indian had murdered an Indian. Because Congress had already determined that the laws of the United States did not extend to offences committed by one Indian on another in Indian Country, the accused was allowed to go free. The judge, however, was of the opinion that the murdered man should have been considered white, for he "was brought up and educated as a white man and pursued the business and habits of whitemen." The jury's decision, nevertheless, was allowed to stand.[15]

The reaction of the mixed-bloods was astonishment, confusion, and anger. They argued that, because they were Indians, they would handle the manner in the Indian way. On 20 July, Daniel P. Bushnell, the La Pointe agent, met with the mixed-bloods, urged them not to seek revenge, and suggested a voluntary expression of condolence (a monetary contribution) on the part of the Indians at the time of their first payment under the Treaty of 1837. The murder, however, had been committed by an Indian from a band that was not a party to the treaty. Furthermore, the agent proposed to withhold the payment of $100,000 to the mixed-bloods until this difficulty (of retribution) was settled peaceably. The next day, the mixed-bloods met in council and selected six of their most prominent men to write a letter of protest to the agent. The government, they wrote, was guided by its own interests; it regarded them as Indians or whitemen, depending on the exigencies of each case. On the one hand, in 1828 the Michigan House of Representatives had acknowledged that mixed-bloods had all the privileges and immunities of citizens of the United States, including the right of suffrage. On the other hand, a supposedly competent tribunal had judged mixed-bloods to be Indians and, therefore, not subject to the laws of the United States. They did not take the agent's threat to withhold the $100,000 lightly and promised to consider the greater good. "None of us will seek the life of Aitken's murderer. This pledge will be rigidly adhered to." In a closing salvo, they added: "From the sense of Justice or Good faith of our self styled Guardians we expect nothing. Every act of theirs towards *this tribe of Indians,* and indeed toward every other tribe, has been marked by injustice & bad faith."[16]

The US government delayed another year in making the payment to the mixed-bloods for the Treaty of 1837. As word got around that the money would finally be distributed in the summer of 1839, people of mixed descent, Ojibwe and other tribes, began to descend on La Pointe in Lake Superior in the hope of getting a share of the money. Lucius Lyon, former US senator from Michigan, was appointed commissioner to take depositions and to apportion the money to all eligible halfbreeds, a category that included "Indians of mixed-blood of whatever degree." What was not clear to those who came to claim a share of the $100,000 was that they were entitled to the money only if they had immediate ties to the people who had ceded the land. They had to establish that their parents belonged to and had been born in the ceded country and that they had not severed connections with the Indians residing there. Mixed-bloods who claimed Chippewa descent came from as far away as Grand River in Michigan and the Red River settlement in British territory. Of the nearly 900 who claimed eligibility, 387 were admitted, 484 were rejected, and some withdrew. Even after Lyon took the testimony of each family head, the names had to be submitted to the chiefs in council, and it was they who had the final say.

Among those who presented themselves to the commissioner were a number of people with connections to Rupert's Land. All, of course, were rejected, but it is interesting to examine who they were and why they came.

Rupert's Land Connections

The two most prominent mixed-bloods with connections to Rupert's Land were Charles Gasper Bruce and Kenneth Mackenzie. Bruce, who had been an interpreter on Stephen Long's expedition in 1823 (the Rupert's Land part), claimed that his wife and four of his children had been born in Pembina (while six others had been born in British territory). The ages of these children indicate that they lived in Pembina between 1830 and 1836. Kenneth Mackenzie's wife was a full Chippewa from Leech Lake, outside the ceded territory. Two of the couple's four children had been born on the Leaf River, also outside the ceded territory, and two had been born at St. Peter's. The mother and the children now resided at Red River, where the children attended school, while the father lived in St. Louis and was associated with the Chouteau Company.[17]

A number of applicants had migrated from Red River to Prairie du Chien, Wisconsin, in the 1830s, when the lumber mills first opened up. Among them were three Desmarais brothers – Jean Baptiste, Louison, and Joseph – all born in Pembina in the time of Alexander Henry the Younger. Their father, Jean-Baptiste, had been one of Henry's traders, and their mother, they claimed, was a Chippewa woman. According to Jean-Baptiste's testimony, he had moved to the falls of the Chippewa River in 1830. He had one son, also named Jean-Baptiste, whose mother was a Chippewa woman from Red Lake and whose wife was the daughter of Peter Pond, likewise a trader from Red Lake. His brother Louison had come at about the same time. Louison's wife was a mixed-blood woman from Fond du Lac, which gave her the right to be admitted to payment, along with the two youngest of her children, who had been born on the Chippewa River and, thus, in the ceded territory. Their descendants are today members of the Lac Courte Oreilles Band of Ojibwe in Wisconsin.[18] At least four other families who had left Pembina for the lumber mills of the Prairie du Chien region applied for mixed-blood money. All were refused.

From Lower Canada, the old retired trader William Morrison tried to get his three children by his second wife (who was of Chippewa descent) accepted. Although born within the ceded territory, they were rejected on the basis of separation from their Chippewa relatives: they had left the country eleven years earlier. Even his two older children by his first marriage were rejected because they had not maintained ties within the ceded country. Morrison's younger brother Allan was somewhat more fortunate. His wife, Charlotte, daughter of the old trader Charles Chaboillez, had been born in Pembina, but because two of the couple's five children had been born in the ceded territory (on Crow Wing River and Swan River), they were accepted.[19]

Sometimes claimants fabricated stories because they were aware that Lucius Lyon did not know when they misspoke; however, they were unaware that the chiefs would review the testimony. Louis Nolin was the grandson of Jean-Baptiste Nolin, a former trader of Sault Ste. Marie who had moved to Red River in about 1816. He claimed that he had been born on the St. Croix River, part of the ceded land, and that his mother was a Chippewa of La Pointe. (Many claimants made this claim, unaware that La Pointe was outside the 1837 cession.) The chiefs in council, however, denied Nolin's claim, saying that he had been born at Sault Ste. Marie or Red River, not on the St. Croix.[20]

Another interesting effort to get recognized was made by four Jourdain brothers from Red Lake, Minnesota, who were the sons of Joseph Jourdain, a Canadian. All had been born at Red Lake and claimed that their mother was a Chippewa of Sandy Lake. "No!" said the chiefs. She was a Muskego from the Hudson Bay territory. Their claim, too, was rejected.[21]

Sometimes there is no accounting for the whims of the chiefs. Charles Chaboillez had been born in Pembina in about 1816, was raised for eleven years in Canada, and had lived for two years at Red Lake, three years at Rainy Lake, seven years at Sandy Lake, three years on Isle Royale, and one year at l'Ance. His mother was a Chippewa from Leech Lake, and his wife was a mixed-blood from Mackinac. His claim was administered, possibly only on the grounds that he had lived for seven years at Sandy Lake.[22]

Another interesting case is that of George D. Cameron, who at the time of the treaty was an independent trader on the Wisconsin River. According to Cameron's testimony, he had been born on the Snake River, a tributary of the St. Croix, in about 1800. He was sent to Canada for a brief time for an education and then worked for the HBC until about 1826, when he seems to have gone to the United States. There, he married (twice) and raised a family. What makes his claim interesting is that other records do not support it, yet, for some reason, possibly his residence on the Wisconsin River, the chiefs admitted him and his two daughters to the payment. His sister Genevieve, two years younger, told a far different story. She, too, claimed that she had been born on the Snake River in ceded territory but that the family had then moved to the north side of Lake Superior and then to Pembina, where she married Joseph Dagnar (Dagnier). She resided at Pembina until 1838, when she and her husband moved to Chippewa Falls. Church records from St. Boniface, Winnipeg, however, cast doubt on her claim. At the time of her death in 1875, it was recorded that she had been born in Manitoba and that her father was Dougald Cameron and her mother Marie l'Esperance. From 1795 to 1805, Cameron had been the NWC factor at Nipigon, and it would have been extraordinary if his children had been born during that time on the Snake River.[23]

In the end, admission to payment came down to residence and birth and acceptance by the chiefs. Each claimant was awarded about $255. Because being of mixed descent entailed monetary advantages in the United States, it was important to determine who was to be considered a halfbreed or mixed-blood. A person of less than one-quarter Indian ancestry was usually considered non-Indian. In 1847, one group of mixed-bloods had enough power to insert an entire article in another treaty made at Fond du Lac. "It is stipulated that the half or mixed bloods of the Chippewa residing with them shall be considered Chippewa Indians, and shall, as such, be allowed to participate in all annuities which shall hereafter be paid to the Chippewas of the Mississippi and Lake Superior." The essential words here are "residing with them." Whether one was considered an Indian was clearly not a mere matter of blood or ancestry but rather about where and how one lived. Fifteen mixed-bloods signed this treaty as chiefs and warriors.[24]

When word of the treaty's provisions reached the La Pointe traders, they were furious that there was to be no compensation for their claims and, worse, that according to article 5 of the treaty an Ojibwe agency would be established on the Upper Mississippi, thereby drawing away from La Pointe all the profits to be made from the Indian payments. The traders convinced a large group of fur trade employees then gathered at La Pointe, most of them mixed-bloods, to sign a statement to the president that denounced the treaty article that allowed them to be considered Indians if they resided with Indians. The mixed-bloods believed that by this article they would have to give up all their rights as United States citizens, "a right we hold dear and not to be sacrificed for money." Clearly, a large portion of mixed-bloods did not see any advantage to being considered Aboriginal, regardless of whether they understood all the implications of the article. Although 103 signatures appear on the petition, most of the signatories were children whose names were signed by their fathers. In reality, members of fewer than twenty families were represented.[25]

Along the Forty-Ninth Parallel

Meanwhile, on the northern border, there arose a problem that threatened the very concept of mixed-blood in the United States. Many Métis, finding the trade restrictions and exorbitant prices of the HBC too onerous to bear, had begun to return to Pembina, where they were not only closer to their hunting grounds but could also take advantage of the longer growing season. More importantly, there was economic opportunity for them in the trade between Pembina and St. Paul. The hunting ground, however, was still disputed territory. The Sioux considered it their own, but Cree, Assiniboin, and, more recently, Ojibwe were also venturing out onto the prairie for buffalo and furs, and hundreds of Métis had now made it their annual hunting ground.

It is evident from reports made to the commissioner of Indian Affairs in the United States in 1845 that the Métis were still an unknown quantity, "the subjects of a foreign power" who "ought not to be permitted to hunt within our boundaries."[26] In 1847, the commissioner asked Henry Schoolcraft for a summary of the situation in the northern borderlands. In a long letter that traced the history of commercial relations between Red River and the Mississippi, Schoolcraft expressed his belief that those who hunted buffalo within the boundaries of the United States were British citizens who had no claim to either the upper portions of the Red River or to the height of land where they hunted. These lands clearly belonged to the Sioux.[27]

And just as American authorities were beginning to wonder who these intruders were, and what to do about them, there arrived in Pembina one who would be their champion. George-Antoine Belcourt (Bellecourt) has been described as an "idealistic but emotionally unstable priest" who unselfishly devoted his life to the Indians and the Métis and who advocated political opposition to – if not the overthrow of – the HBC. In 1848, he joined the Métis in Pembina and began his campaign to have them recognized as American citizens and halfbreeds with the same rights as Indian people.[28]

His first opportunity came during the summer of 1849, when an army officer, Major S. Woods, was sent by the War Department to examine the northwestern frontier of Minnesota to determine whether the area needed a military post. Arriving in Pembina on 1 August, when the Red River was still high, Woods found only one trading establishment, that of Norman Kittson, and no houses. Belcourt lived about one mile down the river on high ground, and the Métis lived in lodges built in the timber along the river. Most of the Indians and Métis were hunting buffalo on the plains and returned by mid-August. According to Woods, the Indians, numbering about five to six hundred, were mostly Chippewa, along with a few Cree and Assiniboin. They came, they said, from the east in pursuit of game and furs, indicating that they must have originally been a hunting band. Because they seemed to lack band organization, though, Woods encouraged them to organize themselves with a principal chief and two second chiefs. There were also Indians from Red Lake who came out to the Prairies to hunt. Woods described the halfbreeds as a distinct class of people, one that was materially different from the Indian and the American in

manners, customs, and pursuits. Belcourt told Woods that the Métis had originally resided on American soil, but when the forty-ninth parallel was marked,
they had been forced to move to Red River. Since the establishment of a fur-
trading post at Pembina, however, they had begun to return, having a "lingering
fondness for the place of their birth." There were at that time 1,026 Métis living
at Pembina, according to Belcourt.[29]

Major Woods was clearly impressed with the Métis of Pembina and saw an
opportunity to strengthen the American presence in the area by allowing them
to own land and farm. "The greater part of these people are descendants of the
Canadian French. They speak the French language, are nearly all Catholics, with
mild and gentle manners, great vivacity, generous and honest in their transactions, and disposed to be a civil and orderly community ... They build log
cabins generally in the timber which they occupy in the winter and leave in the
summer." He found that they possessed "the semblance of a government," a
council of five of their principal men. He believed that, by virtue of their Indian
extraction, those who lived on the American side should be considered as possessing the Indians' rights upon the soil and urged them to organize themselves
into a band.[30]

Along with a report to Governor Alexander Ramsey, dated 10 November
1849, Woods sent a long letter written by Father Belcourt that contained his
observations on the inhabitants of the country. The priest acknowledged that
the Ojibwe "have been for ages in possession of this country" but that before
them the land had belonged to the Sioux. He estimated that there were about
four thousand Indians between Red Lake and Turtle Mountain. "The Chippewas, like all barbarous tribes, are much demoralized, and above all others,
superstitious to excess ... The Chippewas who reside upon the line, or there-
abouts, are generally miserably poor, sluggards, having no aptitude but for the
chase ... Idle and improvident as they are, notwithstanding the abundance of
bison, they are often a heavy charge upon the half-breeds." The Métis, on the
contrary, were "mild, generous, polished in their manners, and ready to do a
kindness." More numerous than the Indians (Belcourt estimated their number
to be over five thousand), the Métis had only been established in Pembina
since about 1818, although many had withdrawn after the HBC threatened to
deny them supplies from its store if they stayed. Nevertheless, Belcourt reported
that they had always had a strong predilection for Pembina and now looked
forward to the protection of the United States. "Originally its citizens and for
so long a time miserable," they hoped to soon "embrace and enjoy the sweets
of liberty."[31]

The governor was impressed with Belcourt's assessment of the Métis and
used it in his annual report to the commissioner of Indian Affairs, Orlando

Brown. This report was the first official acknowledgment that the Métis had settled within the United States and might even be welcome. "I consider these people to be a fine race," Ramsey wrote, "who for several reasons would make a desirable population on our northern frontier." Still, he felt it necessary to explain who they were and to distinguish them from the more familiar halfbreed. They were, he wrote, a superior race that had inherited many of the best qualities of their parent races. "They are industrious, provident, enterprising, honest, and ingenious; and are reported to possess that pre-eminent trait of civilization, a proper care and treatment of their females." He added that the Métis had requested that the United States extend its laws and institutions over them.[32]

Belcourt then took up the cause of the Métis in his frequent letters to the governor, whom he tried to convince that the Métis were already American citizens and, as mixed-bloods, possessed the same rights to the soil as their Indian relatives. Realizing that the lands along the Red River would soon be sold, Belcourt made an extraordinary request: he asked the governor not only to allow the Métis to share in the payment for the Indian lands but also to allow everyone to do so, regardless of their origin. Furthermore, once the land was sold, Belcourt wanted each Métis family to be able to purchase pieces of land six chains wide and one mile in depth along the river at a lower cost than other citizens.[33]

The Indians in the area, however, had other ideas. In August 1850, they told William Dahl, the census taker: "We expected to see some persons here who would interest themselves in our behalf, as the Red River half breeds have taken our lands from us and say it is theirs. As to ourselves, we know no other home but Pembina and Red Lake. But the Half Breeds come over every day from Prince Rupert's Land and settle down on our lands, while we the rightful owners are banished away."[34]

Governor Ramsey knew all this when he arrived in September to treat with the Indians for their lands, thirty miles on either side of the Red River, which would then be opened for settlement. Belcourt stayed away during the treaty negotiations and instead wrote in support of the Métis, asking the governor to remonstrate with the Chippewa and Pillagers, whom he now considered trespassers on Métis lands. "It will be well to remark to those Indians, we do not ask payment for having placed their feet on our lands ... The half breeds consider themselves master of these lands, although the Indians claim a right too, because the half breeds did not drive them from here, but allowed them to establish themselves, and hunt on the mountain as they saw fit."[35]

Red Lake chief Mo-so-mo's testimony to the governor during negotiations contradicted Belcourt's argument: "I think a great deal of the piece of land my Father points to. Upon it is where my father raised me, even up to the place you named (Buffalo River). Just as my father supported me, so that land yet supports me. I love it, I love it, for I live by and on it." Ramsey, although he respected the Métis now settled on the American side of the border, did not share Belcourt's view of their rights. According to instructions received from Washington, he offered the Ojibwe $10,000 a year for twenty years and their mixed-blood relatives a one-time payment of $30,000. The Indians responded to the offer with silence. But the governor was adamant, and the missionaries eventually convinced them to accept the offer. The treaty was made with the Chippewa of Pembina and Red Lake. In a separate addendum to the treaty, the division of the $30,000 was spelled out: "to repay in some measure the kindness and liberality manifested to us by our trader and half blood relatives."[36] The treaty was not ratified by the Senate. It would be another twelve years before a comparable treaty would be made.

The Indians, meanwhile, were more than unhappy with the continued presence of the Métis on what they considered to be their hunting grounds. One of the chiefs, Green Setting Feather, complained in 1852:

In the time past, whenever I looked over my hunting grounds, I ever found a plenty with what to fill my dish, and plenty to give my children; but of late it is not so. I find that my provision bag is fast emptying, my dish is now often empty. And what is the cause of this? It is none other than the children I once raised, that first proceeded from my own loins, that were once fed from my own hands, which child is the half breed.

The manner of his hunt is such as not only to kill, but also to drive away the few he leaves, and waste even those he kills ... When I look at all this, my heart is pained within me. I see my provisions all wasted. I only wish to be master, and do as I please with what is my own. I now say, I hold back, and love all of the Turtle Mountain. From it the half breeds must keep, and stop on the place their father gave them at the Pembina. Also our traders, they must obey our law, not to kill animals or hunt furs, only as we shall tell them. The half breeds of late have been hunting towards the Turtle Mountain without our consent, which we cannot allow any longer. We now close by saying we wish for the half breeds to go get meat from the plains only once a summer, and for them to stay in Pembina and take care of the Preacher. We will take care of our own selves.[37]

But for the Indians, it was too late. Subsequent treaties would be imposed on them, and they would have to accept the inevitable. In 1863, a treaty was made with the Red Lake and Pembina bands. Article 8 stipulated that the United States would grant to each adult halfbreed or mixed-blood related by blood to the said Chippewa of the Red Lake or Pembina bands a homestead of 160 acres of land within the limits of the ceded country. The following year, a supplementary treaty was made by which the mixed-bloods could elect to receive scrip instead of land. Although most of the Métis elected to receive scrip, the names of many others are found on the annuity rolls. "Those who reside among the Indians shall be considered Indians."

The Ojibwe were eventually persuaded to accept mixed-bloods as Aboriginal. There was never a problem with those who lived as Indians, for they had been present since the earliest days of contact, and they had always resided among their mothers' people. The issue of identity was raised only after Aboriginal people began to take on the language, values, and lifestyle of the dominant society and when the US government began to try to use people of mixed descent to help assimilate Indians into Euro-American society. For many today, the issue remains unresolved because they acknowledge the fundamental difference between people who have an Aboriginal ancestor and Aboriginal people.

Notes

1   "Chippewa" and "Ojibwe" are two forms of the same word used since the seventeenth century to designate people who call themselves Anishinaabeg. The name Sauteurs, which referred to the site of their principal village at the Sault (falls) of Ste. Marie, was also used.
2   See "Jay's Treaty – 1794," Archiving Early America, http://earlyamerica.com/earlyamerica/milestones/jaytreaty/text.html.
3   Fort Albany Journal, Hudson's Bay Company Archives (hereafter HBCA), B.3/a/10.
4   The terms "halfbreed" and "mixed-blood" were used interchangeably in the nineteenth century as translations of the French *"métis"* (mixed). I use them in this chapter as they appear in the documents of the period. No disrespect is intended.
5   Schenck, "Against All Odds," 43; and HBCA, E.8/5:131v.
6   For a thorough discussion of these events, see Giraud, *The Metis*, 1:419-87.
7   Kane, Holmquist, and Gilman, eds., *The Northern Expeditions of Stephen H. Long*, 183-84.
8   Dumoulin to Plessis, 13 November 1822, cited in Nute, ed., *Documents Relating to the Northwest Missions*, 378.
9   The United States census of 1850 for the Pembina District, Minnesota Territory, has been published in *Collections of the State Historical Society of North Dakota*, 3:314-405.
10 Consider the words of John H. Fairbanks, who first came to Leech Lake in northern Minnesota in 1818 as a clerk. In the undated memoir that he dictated to J.A. Gilfillan, he commented: "There were no half breeds in those days." Recollections of John H. Fairbanks in Henry M. Rice Papers, Minnesota Historical Society.
11 Wallace, *Jefferson and the Indians*, 223.
12 Kappler, ed., *Indian Affairs*, 2:272-73.
13 See especially a letter written by William Bell for the halfbreeds of the Chippewa Nation and addressed to President Andrew Jackson, 13 November 1836. Correspondence of the Office of Indian Affairs, Letters Received (hereafter COIA-LR), National Archives Microfilm (hereafter NAM), M234, Roll 770.
14 Documents Relating to the Negotiation of Ratified and Unratified Treaties with Various Indian Tribes, 1801-69, NAM, T494, Roll 3.

15 T.P. Burnett to William A. Aitken, 28 May 1838, Henry H. Sibley Papers, Reel 2, Minnesota Historical Society.

16 Daniel P. Bushnell to Henry Dodge, 26 July 1838, enclosing speech of John DuBay and minutes of Half Breed Council, COIA-LR, NAM, M234, Reel 387, (emphasis in original).

17 Affidavits No. 46 and No. 48, Mixed Blood Records, Lucius Lyon Papers, William L. Clements Library, University of Michigan.

18 Affidavits No. 75, No. 152, and No. 174, ibid.

19 Affidavits No. 105 and No. 132, ibid.

20 Affidavit No. 40, ibid.

21 Affidavit No. 79, ibid.

22 Affidavit No. 167, ibid.

23 Affidavits No. 95 and No. 96, ibid.

24 Kappler, ed., *Indian Affairs,* 2:568-69.

25 Half Breed Petition, 21 August 1847, COIA-LR, NAM, M234, Roll 389.

26 Medill to Marcy, 24 November 1845, in *New American State Papers,* 2:118-27.

27 Schoolcraft to Medill, 14 October 1847, COIA-LR, NAM, M234, Roll 760.

28 Gluek, *Minnesota and the Manifest Destiny,* 57-58.

29 Wood, "Report of Major Woods," 9-35.

30 Ibid.

31 Belcourt to Wood, 20 August 1849, Henry H. Sibley Papers, Roll 6, Minnesota Historical Society.

32 Indian Affairs, *Annual Report* (1850), 95-97.

33 Belcourt to Ramsey, 9 January 1850, COIA-LR, NAM, M2234, Roll 438.

34 *Minnesota Pioneer,* 21 November 1850.

35 Belcourt to Ramsey, 15 September 1850, COIA-LR, NAM, M234, Roll 438.

36 "Journal of the US Commission to Treat with the Chippewa Indians of Pembina and Red Lake, 18 Aug.–27 Nov. 1851," COIA-LR, NAM, M234, Roll 438.

37 Quoted in Report No. 86, Isaac I. Stevens to George W. Manypenny, 16 September 1854, in Indian Affairs, *Annual Report* (1855), 189-91.

Bibliography

Archival Sources

Hudson's Bay Company Archives (HBCA)
B.3/a/10, Fort Albany Journal.
E.8/5, Red River Settlement: Papers Related to Disturbances.

Minnesota Historical Society
Henry M. Rice Papers.
Henry H. Sibley Papers.

National Archives Microfilm (NAM)
Correspondence of the Office of Indian Affairs, Letters Received (COIA-LR).
Documents Relating to the Negotiation of Ratified and Unratified Treaties with Various Indian Tribes, 1801-69.

University of Michigan, William L. Clements Library
Lucius Lyon Papers, Mixed Blood Records.

Published Sources

Collections of the State Historical Society of North Dakota, Vol. 3.

Giraud, Marcel. *The Metis in the Canadian West.* Translated by George Woodcock. 2 vols. Edmonton: University of Alberta Press, 1986.

Gluek, Alvin C. *Minnesota and the Manifest Destiny of the Canadian Northwest: A Study in Canadian-American Relations.* Toronto: University of Toronto Press, 1965.

Indian Affairs. *Annual Report of the Commissioner of Indian Affairs, 1849-1850.* Washington: Gideon and Co., 1850.

–. *Annual Report of the Commissioner of Indian Affairs.* Washington: O.P. Nicholson, 1855.

Kane, Lucile M., June D. Holmquist, and Carolyn Gilman, eds. *The Northern Expeditions of Stephen H. Long: The Journals of 1817 and 1823 and Related Documents.* Minneapolis: Minnesota Historical Society Press, 1978.

Kappler, Charles J., ed. *Indian Affairs: Laws and Treaties.* 2 vols. Washington: Government Printing Office, 1904.

New American State Papers. Edited by Thomas C. Cochran. 13 vols. Wilmington, DE: Scholarly Resources, 1972.

Nute, Grace Lee, ed. *Documents Relating to the Northwest Missions.* Minneapolis: Minnesota Historical Society Press, 1942.

Schenck, Theresa M. "Against All Odds ... and with the Help of Our Friends: The Native Role in Establishing the Red River Colony, 1812-1817." *North Dakota Quarterly* 54, 4 (1998): 35-51.

Tanner, John. *A Narrative of the Captivity and Adventures of John Tanner, (U.S. Interpreter at the Saut de Ste. Marie,) during Thirty Years Residence among the Indians in the Interior of North America.* Edited by Edwin James. Minneapolis: Ross and Haines, 1956.

Wallace, Anthony F.C. *Jefferson and the Indians: The Tragic Fate of the First Americans.* Cambridge, MA: Belknap Press of Harvard University Press, 1999.

Woods, Major. "Report of Major Woods, Relative to His Expedition to the Pembina Settlement, and the Condition of Affairs on the North-Western Frontier of the Territory of Minnesota, 10 November 1849." House Executive Document 51, 31st Congress, 1st Session (1850), Serial 577.

10

Edward Ahenakew's Tutelage by Paul Wallace: Reluctant Scholarship, Inadvertent Preservation

David R. Miller

EDWARD AHENAKEW (FIGURE 10.1) was born a Cree of the Ahtahkakoop Cree Nation (Sandy Lake Reserve) in Saskatchewan in 1885 and died seventy-six years later in 1961. When Ahenakew became seriously ill as a child, his parents vowed that they would give him to the church if he survived. He survived, was sent to residential school, and later became an Anglican missionary priest. Throughout his life, Ahenakew was poor and unmarried, and he suffered from periodic illness. Many contemporary Plains Crees consider Ahenakew to be one of their foremost spokespersons and writers because he was among the first to write about Cree culture and history and to be published both during his lifetime and posthumously.[1] A fluent speaker of the Cree language, Ahenakew served as a consultant to Richard Faries for the revision of E.A. Watkins' *Dictionary of the Cree Language* (1865 [1938]), because he was literate in Cree syllabics as well as in English. Ahenakew's major publications include an article, titled "Cree Trickster Tales," which was published in the *Journal of American Folklore* in 1929, and a posthumous publication of selected writings, *Voices of the Plains Cree,* which was published in 1973 and reprinted in 1995. Ahenakew's only publication in the Cree language, written in syllabics, was a mimeographed newsletter titled the *Cree Monthly Guide,* of which only scattered issues have survived.[2]

The posthumous editions of *Voices of the Plains Cree* enabled generations of readers to have access to the writings of this important collector, recorder, and writer. Ruth Matheson Buck, a popular Saskatchewan writer, edited the first edition. She was a long-time friend of the Ahenakew family and daughter of the Anglican priest under whom Edward Ahenakew served following his ordination. Shortly after Ahenakew's death in 1961, his family gave Buck the meagre collection of his papers.[3] Ahab Spence, an employee of the Department of Indian Affairs and fellow clergy, facilitated a modest grant for the preparation of an edition of Ahenakew's writings.[4] A decade after Ahenakew's death, Buck began gathering the material, and she was given free rein to structure, order, shape, and edit the stories. The result was the 1973 edition of *Voices of the Plains Cree.* When this edition was long out of print, *Voices* was reprinted to make it available for classroom instruction.

Recent biographies and histories of indigenous individuals and communities that examine the production of ethnographic texts call for increased reflexivity

Figure 10.1 Edward Ahenakew, 1959. Saskatchewan Archives Board, Photo Collection B-4794.

in fieldwork – that is, fieldworkers and those who study them should carefully assess how their own biases and perspectives shape the material they collect. Recent scholarship also calls for a careful assessment of all the dimensions of authorship, from those who contributed ethnographic information to those who constructed the published work.[5] This chapter applies these standards to the cultural writings of Edward Ahenakew. The processes behind the texts' creation and changes in Ahenakew's writing over time reveal the variety of influences in Ahenakew's life.

The details of Ahenakew's childhood and socialization are not known, and the degree to which he was exposed to Cree cultural knowledge cannot be documented. His writings represent much of what he apparently learned as an adult.[6] Most of Ahenakew's texts contain ethnographic information that he gathered from those who became the subject of his writing. For example, his time with Chief Thunderchild in 1921-23 became the basis for the Thunderchild stories and for elements in the Old Keyam stories, which were both included in *Voices*.

Ahenakew made significant contributions as a natural, albeit untrained, fieldworker. He earned his status as an indigenous expert, akin to an elder's role as an intellectual grandfather, for a myriad of reasons. Male elders were (and are still) often addressed as grandfather. Ahenakew's role as a writer paralleled his role as a white-educated, Cree-speaking Indian. A group of Indian traditionalists elected him to lead the newly formed Saskatchewan chapter of the League of Indians of Canada in 1921. His bishop ordered him to choose between the church and his new political position. He chose the former, but not without some regret. In the fall of 1924, Ahenakew humbly told his friend Paul Wallace that Indian traditionalists had chosen him as a leader and had prayed over him and that he was impressed by this honour. The League of Indians did not blame Ahenakew for withdrawing; rather, many viewed the leaders of the Anglican Church as hypocrites for placing Ahenakew in such a bind. They likened the clergy to paternalist Indian Affairs Department officials, who were unrelenting in their campaign to assimilate Native peoples.[7]

Ahenakew earned his reputation in part because he had collected information from Chief Thunderchild, one of the headmen who had followed Big Bear, and from other elders. Ahenakew's fluency in the Cree language and his facility with linguistics enabled him to listen, comprehend, and record the stories of elders. Unfortunately, no literal transcription of the conversations has survived. Ahenakew was not equipped with the formal skills of linguistic transcription; he instead prepared summaries of the stories in English. His papers do not reveal whether he was aware of the collecting methods of ethnologists and anthropological linguists.

Ahenakew was not trained in historical linguistics, and it was only in the late 1920s, when he was working with Paul Wallace on the trickster stories, that he did perhaps glimpse the merit of studying Indian languages. In this manner, Ahenakew's primary interest in the narratives he collected and wrote down was their cultural, not linguistic, detail. Ahenakew's stories have been venerated as remnants of the knowledge of another age, in particular an era when acculturation was promoted in uncompromising terms. His literary work is imbued with various shades of resistance to acculturation. His work as a collector and editor of traditional stories reflects both his scholarly limitations and his discomfort with programs of acculturation.

One of the most significant influences on Edward Ahenakew and his writings was his friendship with Paul Wallace (see Figure 10.2), a graduate student at the University of Alberta and later professor of English at Lebanon Valley College, Annville, Pennsylvania, who specialized in editing and publishing collections of historical documents.[8] Their friendship began in Edmonton. Wallace was a veteran of the Great War and an eager first-year graduate student from eastern Canada at the University of Alberta when he met the slightly older Cree clergyman at a local literary club. Both men were fascinated by writing and writers and hoped to connect with like-minded souls. Ahenakew had come to the University of Alberta to study medicine. He had been emotionally devastated by his inability to help parishioners and fellow Crees who were among the victims of the influenza pandemic of 1917-18. Feeling that he had failed in his missionary pastorate, Ahenakew decided to learn about physical healing. In the fall of 1918, and at age thirty-three, Ahenakew secured a leave from the Diocese of Saskatchewan and set off to the University of Alberta with the intention of becoming a doctor.

Ahenakew Begins to Write

In Edmonton, Ahenakew's participation in the local literary club, composed of people from the university and the local community, might have caused him to seriously consider writing, possibly as a means to supplement his meagre income. His first writing attempts emulated romantic novels. He later advanced to ethnographic stories of his people, and Wallace assumed the instrumental role of editor. Both men were veterans – Wallace of the First World War and Ahenakew of the influenza epidemic and his tours as a missionary priest – and both were interested in expanding the limits of Canadian literature. Wallace, however, became engrossed with folklore studies and, by 1920, had decided to leave the University of Alberta for the University of Toronto to pursue a graduate degree.[9]

At the same time, toward the end of his second year of courses, Ahenakew developed stomach ulcers and was forced to abandon his studies. He went to stay with a priest's widow on the Thunderchild Reserve and began his long convalescence. When he had partially regained his strength, he took up an almost daily routine of visiting old Chief Thunderchild, and each evening he recorded on paper their conversations from memory.[10] When he recovered fully, Ahenakew accepted a new assignment as general missionary in the diocese, a job that involved travel to a variety of parishes.[11]

The "Old Keyam" Manuscript

Ahenakew's ethnographic work and literary pursuits can be traced in his correspondence with Wallace, which began when the two men parted and continued off and on for thirty years. The precise moment when Ahenakew began the "Old Keyam" manuscript, however, is not clear.[12] In a letter dated 25 August

Figure 10.2   Paul Wallace, 1950. Courtesy of David H. Wallace.

1922, Ahenakew asked Wallace to speak to a Mr. Button in Toronto to whom Ahenakew had sent an unidentified manuscript. In the same letter, Ahenakew reported that he had abandoned his program in Edmonton because of a nervous breakdown, as he called it.[13] Writing again in early December 1922, Ahenakew indicated that an editor at Ryerson Press was interested in his manuscript, and he again asked Wallace to help him communicate with Button, who had promised to review his work. Ahenakew asked Wallace to give Button a little prod, but to read again and correct the manuscript before passing it on to the editor at Ryerson.[14]

In the same letter, Ahenakew mentioned that he had begun a collection of western legends, some of which he had written down; others, he wrote, "are as yet only in my head." Ahenakew promised that he would send a few samples as soon as he was in better health and could retrieve the stories at his old residence. This was the first mention of a second project, and these texts were presumably those published later under the title "Cree Trickster Tales" in the *Journal of American Folklore* in 1929.[15]

In his next letter to Wallace in mid-January 1923, Ahenakew identified the manuscript under consideration by Ryerson as the Old Keyam stories. Keyam, created by Ahenakew, was a composite fictional character who personified a range of behaviour that, on the one hand, was pained and angry and, on the other, humorous and satirical. Ahenakew's Keyam criticized manifestations of the white man's insensitivities toward Indians that had contributed to their dispossession but also voiced protest against the presumed passivity of Indians to the fates they often unwittingly accepted. Certainly, Keyam was more than semi-autobiographical; rather, Ahenakew consciously constructed the persona as a literary device that would permit him to comment freely on a range of topics that would have been difficult for him to discuss directly. Ahenakew created Keyam, in part, to get around the church's censure of his political activities and its attempt to strangle his political voice.

Other compilations of texts provided Ahenakew with models for his collections, even though the remote locations of his missionary assignments restricted his access to libraries. In a letter to Wallace in January 1923, Ahenakew noted that he was looking for published versions of indigenous narratives and cited Alfred Carmichael's *Indian Legends of Vancouver Island* (1922), which he characterized as "nice but there is very little material in it."[16] Presumably, by "material" he meant cultural content. He indicated that he would write a few samples for Wallace's comments when he was again fit to do so. Ahenakew hoped these legends would be a sequel to the Keyam manuscript, but he commented, "that can rest till I feel strong again, i.e., in case 'Old Keyam' is fortunate enough to have a chance of publication."[17]

In February 1923, Ahenakew thanked Wallace for speaking with the editor at Ryerson.[18] In March 1923, as promised, Ahenakew sent two sample Cree legends to Wallace. He provided a lengthy discussion of the trickster Wesakaychak, motifs such as the Flood, and other cultural figures such as the Witiko to illuminate their literary value.[19] He explained that he was providing the texts in English with Cree terms at appropriate places and wrote, "I have many of these now [that] I go daily to hear Chief Thunderchild tell them and I write them down as he tells them. I have left out much of the details and have I am sure lost much beauty through a desire for brevity." But he added, "Hoping that these may prove to be representative."[20] In a letter written in May, Ahenakew explained that he was hard at work on the Wesakaychak stories and had completed five chapters.[21] By July, his correspondence indicated that he had almost finished the Wesakaychak legends and was "feeling very well indeed, almost back to my old self again I think." He intended to forward the stories to Wallace for his response. Ahenakew also asked about Wallace's reaction to the samples he had sent earlier: "How are you getting along with the others? Have you found them unworkable? I should be glad if you would drop me a line and tell me what you think of them."[22]

By the late summer of 1923, Wallace had become instrumental as an editor and a critic, both for the Keyam manuscript and for the collection of Cree legends. Ahenakew wrote:

I am sending the Cree Legends of Wesakaychak. Of course they are rough, but they will show you what they are like. I am sending you on the different paper things that may do for Keyam in addition to what you may find worthy of incorporating in the Legends.

Tell me just what I should do as soon as you are able. I would be glad if it were possible to get something out for Xmas, do you think so?

Cut out whatever you think should be cut out and incorporate what you think should be added to Keyam.

I shall try to do as you advise re: [relative] introductions to talks of Keyam, giving setting to his talks.

I am afraid I have not made much of the "humor" chapter. I have added on "On Keyam at the Saskatoon Fair," I wrote it while at the fair myself, sitting in my rig a little to one side myself ... Please use the greatest freedom in arranging the book and I shall be pleased to abide by what you advise.[23]

The ongoing correspondence between Ahenakew and Wallace revealed the evolving dynamics of their creative relationship. On 5 September 1923, Ahenakew wrote:

I am so glad to hear that the first revision has been completed and that you are getting it typed.

I agree that it should be as authoritative as possible. Some of the statements made [referring to the Old Keyam manuscript] as I told you before have to be modified now, because there have been changes in the working of the I[ndian] Department since some of the articles [pieces] were written. On the other hand I am writing these as things appear to the Indian himself, in Saskatchewan more particularly but I am sure to other provinces in the West at least.[24]

Ahenakew noted that in his last letter he had pressed for "the matter of hurrying publication, but I am inclined to agree with your proposition."[25] Wallace, by inference, had recommended taking more time and putting further effort into the manuscript.

Almost a month later, Ahenakew informed Wallace that he had returned to work and was serving a district that covered the north side of the Saskatchewan River from Battleford to Frog Lake, a round distance of two hundred miles, which he travelled every four weeks. He stated in passing, "Besides this [travelling] I print a monthly paper in Cree Syllabic[s]." Ahenakew referred to the *Cree Monthly Guide,* a mimeographed publication, that he edited and published (he ran the mimeograph machine) and to which he contributed articles. Ahenakew had designed the paper as a spiritual guide and source of information for Cree Anglicans.

Despite his productivity, vigour, and renewed health, Ahenakew was worried about his abilities. In the same letter, he expressed his insecurities over the Keyam manuscript: "I am sorry the new chapters I sent in were not so satisfactory but I did them too hurriedly and were more for the material in them than for the form. If they came up to the requirements as to material I intended to work them up." Ahenakew also was overcome with doubts about his other manuscript project: "The Wesakaychak legends were also written very hurriedly and more to show the material than anything else. If they showed any promise then I felt I would put more time to them ... So at present I do not write but once the winter sets in I shall be able to do whatever is necessary."[26] His worries about the manuscripts extended from their quality to opportunities for publication. He mentioned that he was corresponding with the renowned English Canadian publisher Lorne Pierce but had reached no agreements with him.[27]

Ahenakew became increasingly frustrated with his role as a writer. When Ryerson Press rejected the "Old Keyam" manuscript, his first reaction was to abandon the project altogether. "It was very disappointing to me and I [am] determined to let them all go and attend to my missionary work only." Referring to Wallace's assistance with the project, he wrote, "You yourself have done a great deal of work on it. Did you get any remuneration? I should be sorry to think that you had been put to much trouble and nothing came of it."[28] A large part of Ahenakew's frustration was due to his naïveté about the publishing process. He resented having to adjust his manuscript to standards determined by others and fretted that the texts would not remain central in the book.[29]

In mid-September 1924, when Ahenakew stopped in Toronto on his way to a church meeting in England, he dined at the Wallace home. According to an entry in Wallace's diary, Wallace and Ahenakew sat down "to discuss arrangements for the publishing of his legends of Wissaketchak [sic]. I have promised to rewrite his Ms. next summer, for publication a year from this fall."[30] Ahenakew spent his evening with the Wallace family talking about recent events in his and their lives and Indian customs, folklore, and history. Wallace recounted in his diary that Ahenakew had told him

> of his initiation as a chief four years ago – a most impressive ceremony, in the presence of between seven hundred and eight hundred Indians from Saskatchewan and Alberta. Two chiefs placed their hands on his shoulder, and outside, then two others placed their hands on the shoulders of two past chiefs. For half an hour the ceremony continued, and he walked backward and forward while the chiefs prayed over him. I asked if such prayer was at all like our Christian prayers. "Yes," he replied quickly, "like the prayers of the Old Testament." But he said that he could not tell me the details of the ceremony, for he had been far too much excited to notice much – evidently the Indian's appraisal stolidly is self control.

After discussing Ahenakew's lineage, particularly his relationship to historical chiefs, Wallace recorded in his diary: "He is a 'real chief,' not a 'departmental chief.' The latter are the men elected (with the Indian department's veto) to represent the Indians on the reserve. The real chiefs are elected in accordance with the old traditions of the people. The Department Chiefs are chiefs only on the reserves. 'I am a chief,' he said, 'wherever I go.'"[31]

Wallace recognized that his friend had authentic knowledge and skills to facilitate the preservation of information that would disappear from contemporary existence unless it was collected systematically. Wallace was certainly aware of the contributions of folklorists and of the texts being collected by members of the Boasian school of linguists and ethnologists who were documenting North American Indian cultures.[32] He believed Ahenakew could be a doorway between Cree knowledge and outsiders' appreciation of it.

Wallace, however, compartmentalized his friendship with Ahenakew. The diary entry about how Ahenakew was made a chief demonstrates that Wallace fundamentally misunderstood what Ahenakew had related to him. The entry does not refer to the consequences for Ahenakew, especially that his bishop has forced him to abandon his new office. In addition, Wallace did not understand the purpose of the League of Indians.[33] Wallace assumed that, if Ahenakew was not department chief, he must be a real chief in the traditional sense. Although he was the descendant of chiefs, Ahenakew was not automatically sanctioned to assume a leadership role with political authority. Wallace seems to have missed that Ahenakew was providing him with a first-hand view of a new political movement emerging at the grassroots level among Indians across Canada. Ahenakew had been elected to the top post among the Prairie members (those who held positions in its executive were referred to as chiefs) in a ritual that symbolically paralleled the way that leaders had been chosen in warrior societies and camping bands before the reserve period. In the late 1940s, Wallace began to address Ahenakew with the title "chief" and referred to him as an Indian chief to others. Wallace's diary entry of 1924 illuminates his misunderstanding of Ahenakew. In the newly formed western chapter of the League of Canadian Indians, Ahenakew was elected a political chief, not a traditional headman, of the Cree. Wallace believed Ahenakew was chosen a traditional chief because the investiture involved prayer in a ceremonial context.

Misunderstandings were not restricted to Wallace. Ahenakew certainly must have been able to distinguish a folkloric text from a fictionalized or semi-fictionalized account. However, it was never clear whether Ahenakew considered writing a means to procure additional income or a contribution to scholarly knowledge. What remains indeterminable was whether Ahenakew cared about what was actually published when his purposes seem to have been thwarted by the editorial processes and scholarly standards required.

The Journal of American Folklore

During this time, Wallace began corresponding with C. Marius Barbeau, the Canadian folklorist on the editorial board of the *Journal of American Folklore* (*JAF*), with whom he shared an interest in French Canadian folklore. Wallace wrote to Barbeau about Ahenakew's trickster tales, and on 2 January 1925 Barbeau responded: "I have just written for the second time to Mr. Ahenakew and I have asked him to add some footnotes to his Manebogo [sic] text. These would be necessary for the inclusion of the myth in *The Journal of American Folklore*. I would like to submit it to the General Editor Dr. Boas, if this is agreeable to the author."[34] In a letter written to Wallace on 17 February, Barbeau explained that the *JAF* "never pays its contributors" and "Mr. Ahenakew's chances to publish his article otherwise would not be interfered with here."[35] On 25 February, Ahenakew asked Wallace to write to Barbeau on his behalf. "If you should write to Dr. Barbeau will you please let him know he can have them [the legends]. You are, as I have said at perfect liberty to make what arrangement you think wise re: the ms. Wesahkaychak [sic]. All I would like is to be kept in touch with what is done." Clearly, Ahenakew felt that he was being given mixed signals. "Dr. Barbeau did not say anything about additional notes to increase the scientific value. I shall write him and tell him that I have given you the ms. and that you are in a position to make what arrangements may be required with reference to the publication of it."[36] Presuming that the collaborators intended to submit the manuscript to the *Journal of American Folklore,* Barbeau asked Ahenakew to provide explanatory notes.[37] Wallace, having sought clarification about the kind of explanatory notes needed, received a reply by mid-March from Barbeau:

> The details which Rev. Mr. Ahenakew should furnish are these: The name of the Indian informant from whom he got his interview, or part of the narrative, the tribe, the location; approximately how old was the informant; and in what year the narrative was recorded; either taken down under dictation on the spot, or from memory later on. I am including a little monograph, on the first page of which there is a note of a similar nature, which I have marked off in red. I am also sending to Mr. Ahenakew a copy of my own *Huron and Wyandot Mythology,* in which he will find notes of a similar nature.[38]

Barbeau sent Ahenakew a copy of his edited volume of Huron and Wyandot legends and folklore as a model, and Ahenakew declared, "I can see plainly what he wants. It is almost a verbatim translation of the legends, written more for scientific purposes, I suppose than for anything else."[39] Ahenakew reflected:

> When I wrote mine I was handicapped in that I worked to entertain partly and also to be as near to the actual form of the legends and probably I failed to do either.
>
> I think the only thing to do for Dr. Barbeau would be to rewrite the legends. I may say that there are many other legends among us but I only gave those having to do with Wesaykaychak. A few in the book he sent are very similar to ours and I can recognize expressions in them which are identical with ours, even though we are of a different nation and language and so far removed from each other. For scientific purposes I think I should rewrite the legends with notes, etc. as I find time.[40]

We do not know whether Wallace, the aspiring folklorist and English professor, was at all bothered by Ahenakew's accommodation and concession to

Barbeau that his stories be rewritten. Because no drafts of the manuscript survive, it is impossible to determine who wrote the explanatory notes and arranged the stories. In a letter to Wallace dated 16 June 1925, Ahenakew explained that his itinerant ministry was interfering with his work: "As you say there is probably no hurry for the scientific version of the W. legends. Still I am getting them together slowly, i.e. W. & other legends." He continued, "I am glad you are working on them now and as I said before you are at perfect likely [sic] to arrange them as you think best and also to arrange the business end of it as you think right."[41] Ahenakew still hoped to publish a popular edition of the legends, and Wallace might have suggested securing the illustrator Arthur Heming, whom Ahenakew recognized: "I have seen his work and at the time I felt that he had the knack of making his drawings look intensely Indian." In the same letter, Ahenakew returned to the matter of the Keyam manuscript: "I made too many criticisms of the Indian Department and many of these criticisms are today totally unnecessary as changes in the I.D. policy has set the matters criticized right. In fact as the ms. is now, it is more unfair in places. I can send you the ms. with the condition that nothing goes out of your hand of Old Keyam till I have gone through it again."[42]

No other correspondence survives, and the article "Cree Trickster Tales" was published without explanatory notes in the October-December 1929 issue of the *Journal of American Folklore*. The article acknowledged assistance from the Reverend Canon E.K. Matheson and Chief Thunderchild, but no mention was made of Wallace. Ahenakew and Wallace fell out of touch soon after its publication, each becoming increasingly involved in the other demands of their professional lives. The "Old Keyam" manuscript also languished, unpublished and incomplete.[43]

It was not until the late 1940s that the men resumed their correspondence. Wallace returned his copy of the Keyam manuscript to Ahenakew. In turn, Ahenakew noted that he had, in hindsight, changed his mind about the manuscript that he had criticized years earlier.[44]

The American Philosophical Society

After the Second World War, the American Philosophical Society (APS), the oldest scientific society in North America, shifted its research and collecting priorities toward ethnographic fieldwork among indigenous people in North America. The society wished to create a collection of Indian language materials that would parallel and complement its recent acquisition of the Franz Boas papers and the papers of the Committee on Research in Native American Languages, a special committee of the American Council of Learned Societies.[45]

The society invited Paul Wallace and other scholars to participate in these discussions.[46] Wallace thought of his old friend and, after re-initiating their correspondence, proposed that Ahenakew write a series of texts about Cree culture and history to be supported by the newly reorganized and redefined APS Phillips Fund. Ahenakew responded with cautious interest, explaining that he had recently assumed the position of canon after receiving an honorary doctor of divinity degree in recognition of his many years of missionary service. His commitments had extended considerably.[47] However, in 1948 and 1949 Ahenakew was recruited by Wallace to renew his ethnographic work. As with their previous collaborations, distance and the limitations of their correspondence hampered Ahenakew and Wallace's ability to prepare the APS texts. In the end, Ahenakew wrote nine texts for deposit in the APS (see Appendix).[48] The disparate topics and uneven development of these texts reveal misunderstandings and miscommunications between the two men.

Although they initially demonstrated goodwill, the project broke down as the two men became estranged. Wallace's assumptions about Ahenakew's methods reflected the distance that was growing between the men both personally and intellectually. Ironically, the constituent elements of ethnography as a genre became the contested and disconcerting aspect of the project. Neither man was trained in the practice of anthropology.[49] Ahenakew assumed that Wallace would provide him with a list of topics to research, and Wallace assumed that Ahenakew would be the one to seek the necessary information from Cree elders. However, at the suggestion of APS librarian William Lingelbach, Wallace assumed the role of project manager and intervened in the gathering of data for Ahenakew's texts. To make matters worse, Ahenakew and Wallace did not clarify the nature of their collaboration and respective duties.

Wallace began investigating the ethnographic, linguistic, and archaeological record of Crees, Plains Cree in particular. On a research trip to the Library of Congress, he made a list of references. At Lingelbach's insistence, Wallace asked Ahenakew to help locate publications in the Cree language. The request was unrealistic considering the isolation of Ahenakew's pastoral charges, who were far from libraries and bookstores. Wallace had become aware of Bloomfield's linguistic fieldwork and publication program in the descriptive linguistics of the Plains Cree dialect but had no way to evaluate this kind of linguistic endeavour and its potential relationship to his current collaboration with Ahenakew.

Wallace began by encouraging Ahenakew to write about anything he wanted but ended up suggesting that he start with an autobiographical piece about his own family because, he assumed, the task would be simple and straightforward.

On 3 April 1948, for instance, Wallace wrote to offer Ahenakew some suggestions. He noted that the society's emphasis was on language, archaeology, and history, but "these terms are not to be interpreted too narrowly."[50] Wallace proposed that Ahenakew could gather information on the following topics: the appointment of chiefs (hereditary or elective), government, religion and ethics, social customs, the position of women, family life (food, housing, family relationships, etc.), economics (hunting, agriculture, trade, etc.), medicine, humour, relations with other nations (Blackfeet, Ojibway, etc.), travel, war, and folklore.[51] Wallace then suggested that the texts could be written in Cree with English translations. If Ahenakew approved, Wallace wanted groups of storytellers to speak into a tape recorder provided by the APS. Wallace concluded his letter with an evocation to science: "The American Philosophical Society believes that with your deep understanding you are in a position to do a really great work both in preserving the record of the Cree Language and way of life, and in helping the growth of a better understanding between the Indians and the white people. The Society is ready to cooperate with you whole-heartedly."[52]

In a letter dated 27 April 1948, Wallace told Ahenakew that he had been to Washington, DC, where he had taken stock of the extant ethnology of the Cree and spoken with Canadian and American scholars. He was "amazed at the lifelessness of most of the writing. As if a people could be best described by measuring their bones. You can do a most important work, with your understanding and sympathy in bringing ethnology and history alive by explaining the *motives* behind customs and ritual." Wallace reported that people at the Smithsonian "were impressed with the possibilities of your proposed undertaking, especially with the thought of what you could accomplish in *interpreting* your people."[53] What was meant as encouragement simply increased the expectations placed upon Ahenakew, who also appeared to have a limited sense of what constituted an autobiography.

Ahenakew's first APS text, "Genealogy of the Ahenakew Family," revealed his biases. He named a number of his male Cree relatives but no women or French relatives. Perhaps he assumed that only information about patrilineal descent was important.[54] In a letter written on 30 April 1948, Ahenakew explained that he had refrained from giving French names because of his attention to "matters which are to my mind peculiar to Indian life." He then qualified his statement: "You will please tell me if I err, and give me your guidance." Ahenakew proposed to turn his attention to religious practices. He mentioned the "Meta wi win" but made no reference to the fact that this was predominantly a Saulteaux religio-cultural practice. He asked for direction from Wallace.[55]

Meanwhile, believing that Ahenakew needed the security of a manual to provide direction about methods, Wallace attempted to secure a copy of the second edition of *The Outline of Cultural Materials* (1945), but the volume was out of print. He instead forwarded the much inferior *An Outline of Anthropology* (1940), perhaps on the assumption that this was a comparable volume. In his cover letter, Wallace noted, "I do not know if it will be of any value to you, as it is exceedingly desiccated, but you may find some suggestions here and there."[56] Ahenakew's reaction to this publication, with its heavy emphasis on evolution and race, is not on record, nor do we know whether he related it to the APS project. But this exchange must have been perplexing. When he transmitted his next text, "Cree Theology," Ahenakew noted in passing, "I have been so busy lately in building and getting ready for the Bishop's visit that I have neglected my writing. I am sending a rather poorly written article but if some parts are not clear you can send back after reading and I will rewrite."[57]

In consultation with Lingelbach, Wallace decided that Ahenakew reflected acculturative influences on Cree society and culture and that these influences, by necessity, were represented in Ahenakew's texts. As Ahenakew continued to write, Wallace was not able to provide instructive commentary to help Ahenakew refine the presentation of his information. At one point, in comments to Lingelbach about "Spirit Help," Wallace stated, "I do not know enough about Cree ethnology to express an opinion on the scientific value of the manuscript, but Ahenakew writes with the assurance of a man who know[s] what he is talking about, and I imagine some of the details are new."[58]

It was at this point that Wallace began referring to Ahenakew as "Chief" in his correspondence, a practice that reflected Wallace's misunderstanding of Ahenakew's account of the prayers during the ceremony to mark his election as chief of the Saskatchewan chapter of the League of Indians. Wallace reified this political position, not realizing that Ahenakew had resigned under pressure. Wallace used the title as if it were some sort of an imprimatur by the Cree nation to designate Ahenakew a cultural leader. Wallace undoubtedly equated the title of sachem among the Iroquois with that of chief among the Cree.[59] Wallace's tendency to romanticize Ahenakew and his writing must have made the author increasingly uncomfortable.

After a period of silence, Ahenakew wrote in March 1949 that he had been away on a "long mission trip leaving here beginning of February and arriving back here a couple of weeks ago."[60] In contrast to Wallace's suggestions for their collaboration, Ahenakew proposed that he decide on his own topics for the pieces: "I have mislaid your letter but I would prefer to work by assignment as I waste a good deal of time trying to decide what to write on next. I have a friend, an old man, living close to me and he comes over every evening. I like to have him but he wastes a great deal of my time. He is going away next week, so I will then have the evenings to myself."[61] Wallace met with Lingelbach to compose a response with another set of suggestions:

> He [Ahenakew] would like to have definite assignments. Some time ago I gave him a list of general topics to work on, and I also sent him a book on ethnology to give him further suggestions. In my last letter I did give him a specific proposal (though it is not the one he follows in "Wetikoo," having lost my letter), and this is, I gather, what he likes. He wants me to give him individual assignments *as we go along.* He says that when an opportunity to write comes to him he loses too much time figuring out what to write on.
>
> This being so, I should like to confer with you, if I may, when I am next at the Society, on a plan of procedure to use with our Cree Chief.[62]

This became the pattern of the other texts authored by Ahenakew for the APS through to the fall of 1949. Lingelbach, a semi-retired European and American colonial historian and librarian of the APS, joined with Wallace, the self-trained and -initiated student of Indian histories and cultures and editor of colonial and early American documents, to direct Ahenakew, a Cree Anglican cleric, whom, because of romanticism and limited understanding, they cast as an ethnographic expert.[63] Ahenakew wrote partially from knowledge acquired in the course of his life as a partly assimilated Cree, partially from his position as a missionary priest who was to replace one form of religious ideas and practices with another, and partially from knowledge gained from individuals he sought out in the Cree communities in which he lived about traditional values that had assumed new meanings in the context of resistance to acculturation.

Ahenakew's work for the APS came to a halt in the early fall of 1949, when he suffered a mild stroke. Wallace, writing to Lingelbach in December 1949, reported: "Today a very good letter came from Chief Ahenakew. You will remember he had a stroke a few months ago. He is very much better, and is going back to work; but he says he is not yet back in a mood to write. I fear we may lose the fruits of his contemplated gathering of the old men together to tell tales into a recording machine. Would it not be possible to get someone up into his territory before we lose him as an organizer of research?"[64]

Ahenakew's decline in health brought to an end the APS project (see Appendix). In the spirit of salvage anthropology, Wallace and Lingelbach suggested that someone could be sent to Ahenakew with a first-generation tape recorder to help him complete the work. The most likely candidate was Wallace's son Tony, but this venture never went beyond an initial discussion.[65] The project came to a halt, and the collaboration between Ahenakew and Wallace came to an end.

Conclusion

This chapter has explored how Ahenakew became a writer, particularly the specific opportunities that contributed to his successes and to his limitations. Ahenakew's career as a writer and the texts he produced were complicated by the shifting roles of his collaborators and editors. The progression of influences on Ahenakew's writings is only partially preserved in surviving papers. Yet even this partial record is replete with the dilemmas Ahenakew faced as he tried to write about his own people and their history and culture. Clearly, the relationship between Edward Ahenakew and Paul Wallace was frustrating and fraught with misunderstandings. Wallace's struggle to impose a scholarly style on Ahenakew led to a relationship of tutelage. The disciplinary standards required by the *Journal of American Folklore* for the "Cree Trickster Tales"; the struggle with editors over Ahenakew's other manuscripts, for example, the Thunderchild stories and "Old Keyam"; and, finally, the pressure to become a writer of APS ethnographic texts that would presumably conform to ethnological standards kept Ahenakew under Wallace's tutelage. The tutelage was, for the most part, implicit, but it surfaced explicitly in exchanges between Ahenakew and Wallace and between Wallace and Lingelbach when they discussed Ahenakew's later writings.

This increasingly uneasy relationship between Wallace and Ahenakew was central to the production of Ahenakew's texts. This does not make Wallace or Lingelbach manipulative, nor does it make Ahenakew a dupe. Rather, the situation was much more complicated and unstable. Wallace learned from Ahenakew, and working with Ahenakew's writings quite possibly became the entry point for Wallace's other contributions to Indian cultural history and the history of Indian-white relations on the Pennsylvania frontier. Ahenakew was interested in writing and turned to his academic friend for guidance in the worlds of both scholarly and commercial publishing. With Wallace's help, Ahenakew's writings were produced, preserved, and eventually published. If Wallace had not safeguarded and then returned his copy of the Keyam stories, they may not have survived.

Ahenakew – as storyteller, writer, and recorder – was ultimately accorded the respect of elder, and his writings are read in many contexts. Notwithstanding the extent of his influence, his writings remain a significant contribution to Cree traditional knowledge. His abilities as a fieldworker, building on his obvious facility with his first language, allowed him to communicate the information related to him.

Many questions remain unanswered about Edward Ahenakew. Is there more to be learned from a critical but appreciative probing, from a more nuanced and dialogic understanding of his writings, one that is neither necessarily neat nor complete? Can Ahenakew be taken down from a pedestal and given a balanced treatment? Can his writings about Cree culture and history be viewed as authentic when he wrote for a variety of reasons, including being motivated by the promise of remuneration to offset his often-impoverished life as a missionary priest? Ahenakew translated a lot from Cree in his writings in English. It was only in his newsletter that he wrote in Cree for other Cree people, and then only for those who had become Anglicans. What is the appropriate measure to evaluate the contributions of Ahenakew's erratic and only periodically ordered yet devoted life? Was he conflicted by his choice of vocation and his cultural origins, even though his fellow Indian priests say he was not? What do readers make of him? What can be made of the title, *Voices of the Plains Cree*? Do readers hear Thunderchild, via Old Keyam, and Wesakaychak? And, finally, do readers view Ahenakew as an indigenous anthropologist-cum-informant, albeit a reluctant one, or as a narrator for others? The perplexing question remains: whose voices did Edward Ahenakew present? In the end, perhaps the most significant point is that Ahenakew's writings are available for readers who want to hear the voices.

Appendix

Publications of Edward Ahenakew

1922-   *Cree Monthly Guide* (editor).
1929   Cree Trickster Tales. *Journal of American Folklore* 42 (October-December): 166, 309-53.
1960   An Opinion on the Frog Lake Massacre. *Alberta History* 8, 3: 9-15.
1964   Story of the Ahenakews. *Saskatchewan History* 17 (Spring): 12-23. Edited by Ruth M. Buck.
1973   *Voices of the Plains Cree*. Toronto: McClelland and Stewart. Part 1, The Stories of Chief Thunderchild. Part 2, Old Keyam. Edited with an Introduction by Ruth M. Buck.
1995   *Voices of the Plains Cree*. Regina: Canadian Plains Research Center. Part 1, The Stories of Chief Thunderchild. Part 2, Old Keyam. Edited by Ruth M. Buck and introduced by Stan Cuthand.

This is not a complete list of Ahenakew's church publications – articles in *Canadian Churchman* and various other collections of sermons, commemorations, and so on.

Boas Linguistics Collection of the American Philosophical Society, Philadelphia

418   The Creation of a New Tribe. 1949. Text on the creation of the Assiniboine tribe. 5 pp.
777   A-us-to-yit (Making a Canoe). 1949. 8 pp.
778   The Cree Indians' Theology. 1948. 5 pp.
779   Genealogical Sketch of My Family. 1948. 27 pp.
780   Letter to Paul A.W. Wallace, Re: Additional Genealogy. 1948. 2 pp.
781   Non-Human Personalities. 1949. 10 pp.

782   Spirit Help. 1948. 7 pp.
783   Tanning of Leather. 1948. 8 pp.
784   The We-ti-koo, or He-who-is-alone. 1949. 20 pp.

[Added to the Boas manuscript collection, manuscript numbers within the Boas collection indicated on pp. 114-15:

John E. Freeman, Compiler, with Murphy D. Smith, Editorial Consultant. *A Guide to Manuscripts Relating to the American Indian in the Library of The American Philosophical Society.* Memoir v. 65 of the American Philosophical Society. Philadelphia: American Philosophical Society, 1966].

4187   Correspondence with Paul A.W. Wallace, 25 August 1922–31 July 1961. A. and T.L.S. 60L.
4188   "Genealogical Sketch of My Family," 27 April 1948. T.D. and L. 85 pp. orig. and 2 c.c.

[Manuscript collection numbers not in Freeman, in Kendall p. 36:

Kendall, Daythal, Compiler. *A Supplement to "A Guide to Manuscripts Relating to the American Indian in the Library of the American Philosophical Society."* Memoir v. 65 of the American Philosophical Society. Philadelphia: American Philosophical Society, 1982.]

Notes

This chapter is a revised version of a paper that was delivered at the American Society for Ethnohistory, London, Ontario, 21 October 2000, in an organized session titled "Ethnohistorical Explorations about Cree Grandfathers: Metaphoric, Tangible, and Symbolic." Jennifer Brown provided the commentary. Other portions of this chapter are included in a longer unpublished essay, "Edward Ahenakew's Relationship with Paul Wallace, and Ahenakew's Representation of Plains Cree Culture: Dialogic Shades, Constructed Realities." This research was supported initially by a 1996 Mellon Fellowship at the American Philosophical Society in Philadelphia and later by a research grant from the Humanities Research Institute of the University of Regina.

1   Early attention to Plains Cree culture came largely from linguistic fieldwork. See early texts collected by Leonard Bloomfield in "Sacred Stories" and "Plains Cree Texts" and by the comparative ethnologist Alanson Skinner in "Notes on Eastern Cree and Northern Saulteaux," "Notes on the Plains Cree," "Political Organization," and "The Sun Dance." The most extensive ethnographic attention was given to eastern Plains Cree communities by David G. Mandelbaum during survey fieldwork in the mid-1930s, see "The Plains Cree" and *The Plains Cree*. Mandelbaum's work was followed by Niels Winther Braroe's intensive reserve fieldwork in the 1960s among the Cree of the Nekineet people *(Indian and White)*, David Meyer's work on the Red Earth Crees of east-central Saskatchewan, and, more recently, Dale Russell's study of the *Eighteenth-Century Western Cree.*

2   Ahenakew began his publishing program in 1922 with *The Cree Monthly Bulletin,* printed in set type in syllabics, first produced at "St. Barnabas Indian School, Onion Lake, Saskatchewan." The syllabic writing system was devised by the Reverend James Evans for Ojibwe in 1836. See the discussion of Evans and his influence on writings in Cree and Ojibway in Edwards, *Paper Talk,* 60-70. Many examples are cited in Banks, *Books in Native Languages;* and Walker, "Native Writing Systems," 173-76.

3   Edward Ahenakew Papers, deposited with the Saskatchewan Archives Board, Regina, Saskatchewan.

4 See the Introduction by Stan Cuthand in the 1995 edition of *Voices*. Enigmatic aspects unresolved in this edition can be attributed to the publisher trying to balance the wishes of Ruth Buck and several members of the Ahenakew family, who at that time wanted only the positive emphasized. This concern led to discussion among the editorial board of the Canadian Plains Research Center, of which this author is a member, to provide a wider context to understand Ahenakew, particularly his status as both a Cree person and an Anglican missionary priest. Without knowing that the Ahenakew family was uneasy with this, the board felt Cuthand, a Cree person and also an Anglican priest, could offer insights because Ahenakew had been his role model. The contradictions in the two Introductions were revealing and irresolvable. The Introductions became the exchange of Jennifer Brown's review and the editors' rejoinder in the pages of the *Great Plains Quarterly* in 1997. See Brown, book review; and Leger-Anderson and Mlazgar, "Response to Review."

5 Reflexivity is addressed by Karp and Kendall, "Reflexivity in Fieldwork"; see also Clifford and Marcus, eds., *Writing Culture*; Brettell, ed., *When They Read What We Write*; and Tedlock, *The Spoken Word and the Work of Interpretation*. See the more recent ethical discussions by Indian intellectuals about the contributions of knowledge bearers, Mihesuah, *So You Want to Write about American Indians?*; Mihesuah, ed., *Natives and Academics*; and Mihesuah and Wilson, eds., *Indigenizing the Academy*. Examples of collaborations are Rios and Sands, *Telling a Good One*; and Wilson, *Remember This!*

6 Dr. Ahab Spence, personal communication with the author, September 1996.

7 Cuthand, in his Introduction to the 1995 edition of *Voices*, describes Ahenakew's confrontation with his bishop over his involvement with the League of Indians, xviii-xix; see also Cuthand, "The Native Peoples," 32-33.

8 Paul Wallace's edited publications included *Conrad Weiser, 1696-1760*; and *The Muhlenbergs of Pennsylvania*. He also wrote *The White Roots of Peace*; *Indians in Pennsylvania*; *Pennsylvania: Seed of a Nation*; and *Indian Paths of Pennsylvania*.

9 Wallace to Dean Kerr, 23 December 1920, Paul A.W. Wallace Papers, American Philosophical Society (hereafter APS).

10 Ahenakew's convalescence on Thunderchild Reserve is discussed by Buck in the first pages of her Introduction to the 1973 edition of *Voices* (10-11) and by Cuthand in his Introduction to the 1995 edition (xii-xiii).

11 In January 1923, Ahenakew wrote to Wallace, who had become a graduate student at the University of Toronto, to declare his intention to return to Edmonton to continue his studies and his hope to rejoin the literary club (18 January 1923, Wallace Papers, APS). However, he did not return to university.

12 *"Keyam"* (*"kiyâm"* in standard transcription) is a Cree term for "so what?" or "what does it matter?" or "never mind." It can be used to refer to anything with little meaning or a general state of resignation. Ahenakew translates "Keyam" as "I do not care." This derivation suggests Ahenakew used this term to name his narrator, and this irony simply added further symbolism to the nature of his critical voice. Keith Goulet, personal communication with the author, September 1996; Arok Wolvengrey, personal communication with the author, September 1996; and Neal McLeod, personal communication with the author, August 2006.

13 Actually, it was more likely food poisoning. See the report of him keeping frozen meat outside his window in Buck's Introduction to *Voices* and the report on being "on my feet now," 25 August 1922, Wallace Papers, APS.

14 "As I have given them my work and I hate to break my word or it appear [sic] lacking in promptness to business men who prize such qualities": 22 December 1922, Wallace Papers, APS.

15 Ibid.
16 Carmichael, *Indian Legends of Vancouver Island;* Edward Ahenakew to Paul Wallace, 18 January 1923, Wallace Papers, APS.
17 Edward Ahenakew to Paul Wallace, 18 January 1923, Wallace Papers, APS.
18 Ahenakew to Wallace, 2 February 1923, Wallace Papers, APS.
19 For a basic synonymy of "Wesakaychak" (Ahenakew's spelling) and *"Wîsahkêcâhk"* (standard transcription), see Hodge, *Handbook of North American Indians North of Mexico,* in which "Wisakedjak" is cross-referenced to "Nanabozho," 2:19-23; see also Brightman, "Tricksters and Ethnopoetics," 182-83, and *Grateful Prey,* 38, 40. For "Witiko" (Ahenakew's spelling) or "Wîhtikow" (standard transcription), see Hodge, *Handbook,* "Weendigo," 2:930; and Brightman, "The Windigo," 337-38, which provides context for the exchange, Ahenakew to Wallace, 23 March 1923, Wallace Papers APS.
20 Ahenakew to Wallace, 23 March 1923, Wallace Papers, APS.
21 Ibid., 16 May 1923.
22 Ibid., 17 July 1923.
23 Ibid., 11 August 1923.
24 Ibid., 5 September 1923.
25 Ibid.
26 Ibid., 1 October 1923.
27 Ibid.
28 Ibid., 11 March 1924.
29 Ibid., 16 May 1924.
30 Paul Wallace Diaries, 16 September 1924, United Church Archives. The author thanks Donald Smith for copies of these pages.
31 Ibid.
32 Darnell, "The Boasian Text Tradition"; Darnell, *And Along Came Boas;* Darnell, "Theorizing American Anthropology"; and Darnell, *Invisible Genealogies.* Pioneering publications in which North American texts in translation were welcome were the *Annual Reports and Bulletins of the Bureau of the American Ethnology-Smithsonian Institution; Anthropological Papers of the American Museum of Natural History; Canadian Geographical Survey, Department of Mines, Anthropological Series; National Museum of Canada, Anthropological Bulletins;* the *Columbia University Contributions in Anthropology; Field Columbian Museum Publications, Anthropological Series; International Journal of American Linguistics;* the *Journal of American Folklore;* the *Publications of the American Ethnological Society;* the *Public Museum of the City of Milwaukee Bulletins; University of California Publications in American Archaeology and Ethnology;* and *University of Washington Publications in Anthropology.*
33 The League of Indians, initiated by Mohawk veteran Frederick O. Loft, became a nationwide political organization. Its first congress, held in Sault Ste. Marie in 1919, included in its agenda seeking the vote without penalty of enfranchisement, greater control over band funds and properties, and better standards of education for Indian students. The League and its members were viewed as agitators and were subject to police surveillance; see Dickason, *A Concise History,* 222; and Kulchyski, "A Considerable Unrest." Efforts to organize the League of Indians on the Prairies are discussed by Cuthand, "The Native Peoples," 31-42. See recent reserve histories, Christensen, *Ahtahkakoop;* and Funk, *Outside, the Women Cried.*
34 C. Marius Barbeau, Ottawa, to Paul Wallace, 2 January 1925, Wallace Papers, APS.
35 Ibid., 17 February 1925.
36 Ahenakew to Wallace, 21 February 1925, Wallace Papers, APS.
37 Barbeau to Wallace, 28 February 1925, ibid.

38 Ibid., 13 March 1925.
39 Ahenakew to Wallace, 3 April 1925, ibid.
40 Ibid.
41 Ibid., 16 June 1925.
42 Ibid.
43 Some of the stories that were narrated from the perspective of an imaginary person called Old Keyam were published in the 1973 edition of *Voices of the Plains Cree*.
44 Ahenakew to Wallace, 29 March 1948, Wallace Papers, APS.
45 Harris, "American Indian Linguistic Work" and "Developments in American Indian Linguistics"; and Leeds-Hurwitz, "The Committee on Research in Native American Languages."
46 Kidder, "The Society's Program in American Linguistics and Archaeology," 126; Lydenberg, "The Library's Policy in Regard to American Linguistics and Archaeology."
47 Ahenakew to Wallace, 16 March 1948, Wallace Papers, APS.
48 There are three major manuscript collections: the Ahenakew Papers and Ruth Matheson Buck Papers, both in the Saskatchewan Archives Board in Regina, and the Ahenakew Texts, filed in the Boas Linguistics Collection of the American Philosophical Society Library in Philadelphia. See also the Paul A.W. Wallace Papers at the ASP.
49 Wallace consulted Smithsonian ethnographer William N. Fenton. See their correspondence in the Wallace and Fenton Papers at the APS.
50 Wallace to Ahenakew, 3 April 1948, Wallace Papers, APS.
51 Ibid.
52 Ibid.
53 Ibid., 27 April 1948, emphasis in the original.
54 Ahenakew, "Genealogical Sketch of My Family."
55 Ahenakew to Wallace, 30 April 1948, Wallace Papers, APS.
56 Wallace to Ahenakew, 1 August 1948, ibid.
57 Ahenakew to Wallace, 1 October 1948, ibid.
58 Wallace to Ahenakew, 22 November 1948, ibid.
59 Wallace was a long-time friend of the mixed-blood Mohawk schoolteacher Ray Fadden, who shaped Wallace's view of the Iroquois, which is expressed best in *The White Roots of Peace*.
60 Ahenakew to Wallace, 31 March 1949, Wallace Papers, APS.
61 Ibid.
62 Wallace to William E. Lingelbach, APS, Philadelphia, 6 April 1949, ibid., emphasis in original.
63 See Smith, "Biographical Sketch."
64 Wallace to Lingelbach, 5 December 1949, Wallace Papers, APS.
65 Lingelbach to Wallace, 12 December 1949, Lingelbach-APS Librarians Papers, APS. Paul Wallace's son, Tony, is Anthony F.C. Wallace, the distinguished anthropologist, a graduate student in anthropology at the University of Pennsylvania at this time.

Bibliography

Archival Sources

American Philosophical Society Library (APS), Philadelphia
Franz Boas Linguistics Collection.
Librarians Collection – William Lingelbach Papers.

Paul A.W. Wallace Papers.
William N. Fenton Papers.

Saskatchewan Archives Board, Regina
Edward Ahenakew Papers.
Ruth M. Buck Papers.

United Church Archives, Victoria University, Toronto
Paul Wallace Diaries.

Published Sources

Ahenakew, Edward. "Cree Trickster Tales." *Journal of American Folklore* 42, 166 (1929): 309-53.
–. *Voices of the Plains Cree.* Edited by Ruth M. Buck. Toronto: McClelland and Stewart, 1973.
–. *Voices of the Plains Cree.* Edited by Ruth M. Buck, with introductions by Ruth Buck and Stan Cuthand. Regina: Canadian Plains Research Center, 1995.
An Outline of Anthropology. Brooklyn: Barron's Text Book Exchange, 1940.
Banks, Joyce. *Books in Native Languages in the Collection of the Rare Books and Manuscripts Division of the National Library of Canada.* Ottawa: National Library of Canada, 1980.
Bloomfield, Leonard. "Plains Cree Texts." *Publications, American Ethnological Society.* Vol. 16. New York: Columbia University Press, 1934.
–. "Sacred Stories of the Sweet Grass Cree." *Bulletin 60, Anthropological Series No. 11.* Ottawa: National Museum of Canada, 1930.
Braroe, Niels Winther. *Indian and White: Self-Image and Interaction in a Canadian Plains Community.* Stanford: Stanford University Press, 1975.
Brettell, Caroline B., ed. *When They Read What We Write: The Politics of Ethnography.* Westport: Bergin and Garvey, 1993.
Brown, Jennifer S.H. Review of *Voices of the Plains Cree. Great Plains Quarterly* 17, 1 (1997): 67-68.
Brightman, Robert A. *Grateful Prey: Rock Cree Human-Animal Relationships.* Berkeley: University of California Press, 1993.
–. "Tricksters and Ethnopoetics." *International Journal of American Linguistics* 55, 2 (1989): 179-203.
–. "The Windigo in the Material World." *Ethnohistory* 24, 4 (1988): 327-79.
Carmichael, Alfred. *Indian Legends of Vancouver Island.* Toronto: Musson Book Company, 1922.
Christensen, Deanna. *Ahtahkakoop: The Epic Account of a Plains Cree Head Chief, and Their Struggle for Survival, 1816-1896.* Shell Lake: Ahtahkakoop Publishing, 2000.
Clifford, James, and George E. Marcus, eds. *Writing Culture: The Poetics and Politics of Ethnograpahy.* Berkeley: University of California Press, 1986.
Cuthand, Stan. "The Native Peoples of the Prairie Provinces in the 1920s and 1930s." In *One Century Later: Western Canadian Reserve Indians since Treaty 7,* edited by Ian A.L. Getty and Donald B. Smith, 31-42. Vancouver: UBC Press, 1978.
Darnell, Regna. *And Along Came Boas: Continuity and Revolution in Americanist Anthropology.* Studies in the History of Language Sciences, Vol. 86. Philadelphia: John Benjamins Publishing Company, 1998.
–. "The Boasian Text Tradition and the History of Anthropology." *Culture* 12, 1 (1992): 39-48.

—. *Invisible Genealogies: A History of Americanist Anthropology*. Lincoln: University of Nebraska Press, 2001.

—. "Theorizing American Anthropology: Continuities from the B.A.E. to the Boasians." In *Theorizing the Americanist Tradition*, edited by Lisa Philips Valentine and Regna Darnell, 38-51. Toronto: University of Toronto Press, 1999.

Dickason, Olive Patricia. *A Concise History of Canada's First Nations*. New York: Oxford University Press, 2006.

Edwards, Brendan F.R. *Paper Talk: Print Culture, Libraries and Aboriginal People in Canada before 1960*. Lanham, MD: Scarecrow Press, 2005.

Funk, Jack. *Outside, the Women Cried: The Story of the Surrender by Chief Thunderchild's Band of Their Reserve Near Delmas, Saskatchewan, 1908*. Battleford: TC Publications, 1989.

Harris, Zellig G. "American Indian Linguistic Work and the Boas Collection." *American Philosophical Society Yearbook 1945* (1946): 96-100.

—. "Developments in American Indian Linguistics." *American Philosophical Society Yearbook 1946* (1947): 84-97.

Hodge, Frederick Webb, ed. *Handbook of American Indians North of Mexico*. Bulletin 30, Bureau of American Ethnology, Smithsonian Institution. 2 vols. Washington, DC: Government Printing Office, 1907, 1910.

Karp, Ivan, and Martha B. Kendall. "Reflexivity in Fieldwork." In *Explaining Human Behavior: Consciousness, Human Action and Social Structure*, edited by Paul F. Secord, 249-73. Beverly Hills: Sage, 1982.

Kidder, Alfred V. "The Society's Program in American Linguistics and Archaeology: 2. American Anthropology and Archaeology." *Proceedings of the American Philosophical Society* 92, 2 (1948): 126.

Kulchyski, Peter. "A Considerable Unrest: F.O. Loft and the League of Indians." *Native Studies Review* 4, 1-2 (1988): 95-117.

Leeds-Hurwitz, Wendy. "The Committee on Research in Native American Languages." *Proceedings of the American Philosophical Society* 129, 2 (1985): 129-60.

Leger-Anderson, Ann, and Brian Mlazgar. "Response to Review, *Voices of the Plains Cree*." *Great Plains Quarterly* 71, 3-4 (1997): 263.

Lydenberg, Harry David. "The Library's Policy in Regard to American Linguistics and Archaeology – A Program of Specialization." *Library Bulletin: The American Philosophical Society 1944* (1945): 65-74.

Mandelbaum, David G. "The Plains Cree." *American Museum of Natural History Anthropology Papers* 27, 2 (1940): 155-316.

—. *The Plains Cree: An Ethnographic, Historical, and Comparative Study*. Canadian Plains Studies, Vol. 9. Regina: Canadian Plains Research Center, 1979.

Meyer, David. "The Red Earth Crees, 1860-1960." Mercury Series Paper 100. Canadian Ethnology Service. Hull: National Museum of Man, 1985.

Mihesuah, Devon Abbott, ed. *Natives and Academics: Researching and Writing about American Indians*. Lincoln: University of Nebraska Press, 1998.

—. *So You Want to Write about American Indians? A Guide for Writers, Students, and Scholars*. Lincoln: University of Nebraska Press, 2005.

Mihesuah, Devon Abbott, and Angela Cavender Wilson, eds. *Indigenizing the Academy: Transforming Scholarship and Empowering Communities*. Lincoln: University of Nebraska Press, 2004.

Murdoch, George Peter, Clellan S. Ford, and Alfred E. Hudson. *The Outline of Cultural Materials*. 2nd ed. New Haven: Yale University Press, 1945.

Rios, Theodore, and Kathleen Mullen Sands. *Telling a Good One: The Process of Native American Collaborative Biography*. Lincoln: University of Nebraska Press, 2000.

Russell, Dale R. "Eighteenth-Century Western Cree and Their Neighbours." Mercury Series Number 143, Archaeological Survey of Canada. Hull: Canadian Museum of Civilization, 1991.

Skinner, Alanson. "Notes on Eastern Cree and Northern Saulteaux." *Anthropological Papers, American Museum of Natural History* 9, Part 1 (1911): 1-179.

–. "Notes on the Plains Cree." *American Anthropologist*, new series 16 (1914): 68-87.

–. "Political Organization, Cults and Ceremonies of the Plains Cree." *Anthropological Papers, American Museum of Natural History* 11, Part 6 (1914): 513-42.

–. "The Sun Dance of the Plains-Cree." *Anthropological Papers, American Museum of Natural History* 16, Part 4 (1919): 283-93.

Smith, Donald. "Biographical Sketch of Paul A.W. Wallace and How *The White Roots of Peace* Came to Be Written." In *The White Roots of Peace*, P.A.W. Wallace, 6-23. Ohsweken, ON: Iroqrafts Iroquois Reprints, 1997.

Tedlock, Dennis. *The Spoken Word and the Work of Interpretation*. Philadelphia: University of Pennsylvania Press, 1983.

Wallace, Paul. *Conrad Weiser, 1696-1760: Friend of Colonist and Mohawk*. Philadelphia: University of Pennsylvania Press, 1945.

–. *Indian Paths of Pennsylvania*. Harrisburg: Pennsylvania Historical and Museum Commission, 1965.

–. *Indians of Pennsylvania*. Harrisburg: Pennsylvania Historical and Museum Commission, 1961.

–. *The Muhlenbergs of Pennsylvania*. Philadelphia: University of Pennsylvania Press, 1950.

–. *Pennsylvania: Seed of a Nation*. New York: Harper and Row, 1962.

–. *The White Roots of Peace*. Philadelphia: University of Pennsylvania Press, 1946.

Walker, Willard B. "Native Writing Systems." In *The Handbook of North American Indians*, vol. 17, *Languages*, edited by Ives Goddard, 158-84. Washington, DC: Smithsonian Institution, 1996.

Watkins, E.A. *A Dictionary of the Cree Language: As Spoken by the Indians of the Provinces of Quebec, Ontario, Manitoba, Saskatchewan and Alberta*. Edited and introduced by Richard Faries. Revised, enriched, and brought up to date by J.A. McKay. Toronto: Anglican Book Centre, 1986 [1938].

Wilson, Angela (Waziyatanwin). *Remember This! Dakota Decolonization and the Eli Taylor Narratives*. Lincoln: University of Nebraska Press, 2005.

11
Aboriginal History and Historic Sites: The Shifting Ground

Laura Peers and Robert Coutts

RECENT THEORY ON COLONIAL history has emphasized the idea that there existed, historically, a shared intercultural space of fluid dynamics – a "middle ground," "borderlands," or "contact zone" – within which peoples of different cultural backgrounds interacted, pursued different agendas, and endeavoured to bring other parties within their own sphere of social and political influence.[1] These ideas have been applied especially to situations of historical contact between Aboriginal peoples and peoples of European descent, such as the fur trade, in which cross-cultural relationships, alliances, misunderstandings, and enmities hinged on complex interactions between local realities and global forces. "Contact zones," as defined originally by Mary Louise Pratt, are "social spaces where disparate cultures meet, clash, and grapple with each other, often in highly asymmetrical relations of domination and subordination."[2] They are arenas within which disputing claims to power and sovereignty are negotiated: cross-cultural spaces exist by nature in the tensions between political systems. These ideas have been useful in cohering various strands of scholarship that deal with Aboriginal agency and cultural continuity in contact situations, the relationships and identities of family members in the hybrid societies produced by such situations, and the interactions between Aboriginal and settler histories over time. However useful these theories have been for understanding the past, though, they have not been applied equally to the present situation in which our understanding and commemoration of the past are produced. In the present, just as in the eighteenth and nineteenth centuries that we study, the production of knowledge about the past is set in a network of cross-cultural relationships (both social and political), intersecting agendas, and unequal (or rapidly shifting) relations of power. This has been especially true regarding the representation of Aboriginal histories in public history settings.

Historians who work in the public sector and attempt to bridge scholarly, public, and community-based perspectives to commemorate and represent the past have thus worked in a stimulating, but constantly changing, environment. In this chapter, we explore representations of Aboriginal people and Aboriginal histories at national historic sites in Canada and the way these representations have changed in the past several decades. We link our changing understanding and representation of the past to the changing situation in the present. In part, this chapter has been inspired by Jennifer S.H. Brown's work on familial and other cross-cultural relationships in the fur trade, which has been widely used by public historians in western Canada, and by her own shift from a primary engagement with archival sources to an increasing engagement with Aboriginal people and communities, a pattern that mirrors what has been occurring in public history as a whole. Both of us (Robert Coutts is based at Parks Canada, and Laura Peers works in academia) have worked with Brown over a long period. Our discussions with her have inspired our understanding of the past while complicating our attempts to interpret it to the public. We reflect on these complications and relationships in this chapter. What have been the relationships between scholarly, archivally based histories of Aboriginal communities and the fur trade, Aboriginal communities themselves, new methodologies such as oral history, the increasing involvement of Aboriginal peoples in commemoration and interpretation, and the Aboriginal and non-Aboriginal publics that consume such history? In what situations have the relationships been productive, and when have they revealed underlying tensions or cross-cultural differences in perspective? When have the agendas overlapped, and in which situations have they been completely different? And, in the end, what do these relationships and differences contribute to our understanding of Canadian heritage? We argue that the negotiation and renegotiation of public representations of the Canadian past have been very much a contact zone in the past few decades.

Public History over Time

Since the 1970s, the field of Aboriginal history in Canada, both academic and public, has shifted rapidly. In many ways, the public has tended to follow the academic. Changes in the way Canadian historians have thought about the past have often been reflected in decisions about national commemoration that have been made by public bodies such as the Historic Sites and Monuments Board of Canada (HSMBC). Founded in 1919 and made up of representatives from across the country, the HSMBC advises the federal government on national commemorations. For most of its history, board membership has been dominated by academics. Parks Canada (and its predecessors) is the government agency charged with carrying out the minister's recommendations and the development and administration of those historic sites owned by the federal government.

Both genres of representation – the public and the academic – have been (and continue to be) authoritative spaces within which officially approved values are articulated and sanctioned. In the case of national historic sites and the governmental structures that produced them, both have also been material representations of what John Bodnar calls "public memory," the official version of the past created by social and political leaders: "a body of beliefs and ideas about the past that help a public or society understand both its past, present, and by implication, its future ... The major focus of this communicative and cognitive process is not the past, however, but serious matters in the present such as the ... structure of power in society."[3] Since the 1980s, the nature of public memory and public history representations has shifted along with public debate and policy in mainstream North American society and in academia, which has begun to emphasize the inclusion of minorities, immigrants, and those with very different perspectives to a far greater degree than had been the case in earlier decades. Combined with the determination of Aboriginal people to gain greater control over their lives and the representations of their cultures, this shift has led to the revision of historical narratives communicated by public history sites and to changes in the way that history is chosen for commemoration and interpreted, for instance, to or by Aboriginal audiences and communities.

This has been a significant shift. Canadian history, both academic and public, has tended to emphasize settler narratives of national and regional history and to downplay the perspectives of Aboriginal peoples. Prior to the 1980s, Aboriginal people were seldom mentioned in either scholarly texts or at historic sites; when they were, the discussions emphasized colonial control over Aboriginal people within historical narratives that celebrated the establishment of that control. Thus, the choice of sites, figures, and events for commemoration emphasized "great men" such as explorers and their discoveries, military forts as representations of the establishment of European control in a region, and technological advances associated with nation building such as water locks that facilitated shipping.[4] In the underlying assumptions concerning the selection and interpretation of historic sites at the time, Aboriginal history was always viewed as subordinate to a larger national narrative, to a Euro-Canadian chronicle that could be characterized as colonialist, progressive, and exclusive. Within this perspective, the western fur trade was seen as the extension of capitalism into the wilderness and, thus, as a precursor to the founding of modern Canada rather than as a cross-cultural encounter or a theme in Aboriginal histories.[5] The fur trade fits perfectly into the "nation building" concept as a link between wilderness and civilization.[6] Thus, Lower Fort Garry, a nineteenth-century fur trade and provisioning post in Manitoba, was originally designated as being of historical significance by the federal HSMBC in 1929 not because of its role in the fur trade but because it had been the location where the first western treaty was signed in 1871. The commemoration made no attempt to understand treaty making in its historical context: in fact, it celebrated the end of Aboriginal title and the "clearing of the West" for Euro-Canadian settlement.[7]

Commemoration – the bestowal of national significance by public groups such as the HSMBC – reflected these nation-building narratives and, at the time, represented a national consensus (minus the Aboriginal voice) about what was significant about Canada's past and how the country came to exist in its twentieth-century form. On the rare occasions when they were included in these representations, Aboriginal peoples were portrayed within controlling stereotypes that gave them meaning only in relation to more powerful Europeans: Aboriginal people were depicted as guides, as friends to the whites, or as something inevitably overcome in the course of civilization. Thus, a plaque dedicated to La Vérendrye, unveiled in the 1920s, stated that "his explorations and those of his sons doubled the size of Canada."[8] The statement was not only an anachronism (Canada did not exist in La Vérendrye's time) but also failed to recognize the effort, knowledge, and perspectives of La Vérendrye's Aboriginal guides. Similarly, in Manitoba, Chief Peguis was commemorated in 1924 by a statue with a plaque that was dedicated to him as the "whiteman's special assistant in grateful recognition of his good offices to the early settlers."[9] The memorial makes no mention of Peguis' own goals or of his leadership of his own people, which was the framework within which he negotiated relationships with settlers.

This perspective also influenced the interpretation of individual sites. In preparing a list of topics for interpretation at Lower Fort Garry when it opened to the public for the first time, site director Barbara Johnstone (herself of partly Cree descent) placed European fur traders, exploration history, the founding of the Red River settlement, and the transition from Rupert's Land to Canada well ahead of "Indians." When she did mention Aboriginal people, it was within superficial categories that suggested they were not really important in the trade or at Red River – the topics seen as central to interpretation all concerned Europeans.[10]

The insistent pattern in historical representations of distance between settlers and Aboriginal peoples, of marginalization of Aboriginal peoples, of minimizing their roles in Canadian history, and of denying the legitimacy of Aboriginal perspectives on history and sites of historical importance to Aboriginal peoples mirrored relations between Aboriginal peoples and the dominant society in Canada throughout most of the twentieth century. Aboriginal people were just as marginalized in the present as they were in the past, and their disempowerment in historical representations was part of an unconscious strategy by a settler society that acted to disempower them in the present. The focus on European men and the development of settler society in historical representations functioned to assert a belief in the symbolic importance of these aspects of Canadian society in the twentieth century and a concomitant belief by settler society of the relative unimportance of Aboriginal peoples within Canadian society. These patterns are underscored by Ivan Karp's observation that "the selection of knowledge and the presentation of ideas and images are enacted within a power system. The sources of power are derived from the capacity of cultural institutions to classify and define peoples and societies. This is the power to represent: to reproduce structures of belief and experience through which cultural differences are understood."[11] As a contact zone, public history until the 1980s enacted, as Pratt would have predicted, the "highly asymmetrical relations of domination and subordination" that characterized broad social and political relationships between settler and Aboriginal peoples in Canada.[12]

These dynamics began to shift, however, throughout the 1960s and 1970s, when the rise of social history in both academic and public settings began to augment the great man and colonialist themes of historical narratives. Research on women's history, ethnic and immigrant histories, occupational histories of the working class, and Aboriginal histories slowly began to become available and was incorporated into a broader perspective on Canada's past that informed the criteria for national significance. As Jennifer Brown and Elizabeth Vibert point out, "Before the 1980s there were [judging by the historical literature] no women in the fur trade, and very few Indians."[13] This situation, however, changed rapidly. The production of major texts on Aboriginal history in this era influenced a shift in public history as the texts began to reveal much that had not been well understood and began the process of applying new perspectives and techniques to archival documents to reconstruct Aboriginal perspectives, motivations, and actions. Works that ranged from Arthur Ray's *Indians in the Fur Trade* (1974) to Sylvia Van Kirk's *"Many Tender Ties"* (1980) to Jennifer Brown's *Strangers in Blood* (1980) provided key building blocks for understanding the complexity of actions and interactions in fur trade and Aboriginal histories. Indeed, these explorations of Aboriginal history and of the relations between Europeans and Aboriginal peoples were a crucial turning point that weakened the links between the dynamics of power embedded in earlier constructions of Canadian history, for they made it impossible to deny the complexity of the past or Aboriginal agency and contributions to history.

With this new material, the issue of Aboriginal agency became a dominant theme in scholarly history throughout the 1980s and 1990s. Scholars began to explore historical relations in more nuanced ways, and they focused especially on understanding how Aboriginal peoples had acted according to their own culturally determined motivations and how they had retained core elements of identity and culture as they incorporated new material culture, relationships, and opportunities. Much of this work focused on the fur trade and the role of Aboriginal people within it and, conversely, on the role of the fur trade within Aboriginal histories. As part of these themes, the history of Metis people, who themselves embodied processes of continuity and change, became an important subject in scholarly history in the 1980s and 1990s.

At the same time that these developments were occurring in the academy, public history was breaking new ground as the federal government, through Parks Canada, began to develop new approaches to the changing themes of Canadian history. Gone were the sparse, superficial narratives of the early years of public history; in their place came thematic overviews, social histories, and attempts to link historic sites with a broader view of Canada's past. The numerous and in some cases ground-breaking contributions of historians at Parks Canada in the field of Native studies in the 1970s set the stage for these developments. The work of historians such as Robbie Allen on Indian policy during the War of 1812, the work of Eugene Arima on both West Coast and Arctic material culture and ethnography, the numerous papers on Aboriginal topics written for the HSMBC by David Lee, and the comprehensive work of David Smyth on Blackfoot culture helped push the boundaries of public research and scholarship to a level that rivalled the academy and in some cases actually led the way in providing new perspectives on traditional topics.

In the West, the work of public historians had a significant influence on the interpretation of regional and local history, particularly the community contexts for Metis and First Nations history. For example, the 1980s work of Diane Payment on metis history at Batoche, Walter Hildebrandt's writings on the First Nations of central Saskatchewan, David Neufeld's histories of Yukon First Nations, Frieda Klippenstein's investigations of Stó:lō and Carrier involvement in the fur trade, and Parks Canada's research in the 1990s on the Native peoples of York Factory and the Red River settlement brought a more nuanced and inclusive approach to the way public history characterized Canada's Aboriginal past.

Although public history representations became far more inclusive during this era, control over what was commemorated and how it was commemorated continued to rest with heritage agencies and their largely white, permanent core staff. This is not to say that changes were superficial. The representation of Aboriginal peoples, mixed fur trade families, and individuals who represented the complex identity politics of the eighteenth and nineteenth centuries became a serious goal in this period as sites added new interpretive areas and staff to communicate new understandings about these relationships.

There were, however, serious hindrances to these developments that caused tensions at specific sites and in heritage agencies. The 1970s had been the era of big budgets in historical reconstruction; by the late 1980s and early 1990s, when it became desirable (indeed, sometimes politically urgent) to add Aboriginal history as a theme, drastic budget cuts had severely limited the purchase of interpretive furnishings, the construction of houses and related structures, the revision of introductory exhibits, and the hiring of staff. At some sites, large complexes of European buildings were contrasted with a single Aboriginal structure, unintentionally suggesting that the Aboriginal presence at the site was minimal and unimportant. Some sites had to hire Aboriginal staff at the same time as they were forced to lay off existing staff. Aboriginal staff at many sites tended to be hired solely as seasonal employees who had little say in the themes or content they interpreted and even less power over budgets and program development.

If the situation of change regarding Aboriginal people at historic sites was ambiguous, so was the national framework for change. In 1985, the HSMBC formally acknowledged "the cultural imbalance of the country's National Historic Sites and recommended consultations with First Nations to determine their interest in the national commemoration of their history."[14] At the same time, individual Parks Canada staff and particular sites began to develop relationships with Aboriginal communities that sometimes led to formally articulated relationships such as boards of advisors from local First Nations communities and further shifts in interpretive focus. However, the broader dynamics of control over commemoration and representation (and the choice of themes and sites) remained firmly in the hands of non-Aboriginal managers. Formal consultation between the staff of historic sites and local Aboriginal communities, for instance, often involved little more than sending draft texts, written by Parks Canada's staff on topics decided by Parks Canada's head or regional offices, for community review. And although there were significant shifts in the interpretation of historic sites during this time and a broader set of historical characters and themes interpreted to the public, these themes and characters were still placed within a narrative in which non-Aboriginal, colonialist perspectives prevailed as senior agency staff in Ottawa set the national agenda for historic sites. Overall, historical commemoration's role in constructing a unified nation-state and showing the role of Aboriginal peoples and other minorities within this larger narrative continued to prevail.

Challenge, Controversy, Change

Throughout the 1980s, academic scholarship and public history were challenged to establish reflexive critiques about the production of knowledge about Aboriginal people, its grounding in relations of colonial power, and how it had been used to sustain those relations.[15] The processes of representation in scholarly writing, museum displays, and public history came under sustained scrutiny and were subjected to pointed questions. Who speaks for whom? For what purpose? Who is denied the right to speak for themselves? That the control of commemoration and interpretation rested, in both academia and public agencies such as Parks Canada, with non-Aboriginal people became a serious issue in both theory and practice as the relationships between Aboriginal peoples and those who represented their cultures and histories became increasingly adversarial.[16] These challenges were driven by individuals who felt that the existing frameworks for understanding and representing the past within academia and public history were ethically and intellectually unsatisfactory and by Aboriginal people who had launched a broadly based and profoundly determined movement to reclaim control over their lives. Controlling representations of Aboriginal cultures and histories has been an important symbolic element in this process.

Academic and public trends of thought regarding the representation of Aboriginal histories came together in the controversy over the Olympic exhibition "The Spirit Sings" in the late 1980s, when the Lubicon Cree challenged the Glenbow Museum's decision to create an exhibition that showcased only historical masterpieces of Aboriginal work under the sponsorship of Shell Oil, which was at that time drilling on land claimed by the Lubicon. The use of funds from a company that was damaging contemporary Aboriginal communities created a controversy that challenged the assumed neutrality of scholarship and museums and involved conflict within the anthropological and heritage communities and the active involvement of Aboriginal groups in the debate. In response, the Canadian Museums Association and the Assembly of First Nations created the Task Force on Museums and First Peoples, which held hearings for two years with interested parties from the museum and heritage sector and Aboriginal communities to determine what action was necessary to create a more positive working relationship between the two groups.

Parks Canada made an important submission to the task force in which it acknowledged a fundamental shift regarding Aboriginal participation in the management and presentation of Aboriginal heritage:

> Historical presentations of Canada's special places are incomplete unless they explain any past experiences and present roles of aboriginal peoples at that place ... Co-operation in the collection and presentation of that knowledge will only be earned by persons and agencies that are willing and able to learn from First Peoples how their traditional knowledge and associated objects are to be treated. The Canadian Parks Service will consider its stewardship of Canada's special places incomplete if it fails to pursue this essential element of co-operation with First Peoples.[17]

The dynamic of public historical representations as contact zones between Aboriginal and settler societies was definitely changing. Following its submission to the task force, Parks Canada commissioned a major review of its presentation of Aboriginal history that included a process of consultation with Aboriginal partners and a new system plan to address those areas of Canadian history the government felt were under-represented in Parks Canada's system of national historic sites and commemorations.[18] The three major thrusts of this plan – Aboriginal history, women's history, and ethnocultural history– laid the groundwork for a new approach to historic site commemoration and interpretation.[19] In the North, new sites were designated to commemorate aspects of Aboriginal history, and the sites are managed largely by Inuit and Inuvialuit peoples. At established sites in the south, Aboriginal themes began to be emphasized or brought to the fore, sometimes by hiring Aboriginal staff and reconstructing Aboriginal elements of the sites. In response to concerns about Aboriginal control of and inclusion in heritage management, a further radical change was the development of Aboriginal partnerships in the operation and interpretation of some historic sites.

Following the task force, then, the era of limited inclusion of and token consultation with Aboriginal peoples has evolved into cooperative decision making and the mutual management and operation of many sites. Parks Canada has also begun to place greater emphasis on sites and cultural landscapes that have traditional and spiritual importance to Aboriginal peoples. Sahyoue and Edacho National Historic Sites (also known as Scented Grass Hills and Grizzly Bear Mountain) near Great Bear Lake, Arvia'juaq and Qikiqtaarjuk and Fall Caribou Crossing in Nunavut, and Kejimkujik in Nova Scotia are just some of the sites that have been commemorated and protected because of their traditional historical and cultural value to Aboriginal groups. These commemorations differ dramatically from the old nation-building narratives; they articulate Aboriginal community perspectives about heritage and identity as they relate to place and about the long-term maintenance of a distinct cultural identity as opposed to becoming part of a national history. These new sites and perspectives tend to parallel existing ones, however, rather than integrating Aboriginal views into established historic sites.

In addition to the changing dynamic surrounding the selection of historic sites, the creation of new national parks throughout northern Canada not only helped to protect a fragile Arctic ecology but also employed mechanisms such as traditional knowledge and traditional ecological knowledge to help preserve and interpret the environment and the cultural past. National parks such as Aulavik National Park on Banks Island are administered by co-management structures that involve both the federal government and local people. Tuktut

Nogait National Park, established in 1998 in the western Arctic, protects the calving grounds of the Bluenose-West caribou herd, a resource that is vital to Inuvialuit, Gwich'in, and Sahtu communities that have relied on the herd for hundreds of years. Like other northern national parks, Tuktut Nogait is managed cooperatively through the Tuktut Nogait National Park Management Board and within the context of the Canada National Parks Act, the Inuvialuit Final Agreement, the Tuktut Nogait Agreement, and the cooperative management structures created pursuant to these agreements. These structures guarantee Inuvialuit and community involvement in all park-related decisions. Each of the parties to the Tuktut Nogait Agreement is represented on the board. Through the board, they cooperate in park decision making and ensure that both traditional and scientific knowledge are incorporated into all management decisions.

The Impact of Recent Changes in Historical Representation

These parks and sites challenge received wisdom about commemoration at many levels. At one level, the dynamics of representation have shifted as Aboriginal people have become more involved and as power over decision making has been transferred to Aboriginal groups. At another level, definitions of what is historically significant have changed to include sites of significance to Aboriginal peoples. Indeed, the very purpose of historical designation and interpretation has been questioned. As David Neufeld has noted, "Questions of the legitimacy and utility of a commemoration set within a hostile national historical paradigm have led to a rethinking of the purpose of designation. What social and cultural purposes would a commemoration serve for a First Nation?"[20] The objectives of Aboriginal communities are often quite different from those of the dominant society, and older assumptions about historic sites as valuable entities that provide coherent ideological structure to the nation are not shared by most First Nations people, just as Aboriginal and mainstream narratives communicated about the past still tend to differ.

These different narratives and objectives surfaced in early attempts to involve Aboriginal people more fully in heritage commemoration. Parks Canada initially tried to add what many employees saw as "the Native side of the story" by incorporating Aboriginal perspectives on the past through oral history projects that involved collecting information from First Nations people and adding it to existing national and regional frameworks for historical commemoration and interpretation. These frameworks, however, still retained the older emphasis on European settlement typical of national commemoration; in response, some Aboriginal communities refused to participate in projects that would support these assumptions and ideology. When they did agree to participate, it was largely to pursue their own goals, which often focused on working with a federal agency to prove and narrate community connections and claims to land. David Neufeld's account of his experiences trying to implement changing policy within Parks Canada in Yukon exemplifies these difficulties and differences:

> The Chilkoot Trail Oral History Project did not fulfil the initial expectations of Parks Canada for the "Indian" side of the Stampede story. The attempt to simply throw light on a previously unexplored facet of the national story was a failure. The Carcross Tagish were quick to challenge the project's assumptions of the past. In one instance after an extended set of oral interviews the project anthropologist and an Elder relaxed on a lake shore. The anthropologist found a stone hammer nearby and brought it out to the Elder as proof of the aboriginal presence. The Elder briefly examined the stone and then casually threw it back in the bushes, "What have I been telling you all week?" As the project progressed we watched the First Nation similarly discard the Parks Canada notion of the project objectives. It became clear there was no "Indian" side of the Chilkoot Trail gold rush story, the stampede was simply seen as an annoying but brief interruption of their lives. Community stories instead put forward a parallel historical narrative describing their long use of the area and their connection to it as "home." These were significant messages to Parks Canada about how the Carcross Tagish used their traditional territory to sustain their cultural identity. The First Nation also used the project to make powerful statements about their ownership of the traditional territory returning to the main issue they wished to raise with the federal government.[21]

In the process of making these assertions, elders used oral history to challenge the historiographical framework: "First Nations have used the oral history projects developed with Parks Canada to undermine the constructs of the 'Story of Canada,' to challenge the authority of western cultural and scientific explanations of the world, and to advance their claims – both to the shadow landscapes of the physical world and the intellectual and spiritual landscapes of meaning directly tied to them. Their history is not rationally understandable within the Laurentian thesis, but it doesn't try to be. All that is required is the acknowledgment that it exists."[22] Although Neufeld feels that in some of these partnerships Aboriginal peoples "were able to bring the government of Canada onto a middle ground where there could be a search for accommodation and the development of shared meanings and practices,"[23] he acknowledges that, at least in the commemoration of history, the attempt to simply incorporate Aboriginal stories and histories into traditional, dominant historical frameworks is unacceptable from an Aboriginal perspective: it is possible that there is, in fact, no "shared" national history.

This is not, one would think, an entirely failed experiment in public history, for it points in new directions, toward new relationships and understandings and toward new configurations of the contact zone in which, as James Clifford has suggested for museums, historic sites will become places where people of diverse backgrounds come to attempt to understand one another.[24] This may not, however, be the way of the future, at least not within Parks Canada. That historic sites are in fact contact zones – arenas for battles over issues of power, authority, perspective, and voice – is demonstrated clearly by one particular struggle over what Parks Canada calls the commemorative integrity of historic sites.

Policy regarding commemorative integrity emerged in the early 1990s, when staff at the National Historic Sites Directorate in Ottawa felt that more rigorous measures were required to evaluate and manage historic sites. Commemorative integrity was developed during a period of financial cutbacks and was intended to enable the articulation and review of federal responsibilities toward each national historic site and the manner in which each site's management was fulfilling these responsibilities. Thus, each site within the national system was required to prepare a statement of commemorative integrity in which it set out the ways the site and its interpretation supported the original commemorative intent of the site, that is, the reason the site was *originally* identified by the HSMBC as being of historical significance. According to Parks Canada's policy, "A national historic site possesses commemorative integrity when the resources directly related to the reasons for designation as a national historic site are not impaired or under threat; [when] the reasons for designation as a national historic site are effectively communicated to the public."[25]

For sites designated decades ago by the board, the recent impact of commemorative intent has been substantial. Aboriginal people were deleted from the core interpretation and research programs at the Chilkoot Trail National Historic Site because work on this element of history did not fit the original reasons for commemorating the gold rush site.[26] Aboriginal themes that have been developed over the past several decades for other national historic sites are potentially at risk of being devalued in public presentation. York Factory and Prince of Wales Fort, both fur trade era sites in northern Manitoba, are good examples of older designations that have enjoyed an evolving interpretation that has been deeply influenced by developing scholarship. This recent scholarship has generally revolved around the critical role of Aboriginal peoples within the society and economy of the post, the nature of the interrelationship between Aboriginal peoples and newcomers, and the economic impact of these sites on the Aboriginal people of the region in the more recent past. Telling these stories does more than simply inject Aboriginal history into a traditional dominant-society framework, for these places – especially York Factory – are an integral part of the Cree past in the western Hudson Bay region. But for sites such as York Factory, the policy of commemorative intent imposes a static, fixed, and ultimately conservative view of the past by effectively denying the changes that have occurred in historical understanding since commemoration. Although it is theoretically possible to review and amend commemorative intent statements, this process requires considerable bureaucratic effort because the site in question must be resubmitted to the HSMBC, a practice that has been actively discouraged in the historic sites program.

To illustrate the challenges posed by this policy, we can consider Prince of Wales Fort in Churchill. The fort's designation as a national historic site in 1923 by the HSMBC was one of the first in western Canada. At that time, the federally appointed board – which was made up then, as it is now, of academics and a sprinkling of interested non-professionals – considered the fort's importance to be based solely on its role in the eighteenth-century rivalry between France and England for the territory and resources of Hudson Bay. Given the nature of historical understanding at the time, this commemorative theme was hardly surprising. Themes relating to the establishment of trade with indigenous peoples, and the social and economic impacts that ensued, were of little interest to the board in the 1920s because, arguably, they held little importance within the scholarly community at the time. That the board ignored that the Churchill West Peninsula, where Prince of Wales Fort is situated, contains resources that speak to over three thousand years of occupation by Aboriginal peoples is also hardly surprising, for the cultures of these peoples were little understood at the time. The commemoration of York Factory thirteen years later in 1936 was much the same: the theme of French-English rivalry (although this time focused primarily on seventeenth-century events) dominated the reasons for designation.

Although the nature of these particular designations can be seen as fairly typical of a time in which commemoration concentrated on great men and great battles, it is unfortunate that some seven decades later, through the imposition of commemorative intent, these themes have been resurrected at York Factory and Prince of Wales Fort as, in part, the basis of interpretation. The commemorative intent statement for Prince of Wales Fort, as drafted by Parks Canada in 1995, reiterates the 1923 recommendation that the site was significant for its role in colonial rivalry and adds that the role of the fur trade and its participants, along with the architectural significance of the fort, is relevant to

Figure 11.1 Chief Charles Wastasecoot *(centre)* and councillors after signing Treaty 5 at York Factory, 10 August 1910. Photograph by A.V. Thomas. Archives of Manitoba, Thomas, A.V. 133 (N8207). Image cropped from original.

the commemoration. The commemorative intent statement for York Factory also focuses on French-English rivalry in the fur trade, but it also mentions the site's role as a trading post and its importance as a fur trade entrepot in the nineteenth century (see Figure 11.1). However, if these supporting statements have amplified the designations as originally conceived, there is little doubt that the early focus on colonial rivalry has remained at the core of the commemorative intent for each of these sites.

The impact of these statements within the new policy has been substantial. Whereas in recent years staff at Parks Canada had begun to widen the scope of interpretive themes at northern fur trade sites to reflect the course of Aboriginal and fur trade scholarship after 1970 and new relationships that had been established with Aboriginal peoples, commemorative intent has effectively blunted a number of these new directions. At Churchill, Parks Canada has largely retrenched to interpret only the fort itself and has backed away from initiatives that had begun to focus on the long human history of the Churchill West Peninsula.

Although colonial rivalry is part of the story at Prince of Wales Fort and York Factory, it is, at best, a minor part of that story, especially at York Factory. Moreover, such a narrow emphasis limits the scope for interpretation at these sites and effectively denies that they, like most communities, were dynamic places that changed over time and affected the lives of the people who lived there and nearby. If at York Factory, for instance, commemorative intent places the emphasis on seventeenth-century rivalries or nineteenth-century economic ascendancy, a great many other themes will be missed, such as the impact on local peoples of commercial decline or how a sense of spiritual place at York still resonates with many Cree people in northern Manitoba. To reassert the narratives of an older vision not only ignores the evolution of historical understanding related to the impact of fur trade economies upon local populations but also suggests the continuation of a colonial view of the past.

If, on the one hand, Canada seems to have made steps toward embracing a more inclusive model for historic commemoration in which "national" history is the sum total of local and regional stories and perspectives – perspectives that are national in the sense that they can and should matter to all Canadians and not because they are chosen to represent the view from the centre – then, on the other hand, some elements of heritage commemoration policies clearly reject such a model. How do community considerations affect the communication of national significance, and is this a vision that can only be seen from Ottawa? Is our national narrative simply imposed from Ottawa and from early-twentieth-century understandings of history? If public history representations, like museum representations, function as arenas within which social and political relationships are enacted and contested, then what does the insistence on maintaining original commemorative intent signal about Canadian society? If Canada has accepted the right of Aboriginal peoples to self-determination and has publicly acknowledged the important contributions they have made and continue to make to Canadian society, then do federal heritage agencies not have a responsibility to acknowledge these aspirations and contributions in heritage commemoration? Or, more pointedly, are Aboriginal perspectives on the past not part of Canadian heritage?

History, Power, and Contact Zones

These disputes, questions, explorations, and retrenchments echo battles over authority in textual and museum representations. In anthropology and the social sciences more generally, these shifts in authority have been dramatic as research ethics policies have required consent from descendant populations and as more and more community-based and collaborative research partnerships have emphasized increased Aboriginal authority.[27] These changes have affected the broader relationship between indigenous peoples and the nation-state. Public history sites such as museums, as institutions that symbolize the cultural capital (and power) of the nation-state and the identity of the dominant class, have become important sites of contestation, and the visibility and self-representation of Aboriginal people within museums have proved to be key parts of changing the image and position of Aboriginal people in the broader society as they have challenged stereotypes, academic knowledge/power systems, and social inequalities. Ivan Karp's point that "exhibitions [are] political arenas in which definitions of identity and culture are asserted and contested" is very much about these processes.[28]

In places where new stories about the past are allowed to flourish, the stories are far from the old narrative of the inevitable progress of Western civilization; they instead explore what actually happened when tribal groups and Europeans interacted at different phases of colonization. They explore tribal perspectives on contact, tribal engagement within new relationships, and the effects of historical contact on tribal groups. They explore a process in which both Europeans and Aboriginal peoples borrowed ideas and behaviours from each other, rejected elements of each other's culture, and struggled to maintain their own identities in the midst of change. They tell of individuals and dynamics that bridged settler and Aboriginal communities, such as marriage partnerships, diplomatic efforts to cultivate allies, missionization, trade, and imperial politics. They also tell of the forces and turning points that led to the hardening of cultural boundaries, the sharpening of prejudice, and the heightening of inter-group tensions. They insist on documenting the continuous occupation of territory by Aboriginal peoples and explain some of the inter-relationships between land and Aboriginal culture. They pursue Aboriginal goals for self-determination as well as non-Aboriginal ideas and ideologies. They acknowledge different perspectives on historical events and processes and may, for example, present irreconcilable versions of treaty negotiations or the importance of events.

These stories and the historic sites at which they are told, or suppressed, illustrate Pratt's concept of contact zones as "social spaces where disparate cultures meet, clash, and grapple with each other, often in highly asymmetrical relations of domination and subordination," as arenas in which competing claims to power, control, and sovereignty are negotiated.[29] Historical narratives have partly to do with fulfilling Canadian multicultural policies, partly to do with initiatives by Aboriginal peoples to reclaim control over their lives and lands, partly to do with shifts in theoretical structures of history, and partly to do with reflexive theoretical concerns about power in forms of representation.

Conclusion

Writing about social memory and the legacy of colonialism in Australia, Chris Healy argues that the way in which the past is constructed in the public imagination produces something called history and raises key questions about what history can mean in a postcolonial society.[30] In Canada, the revision of historical narratives and of procedures for commemorating history has been tied to social and political change and changes in the way we understand the nature of Canadian society. Public history sites have come to enact national commitments to social inclusion, multiculturalism, and addressing the legacies of colonial history for Aboriginal peoples. These changes came about as the result of contestation, as Aboriginal people (and many public historians) refused to accept standard narratives of national history and the roles (and powerlessness) assigned to Aboriginal people within them.

Yet according these assertions and parallel historical structures and narratives their proper place within national commemoration schemes is challenging at every level. Parks Canada's mandate remains to "protect and present nationally significant examples of Canada's natural and cultural heritage, and foster public understanding, appreciation and enjoyment in ways that ensure the ... commemorative integrity of these places."[31] At every historic site and commemorative plaque, at every meeting of national heritage managers in Ottawa and discussion by the HSMBC, the federal heritage system acts not only as a symbolic arena for national political and social structures, as an important mechanism constructed of imagined communities past and present, but also as a contact zone, a crossroads, a place where historical narratives intersect and collide, where power is demonstrated in the right to tell narratives, and where, possibly, we can consider one another's stories.

Notes

Thanks to the many colleagues in public history and academia with whom we have discussed these ideas. Laura Peers would especially like to thank David Neufeld for important contributions in personal communications.

1 Pratt, *Imperial Eyes;* Clifford, "Museums as Contact Zones"; White, *The Middle Ground;* and Anzaldua, *Borderlands: La frontera.*
2 Pratt, *Imperial Eyes,* 4.
3 Bodnar, *Remaking America,* 15.
4 See Wallace, "Visiting the Past"; Schlereth, *Cultural History and Material Culture,* 350; Norkunas, *The Politics of Public Memory;* and Neufeld, "Parks Canada, the Commemoration of Canada and Northern Aboriginal Oral History," 24-25.
5 Johnston, "Toward a New Past," 4.
6 See Coutts, "Re-Negotiating the Past," 1.
7 See Coutts, *Lower Fort Garry.*
8 Cited in Taylor, *Negotiating the Past,* 51.
9 Friesen, "Heritage: The Manitoba Experience."
10 Johnstone, "A Broad Outline of Exhibit Stories."
11 Karp, "Introduction: Museums and Communities," 1.
12 Pratt, *Imperial Eyes,* 4.
13 Brown and Vibert, eds., *Reading beyond Words,* xx.
14 Neufeld, "Parks Canada, the Commemoration of Canada and Northern Aboriginal Oral History," 8.
15 Said, *Orientalism;* Fabian, *Time and the Other;* and Clifford, *The Predicament of Culture.*
16 See Spector, *What This Awl Means;* Biolsi and Zimmerman, *Indians and Anthropologists;* and Piker, "Review Essay: Native American Histories," 861-64.
17 Canadian Parks Service, "Submission to Task Force on Museums and First Peoples."
18 Johnston, "Toward a New Past."
19 And see Parks Canada, "National Historic Sites of Canada System Plan."
20 Neufeld, "The Commemoration of Northern Aboriginal Peoples," 31.
21 Neufeld, "Parks Canada, the Commemoration of Canada and Northern Aboriginal Oral History," 11.
22 Ibid., 23.
23 Ibid., 16.
24 Clifford, "Museums as Contact Zones."
25 Parks Canada, "Parks Canada Guide to the Preparation of Commemorative Integrity Statements."
26 David Neufeld, personal communication to Laura Peers, 6 September 2005.
27 Warry, *Unfinished Dreams;* Clifford, "Looking Several Ways"; and Brown and Peers, with members of the Kainai Nation, *Sinaakssiiksi Aotsimaahpihkookiyaawa/Pictures Bring Us Messages.*
28 Karp, "Introduction: Museums and Communities," 1.
29 Pratt, *Imperial Eyes,* 4.
30 Healy, *From the Ruins of Colonialism.*
31 Parks Canada, "Performance Report for Period Ending March 31, 2008," 5.

Bibliography

Archival Sources

Hudson's Bay Company Archives
E.97/53, Johnstone, Barbara A. "A Broad Outline of Exhibit Stories for Lower Fort Garry National Historic Park." 1962.

Published Sources

Anzaldua, Gloria. *Borderlands: La frontera.* San Francisco: Spinster/Aunt Lute, 1987.

Biolsi, Thomas, and Larry J. Zimmerman. *Indians and Anthropologists: Vine Deloria, Jr., and the Critique of Anthropology.* Tucson: University of Arizona Press, 1997.

Bodnar, John. *Remaking America: Public Memory, Commemoration, and Patriotism in the Twentieth Century.* Princeton, NJ: Princeton University Press, 1992.

Brown, Alison K., and Laura Peers, with members of the Kainai Nation. *Sinaakssiiksi Aotsimaahpihkookiyaawa/Pictures Bring Us Messages: Photographs and Histories from the Kainai Nation.* Toronto: University of Toronto Press, 2006.

Brown, Jennifer S.H. *Strangers in Blood: Fur Trade Company Families in Indian Country.* Vancouver: UBC Press, 1983.

Brown, Jennifer S.H., and Elizabeth Vibert, eds. *Reading beyond Words: Contexts for Native History.* Peterborough: Broadview Press, 2001 [1996].

Canadian Parks Service. "Submission to Task Force on Museums and First Peoples," c. 1991. Unpublished document in possession of the author.

Clifford, James. "Looking Several Ways: Anthropology and Native Heritage in Alaska." *Current Anthropology* 45, 1 (2004): 5-30.

–. "Museums as Contact Zones." In *Routes: Travel and Translation in the Late Twentieth Century,* James Clifford, 188-219. London: Harvard University Press, 1997.

–. *The Predicament of Culture: Twentieth-Century Ethnography, Literature, and Art.* Cambridge, MA: Harvard University Press, 1988.

Coutts, Robert. *Lower Fort Garry: An Operational History, 1911-1992.* Ottawa: Parks Canada Microfiche Report Series 495, 1993.

–. "Re-Negotiating the Past: Parks Canada, Commemorative Intent, and Fur Trade History." Paper presented at Old Sites, New Stories: An International Workshop on the Management and Interpretation of Fur Trade Historic Sites, Grand Portage, Minnesota, September 2000.

Fabian, Johannes. *Time and the Other: How Anthropology Makes Its Object.* New York: Columbia University Press, 1983.

Friesen, Jean. "Heritage: The Manitoba Experience." *Prairie Forum* 15, 2 (1990): 199-220.

Healy, Chris. *From the Ruins of Colonialism: History as Social Memory.* Cambridge: Cambridge University Press, 1997.

Johnston, A.J.B. "Toward a New Past: Reflections on the Interpretation of Native History within Parks Canada." Unpublished manuscript, 1994. In possession of the author.

Karp, Ivan. "Introduction: Museums and Communities: The Politics of Public Culture." In *Museums and Communities: The Politics of Public Culture,* edited by Ivan Karp, Christine Kreamer, and Steven D. Lavine, 1-18. Washington, DC: Smithsonian Institution Press, 1992.

Neufeld, David. "The Commemoration of Northern Aboriginal Peoples by the Canadian Government." *George Wright Forum* 19, 3 (2002): 22-33.

–. "Parks Canada, the Commemoration of Canada and Northern Aboriginal Oral History." In *Oral History and Public Memories,* edited by Paula Hamilton and Linda Shopes, 7-29. Philadelphia, PA: Temple University Press, 2008.

Norkunas, Martha K. *The Politics of Public Memory.* Albany, NY: SUNY Press, 1993.

Parks Canada. "National Historic Sites of Canada System Plan." Parks Canada. http://www.pc.gc.ca/docs/r/system-reseau/sec4/sites-lieux47_e.asp.

–. "Parks Canada Guide to the Preparation of Commemorative Integrity Statements." 2008 [2002]. Parks Canada. http://www.pc.gc.ca/docs/pc/guide/guide/index_e.asp.

–. "Performance Report for Period Ending March 31, 2008." Parks Canada. http://www.pc.gc.ca/eng/docs/pc/rpts/rmr-dpr/03312008.aspx.

Piker, Joshua. "Review Essay: Native American Histories: Stories and Theories." *William and Mary Quarterly* 50, 4 (2003): 861-64.

Pratt, Mary L. *Imperial Eyes: Travel Writing and Transculturation.* London: Routledge, 1992.

Ray, Arthur J. *Indians in the Fur Trade: Their Role as Trappers, Hunters, and Middlemen in the Lands Southwest of Hudson Bay, 1660-1870.* Toronto: University of Toronto Press, 1974.

Said, Edward. *Orientalism.* London: Vintage Books, 1978.

Schlereth, Thomas. *Cultural History and Material Culture: Everyday Life, Landscapes, Museums.* Ann Arbor, MI: UMI Research Press, 1990.

Spector, Janet. *What This Awl Means: Feminist Archaeology at a Wahpeton Dakota Village.* St. Paul: Minnesota Historical Society Press, 1993.

Taylor, C.J. *Negotiating the Past: The Making of Canada's National Historic Parks and Sites.* Montreal and Kingston: McGill-Queen's University Press, 1990.

Van Kirk, Sylvia. *"Many Tender Ties": Women in Fur-Trade Society, 1670-1870.* Winnipeg: Watson and Dwyer, 1980.

Wallace, Michael. "Visiting the Past: History Museums in the United States. In *Presenting the Past: Essays on History and the Public,* edited by Susan P. Benson, Stephen Brier, and Roy Rosenzweig, 137-61. Philadelphia: Temple University Press, 1986.

Warry, Wayne. *Unfinished Dreams: Community Healing and the Reality of Aboriginal Self-Government.* Toronto: University of Toronto Press, 1998.

White, Richard. *The Middle Ground: Indians, Empires, and Republics in the Great Lakes Region, 1650-1815.* Cambridge: Cambridge University Press, 1991.

Afterword: Aaniskotaapaan – Generations and Successions

Jennifer S.H. Brown

THIS AFTERWORD HAS SEVERAL starting points. It receives inspiration partly from the perspectives that my friends and colleagues offer in the preceding chapters, as they share their insights and research. In a more personal vein, I also look back at some scholarly and familial influences from previous generations, reflecting on how we organize what we learn from others through language and received categories, and on how we also sometimes take paths that our ancestors would not and could not follow. Across six decades of memory and experience, learning continues and revelations keep coming, often through conversations with the people who speak on these pages and with others of the past and present. Sometimes old words from different places open new angles of vision. Such is the case with the Cree word – *aaniskotaapaan* – that appears in my title.[1]

Translating "Generations"

Recently, Theresa Schenck and I had a conversation about the concept of generations in English and how that idea might be expressed in Algonquian languages. That question has faced her at various times during her work on Anishinaabe historian William Warren's life and writings.[2] Warren, in adapting Ojibwe history for English-speaking readers, reckoned a generation as being forty years in length. This definition is rather different from our common-sense notions of twenty-five to thirty years, the space between parents' and their children's births.[3]

It is not clear why Warren chose forty years as a unit; it is not an Ojibwe notion. It seems to have been his own idea, based perhaps on an estimate of the age at which an adult might become a grandparent. In any case, his use of that figure led him to propose much earlier dates for various events than those indicated by other sources. When, for example, he transposed the generation-based oral history that the elders told him into Christian calendrical dates to calculate the arrival of Europeans at Chequamagon (La Pointe), he arrived at a date of 1612, which was considerably earlier than that indicated by any historical documentation.[4]

When Schenck asked Anishinaabe linguist Roger Roulette for help with the concept, Roulette replied that there was no Ojibwe equivalent for the English word "generation" as a unit that refers to or implies a period of time. Ojibwe speakers use the term *"aanikoobijiganag,"* which evokes units of length that connect successive kin; Roulette explained it in English as "knots on a string."[5] Clearly, Warren had to bridge a conceptual gap when he moved from Ojibwe thinking to writing for an anglophone audience. Speakers of other Algonquian languages also sometimes invoke knots and string to express generational succession; the Ojibwe term parallels a Naskapi (Innu) statement that Frank Speck quoted in translation in his *Naskapi: The Savage Hunters of the Labrador Peninsula:* "From great-grandparents to great-grandchildren we are only knots in a string."[6]

Richard Faries in his 1938 revision of E.A. Watkins' (1865) *Dictionary of the Cree Language* offered another example of this image. He translated the Cree term *"an'iskota'pan,"* as "a knot; a great grandchild." (His "anisk-" corresponds to the Ojibwe cognate "aanik-".) The corresponding verb signifies "he ties one thing to another; he has a great grandchild."[7] When I asked Cree educator and storyteller William Dumas about the terms in Faries' dictionary, he explained that "aaniskotaapaan" referred both to a great-grandchild and to the tying of a knot to extend length or to pull things, as "when you tie one toboggan behind another."[8]

A closer look at the morpheme "aanisko(t)-" adds another dimension. Its association with knots is connotative or implicit, for it does not explicitly refer to knots. Linguist H.C. Wolfart points out that the fuller range of entries in Father Albert Lacombe's Cree dictionary of 1874 gives the focal meaning of "aanisko(t)-" as "abutting end to end, in succession." The notion of knots is "coincidental, for all the lexical entries found with the gloss 'knot' in fact refer to the tying of two (or more) *lengths* of string or rope." The stem recurs in a series of verbs (e.g., *"aaniskoostee-,"* "to be extended"); these verbs "support the meaning of 'extension, succession, articulation'."[9] Wolfart adds, "In its linguistic make-up, the verb *aaniskotaapeew* (from which the noun *aaniskotaapaan* is secondarily derived) is ambiguous. The 'tying' translation suggests *aaniskot-* 'end-to-end' combined with *-aapee-* 'string, rope'; thus 'tie lengths of rope together end to end.'[10] The 'pulling' translation, on the other hand, reflects a different analysis, with *aanisko-* 'end-to-end' construed with *-(i)taapee-* 'drag'; thus, 'drag end to end, pull in succession.' The latent presence of these two competing interpretations makes this a classical instance of homonymy: two words having the same sounds but different meanings."[11] Homonyms offer scope for ambiguity and embellishment, and the image of knots in a string is one way in which this concept of generational succession can be made concrete.

In sum, "aaniskotaapaan" is not a simple word. I decided that "generations and successions" could serve in my title as a gloss of the Cree concept, while images of knots and strings as connecting great-grandparents and great-grandchildren help us to understand the central place that these links hold in the ways that Cree and Ojibwe think about and frame generational relationships. Laura Peers and Carolyn Podruchny, in their Introduction to this book, quote my use, some years back, of the metaphor of chain migration to talk about our scholarly enterprise. That image speaks to the movement of related people following one another across geographical space. "Aaniskotaapaan" also emphasizes extensions, but in a more powerful way, across time; it refers to the making and transmitting of kin relations down the generations (but without implying the passage of any set number of years). Furthermore, the word is personalized when used as a kin term; it is subject to the possessive prefixes ("ni-", "ki-", etc.) that Cree speakers use to refer to or address their relatives: for example, "*nitaaniskotaapaan,*" "my great-grandchild." These terms carry a marker that specifies who is related to whom.[12]

Academic Ancestors

How might the concept of aaniskotaapaan offer fresh ways to think about ourselves as well as others? For me, this concept joins a collection of other Algonquian and anthropological terms that help me to navigate my way into other frames of reference. Aaniskotaapaan challenges us to reflect on our intergenerational relations and their significance, and we can extend those reflections to intellectual and cultural spheres as well. In our mental formations, as in our families, we are all tied to past connections, which may be more or less salient, recognized, or remembered but are nonetheless there. We are all great-grandchildren, and we all had eight great-grandparents. We rarely think of them, and probably few of us could name them all. We may not even have known them (I never met any of mine). But they are tied to us in subtle ways, as we are to them. Then, for those of us blessed with too much education, we have intellectual great-grandparents who have influenced us through those whom they taught, who in turn mentored our teachers. And, of course, there are those who come after us, as we become grandparents and great-grandparents, whether metaphorical or biological.

When we trace kinship ties and their roles in learning and identity formation, we select among the lines we follow. Some stand out in our lives, and others disappear or scarcely remain visible to us. Since I have had some role in knitting together lines of inquiry that are reaching into the future, it may be useful to trace some of those lines back in time, in case anyone is curious about where some of them began. Some strands arrange themselves in linear fashion; others reach out, netlike, to collateral lines, to siblings and cousins, to extend the kin metaphor. For me, a few intellectual lines have been especially important. Certain familial ones have also proved instructive and challenging and have revealed themselves to be more linked to my intellectual endeavours than I would have expected forty years ago.

In the intellectual sphere, I can trace some early strands of learning from my undergraduate days at Brown University in Providence, Rhode Island, to a shifting graduate trajectory (moving from classical archaeology to anthropology) at Harvard University. But the guiding line that set me on course was a research experience in Peru in 1963-64. There I discovered the practice of ethnohistory, thanks to an opportunity to work with the Andean scholar John V. Murra as he mined early Spanish sources for clues to Quechua and Aymara social organization and economic life. As I learned about close reading and listened for indigenous voices in sixteenth-century European colonial documents, I found the sort of work I most wanted to do. A few years later, Murra, single-handedly I think, got me into the PhD program in anthropology at the University of Chicago, his own doctoral alma mater. In 1970, I began my studies with George W. Stocking Jr., Raymond Fogelson, and others and began to find that, for various academic and personal reasons, my research path was leading toward studies of Aboriginal-European relations in the fur trade and mission contexts of northern North America.

Stocking and Fogelson focused on the history of anthropology and North American ethnohistory respectively, but they were intellectual cousins to each other in one striking respect. As graduate students at the University of Pennsylvania, they had both studied with and were influenced by the same senior professor, A. Irving Hallowell. Hallowell (1892-1974) was the author of over thirty important articles on Ojibwe culture and worldview, which grew out of his substantial fieldwork along the Berens River in Manitoba and Ontario in the 1930s, and he was also, in later life, a pioneer in the history of anthropology.[13] I of course read his work as a graduate student at the University of Chicago, but it was in the 1980s that my studies began to focus on his research and writings to a much greater extent. Since I never got to meet him, my link to Hallowell is indirect and involves a generational succession to a descendant he never knew. But I can trace Hallowell's personal influence through George Stocking, whose recollections help to trace lines of transmission that reach from Speck and Hallowell down to the present. Stocking's descriptions of Hallowell, and of Hallowell's influence on him, demonstrate how these connections have worked.

During his graduate studies in American civilization at the University of Pennsylvania in the late 1950s, George Stocking took only two courses in anthropology, both with Hallowell: "Psychology and Culture," and "History of Anthropology." Both courses, he recalled in 1976, "opened up new intellectual vistas: the one, as it were, of anthropology in being, the other, of anthropology in becoming." Both focused on themes to which Hallowell was devoted in the 1950s and 1960s. "Psychology and Culture" explored frameworks for understanding "an alien self [principally Ojibwe] in its culturally constituted behavioral environment"; "The History of Anthropology" seminar discussed "the emergence of a particular form of scientific understanding in Western European culture." Different topics: but Stocking found that, as "products of the same mind," they followed much the same track. In each, Hallowell emphasized the seeking of "emic" or insider understandings, whether held by the Ojibwe themselves or by the denizens of the anthropological past. He asked students to try to grasp the worldviews of "particular groups of historical actors" while looking at how various folk-anthropologies arose in "different historical or cultural contexts."[14]

Hallowell's influence led Stocking to direct his doctoral dissertation toward the history of anthropology. Titled "American Social Scientists and Race Theory, 1890-1915," it was completed in 1960. In the early 1960s, Hallowell and Stocking each began to publish in the history of anthropology, the former as he capped a distinguished career and the latter as he began one. Hallowell was the leading spirit in the organization of a Social Science Research Council conference on the history of anthropology in 1963, and he saw to it that Stocking was invited to participate. In turn, Stocking – in the Preface to his first book, *Race, Culture, and Evolution* (1968), comprised of seven articles he had published in the years 1962-66 – acknowledged Hallowell as "my anthropological godfather, who gave me many insights into both the culture concept and the history of anthropology and introduced me professionally to the world of anthropology."[15]

Fifteen years later, when Stocking published the first edited volume, *Observers Observed* (1983), in his new History of Anthropology series, his Introduction to that volume, "History of Anthropology: Whence/Whither," again evoked Hallowell's worldview and influence. The History of Anthropology series was to encourage, he wrote, "a disciplinary historiography that is both historically sophisticated and anthropologically knowledgeable." It would avoid, however, treating anthropology simply as subject matter to which the methodological orientations of history would be applied. Instead, Stocking proposed an alternative frame of reference: "For the historian of anthropology, [the concepts of anthropology] are not only the object of inquiry, but may provide also a means by which it is pursued. As Hallowell argued several decades ago, the history of anthropology should be approached as 'an anthropological problem.'" Anthropology could furnish many of the tools for analyzing its own past while at the same time situating its tools and concepts historically.[16]

Although I never had the opportunity to meet Hallowell, George Stocking and Raymond Fogelson provided a sense of connection. In 1986, I started to work through Hallowell's papers in the American Philosophical Society Library in Philadelphia. Reading his writings more closely, I and a colleague, Maureen Matthews, also followed his fieldwork trail up the Berens River through his research notes, meeting people who still remembered his sojourns among them. In doing so, I began to realize the significance of two earlier intergenerational ties that had a great influence upon Hallowell. One linked Hallowell to his academic mentor, Frank Speck, and the other to Chief William Berens, the Ojibwe advisor and guide who made his Berens River work possible.

Frank Speck (1881-1950) earned his PhD in 1908 at Columbia University, studying with Franz Boas, the founder of American anthropology. Early in his career, Speck became absorbed in the study of eastern Algonquian languages and ethnology, and he got to meet and learn much from some of the last speakers of those languages. He supervised Hallowell's graduate studies, notably his dissertation (1924) on bear ceremonialism, and the two were colleagues and friends at the University of Pennsylvania until Speck's death in 1950. Hallowell's obituary of Speck in *American Anthropologist* (1951) included a passage that provides clues about the intellectual approaches and standards that his mentor passed on to him:

> The concrete and specific details which ultimately reached the written page were never put down in haste. They were evaluated against a masterly knowledge of relevant linguistic, ethnographic and historical fact covering a much wider area and often subjected to a long process of scrutiny and reflection. One never doubts that Speck knows what he is talking about, so that all his work bears the earmarks of high substantiality. He was never primarily concerned with high-level generalizations or interpretations, but rather with putting well attested facts on record. In this respect he belongs to the classical ethnographic tradition which, broadly speaking, is closely allied to the kind of work many historians have done. So it is not surprising to find throughout his career Speck made considerable use of relevant documentary material in addition to the mass of information he was constantly collecting from Indian informants. Although the term "ethnohistory" appears in some of his later writings, he was always an ethnohistorian.[17]

Hallowell, more often than Speck, did venture into high-level generalizations and theoretical discussions. But as I have noted elsewhere, he became more and more historically oriented in his later writings, while maintaining Speck's bent for "putting well attested facts on record."[18] The works of Speck and Hallowell, consequently, have "the earmarks of high substantiality" that resulted from their combining historical research and fieldwork to produce firmly grounded scholarship of superb quality.

Hallowell's growing historical orientation had another source in the 1930s. This brings me to the other intergenerational link that proved to be of vast importance to his work – his relationship with Chief William Berens (1866-1947). In early July 1930, when Hallowell was travelling up Lake Winnipeg for a summer of fieldwork among the Cree, his lake steamer stopped at Berens River, partway up the eastern shore. Chief Berens met the boat, made Hallowell's acquaintance, and learned of his interest in meeting "un-Christianized Indians." Berens offered to take Hallowell up the river on his next visit and indeed did so in 1932 and in several subsequent summers, becoming, as Hallowell wrote in the 1960s, "my interpreter, guide, and virtual collaborator in the investigations I carried on in subsequent years." As he added, "I have always considered it extremely fortunate that I met William Berens when I did ... Berens himself was bilingual from childhood and as fully acquainted with the ways of white men as Indians. Thus, from the beginning of my association with him, I became historically oriented as a matter of course because we made constant reference to the persons of past generations in the genealogical material we had collected together. This enabled me to integrate data concerning the cultural present with changes in the historic past ... which could be checked in written documents."[19] Berens was in his late sixties, already a grandfather several times, when Hallowell got to know him; Hallowell was in his thirties when the two men met. Berens, in a sense, might have been ready for Hallowell; the moment was right, much as it was when the poet John Neihardt, at about the same time, turned up to record and retell the stories and visions of the Lakota elder Black Elk in South Dakota.[20] Berens had been chief since 1917; he was well versed in dealing with outsiders – traders, commercial fishermen, Indian agents, and others. And his family had a strong connection with Methodism – a link that had begun through his father, Jacob Berens, even before the first mission was established at Berens River in 1874. Jacob and William Berens both sent their children to school when possible, and much of the family grew up bilingual and able to relate to the encroaching outside world.

But as Hallowell learned, William Berens was also steeped in the Ojibwe heritage of his father and grandfathers, which he traced back four generations to his paternal great-grandfather, the powerful medicine man Yellow Legs. Hallowell was keen to learn and hear all that the chief remembered, and Berens was ready and eager to teach this younger newcomer who, unlike most outsiders, was there to focus on the stories and history of Ojibwe people and was not interested in spending time with white folk. While Frank Speck linked Hallowell to his anthropological forefathers and cultural traditions, William

Berens became his link to the culture and history of the Ojibwe. Berens shared legends and stories, explained Ojibwe terms and practices, and took him up the river to meet his Moose clan mates, most notably Fair Wind (Naamiwan), the old medicine man at Pauingassi, Manitoba – and many others.[21] He also told Hallowell about a Berens family missionary connection – a line that leads me back to a great-grandfather of my own.

Familial Ancestors

In the historical section of his ethnography on the Berens River Ojibwe, Hallowell noted the active role that William Berens' father, Jacob, had played "in bringing a resident missionary, Egerton R. Young, to Berens River in 1873."[22] Young, an Ontario Methodist who had served at Norway House from 1868 to 1873, was my father's maternal grandfather. There are some reasons why a scholar of Aboriginal history in the twenty-first century might not want to mention the evangelical Methodism embedded in one of her family lines. But this great-grandfather is one reason for the story line of this essay.

Around 1970, as I was starting doctoral studies at the University of Chicago, my father, Harcourt Brown, recently retired from teaching at Brown University in Providence, Rhode Island, was working to assemble his grandfather's papers to donate as a collection to the Archives of Ontario.[23] He had received a fair quantity of records from his grandmother, Elizabeth Bingham Young (1843-1934). But other materials had gone to cousins and were at risk of being increasingly separated as family lines diverged. As we looked at the papers, I realized that, although my studies to date had scarcely touched on my Canadian heritage, my interest in pursuing ethnohistorical research could find immensely rich outlets in source materials such as these, sources that documented northern Canadian fur trade and mission relations with Aboriginal people, often in remarkable detail.

In the summer of 1972, my father took my husband and son and me on a visit to Norway House, Manitoba. It was a memorable experience for him to see the nearby Rossville mission (now a United Church of Canada parish), where the Youngs had served before going to Berens River. By then, I had realized that, to understand the context in which the Methodist and other northern missions functioned in the mid- to late 1800s, I needed to go back to the fur trade and the earlier history of Rupert's Land, as the old chartered territory of the Hudson's Bay Company was known from 1670 to 1870. I had decided to do my dissertation research on fur traders and their Native families, their familial and marital patterns, and the changes they faced as their lives were increasingly affected by missions and the coming of European settlers.[24] The work led me into the amazing riches of the Hudson's Bay Company Archives and also brought a realization

Figure A.1 Wilson Brown and Jennifer S.H. Brown on Wreck Island near Sans Souci, Georgian Bay, Ontario, August 2001. Photo by George Fulford.

of the significance that those family histories could have for Metis and First Nations research if combined with Aboriginal oral histories and other means of documentation. At the same time, it served to open new angles of vision onto my own family history, adding context and different story lines that reached beyond genealogy.

In 1983, my husband and I left the Chicago area for academic jobs in Winnipeg, Manitoba. I found myself living and working in the homeland of the fur traders and Aboriginal people I was writing about, and numbers of my students at the University of Winnipeg turned out to be descended from those families. Shortly thereafter, when Hallowell's papers became available for research in Philadelphia, I began to mine them for the information that Hallowell had gathered from Ojibwe people about the history of their relations with fur traders and missionaries and about their own history. The papers proved rich in unpublished writings and photographs. Most outstandingly, they held the next to final manuscript of an ethnography of Berens River that Hallowell had written in the 1960s but had never published because the final manuscript was lost in transit to the press. Researching, editing, and annotating this work for its long

Figure A.2 Jacob Owen and Jennifer S.H. Brown, Pauingassi, Manitoba, in front of Jacob Owen's house, October 1992. Photo by Maureen Matthews.

overdue publication in 1992, I found I could bring the fields of fur trade, mission, and Aboriginal history together in a most rewarding way. This work opened the door to many other projects for me and for some of my students and colleagues, particularly as opportunities arose to meet descendants and other relatives of William Berens. In the 1990s, some older Ojibwe people along the Berens River still warmly remembered both him and Hallowell.[25]

In the meantime, my father's quest for E.R. Young's and other family papers had yielded a good many writings that had long sat in drawers and boxes. One of the richest was an autobiographical manuscript by Young's eldest son, E. Ryerson Young (1869-1962). Young was born at the Rossville mission near Norway House during his father's mission service there. As a small child there, and later at Berens River, he was looked after by a Cree nurse whom the family called Little Mary. The first third of Young's memoir focused on his vivid memories of the Cree-style upbringing Mary gave him and on the culture shock he underwent when his family left the mission field for Port Perry, Ontario, and placed him at age seven in a small rural school. This document offered rich material for an essay I wrote in 1987, exploring his childhood experiences and their parallels with the lives of the children of fur traders and their Native wives, women whose values and approaches to learning, discipline, and character formation certainly stood in contrast to those of their European fathers. And it closed a circle, for as a child at Berens River, Eddie, as he was called, knew the Berens family and had some close attachments to Berens River people who befriended him. It has been a privilege to have at hand the writings of this great-uncle, alongside those of his father, Egerton R. Young, and Hallowell.[26] In all these instances, other voices also speak through these texts and can be heard if one listens, just as the sixteenth-century Spanish scribes in Peru told John Murra more than they could have realized, both about the indigenous people of the Andes and about themselves.

This is a small sampling of the lines I can trace – academic, intellectual, and familial – and of the directions in which they have led. What was somewhat unexpected was how they came to be braided together. And yet I shouldn't have been too surprised, for my father, as a professor of French literature and the history of science, had a considerable impact on the course of my academic life. One of the professors who most influenced him at the University of Toronto in the 1920s was George Sidney Brett, whose seminal work on the history of psychology paralleled in some ways the contextualizing approaches that Hallowell and Stocking brought to the history of anthropology (and that my father, Harcourt Brown, applied to his doctoral research on scientific organizations in seventeenth-century France).[27] In 1982, when my son, Matthew, was beginning undergraduate studies at Brown University, his grandfather wrote to him about how, at the University of Toronto, he had found certain "Father Figures," notably Brett, "whose minds were inexhaustible."[28] Brett was interdisciplinary, moving between psychology and history; "he used to emphasize ... that real skill in any field can be used to enter another" (compare Hallowell moving between anthropology and history). Brett also taught his students to "find the point of view from which an author writes and thinks and reconstruct his argument as fully as you can before venturing to criticize his work. That is the way to achieve a fair evaluation of whatever you are looking at, and make your remarks useful."[29]

Of course, my father's other role was in stimulating my interest in the Young papers and in what could be done with such sources. But herein lay a certain challenge. He and I were not Methodists, and he was an avowed agnostic. We could appreciate the many human qualities of Egerton and Elizabeth Young, their good works, and the value of their writings and the information they

preserved. Yet to read the Methodistical prose of a past century requires a leap
into a worldview that sometimes seems as remote from our own as the traditional worlds of Ojibwe people that William Berens was trying to explain and
Hallowell was trying to understand. How does one cope with a great-grandfather who sometimes wrote in his books (as quoted by Hallowell) about the
"superstitious degradation" of the Ojibwe bands along the eastern shore of
Lake Winnipeg and about dangerous conjurors and the dire situation of the
unconverted?[30]

There are ways to meet the challenge. First, the advice of G.S. Brett, quoted
above, is useful: try to understand a writer's viewpoint before offering a criticism. (And, I would add, consider the intended readership when printed works
are involved. The rhetoric of Young's mission-centred books is more general-
izing and stereotypic than his mode of expression in private writings; in fact,
his papers show that he had some significant meetings and conversations with
"conjurors," even though he didn't convert them.)[31] Second, there is no point
in denial: we lose out if we simply ignore the things in our familial (and academic) past that we don't like. To a certain extent, we can choose among our
academic ancestors the mentors whom we decide to follow (although all sorts
of practical constraints enter into our working with certain professors and not
others). But we cannot choose or change our great-grandparents (or grandparents or parents); they are part of us. Sometimes they may influence our
mental development in a reverse way; we react against aspects of their belief
and practice and choose another way. But, while holding true to our own views
and opinions, we have to allow them theirs (which are already part of history)
and try to understand their outlooks and situations.

It helps to acknowledge that, as educated people in this century, we have a
huge advantage over our great-grandparents, missionary or otherwise. We have
imbibed the anthropological concept of cultures in the plural and are steeped
in values that recognize and respect, if imperfectly, other worldviews. We may
vary in our degrees of cultural relativism, but we are schooled in that principle
to an extent that our ancestors could never have fathomed.

There is a spin-off, however, from that relativism. A secular missionary pres-
entism can lead to an easy affixing of judgment and blame on all people of the
past (particularly those of European heritage) who did not exhibit our enlight-
ened perspective toward other cultures and worldviews. Of course, ancestors
(whether well-meaning, naive, or evil) in positions of relative power could do
great damage, as we see, for example, in colonial wars and in Indian residential
schools in Canada. But we can acknowledge the problems of assessing motiva-
tion, character, and intent in our subjects of study and deal honestly and con-
structively with them, as did Victoria Freeman, who had to wrestle with her

ancestors' stories and perspectives in *Distant Relations,* her study of her own familial legacy.[32]

Aboriginal writers also confront these issues as they try to evaluate their ancestors' highly varied relationships with newcomers to this continent and their consequences. Heather Devine expresses the issues well when she writes in her essay for this volume that "the practice of history, like life writing, is also a form of moral deliberation intended to establish ethical relationships to the past, present, and future. Maybe that is why I gravitated to history as a way to explore issues of personal and collective identity in the first place, because history is about trying to understand why past events transpired as they did, how the course of the past has affected our lives in the present, and how the past might influence our decision making in the future."

In this light, with a view to where we are going, we great-grandchildren need to understand all our ancestors better, both the familial and the academic. We are possessed by them and they by us, as those Cree grammatical prefixes make clear. Whether we translate aaniskotaapaan as "succession and extension across the generations" or, metaphorically, as "knots in a string," this Cree concept has helped me to organize these thoughts and reflections. It has provoked me into paying more attention to where we come from and where we are going, as I seek to do work that (quoting A.I. Hallowell on Frank Speck) has "the earmarks of high substantiality" and as I try to help others to do likewise.

Notes

1 Aaniskotaapaan expresses ideas about succession and great-grandchildren as discussed below. It should bear the plural ending, "-ak," to be consistent with the plurals next to it in the title, but the word is long enough already for non-Cree-speakers. In pronunciation, the emphases fall on the last two syllables with double *a*'s.

2 See Schenck, "William W. Warren's *History*," and her biography, *William W. Warren*; also her new, annotated edition of Warren's *History of the Ojibway People,* published in 2009.

3 I use the spelling "Ojibwe," as opposed to "Ojibwa" or "Ojibway," because speakers of the language say that "Ojibwe" with its final "e" elicits a more accurate pronunciation of the word than spellings with a final "-a" or "-ay." On generation length, the *Oxford English Dictionary* proposes thirty years.

4 Schenck, "William W. Warren's *History*," 250.

5 Theresa Schenck to Jennifer Brown, email, 30 April 2007. Nichols and Nyholm, in *A Concise Dictionary of Minnesota Ojibwe,* 18, translate the same term as "ancestor, great-grandparent, great-grandchild."

6 Speck, *Naskapi,* 245. Schenck found one example of string imagery in William Warren's own writings. In an article titled "Brief History of the Ojibways," in the *Minnesota Democrat,* 25 February 1851, he wrote, "The old men of the tribe agree in saying that it is now five generations or 'strings of lives' since their first intercourse with the white race." My thanks to Schenck for this reference, provided by e-mail, 23 September 2007.

7 Faries, *A Dictionary of the Cree Language,* 237.

8   William Dumas in conversation with Jennifer Brown, 5 July 2007. Louis Bird of Peawanuk on Hudson Bay spoke in the same vein. It is like "when you make knots," he said. "Your children are the first knot, your grandchildren are the second, and your great-grandchildren are the third" (in conversation with Jennifer Brown, 29 July 2007). "Aaniskotaapaan" is here spelled (except when quoting) with a double *a*, which signifies a long vowel and follows orthography currently used by Cree and Ojibwe linguists.

9   Wolfart summarized these points in a short unpublished text, "Adjacency, Succession, and Generational Distance in Cree" (2007), with the generous advice of D.H. Pentland, in response to my queries. My warmest thanks to them for their assistance. Along this line, Faries also supplies the verb *"aniska'skowao"* and variants, which mean "he succeeds him" (*A Dictionary of the Cree Language*, 237).

10 According to David H. Pentland in discussion with Wolfart, "-*aapee*- might alternatively be the non-initial form of the root *naapee*- 'male; male offspring.'" Wolfart, personal communication with author.

11 Wolfart adds, "the verbal morpheme -*(i)taapee*- 'drag' also includes the element -*aapee*- 'string, rope.'" He also notes that Cree speakers sometimes invoke the image of great-grandchildren being dragged behind or following behind.

12 As Wolfart points out, standard kin terms in Cree and Ojibwe always require these markers (e.g., one cannot simply say "grandfather" without a possessive). But some lexical sources treat the stem "aaniskotaapaan" as an ordinary noun. Wolfart ("Adjacency") suggests that it may be one example of several marginal terms that he calls quasi-kin terms.

13 For a new collection of most of Hallowell's articles on the Berens River Ojibwe, see Hallowell, *Contributions to Ojibwe Studies* (2010), edited by Jennifer S.H. Brown and Susan Elaine Gray.

14 Stocking, "History of Anthropology," 17-18.

15 Ibid., 19; Stocking, *Race, Culture, and Evolution*, x.

16 Stocking, "History of Anthropology," 6-7. The three paragraphs above are adapted from an unpublished paper, "'An Interdisciplined Spirit': A. Irving Hallowell, Ethnographer, Historian," which I presented in a session in honour of George Stocking at the American Anthropological Association meeting, Washington, DC, 20 November 1997. Raymond Fogelson in 1976 wrote of Hallowell with equal warmth, citing his creativity and ability "to make meaningful connections across traditional disciplinary lines." Furthermore, he commented, "his work reveals discernible threads of continuity, a remarkable sense of integration, and rare authenticity. His career possesses a definite identity that is clearly generative" ("General Introduction," xv).

17 Hallowell, "Frank Gouldsmith Speck," 68.

18 Brown, "Preface," in Hallowell, *The Ojibwa of Berens River*, xv-xvi.

19 Hallowell, *The Ojibwa of Berens River*, 8, 6, 11. The memories, stories, and myths that Berens shared with Hallowell and that Hallowell wrote down have been gathered and annotated in Berens, *Memories, Myths, and Dreams*.

20 For a full account of this encounter and its complex dynamics and results, see DeMallie, *The Sixth Grandfather*.

21 Brown and Matthews, "Fair Wind."

22 Hallowell, *The Ojibwa of Berens River*, 13.

23 The Egerton Ryerson Young Papers became available to researchers at the Archives of Ontario in April 1978. In the early 1990s, as it became evident that the United Church Archives at Victoria University (until moved in 2009), Toronto, would be a more suitable home, the Reverend H. Egerton Young (my father's cousin) and I arranged for the collection to be transferred to them.

24 That work appeared in print as Brown, *Strangers in Blood*.

25 Maurice Berens, a grandson of William, enrolled in my "Metis History" course in the mid-1980s and became greatly interested in Hallowell as a source for Berens family history. In turn, he undertook and shared with me considerable oral and documentary research on his grandfather. See Brown, "A Place in Your Mind for Them All," 223. On pursuing Hallowell and the Ojibwe people who remembered him in the 1990s, see, for example, Matthews, "The Search for Fair Wind's Drum," and Brown and Matthews, "Fair Wind." Susan Gray also built upon some of this work for her graduate work and publications. See her chapter in this book, and her earlier book, *"I Will Fear No Evil."*

26 On Little Mary and her relations with Eddie and the Young family, see Brown, "A Cree Nurse." On Eddie's memories of Cree and Ojibwe people who influenced his childhood, see Brown, "Growing Up Algonquian."

27 G.S. Brett (1879-1944) taught philosophy and ethics at the University of Toronto from 1911 to 1944 and was especially known for his three-volume *History of Psychology*. Brown's dissertation, an important early contribution to the history of science, was published in 1934 as *Scientific Organizations in Seventeenth-Century France*.

28 Harcourt Brown was sensitive to the absence of women professors in his time; he wrote in the same letter, "The chief element of a university is the faculty, the men and women – there were very few in my day." He never had women professors in his university experience; but then neither did I in any of my courses from 1958 to 1972 at three major universities. (Compare, for interest, the gender ratio of the contributors to this volume.) The letter to his grandson Matthew Harcourt Brown was published in 1992 to invite support for the Harcourt Brown Travel Fellowship for University College students; see Brown, "A Letter from a Senior Scholar to His Junior," 8.

29 Ibid. This advice reminds me of my first reading-course experience with George Stocking at the University of Chicago. For our first meeting, I prepared, in the style I had learned at Harvard, a rather slash-and-burn critique of the author he had assigned, only to be quietly rebuked for my lack of attention to the author's own outlook and purposes in writing the book in question.

30 Hallowell, *The Ojibwa of Berens River*, 29.

31 See Lindsay, "Tapastanum," and Brown, "As for Me and My House."

32 Freeman, *Distant Relations*.

Bibliography

Berens, William, as told to A. Irving Hallowell. *Memories, Myths, and Dreams of an Ojibwe Leader*. Edited with introductions by Jennifer S.H. Brown and Susan Elaine Gray. Montreal and Kingston: McGill-Queen's University Press, 2009.

Brett, G.S. *History of Psychology*. London: George Allen and Unwin, 1953 [1912, 1921], abridged one-volume edition.

Brown, Harcourt. "A Letter from a Senior Scholar to His Junior [grandson Matthew Harcourt Brown]." *Alumni Magazine* (spring 1992): 8. University College, University of Toronto.

–. *Scientific Organizations in Seventeenth-Century France, 1620-1680*. Baltimore, MD: Williams and Wilkins, 1934.

Brown, Jennifer S.H. "As for Me and My House: A Traditional Ojibwe Leader Contemplates Methodism at Berens River in the 1870s." In *Papers of the 40th Algonquian Conference* (Minneapolis, October 2008), in press.

–. "A Cree Nurse in a Cradle of Methodism: Little Mary and the Egerton R. Young Family at Norway House and Berens River." In *First Days, Fighting Days: Women in Manitoba History*, edited by Mary Kinnear, 19-40. Regina: Canadian Plains Research Center, 1987.

–. "Growing Up Algonquian: A Missionary's Son in Cree-Ojibwe Country, 1869-1876." In *Papers of the 39th Algonquian Conference, 2007*, edited by Karl S. Hele and Regna Darnell, 72-93. London, ON: University of Western Ontario, 2009.

–. "'An Interdisciplined Spirit': A. Irving Hallowell, Ethnographer, Historian." Paper presented at the meeting of the American Anthropological Association, Washington, DC, November 1997.

–. "'A Place in Your Mind for Them All': Chief William Berens." In *Being and Becoming Indian: Biographical Studies of North American Frontiers,* edited by James A. Clifton, 204-25. Chicago: Dorsey Press, 1989.

–. "Preface." In *The Ojibwa of Berens River, Manitoba: Ethnography into History,* by A. Irving Hallowell, xi-xviii. Fort Worth, TX: Harcourt Brace Jovanovich College Publishers, 1992.

–. *Strangers in Blood: Fur Trade Company Families in Indian Country.* Vancouver: UBC Press, 1980.

Brown, Jennifer S.H., and Maureen Matthews. "Fair Wind: Medicine and Consolation on the Berens River." *Journal of the Canadian Historical Association* 4 (1994): 55-74.

DeMallie, Raymond J., ed. *The Sixth Grandfather: Black Elk's Teachings Given to John G. Neihardt.* Lincoln: University of Nebraska Press, 1984.

Faries, Richard. *A Dictionary of the Cree Language.* Toronto: Anglican Book Centre, 1938.

Fogelson, Raymond D. "General Introduction." *Contributions to Anthropology: Selected Papers of A. Irving Hallowell,* ix-xvii. Chicago: University of Chicago Press, 1976.

Freeman, Victoria. *Distant Relations: How My Ancestors Colonized North America.* Toronto: McClelland and Stewart, 2000.

Gray, Susan Elaine. *"I Will Fear No Evil": Ojibwa-Missionary Encounters along the Berens River, 1875-1940.* Calgary: University of Calgary Press, 2006.

Hallowell, A. Irving. *Contributions to Ojibwe Studies: Essays, 1934-1972.* Edited with introductions by Jennifer S.H. Brown and Susan Elaine Gray. Lincoln: University of Nebraska Press, 2010.

–. "Frank Gouldsmith Speck, 1881-1950." *American Anthropologist* 53, 1 (1951): 67-87.

–. *The Ojibwa of Berens River, Manitoba: Ethnography into History,* edited with a Preface and an Afterword by Jennifer S.H. Brown. Fort Worth: Harcourt Brace College Publishers, 1992.

Lindsay, Anne. "Tapastanum: 'A Noted Conjurer for Many Years, Who Long Resisted the Teachings of Christianity'." In *Papers of the 40th Algonquian Conference* (Minneapolis, October 2008), in press.

Matthews, Maureen, assisted by Jennifer S.H. Brown and Roger Roulette. "The Search for Fair Wind's Drum." *Ideas,* CBC Radio, May 1993.

Nichols, John D., and Earl Nyholm. *A Concise Dictionary of Minnesota Ojibwe.* Minneapolis: University of Minnesota Press, 1995.

Schenck, Theresa M. *William W. Warren: The Life, Letters, and Times of an Ojibwe Leader.* Lincoln: University of Nebraska Press, 2007.

–. "William W. Warren's *History of the Ojibway People:* Tradition, History, and Context." In *Reading beyond Words: Contexts for Native History,* edited by Jennifer S.H. Brown and Elizabeth Vibert, 242-60. Peterborough, ON: Broadview Press, 1996.

Speck, Frank G. *Naskapi: The Savage Hunters of the Labrador Peninsula.* Norman: University of Oklahoma Press, 1977 [1935].

Stocking, George W., Jr. "History of Anthropology: Introduction." In *Contributions to Anthropology: Selected Papers of A. Irving Hallowell,* 17-19. Chicago: University of Chicago Press, 1976.

—, ed. *Observers Observed: Essays on Ethnographic Fieldwork.* Madison: University of Wisconsin Press, 1983.

—. *Race, Culture, and Evolution: Essays in the History of Anthropology.* New York: Free Press, 1968.

Warren, William W. *History of the Ojibway People.* 2nd edition. Edited and annotated with an Introduction by Theresa Schenck. St. Paul: Minnesota Historical Society Press, 2009.

Wolfart, H.C. "Adjacency, Succession and Generational Distance in Cree." Unpublished manuscript, 2007, in possession of the author.

Contributors

Heidi Bohaker is an assistant professor of Aboriginal history in the Department of History at the University of Toronto. Her research interests include treaties and treaty-making practices, the political significance of kinship networks, and Aboriginal writing systems and literacies.

Jennifer S.H. Brown, FRSC, is a professor of history and Canada Research Chair at the University of Winnipeg, where she has taught since 1983. At the university, she also directs the Centre for Rupert's Land Studies, which focuses on the Aboriginal and fur trade history of the Hudson Bay watershed. She has published extensively on many aspects of northern Aboriginal, mission, and fur trade history, with an emphasis on fur traders' Native families and on their Cree, Ojibwe, and Metis connections and related communities.

Kevin Brownlee obtained a master's degree in anthropology from the University of Manitoba. He was hired as the curator of archaeology at the Manitoba Museum in 2003. His research focuses on the archaeology of Manitoba's boreal forest and the emerging field of indigenous archaeology.

Robert Coutts worked as a historian with Parks Canada for over twenty-five years and is currently the manager of external relations and visitor experience in the Western and Northern Service Centre of Parks Canada. His primary research interests focus on First Nations and Metis themes as they relate to fur trade history. In 1996, he co-authored *Voices from Hudson Bay: Cree Stories from York Factory,* and in 2000 he published *The Road to the Rapids: Nineteenth-Century Church and Society at St. Andrew's Parish, Red River.*

Heather Devine is an associate professor in the Department of History at the University of Calgary. Her research and teaching specialties include Canadian Native history, American Indian policy, western Canadian ethnic history, Canadian studies, and museum and heritage studies, with a particular focus on Métis ethnohistory. She is author of *The People Who Own Themselves: Aboriginal Ethnogenesis in a Canadian Family, 1660-1900,* winner of the Harold Adams Innis Prize for 2004-5.

Frederic W. Gleach is a historical anthropologist and curator of the Anthropology Collections at Cornell University. Author of *Powhatan's World and Colonial Virginia: A Conflict of Cultures* and founding co-editor of *Histories of Anthropology Annual,* he works on historical issues of representation and identity in various media with a focus on Virginia Indians, Puerto Rico, and the discipline of anthropology itself.

Susan Elaine Gray is an award-winning scholar of Northern Algonquian history and cultures. She teaches Aboriginal history and is the research associate to the Canada Research Chair in Aboriginal Peoples and Histories at the University of Winnipeg.

David Reed Miller is a professor of indigenous studies at the First Nations University of Canada. He first encountered the contributions of Edward Ahenakew in 1978 when he was utilizing one of his APS texts for a paper on Little People among the Assiniboin and Plains Cree. Besides an interest in northern Plains ethnology, he regularly contributes to the history of ethnological research and ethnohistory for this region. He is currently working on a monograph about Little Bear and his followers in the transborder region between Saskatchewan and Montana.

Laura Peers is reader in material anthropology at the School of Anthropology and Museum Ethnography and curator (Americas) at the Pitt Rivers Museum, University of Oxford. She is interested in material culture (including historic sites) as manifestations of culture and history and in cross-cultural interpretation.

Carolyn Podruchny is an associate professor in the History Department at York University. She works on indigenous and French relations from the sixteenth to the nineteenth centuries, focusing particularly on the fur trade, oral history and folklore, Metis ethnogenesis, and missionaries.

Roger Roulette, raised in an Anishinaabe family in southern Manitoba, is an Anishinaabe oral historian and linguist who teaches at the University of Manitoba.

Theresa Schenck is an associate professor in the American Indian Studies Program at the University of Wisconsin-Madison. She is an enrolled member of the Blackfeet Nation of Montana and of Ojibwe descent through her grandmother. Her recent publications include a biography of William W. Warren and a new annotated edition of his *History of the Ojibwe People.*

Elizabeth Vibert teaches history at the University of Victoria. Her research focuses on racial and gendered identities in colonial settings. Her current project investigates comparative processes of racialization in colonial Nova Scotia, with a focus on the intersections of poverty and race.

Germaine Warkentin is professor emeritus of English at the University of Toronto and a fellow of the Royal Society of Canada. She has published widely in early modern studies, Canadian literature, and book history. She is currently focusing on the manuscript study of early Canadian exploration documents and on the material transmission of Aboriginal knowledge bases. Her edition of the *Voyages and Relations* of Pierre Esprit Radisson will be published by the Champlain Society in 2011.

Cory Willmott is an associate professor in the Department of Anthropology at Southern Illinois University Edwardsville. Her work focuses on visual and material culture of the Great Lakes Algonquians and the Han Chinese in cross-cultural and historical perspective. Her recent publications have dealt with topics that range from fur trade clothing and textiles to an ethnography of Amerindian participation in the garment industry to the representation of Amerindian peoples in museum exhibits.

Index

Printed and bound in Canada by Friesens
Set in Helvetica Condensed and Minion by Artegraphica Design Co. Ltd.
Copy editor: Lesley Erickson
Proofreader: Dallas Harrison
Cartographer: Eric Leinberger